Beginning XSL

Beginning
XSLT and XPath

Transforming XML Documents and Data

Ian Williams

WILEY

Wiley Publishing, Inc.

Beginning XSLT and XPath: Transforming XML Documents and Data

Published by
Wiley Publishing, Inc.
10475 Crosspoint Boulevard
Indianapolis, IN 46256
www.wiley.com

Copyright © 2009 by Ian Williams

Published by Wiley Publishing, Inc., Indianapolis, Indiana

Published simultaneously in Canada

ISBN: 978-0-470-47725-0

Manufactured in the United States of America

10 9 8 7 6 5 4 3 2 1

For general information on our other products and services please contact our Customer Care Department within the United States at (877) 762-2974, outside the United States at (317) 572-3993 or fax (317) 572-4002.

Wiley also publishes its books in a variety of electronic formats. Some content that appears in print may not be available in electronic books.

Library of Congress Control Number: 2009929458

About the Author

Ian Williams is an information designer specializing in XML technologies, and a software technical writer. He worked in the U.K. publishing industry before getting involved in information technology at OWL International, developers of the one of the first commercial hypertext products. Ian was a product manager there, and later a consultant working with large corporate customers.

Since 1998 Ian has worked on technical writing and information-design projects, most recently for Nokia, Reuters, and Volantis. He is co-author with Pierre Greborio of *Professional InfoPath 2003*, also from Wrox Press.

Ian lives with his wife, Helen, in Kent, in a converted lifeboat station overlooking the English Channel.

Credits

Contents

Contents

Contents

Contents

Contents

Contents

Contents

Introduction

Welcome to XSLT and XPath, two members of the W3C XML family of standards. This book concentrates on using XSLT and XPath to solve problems that you are likely to encounter every day in writing XSLT stylesheets. I have tried to focus most attention on the features that you will need frequently, while still treating other aspects of the subject in brief. You can find additional detailed information in the Quick Reference appendixes, and in more advanced works such as Michael Kay's *XSLT 2.0 and XPath 2.0 Programmers Reference*, also in the Wrox list.

Who This Book Is For

I assume that you have a sound knowledge of XML and related web standards, such as XML Schema and XHTML. In an introductory book like this, there isn't enough space to fill in background information on these subjects.

Conversely, I don't assume that you are familiar with a particular programming language, or that you necessarily have a strong programming background. The chapters include a few comparisons with other languages, and as you'll see, XSLT takes a different approach from most of them.

If you are an experienced web author, or a technical writer who works regularly with XML, there is no reason why you can't pick up XSLT, leveraging your existing knowledge and skills. Quite a few practitioners that I know come from this kind of background.

This book aims to give you a good grounding in the basics of XSLT and XPath, concentrating on version 2.0 of both standards. It is *definitely not* aimed at experienced XSLT 1.0 programmers who require a skills update. Explaining the often-very-detailed differences between the two versions would simply confuse matters for beginners, who will do better to learn how to use techniques that are appropriate to the latest version.

XSLT in Outline

According to the W3C specification, XSLT (Extensible Stylesheet Language: Transformations) is a "language for transforming XML documents into other XML documents." Given the widespread use of XML for exchanging data between applications and its success as a means of creating a wide range of document types, it is now easy to see why such a language is useful.

XSLT 1.0 was published as a recommendation late in 1999 shortly after XML 1.0, and at the time it didn't seem obvious that XSLT would become a success. It is probably so successful because it was, and still is, most often used to generate HTML content for the web from XML sources — so much so that XSLT processing was incorporated into browser engines at an early date. XSLT 2.0 was published in January 2007 after a very long development period, which was complicated by some controversy and the need to track the development of XPath 2.0, on which is relies heavily.

The name Extensible Stylesheet Language: Transformations suggests that there is another "branch" to XSL — and there is: Extensible Stylesheet Language: Formatting Objects, or XSL-FO. XSL was initially part of a much more comprehensive project, covering both transformation and formatting semantics. The Formatting Objects recommendation (still formally titled "XSL") was published separately in October 2001. It is essentially an XML vocabulary used to specify the layout and properties of parts of printed pages, but I won't be covering it in this book.

XSLT Is Different

Writing code to handle XML transformations in XSLT differs markedly from the approach used in other programming languages. It is written in XML syntax in a declarative fashion, with processing specified in pattern-matching rules. By *declarative* I mean the opposite of the usual imperative approach; that is, an XSLT programmer does not define a sequence of actions, but specifies a number of rules that the result should satisfy.

XSLT has a type system based on XML Schema, and XPath expressions form an important second language, matching source document objects, selecting content for processing, and performing operations on content.

Compared to some other languages, it is much easier to learn the XSLT basics, but the different syntax and the nature of the XSLT processing model take some getting used to.

The XML source example that follows is written in the DocBook vocabulary (which is widely used in documenting information technology):

```
<?xml version="1.0" encoding="UTF-8"?>
<article>

    <title>A Simple Transform</title>

    <para>Because the transform is an XML document we need to start with an XML
        declaration, specifying the version and the encoding.</para>
    <para>The root element in a stylesheet is
        <emphasis>xsl:stylesheet</emphasis>, though the synonym
            <emphasis>xsl:transform</emphasis> may also be used. You must always
        specify the XSLT namespace, and it is important to set the version
        attribute correctly to match the type of processing required. In this book
        we generally specify version 2.0.</para>

    <programlisting><![CDATA[
<xml version="1.0" encoding="UTF-8"/>
<xsl:stylesheet
```

```
    xmlns:xsl=http://www.w3.org/1999/XSL/Transform
    version="2.0"
    ...
</xsl:stylesheet>]]></programlisting>

    <para>In both cases there are stylesheets available for creating XHTML and
        PDF output. But what if you need to migrate content from one system to
        another?</para
    ...
</article>
```

Shown next is a simple XSLT stylesheet that transforms the XML to HTML:

```
<?xml version="1.0" encoding="UTF-8"?>
<xsl:stylesheet xmlns:xsl="http://www.w3.org/1999/XSL/Transform" version="2.0">
    <xsl:template match="/">
        <html>
            <head>
                <title>
                    <xsl:value-of select="title"/>
                </title>
            </head>
            <body>
                <xsl:apply-templates select="body"/>
            </body>
        </html>
    </xsl:template>
    <xsl:template match="title">
        <h1><xsl:value-of select="."/></h1>
    </xsl:template>
    <xsl:template match="para">
        <p><xsl:apply-templates/></p>
    </xsl:template>
    <xsl:template match="emphasis">
        <em><xsl:value-of select="."/></em>
    </xsl:template>
    <xsl:template match="programlisting">
        <pre>
            <xsl:value-of select="."/>
        </pre>
    </xsl:template>
</xsl:stylesheet>
```

The core HTML elements, highlighted in the preceding code example, form the output structure. They are written literally inside a series of sibling template instructions prefixed with xsl:.

The use of templates is similar to the non-HTML code you may have seen in web pages written using ASP, JSP, or PHP; but here the syntax is entirely XML, and the XSLT elements provide both the framework and the processing instructions.

Importance of XPath Language

XPath 2.0 is an expression language that is absolutely fundamental to XSLT 2.0 in several ways. An expression takes one or more input values and returns a value as output, so everywhere you can use a value you should also be able to use an expression to be evaluated. Usually, expressions are used as the value of attributes on XSLT elements — for example, `<xsl:value-of select="a+b"/>`.

XPath is used to match elements to XSLT template rules.

Another common use of XPath is selecting nodes in an XML document for subsequent processing. You can make a document-wide selection and refer to all the `<list>` elements, or be very specific by pointing to the `class` attribute in the first `<para>` in the third `<section>` of a document.

Then, you can use XPath to load documents, search strings, and manipulate numbers, using a very wide range of built-in functions.

Node Trees

XPath expressions operate on an abstract tree structure. Objects in the tree are nodes, of which there seven types, briefly described here:

❑ **Document:** The root of the tree representing an entire source document. I use the term *document node* to designate this node, to avoid confusing it with the root element of the source document.

❑ **Element:** Defined by pairs of start and end tags (e.g., `<title></title>`) or an empty element tag such as `<img/>` with no content.

❑ **Text:** A character sequence in an element.

❑ **Attribute:** The name and value of an attribute in an element start tag or an empty element tag, including all default value attributes in the schema.

❑ **Comment:** Comments in the XML source document, i.e., `<!-- -->`.

❑ **Processing instruction:** An instruction in the source document contained by `<? ?>`.

❑ **Namespace:** Namespace declaration copied to each element to which the declaration applies.

Figure I-1 shows how part of the tree of nodes for the DocBook article would look, with the document node outside of everything. Only the document, element, and text nodes for one instance of each element are shown. Each node contains the node type at the top, its name in the center in the case of elements, and the string value in the case of text nodes.

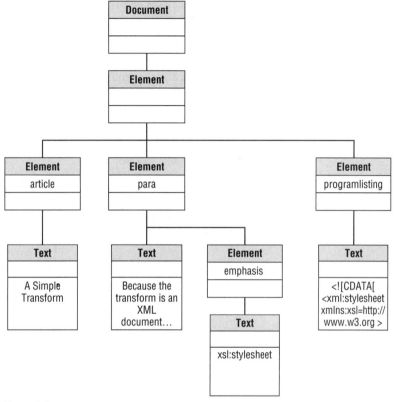

Figure I-1

Processing Overview

The basic work of an XSLT processor is to use a stylesheet as a set of instructions for producing a result document from a source document. Generally, all three documents are XML documents, so XSLT is said to *transform* one input object to an output object of the same kind. Figure I-2 illustrates the process in outline.

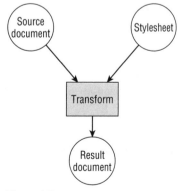

Figure I-2

Introduction

An XSLT processor treats the input and output documents as trees of nodes. You can think of these trees as being something like the W3C document object model, which some XSLT processors indeed use. However, unlike the DOM, there is no defined API in the XSLT specification. Different processors are free to implement this abstract data model in different ways.

The basic processing sequence comprises several steps, shown in Figure I-3.

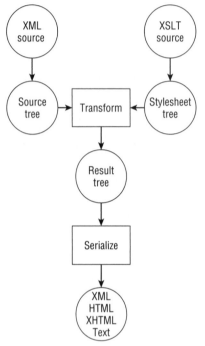

Figure I-3

1. The XML source document is parsed into a source tree.
2. The XSLT stylesheet is parsed to a stylesheet tree.
3. A transform is applied to create a result tree.
4. Serialization is applied to deliver content in the specified output format.

Essentially, the processor traverses the source tree in document order and looks for matching template rules in the stylesheet. If a match is found, then the instructions in the template are used to construct a node in the result tree. By default, the serialization creates an XML document, but specific instructions may be applied to output HTML, XHTML, or plain text.

The process can be more complex, potentially involving multiple sources, stylesheets and result trees, temporary trees held as variables, and multiple serializations. In Appendix B you'll find a more detailed view of how an XSLT processor works.

About the XSLT 2.0 Schema

As you work through the examples in the book, I'll introduce parts of the XSLT 2.0 schema so that you can examine the structure of the individual elements.

This schema is published separately by W3C, and it is not part of the XSLT 2.0 recommendation as such. The full schema is reproduced in Appendix E, and the latest version is also at www.w3.org/2007/schema-for-xslt20.xsd.

XSLT elements are broadly divided into two categories: declarations and instructions. For clarity, I mostly use one or the other of these terms, rather than call them elements.

The <xsl:declaration> and <xsl:instruction> are represented in the schema as abstract elements, which *never* appear in document instances, so you will not use them in a stylesheet; rather, you will use one of the elements in their substitution groups. A substitution group determines where the elements may appear. For example, you can see that <xsl:output> is a declaration from the substitutionGroup attribute value:

```
<xs:element name="output" substitutionGroup="xsl:declaration">
...
</xs:element>
```

This leads to a rather flat structure overall, with very little nesting of elements.

Declarations

Declarations define values such as the location of stylesheets to include or import, the method of output, global parameters, and the templates to use to match the source XML. These are top-level elements that immediately follow the root <xsl:stylesheet> element. They can appear in any order unless there is an <xsl:import> element, which must always appear first.

The schema declares the complex type xsl:generic-element-type with some common attributes:

```
<xs:complexType name="generic-element-type" mixed="true">
   <xs:attribute name="default-collation" type="xsl:uri-list"/>
   <xs:attribute name="exclude-result-prefixes" type="xsl:prefix-list-or-all"/>
   <xs:attribute name="extension-element-prefixes" type="xsl:prefix-list"/>
   <xs:attribute name="use-when" type="xsl:expression"/>
   <xs:attribute name="xpath-default-namespace" type="xs:anyURI"/>
   <xs:anyAttribute namespace="##other" processContents="lax"/>
</xs:complexType>
```

<xsl:declaration> is then defined as a generic-element-type, and the top-level elements are subsequently specified to be in the declaration substitution group:

```
<xs:element name="declaration" type="xsl:generic-element-type" abstract="true"/>
```

Introduction

Here, for example, is the schema definition for the `<xsl:output>` element:

```
<xs:element name="output" substitutionGroup="xsl:declaration">
  <xs:complexType mixed="true">
    <xs:complexContent mixed="true">
      <xs:extension base="xsl:generic-element-type">
        <xs:attribute name="name" type="xsl:QName"/>
        <xs:attribute name="method" type="xsl:method"/>
        <xs:attribute name="byte-order-mark" type="xsl:yes-or-no"/>
        <xs:attribute name="cdata-section-elements" type="xsl:QNames"/>
        <xs:attribute name="doctype-public" type="xs:string"/>
        <xs:attribute name="doctype-system" type="xs:string"/>
        <xs:attribute name="encoding" type="xs:string"/>
        <xs:attribute name="escape-uri-attributes" type="xsl:yes-or-no"/>
        <xs:attribute name="include-content-type" type="xsl:yes-or-no"/>
        <xs:attribute name="indent" type="xsl:yes-or-no"/>
        <xs:attribute name="media-type" type="xs:string"/>
        <xs:attribute name="normalization-form" type="xs:NMTOKEN"/>
        <xs:attribute name="omit-xml-declaration" type="xsl:yes-or-no"/>
        <xs:attribute name="standalone" type="xsl:yes-or-no-or-omit"/>
        <xs:attribute name="undeclare-prefixes" type="xsl:yes-or-no"/>
        <xs:attribute name="use-character-maps" type="xsl:QNames"/>
        <xs:attribute name="version" type="xs:NMTOKEN"/>
      </xs:extension>
    </xs:complexContent>
  </xs:complexType>
</xs:element>
```

Figure I-4 shows a schema diagram for the declaration substitutions.

Instructions

Other XSLT elements known as *instructions* are used to specify the construction of result trees from individual elements and attributes in the source XML.

The `xsl:versioned-element-type` is defined as an extension of the `generic-element-type`, and followed by the instruction declaration. This is because every element except `<xsl:output>` may have a `version` attribute containing the XSLT version number, which may be used to indicate which version of XSLT the processor should apply:

```
<xs:complexType name="versioned-element-type" mixed="true">
  <xs:complexContent>
    <xs:extension base="xsl:generic-element-type">
      <xs:attribute name="version" type="xs:decimal" use="optional"/>
    </xs:extension>
  </xs:complexContent>
</xs:complexType>

<xs:element name="instruction" type="xsl:versioned-element-type" abstract="true"/>
```

`<xsl:output>` *has an attribute with the same name, but this is intended to refer to the XML version specified in the output method.*

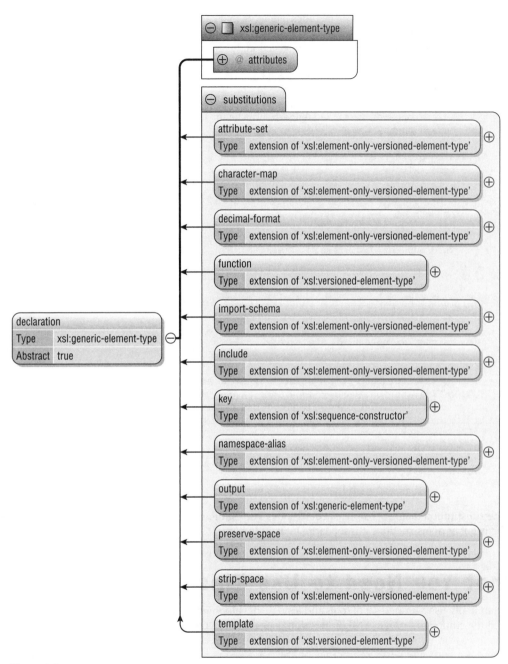

Figure I-4

<xsl:value-of>, which you will meet in Chapter 1, is specified as an instruction. It is also has the type *sequence constructor*, which is a type that contains a series of XSLT instructions. The

`xsl:sequence-constructor` type includes elements that can contain a sequence constructor. The schema extends the `xsl:versioned-element-type`, specifies the content model of a `sequence-constructor` group, and defines the `<xsl:value-of>` instruction:

```
<xs:complexType name="sequence-constructor">
  <xs:complexContent mixed="true">
    <xs:extension base="xsl:versioned-element-type">
      <xs:group ref="xsl:sequence-constructor-group" minOccurs="0"
maxOccurs="unbounded"/>
    </xs:extension>
  </xs:complexContent>
</xs:complexType>

<xs:group name="sequence-constructor-group">
  <xs:choice>
    <xs:element ref="xsl:variable"/>
    <xs:element ref="xsl:instruction"/>
    <xs:group ref="xsl:result-elements"/>
  </xs:choice>
</xs:group>

<xs:element name="value-of" substitutionGroup="xsl:instruction">

  <xs:complexType>
    <xs:complexContent mixed="true">
      <xs:extension base="xsl:sequence-constructor">

        <xs:attribute name="select" type="xsl:expression"/>
        <xs:attribute name="separator" type="xsl:avt"/>
        <xs:attribute name="disable-output-escaping" type="xsl:yes-or-no"
          default="no"/>
      </xs:extension>
    </xs:complexContent>
  </xs:complexType>
</xs:element>
```

The substitution diagram for instructions looks very similar to the one for declarations, but because of the number of instructions it is too large to include here.

What You Need to Use This Book

I habitually use a limited set of tools and a single development environment: the open-source Eclipse IDE, and the edition of Oxygen XML Editor that goes with it. Now and then I'll refer to them in particular.

There is a wide and very useful range of XSLT processors and XML editors out there; and while I don't want to endorse one rather than another, there are some arguments for using Oxygen as you work through this book, even if only temporarily:

❑   Oxygen is a multiplatform Java application.

❑   Both the basic and schema-aware versions of the Saxon XSLT processor are bundled with it.

❑   The IDE tools considerably ease the task of working with XSLT.

❑   You can get an evaluation license free.

❑   You can obtain the academic edition at a low cost.

Regardless of which processor you choose, make sure that it supports XSLT 2.0 and XPath 2.0. Ideally, it should also be schema-aware, or you will miss out on many important aspects of this book.

Choosing a Processor

Although the W3C recommendation for XSLT 2.0 was published early in 2007, not many processor implementations are available. I'll mention a few here.

One of the best-known processors is Michael Kay's Saxon, currently at version 9.x. The basic, or "B," versions of Saxon are free, and open source; the "SA" (schema-aware) versions will cost you something, either as a standalone tool from Saxonica, or as a bundled component in a commercial IDE.

AltovaXML 2008 is a free XML toolkit that includes a validating parser, an XSLT 1.0 engine, and XSLT 2.0 and XQuery 1.0 engines, which are both schema-aware. These tools are also part of Altova's commercial XMLSpy 2008 IDE.

The Gestalt command-line processor for XSLT 2.0 is still under development. You can find about its current status at `http://gestalt.sourceforge.net/doc/gexslt/index.html`.

The XML team at Microsoft seems to have concluded that developer demand will be greater for the SQL-like syntax of XQuery than for XSLT 2.0, although because XQuery depends on XPath 2.0 being in place, they will be more than part of the way once the XPath implementation is done. Any development will be implemented in the `System.Xml` classes rather than a Windows COM component.

Don't expect to see support for built-in XSLT parsing in browsers anytime soon. MSXML 6.0 continues to provide support for XSLT version 1.0, as does Mozilla 1.9, with JavaScript interfaces. Safari and Opera 9.0 will handle `xml-stylesheet` instructions.

Interface Options

XSLT processors can be invoked in several ways: from a browser using an `xml-stylesheet` processing instruction, from an XML IDE, from the command line, or from an API.

I've generally used version 10.x of the Oxygen IDE, Eclipse Edition, for the examples in this book. Please note that the user interface in Windows, Linux, and Mac OS X desktop editions differs somewhat from the Eclipse interface.

How This Book Is Structured

This book contains 11 chapters, 7 appendixes, and a glossary.

It is important that you read the chapters sequentially for two reasons. First, you will add to your knowledge in increments that build on what you picked up in the previous chapters. Second, and especially true in the first half of the book, the stylesheet code examples use XML source documents with a similar structure to progressively produce more complex output, making the new material easier to understand.

Chapter 1, "First Steps with XSLT" — This chapter shows you how to write two stylesheets: the first generates a web page from an XML document, and the second illustrates how to transform one XML data format to another. You'll learn about key XSLT elements and structures, XPath expressions for matching and selection, and different ways to invoke a stylesheet processor.

Chapter 2, "Introducing XPath" — In this chapter you'll take a short break from creating stylesheets to learn about the basics of XPath, node types, and properties, the XPath data model, and the important topic of path expressions used to navigate the node trees in your source documents.

Chapter 3, "Templates, Variables, and Parameters" — In this chapter you'll extend your knowledge about template rules, learning how to apply them using match patterns, modes, and priorities. You will also work with named templates, and learn about variables and parameters with both local and global scope.

Chapter 4, "Using Logic" — There are often cases when you want to use a more imperative style of programming, and exercise specific control over the processor. This chapter shows you how to use logic to test for simple or complex conditions, and direct processing accordingly. You'll also learn that when the source data is repetitive in nature, often the most straightforward thing to do is iterate over it rather than use template rules.

Chapter 5, "Sorting and Grouping" — This chapter examines the options available to you in sorting and grouping. Along the way, you'll learn about the significance of datatypes and languages in sorting, see how to use variables and attribute-value templates to create run-time values, and encounter part of a play by William Shakespeare, marked up in XML.

Chapter 6, "Strings, Numbers, Dates, and Times" — This chapter takes you through a mix of XSLT elements and XPath functions that you can use to manipulate string, numeric, and datetime values. XPath 2.0 has a very handy set of string-processing tools, including ones to match, tokenize, and replace regular expressions, and others to normalize text values and escape URIs. You'll learn how to generate simple and hierarchical numbering and how to format the generated values. Also included are many valuable XPath functions, which you'll use to generate and format dates.

Chapter 7, "Multiple Documents" — In this chapter you'll take a look at ways to deal with multiple documents. You'll learn how to include stylesheet modules and how to override existing stylesheets by importing them into a new one that provides alternative parameters, variables, and template rules. You'll also create multiple document output in different formats, and "chunk" a source file into separate web pages.

Chapter 8, "Processing Text" — Although XSLT is primarily designed to generate XML markup, in this chapter you will learn use XSLT to produce plain text without markup in any convenient output format. You will process raw text with XSLT by loading a text file and analyzing the content to find markers that you can use to construct XML elements or attributes.

Chapter 9, "Identifiers and Keys" — XSLT and XPath between them provide several ways to make use of identifiers and keys to locate items, which you can then use to support indexing and linking processes. In this chapter you'll learn about some limitations of using XML identifiers, and work with a variety of techniques, including one provided by XSLT's built-in ID generator.

Chapter 10, "Debugging, Validation, and Documentation" — In this chapter you'll learn how to make use of IDE debugging features that will help locate problems in your code, and make use of inline messaging and error-tracing features in XSLT. You will learn how to validate both source and result documents within an XSLT processor. You will also see how easy it is to add documentation to your stylesheets and process them using XSLT.

Chapter 11, "A Case Study" — The case study in this chapter builds on the work you have already done with the templates for processing the documents used in the XSLT 2.0 Quick Reference in Appendix D. The link processing uses a small library of modules that operate on both resource and subject metadata. This chapter explains the reference and metadata schemas, and how a link module and a related function module together provide link processing. Subject metadata is processed in a similar way to create a glossary, and inline definitions. The chapter ends by illustrating the production of a quick-reference website, and how to output a sitemap conforming to the Sitemaps protocol for consumption by web crawlers.

Appendix A, "Answers to Exercises" — Contains solutions to exercises for Chapters 2–10.

Appendix B, "Extending XSLT" — Examines the resources available in third-party function libraries built with XSLT and XPath, and vendor-provided extensions.

Appendix C, "XSLT Processing Model" — Reviews the XSLT processing model, drawing on the knowledge and experience that you have gained in working through the book.

Appendix D, "XSLT 2.0 Quick Reference" — This reference provides brief details about the XSLT 2.0 elements and functions. It is derived from the same XML source as the material used in the case study in Chapter 11. If you choose to build the reference website described there, you can make use of the online version too.

Appendix E, "XSLT 2.0 Schema" — This is a copy of the XSLT schema published by the W3C.

Appendix F, "XPath 2.0 Function Reference" — This reference provides brief details of the XPath 2.0 functions. These are distinct from functions that apply only to XSLT, and which are detailed in Appendix D.

Appendix G, "References" — A consolidated list of online resources found in various chapters and appendixes.

Glossary — A glossary of key terms, based on definitions published in the XSLT specification.

Conventions

To help you get the most from the text and keep track of what's happening, a number of conventions are used throughout the book.

Try It Out

The *Try It Out* is an exercise you should work through, following the text in the book.

1. They usually consist of a set of steps.
2. Each step has a number.
3. Follow the steps through with your copy of the database.

_____

> **Boxes like this one hold important, not-to-be forgotten information that is directly relevant to the surrounding text.**

Notes, tips, hints, tricks, and asides to the current discussion are offset and placed in italics like this.

As for styles in the text:

- ❑   We *italicize* new terms and important words when we introduce them.
- ❑   We show keyboard strokes like this: Ctrl+A.
- ❑   We show filenames, URLs, and code within the text like so: `persistence.properties`.
- ❑   We present code in two different ways:

```
We use a monofont type with no highlighting for most code examples.
We use gray highlighting to emphasize code that is of particular importance.
```

Source Code

As you work through the examples in this book, you may choose either to type in all the code manually or to use the source code files that accompany the book. All of the source code used in this book is available for download at `www.wrox.com`. Once at the site, simply locate the book's title (either by using the Search box or by using one of the title lists) and click the Download Code link on the book's detail page to obtain all the source code for the book.

Because many books have similar titles, you may find it easiest to search by ISBN; this book's ISBN is 978-0-470-47725-0.

Once you download the code, just decompress it with your favorite compression tool. Alternately, you can go to the main Wrox code download page at `www.wrox.com/dynamic/books/download.aspx` to see the code available for this book and all other Wrox books.

Errata

We make every effort to ensure that there are no errors in the text or in the code. However, no one is perfect, and mistakes do occur. If you find an error in one of our books, like a spelling mistake or a faulty piece of code, we would be very grateful for your feedback. By sending in errata, you may save another reader hours of frustration, and at the same time you will be helping us provide even higher quality information.

To find the errata page for this book, go to `www.wrox.com` and locate the title using the Search box or one of the title lists. Then, on the book details page, click the Errata link. On this page you can view all errata that has been submitted for this book and posted by Wrox editors. A complete book list, including links to each book's errata, is also available at `www.wrox.com/misc-pages/booklist.shtml`.

If you don't spot "your" error on the Errata page, click the Errata Form link and fill out the form that appears. We'll check the information and, if appropriate, post a message to the book's errata page and fix the problem in subsequent editions of the book.

p2p.wrox.com

For author and peer discussion, join the P2P forums at p2p.wrox.com. The forums are a Web-based system for you to post messages relating to Wrox books and related technologies and interact with other readers and technology users. The forums offer a subscription feature to e-mail you topics of interest of your choosing when new posts are made to the forums. Wrox authors, editors, other industry experts, and your fellow readers are present on these forums.

At http://p2p.wrox.com you will find a number of different forums that will help you not only as you read this book, but also as you develop your own applications. To join the forums, just follow these steps:

1. Go to p2p.wrox.com and click the Register link.
2. Read the terms of use and click Agree.
3. Complete the required information to join, as well as any optional information you wish to provide, and click Submit.
4. You will receive an e-mail with information describing how to verify your account and complete the joining process.

You can read messages in the forums without joining P2P; but in order to post your own messages, you must join.

Once you join, you can post new messages and respond to messages other users post. You can read messages at any time on the Web. If you would like to have new messages from a particular forum e-mailed to you, click the Subscribe to this Forum icon by the forum name in the forum listing.

For more information about how to use the Wrox P2P, be sure to read the P2P FAQs for answers to questions about how the forum software works as well as many common questions specific to P2P and Wrox books. To read the FAQs, click the FAQ link on any P2P page.

First Steps with XSLT

In this chapter you will get started with XSLT by developing two stylesheets. In the first stylesheet you'll see how to generate an XHTML web page from an XML document.

The second stylesheet illustrates how to transform one XML data format to another, in this case from the Atom 1.0 syndication format to RSS 1.0.

You'll learn about:

❑ Key XSLT elements and structure

❑ Built-in template rules

❑ XPath expressions for matching and selection

❑ Different ways to invoke a stylesheet processor

Transforming an XML Document to a Web Page

Probably the most common application of XSLT is to generate one or more pages of a website from an XML source of some kind. For example, you might want to split a large file into chapters, each with a separate page, or display a news feed.

There are a couple of ways to accomplish this: You might want to rely on a browser's client-side processor to transform the content; alternatively, you could generate static content for a server to render.

Let's start with an example that relies on a browser's built-in processor. It is drawn from the case study that you will work on later in this book.

The case study in Chapter 11 illustrates the production of a website from a set of XML source documents that describe each of the XSLT elements and functions. The same information was used to produce the XSLT Quick Reference in Appendix C.

If you haven't already done so, download the source code for this book from this book's web page at www.wrox.com. You'll be using the source files from now on in the examples that follow. When you've unzipped the download, open the folder for Chapter 1 and locate the file xml_stylesheet.xml.

Listing 1-1 shows a pared-down version of the source document describing the <xsl:stylesheet> element.

Listing 1-1

```
<?xml version="1.0" encoding="UTF-8"?>
<reference>
  <body>
    <title>xsl:stylesheet</title>
    <purpose>
       <p>The root element of a stylesheet.</p>
    </purpose>
    <usage>
       <p>The <element>stylesheet</element> is always the root element, even if
a stylesheet is included in, or imported into, another. It must have a
<attr>version</attr> attribute, indicating the version of XSLT that the
stylesheet requires.</p>
       <p>For this version of XSLT, the value should normally be "2.0". For a
stylesheet designed to execute under either XSLT 1.0 or XSLT 2.0, create a core
module for each version number; then use <element>xsl:include</element> or
<element>xsl:import</element> to incorporate common code, which should specify
<code>version="2.0"</code> if it uses XSLT 2.0 features, or
<code>version="1.0"</code> otherwise.</p>
          <p>The <element>xsl:transform</element> element is allowed as a synonym.</p>
          <p>The namespace declaration <code>xmlns:xsl="http//www.w3.org/1999/XSL/
Transform</code> by convention uses the prefix <code>xsl</code>.</p>
          <p>An element occurring as a child of the <element>stylesheet</element>
element is called a declaration. These top-level elements are all optional, and
may occur zero or more times.</p>
    </usage>
  </body>
</reference>
```

In the quick reference documents I use an XML grammar based on the Darwin Information Typing Architecture (DITA) reference content model. DITA is finding increasing support among the larger publishers of technical documentation. It differs considerably from the longer-established DocBook format, using a more modular approach, covering the concept/task/reference pattern often found in software help systems. You can look ahead to see details of the schema in Chapter 11. In addition to markup like <body>, <p> and <code>, which you'll recognize from XHTML, note that the root element in this example is <reference>. To keep the example simple, only the sections on <purpose> and <usage> are included, as are the inline <attr> (attribute) and <element> names. In later chapters I'll introduce more elements from the reference vocabulary.

Using a Browser

To run any transform inside a browser, you need to add a processing instruction to the source document, which will give the browser the location of the stylesheet you want to use. This goes immediately after the XML declaration in xsl_stylesheet.xml. Save the update while you start work on the stylesheet.

```
<?xml version="1.0" encoding="UTF-8"?>
<?xml-stylesheet href="browser.xsl" type="text/xsl"?>
<reference>
...
</reference>
```

You may have used processing instructions in other XML applications; what appear to be attributes in the instruction are in fact known as *pseudo-attributes*. The `href` pseudo-attribute locates the stylesheet (`browser.xsl`). The file extension `.xsl` is a convention, which some applications may rely on for identification. The `type` pseudo-attribute defines the content type (text/xsl). In this case you use a relative URI, for a stylesheet in the same directory as the source document. (In this book I use the more general term URI, which is an identifier that may not imply a specific location, whereas the term URL implies a location from which you can obtain a representation of a resource such as an HTML page.

The W3C recommendation for this processing instruction is separate from the XSLT specifications, and is at www.w3.org/TR/xml-stylesheet/.

> *The semantics of pseudo-attributes is the same as that of the attributes used in* `<link rel="stylesheet">` *in HTML.*

> *The content type expressed need not be XSLT, and this processing instruction is often used to specify multiple CSS files to handle different types of media using the value* `'text/css'`. *The content type for XSLT 1.0 was never specified in the W3C recommendation. Microsoft invented the* `'text/xsl'` *value for Internet Explorer, which seems to have stuck in practice, though browsers may also accept other values, such as* `'text/xml'`. *The XSLT 2.0 recommendation formally registers the media type* `'application/xslt+xml'`.

Built-in Rules

We can now process the sample by writing a bare-bones transform. It is not very exciting, but it illustrates the default behavior of a processor using a built-in template rule, specified in the XSLT specification.

XSLT defines built-in rules for processing templates, and the rule for document and element nodes ensures that the root element and all of its children will be handled recursively, even if there are no element-specific templates.

This book generally specifies XSLT version 2.0 for stylesheets. However, in the following Try It Out you'll create an XSLT 1.0 transform using a single root `<xsl:stylesheet>` element to demonstrate this built-in behavior.

Try It Out   A Root Element Stylesheet

To create the transform, follow these steps:

1. In the Oxygen IDE, mentioned in this book's Introduction, create a new document by choosing New ➤ Stylesheet (XSL) File.
2. In the dialog that appears, select 1.0 as the Stylesheet version.

3.   Enter **browser.xsl** as the filename and click Finish. The new file should open with the following contents:

```
<?xml version="1.0" encoding="UTF-8"?>
<xsl:stylesheet xmlns:xsl="http://www.w3.org/1999/XSL/Transform" version="1.0">

</xsl:stylesheet>
```

Because this stylesheet is an XML document, it must begin with an XML declaration, specifying the version number and the encoding. The root element in a stylesheet is `<xsl:stylesheet>`, though the synonym `<xsl:transform>` may also be used. You must always specify the XSLT namespace, and it is important to set the `version` attribute correctly to match the type of processing required.

After you've declared the namespace, all the XSLT element names require the namespace prefix, which is `xsl:` by convention. The prefix also makes it clear which element is referenced if other namespaces are in use.

Browsers that I have used will not complain about the version number, and many version 1.0 features are unchanged in version 2.0. In any case, it is good practice to document your intentions.

You can now process the sample. Open the `xsl_stylesheet.xml` file from a browser using the File ➤ Open menu command. You should see something like the output shown in Listing 1-2.

Listing 1-2

```
xsl:stylesheetThe root element of a stylesheet.The xsl:stylesheet element is
always the root element, even if a stylesheet is included in, or imported
into, another. It must have a version attribute, indicating the version of
XSLT that the stylesheet requires. For this version of XSLT, the value should
normally be "2.0". For a stylesheet designed to execute under either XSLT 1.0
or XSLT 2.0, create a core module for each version number; then use xsl:include
or xsl:import to incorporate common code, which should specify version="2.0" if
it uses XSLT 2.0 features, or version="1.0" otherwise.The xsl:transform element
is allowed as a synonym.The namespace declaration
xmlns:xsl="http//www.w3.org/1999/XSL
/Transform by convention uses the prefix xsl. An element occurring as a child of
the xsl:stylesheet element is called a declaration. These top-level elements are
all optional, and may occur zero or more times.
```

What has happened here? Without any further instructions, the processor has output all the text nodes from the source document.

Safari 3.4 on Windows reports an empty stylesheet error and renders nothing, which suggests that something may not be quite right with the implementation of built-in rules. Google Chrome produces the same result, presumably because it is based on the same core engine.

Defining an Output Method

You can provide hints to the stylesheet processing by adding some output specifications to your stylesheet. Unless otherwise specified as HTML or XHTML, the output will be in XML format. It is also possible to add user-defined methods.

You can define the type of output in the declaration `<xsl:output>`. You saw the schema definition in this book's introduction, but here it is as a reminder. The attribute list is quite extensive, but for now I'd like to focus on just a few attributes:

```
<xs:element name="output" substitutionGroup="xsl:declaration">
   <xs:complexType mixed="true">
      <xs:complexContent mixed="true">
         <xs:extension base="xsl:generic-element-type">
            <xs:attribute name="name" type="xsl:QName"/>
            <xs:attribute name="method" type="xsl:method"/>
            <xs:attribute name="byte-order-mark" type="xsl:yes-or-no"/>
            <xs:attribute name="cdata-section-elements" type="xsl:QNames"/>
            <xs:attribute name="doctype-public" type="xs:string"/>
            <xs:attribute name="doctype-system" type="xs:string"/>
            <xs:attribute name="encoding" type="xs:string"/>
            <xs:attribute name="escape-uri-attributes" type="xsl:yes-or-no"/>
            <xs:attribute name="include-content-type" type="xsl:yes-or-no"/>
            <xs:attribute name="indent" type="xsl:yes-or-no"/>
            <xs:attribute name="media-type" type="xs:string"/>
            <xs:attribute name="normalization-form" type="xs:NMTOKEN"/>
            <xs:attribute name="omit-xml-declaration" type="xsl:yes-or-no"/>
            <xs:attribute name="standalone" type="xsl:yes-or-no-or-omit"/>
            <xs:attribute name="undeclare-prefixes" type="xsl:yes-or-no"/>
            <xs:attribute name="use-character-maps" type="xsl:QNames"/>
            <xs:attribute name="version" type="xs:NMTOKEN"/>
         </xs:extension>
      </xs:complexContent>
   </xs:complexType>
</xs:element>
```

In XSLT 1.0, the `method` attribute can take the values `"xml"`, `"html"`, or `"text"`. For instance, you would use the `"text"` method to output a CSV file, which you'll learn how to do in Chapter 9. You would use `"xml"` as a value for SVG output, and also for PDF because it requires transforming to the XSLFO format as an intermediate step. The XSLT 2.0 specification adds `"xhtml"` to the possible attribute values.

However, in the next XSLT 1.0 example you'll use `"xml"` as a value, as the output is XHTML.

The `version` attribute on the `<xsl:stylesheet>` element is rather confusing. It has absolutely nothing to do with the version of XSLT; rather, it refers to the version of XML to be output.

You can define an `encoding` attribute, which specifies the preferred character encoding of the output document. All XSLT processors (and XML parsers) are required to support UTF-8 and UTF-16. Clearly, processing Chinese or Japanese content with UTF-8 encoding would produce corrupt output.

On this occasion, you'll set it to `'UTF-8'`. You can also add two more attributes specifying the XHTML `doctype-system` and `doctype-public` attribute values. These will result in the processor generating correct declarations in the output, before the `<html>` element:

```
<xml version="1.0" encoding="UTF-8"/>
<xsl:stylesheet
   xmlns:xsl=http://www.w3.org/1999/XSL/Transform
```

```
              version="1.0">
<xsl:output
   method="xml"
   encoding="UTF-8"
   doctype-system="http://www.w3.org/TR/xhtml1/DTD/xhtml1-transitional.dtd"
   doctype-public="-//W3C//DTD XHTML 1.0 Transitional//EN"/>

...
</xsl:stylesheet>
```

An XSLT 2.0 stylesheetstylesheet may contain multiple `<xsl:output>` declarations and may include or import stylesheet modules that also contain `<xsl:output>` declarations. This enables you to use one or more stylesheets to output results using different methods. So you might, for instance, output both a CSV file and a web page in one pass.

If you use multiple declarations in this way, the `name` attribute must be specified on each `<xsl:output>` element to identify it. These names should match a set of `format` attribute values on `<xsl:result-document>` instructions, which I discuss in Chapter 7, in the stylesheet. The following snippet briefly illustrates how this might work:

```
<xsl:output name="web" method="xhtml" encoding="UTF-8"/>
<xsl:output name="csv" method="text"/>

<xsl:template match="/">
   <xsl:result-document format="web">
      ...
   </xsl:result-document>
   <xsl:result-document format="csv">
      ...
   </xsl:result-document>
</xsl:template>
```

The form of name *attributes on XSLT elements is defined as a lexical* QName *or namespace qualified name. It applies, for example, to templates, attribute sets, variables, parameters, and so on. Typically this is a simple name, but it may also be qualified with a namespace prefix such as* `<xsl:function name="xm:getentry-by-id">`. *If two qualified names are compared, the namespace URI that is declared with the prefix and the local name is used.*

Main Template

The `<xsl:template>` element, which is covered in more detail in Chapter 3, is a basic building block of a stylesheet. This element is used to declare templates that match elements in the XML source, and to generate nodes in a result tree. Usually a stylesheet has a main template with the `match` attribute, set to `"/"`:

```
<xsl:template match="/">
   ...
   <xsl:apply-templates select="reference/body"/>
   ...
</xsl:template>
```

This value is an XPath expression that means "match the root of the source tree." Note that this is *not* the same thing as the root element of the source document. The root of the source tree is outside of everything, including the containing top-level element.

This means that processing will begin right at the start of the XML source tree, outside the `<reference>` element. Path expressions in this context will be relative to this location.

The contained `<xsl:apply-templates>` instruction selects the `<body>` element in the source document (see Listing 1-1) for processing, showing the relative XPath expression `"reference/body"` in the `select` attribute. This means that the `<body>` element and everything inside it have been selected for processing. This instruction simply defines a set of nodes to be processed using the template rules for each source node to be matched.

> *You are not restricted to following the nested nodes as shown in this example. You might want to select all the paragraphs in the source document for processing, in which case you would use* `<xsl:apply-templates select= "//p"/>`*. There's more on XPath expressions in Chapter 2.*

Literal Result Elements

You have two options when it comes to generating the element names that will be output. Usually, the most straightforward is to create what is called a *literal result element* by typing the element name with start and end tags straight into the stylesheet, and then populating the new elements with selected content from the source XML.

Literal result elements are treated as data to be copied from the result tree directly to the output. These elements can have any name, and the content may be XSLT instructions, nested literal result elements, or text. If you set attributes on the literal result elements, they will also be copied to the output.

This gives you considerable freedom to construct output from any source in your target XML vocabulary. For this XHTML page, you will start with something like the following skeleton:

```
<xsl:template match="/">
   <html>
   <head>
      <title>
         <xsl:value-of select="reference/body/title"/>
      </title>
   </head>
   <body>
      <p>The body goes here</p>
   </body>
</html>
</xsl:template>
```

The preceding code will render the following output:

```
<html>
   <head>
      <meta http-equiv="Content-Type" content="text/html; charset=UTF-8">
      <title>xsl:stylesheet</title>
   </head>
   <body>
      <p>The body goes here.</p>
   </body>
<html>
```

Selecting Source Content

To output source content, you select from the element to be transformed, using the `<xsl:value-of>` instruction. The `select` attribute defines the XPath expression to use. The next code snippet shows how:

```
<h1 class="section"><xsl:value-of select="title"/></h1>
```

As you learned in the introduction to this book, the `<xsl:value-of>` element is a sequence constructor, which is a series of XSLT instructions. This is the schema declaration:

```
<xs:element name="value-of" substitutionGroup="xsl:instruction">
  <xs:complexType>
    <xs:complexContent mixed="true">
      <xs:extension base="xsl:sequence-constructor">
        <xs:attribute name="select" type="xsl:expression"/>
        <xs:attribute name="separator" type="xsl:avt"/>
        <xs:attribute name="disable-output-escaping" type="xsl:yes-or-no" default=
          "no"/>
      </xs:extension>
    </xs:complexContent>
  </xs:complexType>
</xs:element>
```

Processing Specific Source Elements

The processor's built-in template rules have a lower priority than other templates, so by adding rules for individual elements, you can override the defaults.

Now you can add specific templates for the structural elements in the XML source: `<title>`, `<purpose>`, `<usage>`, and `<p>`. The `match` attribute identifies the element, and the output is specified with literal result elements. The `select` attribute value `"."` for the `<title>` element is an XPath expression that refers to the current node being processed. Because both the `<purpose>` and the `<usage>` elements can contain paragraphs, we apply processing to all the `<p>` content and its inline markup.

These templates are located at the top level like the main template you have just written, but their order is not significant. The XSLT processor treats the source elements in document order and will look in the templates for matches as it goes. I generally put them in rough document order in simple stylesheets:

```
<xsl:template match="title">
   <h1>
      <xsl:value-of select="."/>
   </h1>
</xsl:template>

<xsl:template match="purpose">
   <h2>Purpose</h2>
   <xsl:apply-templates select="p"/>
</xsl:template>

<xsl:template match="usage">
   <h2>Usage</h2>
   <xsl:apply-templates select="p"/>
</xsl:template
```

```
<xsl:template match="p">
   <p><xsl:apply-templates/></p>
</xsl:template>
```

In the next template you match the XML source `<attr>` (attribute) and `<element>` names using the XPath union operator `"|"`, and output a containing `<code>` literal result element. The union operator performs a logical OR, matching either of the source element names:

```
<xsl:template match="attr | element">
   <code>
      <xsl:value-of select="."/>
   </code>
</xsl:template>
```

The output for an element name will look like this:

```
<p>An element occurring as a child of the
   <code>xsl:stylesheet</code> element is called a
   declaration. These top-level elements are all optional, and may
   occur zero or more times.
</p>
```

Copying Content

When content in both the source and the output should be identical, you can simply copy the source nodes to the result. With the `<xsl:copy>` instruction, you copy the source `<code>` element name *and* its content to the output:

```
<xsl:template match="code">
     <xsl:copy>
         <xsl:apply-templates/>
     </xsl:copy>
</xsl:template>
```

Here is the schema definition:

```
<xs:element name="copy" substitutionGroup="xsl:instruction">
  <xs:complexType>
    <xs:complexContent mixed="true">
      <xs:extension base="xsl:sequence-constructor">
        <xs:attribute name="copy-namespaces" type="xsl:yes-or-no" default="yes"/>
        <xs:attribute name="inherit-namespaces" type="xsl:yes-or-no" default=
          "yes"/>
        <xs:attribute name="use-attribute-sets" type="xsl:QNames" default=""/>
        <xs:attribute name="type" type="xsl:QName"/>
        <xs:attribute name="validation" type="xsl:validation-type"/>
      </xs:extension>
    </xs:complexContent>
  </xs:complexType>
</xs:element>
```

There are two copy instructions in XSLT. The `<xsl:copy>` instruction is a *shallow copy*, and copies only the context node, but nothing under it. You specify the output in the sequence constructor inside `<xsl:copy>`. This instruction is most useful when copying element nodes.

It causes the current XML node in the source document to be copied to the output. The actual effect depends on whether the node is an element, an attribute, or a text node. For an element, the start and end element tags are copied; the attributes, character content, and child elements are copied only if `xsl:apply-templates` is used within `xsl:copy`.

In contrast, if you use `<xsl:copy-of>`, each new node will contain copies of all the children, attributes, and namespaces of the original node, recursively. This is often called a *deep copy*. This instruction has a `select` attribute, providing you with more flexibility in selection:

```
<xs:element name="copy-of" substitutionGroup="xsl:instruction">
  <xs:complexType>
    <xs:complexContent mixed="true">
      <xs:extension base="xsl:versioned-element-type">
        <xs:attribute name="select" type="xsl:expression" use="required"/>
        <xs:attribute name="copy-namespaces" type="xsl:yes-or-no" default="yes"/>
        <xs:attribute name="type" type="xsl:QName"/>
        <xs:attribute name="validation" type="xsl:validation-type"/>
      </xs:extension>
    </xs:complexContent>
  </xs:complexType>
</xs:element>
```

Listing 1-3 shows the completed stylesheet. Save this version as `local.xsl`.

Listing 1-3

```
<?xml version="1.0" encoding="UTF-8"?>
<xsl:stylesheet xmlns:xsl="http://www.w3.org/1999/XSL/Transform"
    version="1.0">
  <xsl:output method="html"
      encoding="UTF-8"
      doctype-system="http://www.w3.org/TR/xhtml1/DTD/xhtml1-transitional.dtd"
      doctype-public="-//W3C//DTD XHTML 1.0 Transitional//EN"/>

  <xsl:template match="/">
    <html>
      <head>
        <title>
          <xsl:value-of select="reference/body/title"/>
        </title>
      </head>
      <body>
        <xsl:apply-templates select="reference/body"/>
      </body>
    </html>
  </xsl:template>

  <xsl:template match="title">
    <h1>
      <xsl:value-of select="."/>
    </h1>
  </xsl:template>

  <xsl:template match="purpose">
    <h2>Purpose</h2>
    <xsl:apply-templates select="p"/>
  </xsl:template>
```

```
    <xsl:template match="usage">
       <h2>Usage</h2>
       <xsl:apply-templates select="p"/>
    </xsl:template>

    <xsl:template match="p">
       <p>
          <xsl:apply-templates/>
       </p>
    </xsl:template>

    <xsl:template match="attr | element">
       <code>
          <xsl:value-of select="."/>
       </code>
    </xsl:template>

    <xsl:template match="code">
       <xsl:copy>
          <xsl:apply-templates/>
       </xsl:copy>
    </xsl:template>

</xsl:stylesheet>
```

Transforming Locally

This time you'll run the stylesheet processor "locally," rather than on the browser. The setup suggestions that follow make further use the Oxygen IDE . You'll also look briefly at invoking the Java command-line interface for the Saxon processor.

Try It Out   Configuring a Transformation

You can use the Oxygen IDE to set up a transformation, providing a range of configuration values. Essentially, you provide input and output values, which are associated with the source file and saved automatically for reuse. To avoid typing long paths, you can use editor variables recognized by the application, such as "${cfdu}" for "current file directory URL."

   1.   Open xsl_stylesheet.xml in the XML editor.

   2.   Choose XML ➤ Configure Stylesheet Transformation.

   3.   Click New in the dialog that opens, and name the scenario **xml2xhtml** in the Edit Scenario dialog that appears, as shown in Figure 1-1. By default, the variable **"${currentFileURL}"** is used for the XML URL setting.

   4.   On the XSLT tab, insert **${cfdu}local.xsl** in the XSL URL control.

   5.   Choose Saxon6.5.5 in the Transformer drop-down. Figure 1-1 shows the settings.

   6.   On the Output tab, accept the default setting Save as **${cfn}.html**, which will save the XHTML file in the same directory as the source, with the current filename.

   7.   Check Show in Browser and click OK.

   8.   In the main dialog, click Transform Now.

Figure 1-1

The transformed document should open in your browser.

Figure 1-2 shows the browser output, and Listing 1-4 shows the XHTML source code.

xsl:stylesheet

Purpose

The root element of a stylesheet.

Usage

The xsl:stylesheet is always the root element, even if a stylesheet is included in, or imported into another. It must have a version attribute, indicating the version of XSLT that the stylesheet requires.

For this version of XSLT, the value should normally be "2.0". For a stylesheet designed to execute under either XSLT 1.0 or XSLT 2.0, create a core module for each version number; then use xsl:include or xsl:import to incorporate common code. which should specify version="2.0" if it uses XSLT 2.0 features, or version="1.0" otherwise.

The xsl:transform element is allowed as a synonym.

The namespace declaration xmlns:xsl="http//www.w3.org/1999/XSL/Transform by convention uses the prefix xsl.

An element occurring as a child of the xsl:stylesheet element is called a declaration. These top-level elements are all optional, and may occur zero or more times.

Figure 1-2

Listing 1-4

```xml
<?xml version="1.0" encoding="UTF-8"?>
<!DOCTYPE html
    PUBLIC "-//W3C//DTD XHTML 1.0 Transitional//EN"
    "http://www.w3.org/TR/xhtml1/DTD/xhtml1-transitional.dtd">
<html>
    <head>
        <title>xsl:stylesheet</title>
    </head>
    <body>
        <h1>xsl:stylesheet</h1>
        <h2>Purpose</h2>
        <p>The root element of a stylesheet.</p>
        <h2>Usage</h2>
        <p>The <code>stylesheet</code> is always the root element, even if a
stylesheet is included in, or imported into, another. It must have a <code>
version</code> attribute, indicating the version of XSLT that
the stylesheet requires.</p>
        <p>For this version of XSLT, the value should normally be <code>"2.0"</code>.
For a stylesheet designed to execute under either
XSLT 1.0 or XSLT 2.0, create a core module for each version number;
then use <code>xsl:include</code> or <code>xsl:import</code> to
incorporate common code, which should specify <code>version="2.0"</code> if it uses
XSLT 2.0 features, or <code>version="1.0"</code> otherwise.</p>
        <p>The <code>xsl:transform</code> element is allowed as a synonym.</p>
        <p>The namespace declaration <code>xmlns:xsl="http//www.w3.org/1999/XSL
/Transform</code> by convention uses the prefix <code>xsl</code>.</p>
        <p>An element occurring as a child of the <code>stylesheet</code> element is
called a declaration. These top-level elements are all optional, and may occur
zero or more times.</p>
    </body>
</html>
```

Using the Command Line

Another way to invoke a stylesheet processor is to use a command-line interface. The specifics of the interface will vary according to which processor you use.

The next example uses the Saxon CLI for the open-source version on the `local.xsl`. If you intend to use the CLI frequently, you may prefer to run it from an open-source tool like jEdit (`www.jedit.org`), rather than from the file system console.

If you are using the Oxygen IDE and just want to experiment with the CLI, you will find the `.jar` file in the `lib` directory. If you are not using a bundled version of Saxon, you can download the Java version of the Saxon processor from SourceForge (`http://sourceforge.net/project/showfiles.php?groupid=29872`).

Unzip the download to a convenient directory. Add the `saxon9.jar` file to the classpath so that the command in the following Try It Out will locate the main program `net.sf.saxon`. The schema-aware version is `com.saxonica`.

Full documentation is available on the Saxonica site, which you should consult for installation and configuration instructions (`www.saxonica.com/documentation/contents.html`).

The Saxon CLI

Enter the following code on the command line and execute it:

```
java net.sf.saxon.Transform -s:xsl_stylesheet.xml -xsl:local.xsl
-o:xsl_stylesheet.html
```

The options in the example have the following meanings:

- `-s:filename`: The source XML file

- `-xsl:filename`: The XSL stylesheet to use

- `-o:filename`: The output filename

The remaining Saxon CLI options are extensive and quite powerful. If you are interested in pursuing the CLI approach, you should review the Saxon documentation at your leisure before using them.

Transforming XML Data to XML

The next example illustrates how simple it can be to transform content from one XML format to another. A common transform problem is that two similar schemas will use different names for identical content values. Another problem is that in one case an attribute is used for a value, while another uses an element for the same purpose.

The next stylesheet uses two common metadata vocabularies that express information in roughly the same manner. One is the Atom 1.0 format, increasingly used for blogs and news feeds; the other is RSS 1.0, which uses a combination of the Dublin Core Metadata Initiative vocabulary and RDF/XML.

There is also a version 2.0 "branch" of RSS. Although it is often assumed that RSS 2.0 supersedes RSS 1.0, it doesn't; and the versions are incompatible in several ways. RSS 2.0 is also in widespread use, but we won't be using it in this chapter. If you want to explore the structure of RSS 2.0, go to `http://cyber.law.harvard.edu/rss/rss.html`.

Of course, you wouldn't bother serializing either of these feeds to XML if the data were in a SQL database or an RDF triple store. However, if you are aggregating the data from feed URLs, or you have been provided with source data in XML, you won't have much choice.

Atom and RSS Elements

The next two tables compare the feed elements and entry elements in the Atom 1.0 schema with the equivalents in RDF Site Summary (RSS) 1.0. The pros and cons of the different ways to describe metadata can be a contentious issue, but just now we need not be concerned with the details.

The following table lists the top-level elements that define the properties of the Atom feed in the `<feed>` and RSS 1.0 `<channel>` elements. The matches are quite weak at this level, perhaps reflecting the history of how these structures were developed. The Atom specification provides a richer set of values on the whole.

Atom	RSS 1.0	Description
feed	channel	Root element of the feed document
title	title	Feed title
id		Feed identifier
updated		Date the feed was most recently updated
subtitle		Feed subtitle
generator		Application that generated the feed
link	link	URL for the HTML version of the feed
	description	Feed description
logo, icon	image	URI for a feed image
	items	RDF sequence acting as a table of contents
entry	item	Feed entry container

The next table shows elements in the Atom `<entry>` and RSS 1.0 `<item>` elements. The "item" contents for RSS 1.0 are in the Dublin Core (DC) namespace. The matches between the schemas are much closer here, and the differences reflect the fact that the DC format has strong origins in the library community, and Atom was primarily developed for the requirements of web logs.

Atom	DC	Description
id	identifier	Identifier of the resource
title	title	Name by which the resource is known
published	date	Date of publication
updated		Date updated
author		Container for name, e-mail, and URI elements
name	creator	The person or organization responsible for creating the resource
email		Author's e-mail address
uri		URI associated with the author
contributor	contributor	Contributor to a work; same structure as author.

Continued

15

Atom	DC	Description
summary	description	Description of the resource
	language	Principal language of the resource
content/@type	format	File format
	type	Defines either the genre or intellectual type of the resource
	publisher	Supplier of the resource
source	source	Identifier for source material for the resource, assuming it is derived from another format
content		Container of or link to the content
	coverage	Locations or periods that are subjects of the resource
category	subject	Subjects of the resource
rights	rights	Rights information
	relation	Reference to a related resource

Listing 1-5 shows part of an Atom feed from the xml.com website. We'll use this document as the source for the transformation. Some content, an additional namespace declaration, and stylesheet-processing instructions have been removed for clarity.

The listing shows the <feed> element and its content to the end of the first <entry> element. The code download is in the file atom.xml.

Listing 1-5

```
<?xml version="1.0" encoding="UTF-8"?>
<feed xmlns="http://www.w3.org/2005/Atom">
   <title>O'Reilly News: XML</title>
   <link rel="alternate" type="text/html" href="http://news.oreilly.com/"/>
   <id>tag:news.oreilly.com,2008-08-01://44</id>
   <updated>2008-12-17T07:32:30Z</updated>
   <subtitle>O'Reilly News - Spreading the knowledge of innovators</subtitle>
   <generator uri="http://www.sixapart.com/movabletype/">Movable Type Pro 4.21-en
     </generator>
   <link rel="self" href="http://feeds.oreilly.com/oreilly/xml"
      type="application/atom+xml"/>
   <entry>
      <title>Defining markup languages using Unicode properties</title>
      <link rel="alternate" type="text/html"        href="http://feeds.oreilly.com
         /~r/oreilly/xml/~3/487372046/defining-markup-languages-usin.html"/>
      <id>tag:broadcast.oreilly.com,2008://53.34679</id>
      <published>2008-12-17T03:01:23Z</published>
      <updated>2008-12-17T07:32:30Z</updated>
```

```
        <summary>Can we define a family of markup languages that used the Unicode
          properties and which could accept a fair imitation of XML and produce
          a SAX-like event stream?</summary>
        <author>
            <name>Rick Jelliffe</name>
        </author>
        <category term="xml" label="xml"
          scheme="http://www.sixapart.com/ns/types#tag"/>
        <content type="html" xml:lang="en" xml:base="http://broadcast.oreilly.com/">
          Can we define a family of markup languages that used the Unicode
          properties and which could accept a
          fair imitation of XML and produce a SAX-like event stream?
          &lt;img src="http://feeds.oreilly.com/~r/oreilly/xml/~4/487372046"
height="1" width="1"/&gt;</content>
    </entry>
    ...
</feed>
```

This feed will be well out of date when you read this. To get a current version, go to http://feeds.oreilly.com/oreilly/xml, *copy the source, and save it as a replacement. Alternatively, you can load the data directly from the feed site using the URL containing the feed source.*

Developing the Stylesheet

As with the XML to HTML transform, we'll take the development one step at a time. The approach is essentially the same, with XML as the target rather than HTML. The vocabularies are, of course, different, but the matching process will work similarly. It is not too important at present to absorb the details of the Atom and RSS 1.0 formats, but if you would like to do so here are the relevant URLs:

Atom 1.0 www.atomenabled.org/developers/syndication/atom-format-spec.php

RSS 1.0 http://web.resource.org/rss/1.0/spec

I'll call the top-level elements "feed elements," and the individual entries "entry elements," using the Atom terminology.

Preliminaries

Let's start with the basics of the stylesheet rss_feed.xsl. This time you'll set "2.0" as the value of the stylesheet's version attribute. Inside the <xsl:stylesheet> element are two namespaces to declare using the rdf and dc prefixes.

> **Always check the source file for a default namespace declaration: In this case it is "http://www.w3.org/2005/Atom". You need to set the xpath-default-namespace attribute on the <xsl:stylesheet> element to this value; otherwise, *nothing* from the source file will be output.**

Next, declare the output method as `"xml"` and the encoding as `"UTF-8"`. In the main template, create the literal result elements `<rdf:RDF>` and `<channel>`, in that order, as the container for your output. The namespaces must be declared again on the `<rdf:RDF>` element:

```
<?xml version="1.0" encoding="UTF-8"?>
<xsl:stylesheet version="2.0"
   xmlns:xsl="http://www.w3.org/1999/XSL/Transform"
   xmlns:rdf="http://www.w3.org/1999/02/22-rdf-syntax-ns#"
   xmlns:dc="http://purl.org/dc/elements/1.1/"

xpath-default-namespace="http://www.w3.org/2005/Atom">

   <xsl:output method="xml" encoding="UTF-8"/>
   <xsl:template match="/">
      <rdf:RDF
        xmlns:rdf="http://www.w3.org/1999/02/22-rdf-syntax-ns#"
        xmlns:dc="http://purl.org/dc/elements/1.1/"
        <channel>
        ...
        </channel>
      </rdf:RDF>
   </xsl:template>
   ...
</xsl:styleheet>
```

Specifying Attributes

Both the `<channel>` and `<item>` elements require the `rdf:about` attribute.

An attribute can be set directly on a literal result element if you know its value ahead of time, but in this case you need to use another approach, with the `<xsl:attribute>` instruction. This element should always come first in any set of sequence constructor instructions. You can use either the element content or the `select` attribute, but note that these approaches are mutually exclusive.

The XSLT 2.0 schema definition looks like this:

```
<xs:element name="attribute" substitutionGroup="xsl:instruction">
  <xs:complexType>
    <xs:complexContent mixed="true">
      <xs:extension base="xsl:sequence-constructor">
        <xs:attribute name="name" type="xsl:avt" use="required"/>
        <xs:attribute name="namespace" type="xsl:avt"/>
        <xs:attribute name="select" type="xsl:expression"/>
        <xs:attribute name="separator" type="xsl:avt"/>
        <xs:attribute name="type" type="xsl:QName"/>
        <xs:attribute name="validation" type="xsl:validation-type"/>
      </xs:extension>
    </xs:complexContent>
  </xs:complexType>
</xs:element>
```

To add the `rdf:about` attribute to the `<channel>` element, enter the `<xsl:attribute>` element right after the `<channel>` element, and use the `<xsl:value-of>` instruction to obtain the link URL `http://news.oreilly.com/` from the `href` attribute on the source feed's `<link>` element:

```
<channel>
   <xsl:attribute name="rdf:about">
      <xsl:value-of>feed/link/@href<.xsl:value-of>
   </xsl:attribute>
   ...
</channel>
```

Completing the Feed Elements

Adding a title is straightforward, again using the element `<xsl:value-of>`; you could also have used `<xsl:copy-of>` because the elements are identical in each vocabulary:

```
<title>
   <xsl:value-of select="feed/title"/>
</title>
```

There's nothing you can use to fill the `<description>` element except perhaps the feed's subtitle, but that might not be a good idea because it is optional in the Atom schema.

Next you come to the `<link>` element in the RSS feed ... but wait — you've just used the required value in the `rdf:about` attribute. Let's backtrack and create a reusable template variable `$feedurl`.

You can also refine the selection to choose the link that has the `rel` attribute set to `'self'`, because there are two link elements in the source. To do this you use a predicate inside square brackets: `"[]"`. You'll learn more about predicates in the next chapter. Change the code to look like this:

```
<channel>
   <xsl:variable name="feedurl" select="feed/link[@rel='self']/@href"/>
   <xsl:attribute name="rdf:about">
      <xsl:value-of select="$feedurl"/>
   </xsl:attribute>
   <title>
      <xsl:value-of select="feed/title"/>
   </title>
   <link><xsl:value-of select="$feedurl"/></link>
   ...
</channel>
```

Item Listing

To create an item listing to act as a table of contents, enter the literal result element `<items>` and an RDF sequence element, `rdf:Seq`. The sequence constructor `<xsl:for-each>` will take the processor to all of the matching nodes one by one, changing the context node as it goes. You will learn more about `<xsl:for-each>` in Chapter 4.

By selecting with the XPath expression `feed//entry` (using `"//"`), you operate on *all* the entry elements in the feed. For each entry, you add an RDF list item, `rdf:li`, and set its `rdf:resource` attribute value from the `<link>` element in each individual entry:

```
<items>
   <rdf:Seq>
```

```
    <xsl:for-each select="feed//entry">
       <rdf:li>
          <xsl:attribute name="rdf:resource">
           <xsl:value-of select="link/@href"/>
          </xsl:attribute>
       </rdf:li>
    </xsl:for-each>
  </rdf:Seq>
</items>
```

Entry Elements

Still in the main template, you need to loop through the entries again to create a series of complete `<item>` elements in the output:

```
<xsl:for-each select="//entry">
   <xsl:apply-templates select="."/>
</xsl:for-each>
```

In a template matching `<entry>` elements, you can handle the translation from Atom to Dublin Core. Most of the translations are straightforward. Dublin Core doesn't have an equivalent of the `<atom:updated>` element, so you use that value in `<dc:date>`. The language can be obtained from the `<content>` element's `xml:lang` attribute. Another point to note is that there can be multiple categories in entries, just as there can be multiple `<dc:subject>` elements. Therefore, you need to select the `label` attribute on the `<category>` element inside another `<xsl:for-each>` loop that creates the subject elements.

In neither of these two schemas does the order of elements matter, or the number of occurrences, so you can simply let the source sequence drive the process:

```
<xsl:template match="entry">
   <item>
    <xsl:attribute name="rdf:about">
       <xsl:value-of select="id"/>
    </xsl:attribute>
    <link>
       <xsl:value-of select="link/@href"/>
    </link>
    <dc:identifier>
       <xsl:value-of select="id"/>
    </dc: identifier >
    <dc:language>
       <xsl:value-of select="content/@xml:lang"/>
    </dc:language>
    <dc:title>
       <xsl:value-of select="title"/>
    </dc:title>
    <dc:date>
       <xsl:value-of select="published"/>
    </dc:date>
    <dc:creator>
       <xsl:value-of select="author/name"/>
    </dc:creator>
```

```
    <dc:description>
       <xsl:value-of select="summary"/>
    </dc:description>
    <dc:format>
       <xsl:value-of select="content/@type"/>
    </dc:format>
    <xsl:for-each select="category">
       <dcsubject>
       <xsl:value-of select="./@label"/>
       </dc:subject>
       </xsl:for-each>
    </item>
  </xsl:template>
```

The full stylesheet is shown in Listing 1-6.

Listing 1-6

```
<?xml version="1.0" encoding="UTF-8"?>
<xsl:stylesheet version="2.0" xmlns:xsl="http://www.w3.org/1999/XSL/Transform"
   xmlns:dc="http://purl.org/dc/elements/1.1/"
   xmlns:rdf="http://www.w3.org/1999/02/22-rdf-syntax-ns#"
   xpath-default-namespace="http://www.w3.org/2005/Atom">
<xsl:output method="xml"/>
<xsl:variable name="site">testurl</xsl:variable>
<xsl:template match="/">
    <rdf:RDF xmlns:rdf="http://www.w3.org/1999/02/22-rdf-syntax-ns#"
       xmlns:dc="http://purl.org/dc/elements/1.1/">
       <channel>
          <xsl:variable name="feedurl" select="feed/link[@rel='self']/@href"/>
          <xsl:attribute name="rdf:about">
             <xsl:value-of select="$feedurl"/>
          </xsl:attribute>
          <title>
             <xsl:value-of select="feed/title"/>
          </title>
          <link>
             <xsl:value-of select="$feedurl"/>
          </link>
          <items>
             <rdf:Seq>
                <xsl:for-each select="feed//entry">
                   <rdf:li>
                      <xsl:attribute name="rdf:resource">
                         <xsl:value-of select="id"/>
                      </xsl:attribute>
                   </rdf:li>
                </xsl:for-each>
             </rdf:Seq>
          </items>
          <xsl:for-each select="//entry">
             <xsl:apply-templates select="."/>
          </xsl:for-each>
       </channel>
```

Continued

Listing 1-6: *(continued)*

```
        </rdf:RDF>
    </xsl:template>
    <xsl:template match="entry">
        <item>
            <xsl:attribute name="rdf:about">
                <xsl:value-of select="id"/>
            </xsl:attribute>
            <link>
                <xsl:value-of select="link/@href"/>
            </link>
            <dc:language>
                <xsl:value-of select="content/@xml:lang"/>
            </dc: language >
            <dc:title>
                <xsl:value-of select="title"/>
            </dc:title>
            <dc:date>
                <xsl:value-of select="updated"/>
            </dc:date>
            <dc:creator>
                <xsl:value-of select="author/name"/>
            </dc:creator>
            <dc:description>
                <xsl:value-of select="summary"/>
            </dc:description>
            <dc:format>
                <xsl:value-of select="content/@type"/>
            </dc:format>
            <xsl:for-each select="category">
                <dc:subject>
                    <xsl:value-of select="./@label"/>
                </dc:subject>
            </xsl:for-each>
        </item>
    </xsl:template>
</xsl:stylesheet>
```

RSS 1.0 Results

To run the transform, add a scenario in the Oxygen IDE, using `atom.xml` as the source, and `rss_feed.xsl` as the stylesheet.

Listing 1-7 shows a matching fragment of the transformed RSS 1.0 feed.

Listing 1-7

```
<?xml version="1.0" encoding="UTF-8"?>
<rdf:RDF xmlns:dc="http://purl.org/dc/elements/1.1/"
    xmlns:rdf="http://www.w3.org/1999/02/22-rdf-syntax-ns#">
    <channel rdf:about="http://feeds.oreilly.com/oreilly/xml">
        <title>O'Reilly News: XML</title>
```

```
<link>http://feeds.oreilly.com/oreilly/xml</link>
<items>
    <rdf:Seq>
        <rdf:li rdf:resource="tag:broadcast.oreilly.com,2008://53.34667"/>
        <rdf:li rdf:resource="tag:broadcast.oreilly.com,2008://53.34679"/>
        <rdf:li rdf:resource="tag:broadcast.oreilly.com,2008://53.34620"/>
        <rdf:li rdf:resource="tag:broadcast.oreilly.com,2008://53.34524"/>
        <rdf:li rdf:resource="tag:broadcast.oreilly.com,2008://53.34508"/>
        ...
    </rdf:Seq>
</items>
<item rdf:about="tag:broadcast.oreilly.com,2008://53.34667">
    <link>http://feeds.oreilly.com/~r/oreilly/xml/~3/487860677
      /xforms-a-pause-for-reflection.html</link>
    <dc:language>en</dc: language >
    <dc:title>XForms, a pause for reflection</dc:title>
    <dc:date>2008-12-17T18:05:12Z</dc:date>
    <dc:creator>Philip Fennell</dc:creator>
    <dc:description>The other day I had what could only be described as a
'Roy Scheider moment', you know the bit in the film Jaws where the camera
tracks-in whilst zooming-out at the same time. Well, whilst debugging an
XForms enabled application, the Mozilla XForms plug-in had exposed the host
document, XForms and all, as the content of the empty xf:instance. How odd.
I mean, what good is that? That's when it struck me in a Roy Scheider sort
of way; this was Reflection, the ability of a program to look at itself and
change its behaviour.</dc:description>
    <dc:format>html</dc:format>
    <dc:subject>xforms</dc:subject>
    <dc:subject>xml</dc:subject>
    <dc:subject>xrx</dc:subject>
</item>
    ...
</channel>
</rdf:RDF>
```

Summary

In this chapter you created two stylesheets, the first of which handled a typical document transformation from XML to XHTML.

The second transform was a little more complex, involving two different schemas. You used an XSLT version 2.0 stylesheet with XML output, and learned about using the `<xsl:for-each>` instruction to handle repeating uniform data structures.

You used three methods to invoke your first stylesheet: the `<?xsl-stylesheet?>` processing instruction, the Oxygen IDE, and the Saxon CLI.

Along the way, you learned about the main structural XSLT elements, defining output methods, matching nodes in source documents, and selecting content to transform. You also encountered some common XPath syntax, more of which is introduced in Chapter 2.

Key Points

- ❑   A stylesheet processor uses built-in rules for processing by default.

- ❑   You override these rules by using specific template rules to match elements in an XML source document with XPath expressions.

- ❑   You can specify different output methods in a stylesheet — XML, XHTML, HTML and text — and define the preferred character encoding too.

- ❑   Literal result elements and attributes are often used to define output structures.

- ❑   Output element content is usually specified by selecting values in the source with XPath expressions.

- ❑   Always check for default namespace declarations in source files and set the `xpath-default-namespace` attribute on the `<xsl:stylesheet>` element to this value.

Introducing XPath

XPath 2.0 is an expression language that is absolutely fundamental to XSLT 2.0 in several important ways.

A common use of XPath in XSLT is selecting nodes in an XML document. For example, you can make a very wide selection and refer to all the `<li>` elements in a document using the expression `select="//li"`, or be very specific by pointing to the class attribute in the first `<p>` in the third `<div>` of a document using `div[3]/p[1]/@class`.

XPath expressions are also used by an XSLT processor to match source tree nodes to template rules. As the XSLT processor traverses the element nodes in an XML source document, it looks for a corresponding XPath expression that you set in the `match` attribute of an `<xsl:template>` declaration.

XPath functions provide you with a wide range of features, enabling you to manipulate strings, dates and times, numbers, and nodes.

In this chapter you take a break from creating full-scale stylesheets and look into some XPath 2.0 features in some detail. You'll do all of the following:

- ❑ Review node types and properties.
- ❑ Look at the XPath data model.
- ❑ Tackle the important topic of path expressions used to navigate the node trees in your source documents.
- ❑ Get a brief overview of using the XPath Analyzer — a tool that can help you avoid problems along the XPath trail.
- ❑ Study a rich set of XPath functions that you will encounter repeatedly as you develop your XSLT skills.

Nodes

In the introduction you saw that XPath models the XML document as a tree of typed nodes. Here you'll look at the node types in more detail, including their properties.

Let's consider another partial document from the case study, this one describing the <xsl:apply-templates> instruction. In this example, a namespace for a different XML vocabulary is declared and used in the paragraph under the <purpose> element to mark the phrase "template rule" as a <xm:term> element. A figure contains a reference to a diagram illustrating the content model of <xsl:apply-templates>. I'll refer to this example in the section on node types that follows.

```
<reference>
  <body>
<title>xsl:apply-templates</title>
      <purpose>
          <p>A template instruction used to override a <xm:term
   xmlns:xm="http://xm.net/2007/xsl/term"> template
          rule</xm:term> in an importing module with one of the same name in
          an imported module.</p>
      </purpose>
      <usage>
          <p><element>xsl:apply-imports</element> is useful when you want to
   partially override a rule rather than replace it.</p>
      </usage>
      <!-- content model diagram -->
      <figure><object src="stylesheet_cm.jpg"/></figure>
      ...
  </body>
</reference>
```

Node Types

XPath defines a number of node types:

- ❑ **Document:** The root of the tree representing the entire document contents, represented by the "/" character in an XPath expression. I use the term "document" to designate this node, which is often called the *root node*, because I find that using "root node" makes it easy to confuse the document node with a document's root, or outermost, element.

- ❑ **Element:** Element nodes are defined by pairs of start and end tags such as <title> </title> or an empty element tag such as <object/> with no content. Often you will see "tag" used as a synonym for "element," but I won't follow that usage.

- ❑ **Text:** A character sequence in an element, comment, processing instruction, or namespace, such as the content "XSLT 2.0" in <title>XSLT 2.0</title>.

- ❑ **Attribute:** The name and value of an attribute in an element start tag or an empty element tag, such as <object src="stylesheet_cm.jpg"/>.

- ❑ **Comment:** Comments in an XML source document, such as <!--content model diagram -->.

- ❑ **Processing instruction:** An instruction in the source document, such as the stylesheet instruction <?xml-stylesheet href="step1.xsl" type="text/xsl"?>.

- ❑ **Namespace:** A namespace declaration is copied to each element to which the declaration applies. In this case it is http://xm.net/2007/xsl/term, copied to the <xm:term> element.

Node Properties

A node may have a number of properties. The following table shows how they apply to each node type.

Property	Description	Applies to Node Type(s)
Name	Qualified by the namespace, such as `<xm:term>`; the prefix `"xm"` precedes the colon, followed by the local part of the name, here `"term"`. The two parts of the node may be accessed using the functions `namespace-uri()` and `local-name()`.	Element, attribute, namespace, processing instruction
String value	The value of the element, attribute, comment, and so on. You can use the `string()` function to access this property.	All
Typed value	The content of the node after it has been validated against the schema. Applies only to element and attribute nodes; otherwise, it is identical to the string value. Most operations extract this value automatically.	Element, attribute
Type annotation	The datatype of the node content, set by the schema processor, as distinct from the node type.	Element, attribute
Base URI	The base URI of the document from which the node data was read, or, if present, the value of the `xml:base` attribute on the element.	Document, element, processing instruction
Parent	Refers to the parent node. It does not apply to the document node.	All except document
Children	A list of child nodes.	Document, element
Attributes	The order of attributes is undefined.	Element
Namespace	The namespace nodes of an element.	Element

Data Model

The XPath value that results from evaluating an expression is known as a *sequence*. Sequences are ordered collections of items, and may contain atomic values as well as nodes.

For example, if you were to select all the `<property>` elements in a document using the expression `"//property"`, the processor would return a sequence of the elements.

The numbering of items always starts at 1. You can access individual items in this sequence using XPath functions such as `position()`, `count()`, and `last()`. The next snippet shows a test for the count of elements in the sequence. If it is greater than 1, then an "s" is added to the literal text value of `Attribute`:

```
<h2>Attribute<xsl:if test="count(//property) gt 1">s</xsl:if></h2>
```

By *atomic values* I mean things such as numbers of various kinds, strings, and Boolean values. These are typed values, using an extension of the W3C XML Schema 1.0 datatypes recommendation. In addition to some 20 primitive datatypes, there are many derived types as well, with the namespace prefix xs. XPath 2.0 defines five additional datatypes in the XML Schema 1.0 namespace, with the same prefix — namely, `anyAtomicType`, `untyped`, `untypedAtomic`, `dayTimeDuration`, and `yearMonthDuration`.

These types may be extended further by specifying user-defined types in an XML schema. With a schema-aware processor you can access them in XSLT 2.0 using the `<xsl:import-schema>` declaration.

Examples of these datatypes include `xs:anyURI`, `xs:dateTime`, and `xs:string`. The following table provides descriptions of the frequently used atomic types supported in XPath functions.

Atomic Type	Description
`xs:anyURI`	Absolute and relative URIs, including those with a fragment identifier.
`xs:date`	A date in the ISO 8601 format yyyy-mm-dd.
`xs:dateTime`	A DateTime value in the ISO 8601 format yyyy-mm-ddThh:mm:ssZ. A fractional seconds part containing at least three digits may be provided.
`xs:decimal`	Numbers that can be represented in decimal notation.
`xs:double`	Double-precision, floating-point numbers.
`xs:integer`	Positive and negative natural numbers up to 20 digits.
`xs:QName`	A simple local name, or a namespace-prefixed local name.
`xs:string`	A sequence of zero or more characters.
`xs:time`	A time in ISO 8601 format hh:mm:ss.
`xs:dayTimeDuration`	Duration in the ISO 8601 format PnDnHnMnS.
`xs:yearMonthDuration`	Duration in the ISO 8601 format PnYnM.

The W3C XML Schema working group has developed XML Schema 1.1 to address commonly requested features and shortcomings of XML Schema 1.0. To align the type systems of XML Schema with XPath 2.0, the new datatypes specification that is currently at working draft status, introduces three of these datatypes: `xs:anyAtomicType`, `xs:dayTimeDuration`, *and* `xs:yearMonthDuration`.

You can find the working draft at www.w3.org/TR/xmlschema11-2/.

Path Expressions

You've already encountered several path expressions in the XSLT stylesheets that you have seen so far. Expressions like `reference/body` from the first stylesheet in Chapter 1 are used to select nodes in a tree in a series of steps.

Paths are interpreted with respect to the current *context*, which, broadly speaking, is the node in the tree being processed, or the location. It also consists of other information, such as the variables, functions, and namespaces that are in scope, and a good deal more as well.

Simple location expressions include "/", which by itself selects the document node, mentioned earlier. Other examples include ".", which is shorthand for the current context, and "..", which will select the parent of the context node.

Step expressions "navigate" the node tree, in the sense that they describe absolute or relative positions. These steps are separated by the "/" character, which you will recognize from the naming of paths in file systems.

Each step may have three parts — axis, test, and predicate:

❑   **Axis:** Specifies a directional relationship in the node tree such as parent:: or child:: This is often implied — for example, p/code is the shorthand for the code element on the child axis.

❑   **Test:** Defines the nodes to select using the node name or type.

❑   **Predicate:** May be used to filter a selection by some other property.

The following example refers to the parent:: axis, testing for an element <p> with the predicate class attribute equal to "highlight":

```
parent::p[@class= "highlight"]
```

Absolute paths start at the document node of the tree containing the context. Relative paths select nodes relative to the context node.

Using an XPath Analyzer

A quick way to experiment with path expressions is to use an analysis tool. These tools are invaluable for debugging, too. When I write some XSLT that fails to make the expected selection the first time, I often go to an analyzer to help me get the syntax right.

Here's how to use the tool that is built into the Oxygen IDE, which you can use to get feedback as you work through the book:

1.   Open atom.xml from Chapter 1 in the XML editor.

2.   Choose XML ➤ XPath to open the XPath dialog.

3.   Choose XPath 2.0 from the drop-down list.

4.   Type an expression in the Expression control; the following example uses **"/feed/id"**.

5.   Click Execute. Figure 2-1 shows the XPath Results window.

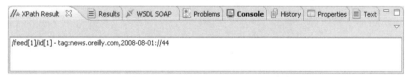

Figure 2-1

The analyzer reports the relative path from the document root, providing the position — in square brackets "[]" — of each node that matches the expression, followed by the relevant text node.

If you click on an item in the report, the matching item in the source code is highlighted.

Try another analysis, this time with the expression `//content/@xml:lang`. You should get a list of all the entry nodes with the attribute `xml:lang` and its value:

```
/feed[1]/entry[1]/content[1]/@xml:lang - en
/feed[1]/entry[2]/content[1]/@xml:lang - en
/feed[1]/entry[3]/content[1]/@xml:lang - en
/feed[1]/entry[4]/content[1]/@xml:lang - en
/feed[1]/entry[5]/content[1]/@xml:lang - en
/feed[1]/entry[6]/content[1]/@xml:lang - en
...
```

Axes

The following tables summarize the axis relationships and demonstrate two groups of selections from `xsl_stylesheet.xml`, which you have already seen:

```
<reference xml:id="xsl_stylesheet">
    <body>
        <title>xsl:stylesheet</title>
        <purpose>
            <p>The root element of a stylesheet.</p>
        </purpose>
        <usage>
            <p>The <element>xsl:stylesheet</element> is always the root element,
                even if a stylesheet is included in, or imported into, another. It
                must have a <attr>version</attr> attribute, indicating the version
                of XSLT that the stylesheet requires.</p>
            <p>For this version of XSLT, the value should normally be
                <code>"2.0"</code>. For a stylesheet designed to execute under either
                XSLT 1.0 or XSLT 2.0, create a <xm:term
                xmlns:xm="http://xm.net/2007/xsl/term">core module</xm:term> for each
                version number; then use <element>xsl:include</element> or
                <element>xsl:import</element> to incorporate common code, which should
                specify <code>version="2.0"</code> if it uses XSLT 2.0 features, or
                <code>version="1.0"</code> otherwise.</p>
            <p>The <element>xsl:transform</element> element is allowed as a
                synonym.</p>
            <p>The namespace declaration
                <code>xmlns:xsl="http//www.w3.org/1999/XSL/Transform</code> by
                convention uses the prefix <code>xsl</code>.</p>
            <p>An element occurring as a child of the
                <element>xsl:stylesheet</element> element is called a
                declaration. These top-level elements are all optional, and may
                occur zero or more times.</p>
        </usage>
    </body>
</reference>
```

The first table that follows shows the `self::` axis, which identifies the starting node from which any relationship is expressed, together with five axes that work "up" the tree from the start node. These axes select either ancestor or preceding nodes. The fourth column in the table lists the elements selected from the XML source when the start node is the third `<code>` element in the second paragraph under `<usage>`. The number inside square brackets ("[]")shows the position of the elements.

Axis	Selects	Start	Elements
self::	The start node from which any relationship is expressed	/usage/p[2] /code[3]	code[3]
parent::	Single parent of the start node		p[2]
ancestor::	All the elements that enclose the start node, up to and including the root node		reference, body, usage, p[2]
ancestor-or-self::	The start node as well as all the ancestors		reference, body, usage, p[2] code[3]
preceding::	Preceding nodes (excluding ancestors) in document order, excluding attribute and namespace nodes		p[1]
preceding-sibling::	All nodes with the same parent that precede the start node		code[1], element [1], element[2], code[2]

The next table shows axes with child and following sibling nodes.

The last two axes in the table, attribute:: and namespace::, apply only to element nodes, and are not directional in any meaningful sense. This time several different start nodes are given to illustrate all the axis relationships.

Axis	Selects	Start	Elements
child::	All of the children of the start node	/usage	p[1], p[2], p[3], p[4], p[5]
descendant::	Children of the start node, and all their children recursively		All the individuals under usage
descendant-or-self::	The start node and all the descendants		usage and all the individuals under usage
following::	Following nodes in document order, excluding attribute and namespace nodes	/usage/p[4]	p[5], element
following-sibling::	All nodes with the same parent that follow the start node	/title	purpose, usage
attribute::	Attributes of the start node	/reference	xml:id
namespace::	Namespace nodes of the start node	/usage/p[2] /xm:term	http://xm.net/2007 /xsl/term

According to the XPath 2.0 recommendation, "In XPath Version 2.0, the namespace axis is deprecated and need not be supported by a host language," so you may find that a processor does not support this representation. However, the Saxon processor will return values on this axis.

Node Tests

A node test defines the nodes to select. The syntax is usually in the shorthand form of the axis to follow — typically an element name, but some tests select on the basis of the node type. Here are just a few examples.

Name Tests

Consider the instruction `<xsl:apply-templates select="reference/body">`. In this case, the selection is implicitly on the child axis, where the full syntax is `child::reference/child::body`. This is certainly the most common axis relationship, and one that you have used in your stylesheets so far (probably without noticing it).

Another example of shorthand notation is for the attribute axis, where an expression such as `"@src"` replaces the full syntax `attribute::src`.

`"//"` selects *all* the nodes in the specified context — for example, `body//p` selects the `<p>` element descendants of the `<body>` element.

`"*"` is a useful wildcard to apply. The following table shows some name test examples.

Expression	Description
`*`	Matches all elements
`@*`	Selects all the attributes
`xm:*()`	Matches all element nodes in the namespace with the `"xm"` prefix
`*:term`	Any name matching the local name `"term"`, regardless of namespace

Type Tests

Node type tests look like `element(div)` or `comment()`, which will match any `<div>` element or all comments, respectively. The following table presents some examples.

Expression	Description
`node()`	Matches any node
`element()`	Matches any element node
`attribute(src)`	Any attribute node named "src"
`section//comment()`	All comments under the `<section>` element

Predicates

A step may be qualified with a predicate that acts as a filter on the selected nodes. For example, p/img[@src="icon.png"] will select only the <img> element with exactly the specified src attribute value.

In a predicate, the position is expressed as item[integer] — for example, div[3]. Note that numbering starts at 1, not zero.

The resulting sequences are always in document order, regardless of the direction of the path. Have another look at xsl_stylesheet.xml. If the start node is in /usage/p[5] and you select preceding-sibling::p/element, the result will be as follows:

```
<element>xsl:stylesheet</element>
<element>xsl:include</element>
<element>xsl:import</element>
<element>xsl:transform</element>
```

Note also that the position works in the same direction as the relationship. For example, preceding-sibling
::p[3]/element will return the element nodes three paragraphs back; that is, those from the second paragraph in our example:

```
<element>xsl:include</element>
<element>xsl:import</element>
```

Operators

In XPath expressions, you can use several groups of operators. The examples make use of XPath functions described in the following sections of this chapter. I'll defer a discussion of type operators until Chapter 11, when I consider validation with a schema-aware processor.

Arithmetic

Of the arithmetic operators +, -, *, div, idiv, and mod, the use of the first four will be familiar from other languages. The idiv operator performs integer division, and the mod operator provides the resulting remainder. The following table shows some examples.

Expression	Description
count($metadata) + 1	One greater than the number of nodes in the $metadata variable
last() -1	The next-to-last node in a sequence of items
@width idiv 2	Half of the value of the width attribute
@height * 3	Three times the value of the height attribute

Value Comparison

XPath 2.0 has introduced a new set of value-comparison operators for reasons related to XQuery optimization (see the following table for examples). Therefore, it is recommended that you use "gt" instead of ">" for comparing single atomic values, along with "eq", "ne", "lt", and "ge".

33

Expression	Description
`position() ne last()"`	Compares the position in the current sequence with the last position
`count(//property) gt 1`	Evaluates to true if the number of property nodes is greater than 1
`current-date() ne published`	Returns true if the current date is not equal to the published date

General Comparison

General comparison operators allow the operands to be sequences of items, unlike the value-comparison operators, which can compare only atomic values. Usually you will be making one-to-many comparisons, rather than many-to-many comparisons, which can be computationally expensive for long sequences.

Comparing sequences can be quite tricky in some circumstances, so think carefully about your logic, and especially about the possible effect of any empty nodes on what is returned. Here are some examples.

Expression	Description
`count(preceeding-sibling::p) eq 5`	Returns true when there are five preceding nodes with the same parent as the current node.
`sum(employees) < 10`	Tests whether the number of `employee` children is less than 10.
`$value != 5`	Returns true if any item in the `$value` sequence is not equal to 5.
`$list = $titles`	Returns true if `$list` and `$titles` have any value in common; for example, `(a,b,c) = (b,e,k)` is true.
`@src != @href`	Returns false if no `src` attribute is present.

Boolean Expressions

The order of operands in AND and OR expressions is not significant because the XPath rules allow implementations to optimize the processing of large sequences by indexing. Here are some examples of Boolean expressions.

Expression	Description
`@values and @required`	True if both attributes are present
`@values or @required`	True if either or both attributes are set
`exists(preceding-sibling::topicref[1]) and exists(following-sibling::topicref[1])`	True if there is both an adjacent preceding and an adjacent following sibling `<topicref>` element

Combining Node Sets

You can combine two sets of nodes using three XPath operators: union (or " | "), intersect, and except. These sets of nodes are just sequences, not ordered sets in the mathematical sense, and they may contain duplicates (see the following table for examples).

Expression	Description
`@a* except scheme`	Selects all attributes except the `scheme` attribute
`sum(employees | managers)`	Returns the number of `employee` and `manager` children
`$members intersect $visitors`	Returns a sequence of nodes containing the `$visitors` variable values that are also in `$members`

XPath Functions

In working with XSLT you'll come across several different kinds of function. Some are specific to XSLT, such as the `document()` function, and cannot be used in XPath expressions in XQuery. Others are so-called constructor functions such as `xs:date()`, which use built-in schema types or user-defined schema types to cast values, or extension functions you have developed using `<xsl:function>` declarations.

The XPath 2.0 functions discussed here are distinct from any of these and are specified in *XQuery 1.0 and XPath 2.0 Functions and Operators*, which is available at `www.w3.org/TR/2007/REC-xpath-functions-20070123/`.

An A–Z list is provided in the XPath 2.0 Function Reference in Appendix F. The following sections review some of the functions you'll encounter frequently in this book. They are divided into the following broad categories:

❑ Strings

❑ Dates, Times, and Durations

❑ Nodes and Documents

❑ Numbers

The examples are set in the context of their use in XSLT.

Strings

String functions will possibly be used more often than any other in your stylesheets. XPath 2.0 provides a very full range of string functions, bringing it closer to languages like Perl and JavaScript.

Concatenation

Concatenation is the string function I seem to need most frequently. The `concat()` function takes two or more comma-separated values, converts them into strings, and joins them with no punctuation or spacing. Typically, you'll use it in a `select` attribute value as shown in the following example, which you'll see in later chapters. It sets the value of an `href` attribute by concatenating a metadata URI with an identifier and a string:

```
<xsl:template match="link">
   <xsl:variable name="linkID" select="@href"/>
   <xsl:variable name="linkmeta" select="$resourcelist//entry[@xml:id=$linkID]"/>
   <a>
```

35

```
        <xsl:attribute name="href">
            <xsl:value-of select="concat($linkmeta/content/@src,$linkID,'.html')"/>
        </xsl:attribute>
        <xsl:value-of select="$linkmeta/title"/>
    </a>
</xsl:template>
```

If the arguments are the URI of a file on the path `"../xslt_reference/"`, a document identifier `"xsl_if"`, and the file extension `"html"`, the result passed will be as follows:

```
../xslt_reference/xsl_if.html
```

An alternative to `concat()` is `string-join()`. It enables you to provide a separator to use between values as a final argument, but it has the disadvantage that you need to explicitly convert any non-string values to strings using the `string()` function beforehand.

The next snippet uses `string-join()` with the `"/"` separator, converting a number in the nested `string()` function:

```
<p><xsl:value-of select="string-join(('my', 'string', 'join',
    string(4.00)), '/')"/></p>
```

The output will look like the following:

```
<p>my/string/join/4</p>
```

Substrings

You can use several useful string functions to handle partial strings.

You can test for the existence of one string within another using the `contains()` function. The first argument is the containing string to test, and the second is the value to find.

Suppose a source XML `<link>` element has a `contexts` attribute that may contain multiple space-separated values. If either of the values "meta" or "test" are present, then the link will be generated; otherwise not:

```
<related>
    <link href="entry" contexts="meta test"/>
    ...
</related>
```

The following expression tests for the existence of one of the values and returns true if it is present. The `<xsl:if>` instruction, which is covered in more detail in Chapter 4, provides a simple condition test:

```
<xsl:if test="contains(contexts,'meta')">
...
</xsl:if>
```

The functions `substring-before()` and `substring-after()` do what you would expect. The next snippet shows a metadata entry for an XSLT quick reference element:

```
<entry xml:id="xsl_output">
   <title>xsl:output</title>
   <content src="../xslt_reference/"/>
   <category term="element_reference" scheme="resource"/>
   <published>2008-12-19T20:13:28Z</published>
</entry>
```

The next example extracts the date part of a string representation of a DateTime value:

```
<xsl:variable name="tagdate"
              select="substring-before(published,'T')"/>
```

The first parameter is the value to analyze, and the second is the substring delimiter. In this case, the variable $tagdate would be set to "2008-12-19".

You can use index and length values on strings with the more general substring() function, which is useful when you need to work character by character, and you know the structure of the input. For example, you might select area-code prefixes from North American telephone numbers using the following:

```
<xsl:value-of select="substring($code,1,3)"/>
```

The index starts at 1. The length argument is optional; if you omit it, the entire string following the index value is returned.

When content entered by users has not been validated, it is good practice to remove leading and trailing whitespace before you start working with string values. The normalize-space() function does just that; in addition, it replaces multiple internal spaces with single space characters. If you have validated, structured values to work with this shouldn't be necessary.

Given some source content like " A History of France " in a list of book titles, you could prepare it for matching against another title, or for accurate sorting, by setting a value as shown in this example:

```
<xsl:value-of select="normalize-space($title)"/>
```

Dates, Times, and Durations

A host of functions are available for manipulating date and time values. Three of them simply return the values from your system. You can then go to town with extracting subsets or getting day values. You can also work with durations.

Contextual Dates

The contextual current-date(), current-dateTime(), and current-time() functions, along with any values in the source data, will get you to the starting point for your calculations.

Here's a fragment that timestamps an update to some feed metadata. It returns an xs:dateTime such as "2008-11-04T16:01:12.451Z":

```
<updated>
   <xsl:value-of select="current-dateTime()"/>
</updated>
```

All the DateTime functions always return the same result from multiple calls for any given transforma-tion, so you can't get one value for the beginning of a process and another for the end, for example.

Formatting

None of the DateTimes returned can be processed using XPath expressions. If you want to format the information differently, you can use the one of the XSLT formatting functions such as `format-date()`, which you'll examine further in Chapter 6.

Options include 12- or 24-hour clocks, time zones, and even calendars. A picture is used to specify the options. In the following example, `"[M]/[D]/[Y]"` returns the month/ day /year format:

```
<xsl:variable name="date"
        select="format-date(current-date(),'[M]/[D]/[Y]')"/>
```

Durations

For calculating durations you can use a function like `subtract-dates-yeilding-dayTimeDuration()`, or just use the subtraction operator `"-"` with two date values:

```
<xsl:value-of select="subtract-dates-yeilding-dayTimeDuration(xs:date("2008-06-24")
, xs:date("2008-06-22"))"/>
```

The result is an `xs:dayTimeDuration` value of `"P2D"`. Duration functions work in the opposite direction. For example, you can use the `hours-from-duration()` function on `"P2D"` to get `"48"`:

```
<xsl:variable name="hours"
        select="hours-from-duration(xdt:dayTimeDuration('P2D'))"/>
```

Nodes and Documents

Several functions are available that enable you to operate on nodes or entire documents, and provide context information, as described in the following sections.

Node Properties

You can access the properties of nodes with a number of functions (see the following table for examples). For example, the `root()` function will return the document node of a source tree.

Expression	Description
name()	For elements and attributes, returns the name of the context node, including the namespace prefix if present
data(author, title)	Returns the atomized values of the given sequence
namespace-prefix-for-uri(xm)	Returns the URI for the namespace prefix "xm"

Counting and Position

You can count nodes in a sequence, and determine positions in the sequence too.

The `count()` function returns the number of items in a sequence. If the sequence consists of nodes, each node counts as one item.

Here's an example of a test that handles *some* English-language plurals. The XPath expression uses the `count()` function to check whether multiple `<property>` elements need to be processed. If the count is greater than one, then an `"s"` is appended to the `<h2>` content:

```
<h2>Attribute<xsl:if test="count(//property) gt 1">s</xsl:if></h2>
```

Given a sequence of nodes made in a selection, two functions, `position()` and `last()`, will return the path position and the size of the sequence, respectively.

The following example shows the use of both functions to check on the current context, testing for inequality with `"ne"`, and rendering a separator character until the last item in a sequence of nodes is detected. If `$separator` is a comma followed by a space, you would get a result like `"a, b, c, d"`:

```
<xsl:if test="position() ne last()">
   <xsl:value-of select="$separator"/>
</xsl:if>
```

Documents

To return an external document you can use the `doc()` function. It is a simplified form of the `document()` function in XSLT. You provide the URI of the source document of a single document, and it returns the document node, ready to process. Fragment identifiers are not supported. Here is an example:

```
<xsl:variable name="metadata" select="doc('../reslist_xsl.xml')"/>
```

The XSLT `document()` function, by comparison, enables you to reference a sequence of nodes containing the URIs to process, and to use document-fragment identifiers.

Numbers

Numeric functions are fairly limited in comparison to other categories. Here are a few examples.

Expression	Description
`avg((2,4,6))`	Returns the average of the values in the sequence in the same primitive type as the values in the input sequence
`sum(@width,@height)`	Returns the total of the `width` and `height` attributes
`max((5,22,8))`	The maximum value in a numeric sequence

Summary

In this chapter you learned more about the XPath node types and their properties. You saw how you can use path expressions to select nodes in a source tree, and how these expressions are composed of axes, node tests, and predicates.

An XPath analyzer is a valuable tool that will help you validate path expressions, and you learned how the analyzer in the Oxygen IDE works.

XPath functions provide the basis for a very wide range of expressions. You reviewed a subset of these functions, especially string, date, node, and number functions, giving you a flavor of some of the most common functions you can expect to use in XSLT.

In the next chapter, you'll return to stylesheet development, focusing on templates, variables, and parameters. Before moving on, try answering the questions that follow to test your understanding of XPath.

Key Points

❑ XPath is central to XSLT processing for matching, selection, and functions.

❑ Work on the axis/test/predicate pattern, using both the shorthand and full axis relationship syntax, because it is the key to precise selection.

❑ Add an XPath analysis tool to your kit. It will save time and help to hone your skills.

❑ XPath functions are distinct from those that are reserved for XSLT. Familiarize yourself with the details of the function library, which provides a wide range of valuable processing features.

Exercises

You'll find solutions to these exercises in Appendix A.

1. Name some common XPath axes used to select element and attribute nodes.

2. Assume that the context is in an element node. Write the expression that selects the xml:id attribute node for the element using the full and shortcut syntaxes (you can use any element name you like).

3. After reviewing the string functions in XPath, create a simple XSLT stylesheet that you can use as a function test bed. Include several additional examples inside <p> elements using the following code as a guide:

```
<?xml version="1.0" encoding="iso-8859-1"?>
<xsl:stylesheet xmlns:xsl="http://www.w3.org/1999/XSL/Transform    version="2.0">
   <xsl:output method="xml" indent="yes" encoding="utf-8"/>
   <xsl:template match="/">
```

```
<output>
  <p>
    <xsl:value-of
        select="string-join(('my', 'string', 'join', string(4.00)), '/')"/>
  </p>
</output>
  </xsl:template>
</xsl:stylesheet>
```

Hint: You can transform the stylesheet by using itself as the source document.

Templates, Variables, and Parameters

When you are writing a stylesheet, some of the intended output, excepting the case of text, will come from generating elements and attributes that conform to the schema of the resulting document.

However, most of the output content will come from the source tree that the processor has loaded, and will be obtained (as a first step) by matching source tree nodes to patterns in the stylesheet templates.

Templates, specified with the `<xsl:template>` element, are core structures in XSLT. You use them as containers for the sequences of instructions that select values from the source tree and write them to the result tree. In addition to specifying matching patterns, you can give templates priority values to cover cases when several templates match the same source node. You can also specify different modes of processing for a given match. Named templates can be called explicitly, providing a degree of control over the processing sequence.

In XSLT you can use both global and local variables, defined with the `<xsl:variable>` element. As in any programming language, they enable you to set or calculate a value once and then use it in many places. They also have other uses, including storing temporary trees of nodes. However, in XSLT variables cannot be updated. XSLT is designed to be free of side effects. A side effect of assigning variable values as you might in other languages is that the processor would have to handle instructions in a particular order.

Parameters can also be defined globally, with predefined values set or passed in as the stylesheet is invoked. They can also be specified within templates or user-defined functions and passed as part of the calling process.

In this chapter you'll do the following:

- ❑ Extend your knowledge about template rules, and how to apply them using match patterns, modes, and priorities.
- ❑ Work with named templates.
- ❑ Learn about variables and parameters, including how to use those with global scope and those with local scope that are used in both template rules and named templates.

About Templates

The XSLT specification notes that the `<xsl:template>` element may define either a *template rule*, which matches source tree nodes against a pattern, or a *named template*, called explicitly by name.

Each template contains a sequence constructor containing instructions like those you used in Chapter 1, usually used to create element nodes.

Template rules operate rather like filters, matching specific criteria in the source tree. You don't direct the processor to use a template rule; it will automatically compare nodes in the source tree to the rules. Having found a match, the contained instructions are followed, writing the transformed values to the result tree.

Named templates, conversely, are called explicitly, and operate more like procedural calls, returning to the calling context after the output has been added to the result tree. This additional control makes them most suited for data-driven stylesheets, where structures in source instances are quite uniform.

All template elements require either a `match` attribute, in the case of a template rule, or a `name` attribute, in the case of a named template. The `<xsl:template>` declaration may have both attributes set, but that is unusual.

All templates are in the declaration substitution group and are therefore top-level elements. Their order in a stylesheet is not significant. Here's a reminder of the element structure:

```
<xs:element name="template" substitutionGroup="xsl:declaration">
  <xs:complexType>
    <xs:complexContent mixed="true">
      <xs:extension base="xsl:versioned-element-type">
        <xs:sequence>
          <xs:element ref="xsl:param" minOccurs="0" maxOccurs="unbounded"/>
          <xs:group ref="xsl:sequence-constructor-group" minOccurs="0"
            maxOccurs="unbounded"/>
        </xs:sequence>
        <xs:attribute name="match" type="xsl:pattern"/>
        <xs:attribute name="priority" type="xs:decimal"/>
        <xs:attribute name="mode" type="xsl:modes"/>
        <xs:attribute name="name" type="xsl:QName"/>
        <xs:attribute name="as" type="xsl:sequence-type" default="item()*"/>
      </xs:extension>
    </xs:complexContent>
  </xs:complexType>
</xs:element>
```

Template Rules

First let's consider the template rule, characterized by a `match` attribute pattern that is used to identify the source node or nodes to which the rule applies. Actually, there is more to rule evaluation than patterns. Modes, import precedence, and priorities may also come into play, but the match pattern is the most commonly seen.

Template rules can have three parts: a pattern that is matched against nodes, a set of template parameters, and a sequence constructor that produces a sequence of new nodes intended to be written to a result tree.

The XSLT 2.0 schema specifies `xsl:pattern` as the type for the `match` attribute. A pattern is an XPath expression that will return a sequence of nodes.

Some matches seem intuitive. You saw several examples in the discussion of XPath in Chapter 2, where I discussed steps, axes, predicates, and so on; but let's add a few more match examples here as an aid to memory:

❑ `purpose/p`: Matches paragraphs inside the `<purpose>` element

❑ `usage/p[3]`: Matches the third paragraph in any `<usage>` section

❑ `element[@xml:id="xsl_stylesheet"]`: Matches an element with an `xml:id` attribute equal to "xsl_stylesheet"

❑ `$resourcelist/entry`: Matches any `<entry>` element contained in the nodes assigned to the variable `$resourcelist`

The rules for the some of the more complex patterns, and those related to resolving conflicts between apparently similar nodes, are quite complex and therefore beyond the scope of this book. If you want to dig in to this subject, I suggest you read Chapter 12, ''XSLT Patterns,'' in Michael Kay's *XSLT 2.0 and XPath 2.0 Programmer's Reference, 4th Edition* (Wrox, 2008).

You'll encounter patterns again when looking at `<xsl:number>` in Chapter 6, in the sections on grouping in Chapter 5, and with `<xsl:key>` in Chapter 9.

This template rule approach is very flexible. It supports reuse, and it is simple to maintain when changes take place in the source or target schemas, because you can isolate the processing of source components so readily. It works especially well for quite complex documents with unpredictable instance structures, especially if they may be nested in different ways.

You may well know a great deal about the potential source content; you have the schema, after all. But schema compliance is not the same thing as consistency from one document instance to another. Take a schema like DocBook, which is widely used in technical documentation. The schema is very open, and a large number of elements may appear in a very wide range of contexts. For instance, the `<cmdsynopsis>` element provides a syntax summary for a software command. Its content model seems compact, but the element itself may appear in over 90 different contexts. A look at its child element shows similar characteristics.

Invoking a Rule

As you have seen, you invoke the evaluation of a rule by using the `<xsl:apply-templates>` instruction inside a template that already matches a context node. The instruction selects a set of nodes and causes them to be processed by selecting a rule for each one. It is therefore commonly used to process nodes that are descendants of the context node. A rule is evaluated when the `<xsl:apply-templates>` instruction selects a node that matches the pattern in the `match` attribute value. The context *always* moves to the matched node. Here is the schema definition.

```
<xs:element name="apply-templates" substitutionGroup="xsl:instruction">
  <xs:complexType>
```

```
    <xs:complexContent>
      <xs:extension base="xsl:element-only-versioned-element-type">
        <xs:choice minOccurs="0" maxOccurs="unbounded">
          <xs:element ref="xsl:sort"/>
          <xs:element ref="xsl:with-param"/>
        </xs:choice>
        <xs:attribute name="select" type="xsl:expression" default="child::node()"/>
        <xs:attribute name="mode" type="xsl:mode"/>
      </xs:extension>
    </xs:complexContent>
  </xs:complexType>
</xs:element>
```

Immediately after the start tag of the `<xsl:apply-templates>` element you may specify a way of sorting the resulting output using `<xsl:sort>`, as the following snippet illustrates:

```
<xsl:apply-templates select="book">
   <xsl:sort select="author"/>
<xsl:apply templates>
```

Information on sorting is covered in Chapter 5.

You can optionally provide a number of patterns to match in the `select` attribute:

```
<xsl:apply-templates select="attr | element"/>
```

Normally the XSLT processor will treat the selected nodes in the source document order, but if you want to define a different order, you can provide space-separated values in the `select` attribute, and the specified sequence will be followed:

```
<xsl:apply-templates select="element attr"/>
```

Using Modes

Modes enable you to process the same content more than once in different ways. One use of modes is to process a node in a source tree multiple times, each time producing a different result. Another use is to enable different sets of template rules to be active when processing different trees.

The modes in a template are defined by the `mode` attribute on the `<xsl:template>` element. In this case, the `<xsl:apply-templates>` instruction that invokes the template must specify both a `select` and a `mode` attribute. The `mode` attribute value may be a specific name or it can specify `#current`, which means "use the current mode." Using `#current` ensures that your templates work even if there are any subsequent changes or additions to mode names.

`mode` attributes on templates can contain a list of modes; the value `#default`, which means "use the default (unnamed mode)"; or the value `#all` to show that it matches all modes. Templates without modes are processed using the default mode.

The following Try It Out develops a simple example based on the template `local.xsl`. It makes a second pass through the source to create an index of element names.

Try It Out   Using Modes

Open `local.xsl`, save it as `modes.xsl`, and add the code that is highlighted in Listing 3-1, which will select all the nodes named ``element`` and apply the template with the mode attribute set to ``index.``

The template is used to produce an unordered list of the element occurrences, following the other output. The list is in document order and multiple instances are shown. An enhanced process could remove duplicates, sort the output, and merge it with index data from other source files.

Listing 3-1

```
<?xml version="1.0" encoding="UTF-8"?>
<xsl:stylesheet xmlns:xsl="http://www.w3.org/1999/XSL/Transform" version="2.0">
    <xsl:output method="xhtml" encoding="UTF-8"
        doctype-system="http://www.w3.org/TR/xhtml1/DTD/xhtml1-transitional.dtd"
        doctype-public="-//W3C//DTD XHTML 1.0 Transitional//EN"/>

    <xsl:template match="/">
        <html>
            <head>
                <title>
                    <xsl:value-of select="reference/body/title"/>
                </title>
            </head>
            <body>
                <xsl:apply-templates select="reference/body"/>
                <p><strong>Element index</strong>:
                    <xsl:apply-templates select="//element" mode="index"/>
                </p>
            </body>
        </html>
    </xsl:template>
    <xsl:template match="title">
        <h1>
            <xsl:value-of select="."/>
        </h1>
    </xsl:template>
    <xsl:template match="purpose">
        <h2>Purpose</h2>
        <xsl:apply-templates select="p"/>
    </xsl:template>

    <xsl:template match="usage">
        <h2>Usage</h2>
        <xsl:apply-templates select="p"/>
    </xsl:template>

    <xsl:template match="p">
        <p>
            <xsl:apply-templates/>
        </p>
    </xsl:template>
```

Continued

Listing 3-1: *(continued)*

```
    <xsl:template match="attr | element">
       <code>
          <xsl:value-of select="."/>
       </code>
    </xsl:template>

    <xsl:template match="element" mode="index">
          <ul>
          <xsl:for-each select=".">
             <li>
                 <xsl:value-of select="."/>
             </li>
          </xsl:for-each>
          </ul>
    </xsl:template>

    <xsl:template match="code">
       <xsl:copy-of select="."/>
    </xsl:template>
</xsl:stylesheet>
```

Now run the modified transform against the original file `xsl_stylesheet.xml`. The output of the index should look like this:

```
<p><strong>Element index</strong>: <ul>
       <li>xsl:stylesheet</li>
    </ul><ul>
       <li>xsl:include</li>
    </ul><ul>
       <li>xsl:import</li>
    </ul><ul>
       <li>xsl:transform</li>
    </ul><ul>
       <li>xsl:stylesheet</li>
    </ul>
</p>
```

Setting Priorities

You can apply `priority` attribute values to `<xsl:template>` elements to resolve cases for which there are several possible candidates for a match.

Some patterns are more specific than others. For example, `section/p` is more specific than p, as it applies to all paragraphs within sections, not to just any paragraph. It should logically have a higher priority allocated to it by the XSLT processor.

As a last step in evaluating a match, the processor allocates a default priority in the range −0.5 to +.0.5 using rules based on the pattern syntax. These rules are chosen carefully, but a clear "best match" solution cannot always be guaranteed. For example, `section/p` and `section/p[1]` both have a default priority of +0.5.

If more than one matching template has the same priority, the processor can either choose the last template declared or report an error. In these circumstances you should verify that the result is what you expect, or better still, specify your own priority values for a more certain result.

You can use the `priority` attribute to set an absolute priority value on templates with the same precedence. The attribute value is a positive or negative `xs:decimal` number — such as "3" or "-1.6" — that the processor will use rather than the default rules when there are several candidate nodes in the same source tree with the same namespace URI.

Priority values are the last to be considered in a match after mode, pattern, and import precedence.

Built-in Rules

If there is no rule with a matching pattern, a built-in template rule is used. You encountered built-in template rules in your first transform, where you saw that one set of default behaviors was for the XSLT processor to apply templates to all the children of the document node, and element nodes and their children. A nodes rule ensures that these nodes are processed regardless of any mode that might be current.

Four additional built-in rules are applied to nodes when no matching rule is present. Attribute and text nodes will be copied to the result tree as text, not as nodes, provided they are explicitly selected — for example, in a `select` attribute value such as "select='@*'". Comments, processing instructions, and namespace nodes are ignored.

Named Templates

A named template is one defined by the `name` attribute value. One of the advantages of named templates is reuse for common markup tasks, so when the look and feel of a website is changed there is little maintenance work to do.

Another benefit is the degree of control you can obtain by explicitly calling a template, rather than relying on the match processing sequence that typifies template rules.

Named templates are invoked with the `<xsl:call-template>` instruction. This instruction has a required `name` attribute that identifies the target `<xsl:template>` element. It is an error if there is no named template with a matching name. Here is the schema definition:

```
<xs:element name="call-template" substitutionGroup="xsl:instruction">
  <xs:complexType>
    <xs:complexContent>
      <xs:extension base="xsl:element-only-versioned-element-type">
        <xs:sequence>
          <xs:element ref="xsl:with-param" minOccurs="0" maxOccurs="unbounded"/>
        </xs:sequence>
        <xs:attribute name="name" type="xsl:QName" use="required"/>
      </xs:extension>
    </xs:complexContent>
  </xs:complexType>
</xs:element>
```

When you call a named template, the context node does not change as it does when a template rule is invoked with `<xsl:apply-templates>`.

In the last section of this chapter you will find a Try It Out that creates an XHTML `<head>` element, passing title and style parameter values.

Variables

Variables in XSLT have a number of uses. On the surface, they are used like variables in conventional languages. They can be used to specify global constants that are available throughout a stylesheet, or to set or calculate a locally used value with restricted scope.

A critical difference from conventional languages is that you cannot assign a new value to a variable once it has been set. So why call them variables? Consider the mathematical use of the term: It defines a name that may be used to express different values at different times. With an equation like $a = b \times c$, the names represent values expressing a relationship. They are variables because they can contain different values each time the equation is applied, not because the relationship is somehow changing dynamically.

Variables also have less obvious uses in XSLT, such as storing intermediate results in temporary trees of nodes, capturing context-sensitive values to call upon when the processing context has changed, and convenience values used just to simplify and clarify code.

You define a variable with the `<xsl:variable>` element, either as a top-level element or in a template. The schema defines it as content both in the `<xsl:transform>` substitution and in the sequence-constructor-group:

```
<xs:element name="variable">
  <xs:complexType>
    <xs:complexContent mixed="true">
      <xs:extension base="xsl:sequence-constructor">
        <xs:attribute name="name" type="xsl:QName" use="required"/>
        <xs:attribute name="select" type="xsl:expression" use="optional"/>
        <xs:attribute name="as" type="xsl:sequence-type" use="optional"/>
      </xs:extension>
    </xs:complexContent>
  </xs:complexType>
</xs:element>
```

One way to specify a variable is to use the `select` attribute with an XPath expression. The other way is to define the `<xsl:variable>` value in a contained sequence constructor.

The `name` attribute is required in each case, and must be unique within the scope of the variable, unless one of them is in an imported stylesheet.

Any variable defined at top level has a global scope, which means that you can access the value from anywhere in your stylesheet, and you may refer to it before it is declared, a so-called *forward reference*. That said, it seems to me good practice to set global variables near the beginning of a transform, or even in an included stylesheet module, rather than scattering the declarations about.

The scope of a template, or local, variable may be referenced in any *following* sibling element or any of those siblings' descendants. If the name of a local variable is the same as a global variable, then the local value is used. You cannot access the variable from one of its own descendant elements. Forward references are not allowed.

In the next Try It Out you'll use part of another reference document for the `<xsl:choose>` element that shows three elements — `<contains>`, `<containedby>` and `<link>` — used to express the content model. The link elements identify metadata for the related elements.

The stylesheet will use both global and local variables to generate an XHTML web page, in which title and URI values from the metadata are transformed into `<a>` elements content and `href` attribute values that link to the related pages.

`xsl_choose.xml` is shown in Listing 3-2.

Listing 3-2

```
<?xml version="1.0" encoding="UTF-8"?>
<reference>
   <body>
       <title>xsl:choose</title>
       <purpose>
           <p>An instruction that specifies a choice between alternatives which are
               defined by multiple <element>xsl:when</element> instructions, and an
               optional, terminal, <element>xsl:otherwise</element> element. Each
               <element>xsl:when</element> instruction has a <attr>test</attr>
               attribute containing an expression to evaluate.</p>
       </purpose>
       <usage>
           <p>A single <element>xsl:when</element> has the same result as though you
               had used <element>xsl:if</element> for a single test.</p>
       </usage>
       <contains label="contains">
           <link href="xsl_when"/>
           <link href="xsl_otherwise"/>
       </contains>
       <containedby label="containedby">
           <link href="xsl_instruction"/>
       </containedby>
   </body>
</reference>
```

Try It Out   Using Variables

Make another copy of `local.xsl`, saved as `content_model.xsl`.

At the top level, specify a global variable named `resourcelist`. In the `select` attribute, use the XSLT `document()` function to refer to the metadata file, `reslist-xsl.xml`, to be loaded by the processor. This function returns the document node specified. When the stylesheet is run, you can use the variable

$resourcelist (identified with the $ prefix) for operations on the metadata entries in this second source tree:

```
...
<xsl:variable name="resourcelist"
    select="document('reslist_xsl.xml')"/>
...
```

Next, add the following template rule to the new stylesheet. The <h2> literal result element is followed by an <xsl:choose> instruction that selects the section heading, based on the value of the label attribute. The paragraph element, <p>, will contain the XHTML links. In an <xsl:for-each> instruction, which will step through the <link> element nodes, the <link> elements inside both containers are selected for processing with the select attribute value "//link":

```
<xsl:template match="contains ! contained by">
    <h2>
        <xsl:choose>
            <xsl:when test="@label='contains'">Contains</xsl:when>
            <xsl:otherwise>Contained by</xsl:otherwise>
        </xsl:choose>
    </h2>
        <p>
            <xsl:for-each select="//link">
                <xsl:apply-templates select="."/>
            </xsl:for-each>
        </p>
</xsl:template>
```

The metadata entries contained in the $resourcelist variable are based on the Atom 1.0 recommendation, though they are not identical. The entry for the <xsl:when> element shows the structure. The xml:id attribute and the <title> and <content> elements exemplify the values to be processed:

```
...
<entry xml:id="xsl_when">
    <title>xsl:when</title>
    <content src="../xslt_reference/"/>
    <category term="element_reference" scheme="resource"/>
</entry>
...
```

In another template rule you can handle the links by first declaring two template variables:

```
<xsl:template match="link">
    <xsl:variable name="linkID" select="@href"/>
    <xsl:variable name="linkmeta"
        select="$resourcelist//entry[@xml:id=$linkID]"/>
        <a>
            <xsl:attribute name="href">
                <xsl:value-of
                    select="concat($linkmeta/content/@src,$linkID,'.html')"/>
            </xsl:attribute>
            <xsl:value-of select="$linkmeta/title"/>
        </a>
</xsl:template>
```

Naming the first variable $linkID gives us a meaningful, reusable value to work with, and selects the href attribute on the <link> element. The second variable, named $linkmeta, gives us a simplified value for the complex pattern $resourcelist//entry[@xml:id=$linkID].

Let's break down the second select expression. $resourcelist is the same global variable shown earlier in this section. It causes the file reslist_xsl.xml to be loaded and parsed. "//" selects all the entry element nodes, qualified by a predicate that matches the xml:id attribute in the metadata with the $linkID variable you specified first.

Inside the <a> element you set the href attribute value using the concat() function you learned about in Chapter 2. You also set the title in the link content.

Because the link template rule is being invoked from inside the <xsl:for-each> loop in the first template rule, both of the $linkID and $linkmeta select expressions in the second rule are evaluated each time the context node changes from one link element to another. This is *not* a change in the values of the two variables; rather, they are fresh instances within the scope of a given link node to be processed.

Before running the modified transform, change the stylesheet version to "2.0" and the output method to "xhtml".

Listing 3-3 shows the updated stylesheet.

Listing 3-3

```xml
<?xml version="1.0" encoding="UTF-8"?>
<xsl:stylesheet xmlns:xsl="http://www.w3.org/1999/XSL/Transform" version="2.0">

    <xsl:output method="xhtml" encoding="UTF-8"
        doctype-system="http://www.w3.org/TR/xhtml1/DTD/xhtml1-transitional.dtd"
        doctype-public="-//W3C//DTD XHTML 1.0 Transitional//EN"/>

    <xsl:variable name="resourcelist"
        select="document(concat('reslist_',reference/@scheme,'.xml'))"/>

    <xsl:template match="/">
        <html>
            <body>
                <h1>
                    <xsl:value-of select="reference/body/title"/>
                </h1>
                <xsl:apply-templates select="reference/body"/>
            </body>
        </html>
    </xsl:template>

    <xsl:template match="purpose">
        <h2>Purpose</h2>
        <xsl:apply-templates select="p"/>
    </xsl:template>

    <xsl:template match="usage">
        <h2>Usage</h2>
```

Continued

Listing 3-3: *(continued)*

```
        <xsl:apply-templates select="p"/>
    </xsl:template>

    <xsl:template match="contains | containedby">
        <h2>
            <xsl:choose>
                <xsl:when test="@label='contains'">Contains</xsl:when>
                <xsl:otherwise>Contained by</xsl:otherwise>
            </xsl:choose>
        </h2>
        <p>
            <xsl:for-each select="link">
                <xsl:apply-templates select="."/>
                <xsl:text> </xsl:text>
            </xsl:for-each>
        </p>
    </xsl:template>

    <xsl:template match="p">
        <p>
            <xsl:apply-templates/>
        </p>
    </xsl:template>

    <xsl:template match="attr | element">
        <code>
            <xsl:value-of select="."/>
        </code>
    </xsl:template>

    <xsl:template match="attr | element" mode="index">
        <code>
            <xsl:value-of select="."/>
        </code>
    </xsl:template>

    <xsl:template match="code">
        <xsl:copy-of select="."/>
    </xsl:template>

    <xsl:template match="link">
        <xsl:variable name="linkID" select="@href"/>
        <xsl:variable name="linkmeta"
            select="$resourcelist//entry[@xml:id=$linkID]"/>
        <a>
            <xsl:attribute name="href">
                <xsl:value-of

                    select="concat($linkmeta/content/@src,$linkID,'.html')"/>
            </xsl:attribute>
            <xsl:value-of select="$linkmeta/title"/>
        </a>
    </xsl:template>
</xsl:stylesheet>
```

When you run the stylesheet with `xsl_choose.xml` as source, set the stylesheet processor to be Saxon-B version 9x. You should see the following XHTML output at the end of the page:

```
...
<h2>Contains</h2>
    <p>
        <a href="../xslt_reference/xsl_when.html">xsl:when</a>
        <a href="../xslt_reference/xsl_otherwise.html">xsl:otherwise</a> </p>
<h2>Contained by</h2>
    <p>
        <a href="../xslt_reference/xsl_instruction.html">xsl:instruction</a>
    </p>
...
```

Parameters

Like variables, parameters can be defined globally at top level. They can also be specified within templates or user-defined functions, and passed as part of the calling process. The scoping rules are identical too. Here is the schema definition:

```
<xs:element name="param">
  <xs:complexType>
    <xs:complexContent mixed="true">
      <xs:extension base="xsl:sequence-constructor">
        <xs:attribute name="name" type="xsl:QName" use="required"/>
        <xs:attribute name="select" type="xsl:expression"/>
        <xs:attribute name="as" type="xsl:sequence-type"/>
        <xs:attribute name="required" type="xsl:yes-or-no"/>
        <xs:attribute name="tunnel" type="xsl:yes-or-no"/>
      </xs:extension>
    </xs:complexContent>
  </xs:complexType>
</xs:element>
```

Global Parameters

Generally, my preference is to use parameters rather than variables to set global values because they can also be passed in from an IDE interface or the command line, on a per-stylesheet basis if required.

The `<xsl:param>` element defines the name and value of a global parameter. As with a variable, the `name` attribute is required, and the value can be specified either by the `select` attribute or in the content of the element.

In the next exercise, you'll make use of a set of global parameters to do some "preprocessing," and experiment with the Oxygen IDE to view or modify the values you have set.

Try It Out   **Setting Global Values**

You can place global parameters in the main stylesheet module, or in a reusable included stylesheet.

Save a copy of `content_model.xsl` as `global.xsl`, delete the existing `$resourcelist` variable definition, and add the following global parameters:

```
. . .
<xsl:param name="identifier" select="reference/@xml:id"/>
<xsl: param name="resourcelist"
   select="document(concat('reslist_',reference/@scheme,'.xml'))"/>
<xsl:param name="meta"
   select="$resourcelist//entry[@xml:id eq $identifier]"/>
<xsl:param name="title" select="$meta/title"/>
<xsl:param name="style">reference.css</xsl:param>
. . .
```

`$identifier` is a copy of the `xml:id` attribute on the reference element. For the `$resourcelist` variable, the document URI is concatenated from the prefix `` `reslist_` ``, the `scheme` attribute on the reference element, and the file extension `` `.xml` ``. In turn, `$meta` and `$title` will extract the document title from the metadata entry that matches the `xml:id` attribute value. The `$style` variable value is used to specify a CSS stylesheet.

There are some variations in the manner global parameters are passed in by different processors, so check your documentation for the details.

With the Oxygen IDE you can set parameter values for each transformation scenario that you define. The user interface lists all the parameter values that are currently set in the main stylesheet and any included and imported stylesheets, with their default values. You can modify the default values for any processing run.

Take the following steps to set up parameters:

1. Open `xsl_choose.xml` in the XML editor.

2. Choose XML ➤ Configure Stylesheet Transformation.

3. On the XSLT tab, link it to `global.xsl`.

4. Click the Parameters button. The Configure parameter dialog, shown in Figure 3-1, will open, listing the existing parameters.

5. Double-click in the Value column to override a default parameter value. The changed parameter is highlighted.

6. Click Add to enter a new parameter name, and then enter the parameter value in the Value column.

Click Remove to remove a new parameter, or Disable to revert to the default value.

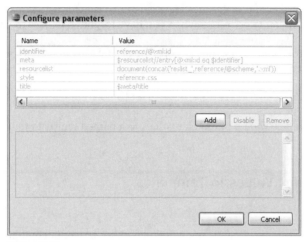

Figure 3-1

Template Parameters

In contrast to the similarities between a global variable and a parameter, the use of `<xsl:param>` in template rules or named templates differs considerably from the use of variables.

In templates, the `<xsl:param>` instruction must come immediately after the `<xsl:template>` declaration.

The `required` attribute indicates whether or not the parameter is required. The default value is ``no''.

The `<xsl:with-param>` instruction specifies the target parameter name and the value to be passed to a template. Zero or more such instructions may be used inside the `<xsl:apply-template>`, `<xsl:call-template>`, `<xsl:apply-imports>`, and `<xsl:next-match>` elements. This is the schema definition:

```
<xs:element name="with-param">
  <xs:complexType>
    <xs:complexContent mixed="true">
      <xs:extension base="xsl:sequence-constructor">
        <xs:attribute name="name" type="xsl:QName" use="required"/>
        <xs:attribute name="select" type="xsl:expression"/>
        <xs:attribute name="as" type="xsl:sequence-type"/>
        <xs:attribute name="tunnel" type="xsl:yes-or-no"/>
      </xs:extension>
    </xs:complexContent>
  </xs:complexType>
</xs:element>
```

It is an error to pass a parameter value that is not declared on a template rule or a named template. If the required attribute on the template is set to ``yes'', the processor will stop, reporting an error. To avoid this potential problem, you can optionally provide a default parameter value in a template — for example, a debug message to alert you to occasions when you have forgotten to pass them.

Any parameters are followed by a sequence constructor that is evaluated to produce a sequence of items, which are then written to a result tree:

```
<xsl:with-param name="title" select="$title"/>
```

In the next Try It Out, you'll pass parameter values to a named template that generates the <head> element in the output.

Try It Out   **Passing Values to Templates**

Save a copy of global.xsl as param.xsl.

Set up a template named "head" with some default values, immediately following the template's start tag:

```
<xsl:template name="head">
    <xsl:param name="title">title</xsl:param>
    <xsl:param name="style"/>css</xsl:param>
    <head>
        <meta http-equiv="Content-Type" content="text/xml;charset=UTF-8"/>
        <title>
            <xsl:value-of select="$title"/>
        </title>
        <link rel="stylesheet" type="text/css">
            <xsl:attribute name="href">
                <xsl:value-of select="$style"/>
            </xsl:attribute>
        </link>
    </head>
</xsl:template>
```

In the main template, use the <xsl:call-template> instruction to pass the $title and $style values you defined earlier using <xsl:with-param>:

```
<xsl:template match="/">
    <html>
        <xsl:call-template name="head">
            <xsl:with-param name="title" select="$title"/>
            <xsl:with-param name="style" select="$style"/>
        </xsl:call-template>
        <body>
            <h1>
                <xsl:value-of select="$title"/>
            </h1>
            <xsl:apply-templates select="reference/body"/>
        </body>
    </html>
</xsl:template>
```

Before you run the modified transform, remember to remove the `<title>` element from the source XML; you no longer need it for any of the quick reference documents, provided you accept the dependency on the metadata.

The modified output should look like the following:

```
...
<head>
   <meta http-equiv="Content-Type" content="text/xml;charset=UTF-8"/>
   <title>xsl:choose</title>
   <link rel="stylesheet" type="text/css" href="reference.css"/>
</head>
...
```

Tunnel Parameters

Before leaving this discussion of parameters, I want to mention tunnel parameters, which can also be passed using the `<xsl:with-param>` instruction. When a tunnel parameter is passed to a template, it is silently passed on to any templates called from the first one:

```
<xsl:apply-templates select="//figure">
   <xsl:with-param name="default_scheme" select="$scheme" tunnel="yes"/>
</xsl:apply-templates>
```

The `tunnel` attribute specifies whether or not this is a tunnel parameter.

To declare an interest in this parameter value in a template, you add a matching attribute value to the nested `<xsl:param>` element:

```
<xsl:template match="figure">
   <xsl:param name=" default_scheme" tunnel="yes" required="yes"/>
<!-- do something with the parameter value →
   <xsl:apply-templates select="object"/>
</xsl:template>
```

The parameter name must be unique within the sending and receiving contexts, but otherwise you need not worry about name clashes on any intermediate stages in the chain.

Summary

In this chapter you looked in more detail at the structure of both template rules and named templates, exploring modes and priorities as they apply to template rules.

You learned how to specify variables and parameters at both global and local levels. You also saw how to pass global parameters using an IDE, and how to use the `<xsl:with-param>` instruction in the case of local parameter values.

Along the way, you developed a more complex stylesheet that made use of the XSLT `document()` function to access metadata about the main document and other linked documents.

Key Points

❏   XSLT templates take two forms: template rules that specify matching patterns, and named templates that are called explicitly with the `<xsl:call-template>` instruction.

❏   In addition to pattern matching, template rules may use modes to specify multiple templates for the same basic pattern.

❏   You can use `priority` attribute settings in template rules to make the most important criteria explicit, rather than rely on specificity rules used by the processor.

❏   Variables and parameters appear to be similar in many respects, especially at a global level. However, within templates their purpose and use differ noticeably.

Exercises

You'll find solutions to these exercises in Appendix A.

1.   List some of the characteristics that distinguish template rules from named templates.

2.   In the `modes.xsl` stylesheet, I suggested one way of formatting index values for element names. Try out two additional modes — one that produces a simple space-separated list layout, and one that indexes additional element names.

Using Logic

The declarative nature of XSLT programming and the complex nature of many XML source documents often leads to stylesheets that make extensive use of template rules.

In some cases, however, you will want to use a more imperative style of programming, exercising specific control over the processor. One of these cases is when you want to use logic to test for simple or complex conditions, and direct processing accordingly. Another is when the source data is repetitive in nature, and the most straightforward thing to do is iterate over it.

In this short chapter you'll do the following:

❑ Learn more details about how you can control processing using `<xsl:if>`, `<xsl:choose>`, and conditional expressions in XPath.

❑ Learn when best to use `<xsl:for-each>` for iterative processing, rather than `<xsl:apply-templates>`.

❑ Apply the `<xsl:attribute-set>` declaration to define attribute values to be used in creating tabular output in XHTML.

❑ Process CDATA sections to display code examples that illustrate the use of XSLT elements.

Conditional Processing

There are two instructions in XSLT that enable you to perform actions based on data values conditionally. The `<xsl:if>` instruction provides a simple test, with a single outcome if the test is positive; the `<xsl:choose>` instruction supports the selection of one choice when there are several possibilities. They are conceptually similar to the if and case constructs you have encountered in other languages.

A Simple Choice

The `<xsl:if>` instruction has a required `test` attribute containing an XPath expression. If the attribute value evaluates to the Boolean value `"true"`, then the sequence constructor inside

the instruction is processed and the resulting node sequence is returned. Otherwise, an empty sequence is returned and processing continues. The XML schema definition looks like the following:

```
<xs:element name="if" substitutionGroup="xsl:instruction">
  <xs:complexType>
    <xs:complexContent mixed="true">
      <xs:extension base="xsl:sequence-constructor">
        <xs:attribute name="test" type="xsl:expression" use="required"/>
      </xs:extension>
    </xs:complexContent>
  </xs:complexType>
</xs:element>
```

The next example shows a test from a website build stylesheet. The code constructs a link in the table of contents. If the current document has a match in the table of contents, then a highlight style `"currentref"` is applied to the link in the `class` attribute on the `<a>` element, providing the user with a visual guide to his or her location in the site.

The `href` attribute on the link is constructed by concatenating URI and identifier values from metadata, in a similar manner to what you used to create links in Chapter 4. The variable `$thistopic` contains the document's identifier. The XSLT `current()` function returns the current context item:

```
<a>
   <xsl:attribute name="href">
      <xsl:value-of select="concat($topic/content/@src,@href,'.html')"/>
   </xsl:attribute>
   <xsl:if test="$thistopic=current()/@href">
      <xsl:attribute name="class">currentref</xsl:attribute>
      <xsl:value-of select="$topic/title"/>
   </xsl:if>
</a>
```

You can also use `<xsl:if>` to simply test whether a node exists, before continuing with some processing:

```
<xsl:if test="//purpose">
   <h2>Purpose</h2>
   <xsl:apply-templates select="//purpose"/>
</xsl:if>
```

Multiple Choices

For more complex situations you can make use of the `<xsl:choose>` instruction. It may have occurred to you that the last example was logically incomplete. What happens if there is no match between the table-of-contents entry and the current topic? A link is still needed, but in the basic unhighlighted style. Here is a little more context for the link test, showing how it is set within `<xsl:choose>`:

```
<xsl:choose>
   <xsl:when test="@href">
      <xsl:variable name="topic"
select="$resourcelist//entry[@xml:id=current()/@href]"/>

         <a>
            <xsl:attribute name="href">
               <xsl:value-of
select="concat($topic/content/@src,@href,'.html')"/>
            </xsl:attribute>
            <xsl:if test="$thistopic=current()/@href">
               <xsl:attribute
name="class">currentref</xsl:attribute>
               <xsl:value-of select="$topic/title"/>
            </xsl:if>
         </a>
   </xsl:when>
   <xsl:otherwise>
      <xsl:value-of select="."/>
   </xsl:otherwise>
</xsl:choose>
```

With this kind of structure there are no attributes to set. The content of `<xsl:choose>` is a sequence of one or more `<xsl:when>` instructions, and an optional, single `<xsl:otherwise>` instruction.

Each of the `<xsl:when>` instructions has a required `test` attribute value, evaluated in just the same way as described previously for `<xsl:if>`. These expressions are evaluated in document order: when one expression evaluates to `true`, all the subsequent tests are ignored.

You may use `<xsl:otherwise>` to handle a fallback result, should all the "when" tests fail, provided it appears last inside `<xsl:choose>`.

All three schema definitions follow:

```
<xs:element name="choose" substitutionGroup="xsl:instruction">
   <xs:complexType>
      <xs:complexContent>
         <xs:extension base="xsl:element-only-versioned-element-type">
            <xs:sequence>
               <xs:element ref="xsl:when" maxOccurs="unbounded"/>
               <xs:element ref="xsl:otherwise" minOccurs="0"/>
            </xs:sequence>
         </xs:extension>
      </xs:complexContent>
   </xs:complexType>
</xs:element>
```

```
<xs:element name="when">
  <xs:complexType>
    <xs:complexContent mixed="true">
      <xs:extension base="xsl:sequence-constructor">
        <xs:attribute name="test" type="xsl:expression" use="required"/>
      </xs:extension>
    </xs:complexContent>
  </xs:complexType>
</xs:element>

<xs:element name="otherwise" type="xsl:sequence-constructor"/>
```

Using XPath for Conditional Tests

If using `<xsl:choose>` testing starts to make your code hard to follow, you can shrink it considerably by using an if-then-else comparison inside a `select` attribute. Depending on the result of the evaluation, either the `then` or the `else` branch is returned. Both branches must be present, so you have to use an empty `else()` sequence, even if you don't need it.

In the following example, one attribute value is used to determine which of two other attribute values is selected:

```
<xsl:value-of select="if (@scheme eq `resource´) then @term else @label"/>
```

Iteration

You have already seen something of the use of `<xsl:for-each>` in earlier chapters. Typically it is used to select a sequence of nodes and iterate over them. Examples include report writing from uniform data structures, and XML-based e-commerce documents containing product information or billing data.

Whether you use this approach or simply use the more declarative `<xsl:apply-templates>` and template rules is often a question of personal preference. I tend to use `<xsl:for-each>` for data-oriented processing when there is a very predictable source content, such as news feeds or other tablelike representations. Sometimes it simply helps to see what your code is doing.

Using `<xsl:for-each>` is not like applying a for-next loop, where you can set the size of the loop or test for a terminal value. Rather, you use this instruction to select a sequence of nodes for processing in an identical manner. The term *iteration* is meaningful only in the context of a node sequence, in which variables will fall out of scope and cannot be updated.

Using Attribute Sets

Attribute sets provide a convenient way to group attribute definitions together for subsequent use in result trees. Quite often they are used to apply style properties to elements in XHTML pages, but they can be used for any purpose.

You declare attribute sets with the `<xsl:attribute-set>` element, with one or more nested `<xsl:attribute>` elements:

```
<xsl:attribute-set name="row">
   <xsl:attribute name="scope">row</xsl:attribute>
</xsl:attribute-set>
```

Having made this declaration, you can use it in a literal result element with a `use-attribute-sets` attribute as illustrated in the next snippet. Note that because the elements themselves are in the XHTML namespace, you need to specify the `xsl:` namespace prefix explicitly on the attributes:

```
<td xsl:use-attribute-sets="row">
   <xsl:apply-templates select="description"/>
</td>
```

Here is the XSLT schema definition for `<xsl:attribute-set>`. You'll see that one of its own attributes is `use-attribute-sets`, so you can combine attribute sets in a declaration:

```
<xs:element name="attribute-set" substitutionGroup="xsl:declaration">
  <xs:complexType>
    <xs:complexContent>
      <xs:extension base="xsl:element-only-versioned-element-type">
        <xs:sequence minOccurs="0" maxOccurs="unbounded">
          <xs:element ref="xsl:attribute"/>
        </xs:sequence>
        <xs:attribute name="name" type="xsl:QName" use="required"/>
        <xs:attribute name="use-attribute-sets" type="xsl:QNames" default=""/>
      </xs:extension>
    </xs:complexContent>
  </xs:complexType>
</xs:element>
```

The next Try It Out uses as a source another quick reference document describing the `<xsl:for-each group>` instruction, which you'll learn about in Chapter 5. Many of these reference documents contain attribute descriptions, which are a good example of highly structured content suited to processing with the `<xsl:for-each>` instruction. This source document also provides a good use case for applying attribute sets.

The structure provides `<name>`, `<description>`, `<type>`, `<values>`, and `<required>` elements within a set of `<property>` elements, nested inside a `<properties>` container.

Listing 4-1 shows the attribute descriptions from `xsl_for-each_group.xml`:

Listing 4-1

```
<properties type="attribute">
   <property xml:id="select">
      <name>select</name>
      <description>The sequence of items to group</description>
      <type>xsl:expression</type>
      <required state="required"/>
```

Continued

Listing 4-1: *(continued)*

```
        </property>
        <property xml:id="group_by">
            <name>group-by</name>
            <description>The common value or values to use</description>
            <type>xsl:expression</type>
            <required state="optional"/>
        </property>
        <property xml:id="group_adjacent">
            <name>group-adjacent</name>
            <description>The common value to use if items are adjacent</description>
            <type>xsl:expression</type>
            <required state="optional"/>
        </property>
        <property xml:id="starting">
            <name>group-starting-with</name>
            <description>The pattern that starts a group of following items</description>
            <type>xsl:pattern</type>
            <required state="optional"/>
        </property>
        <property xml:id="ending">
            <name>group-ending-with</name>
            <description>The pattern that ends a group of preceding items</description>
            <type>xsl:pattern</type>
            <required state="optional"/>
        </property>
        <property xml:id="collation">
            <name>collation</name>
            <description>The URI of a collation to use for string
                comparison</description>
            <type>xs:anyURI</type>
            <required state="optional"/>
        </property>
    </properties>
```

In the stylesheet, you will modify an existing template by specifying several attribute sets and combining them. You will also add two templates to process the <property> elements, which will be displayed in a <table> element.

Try It Out   Quick Reference Properties

First save a copy of param.xsl as for-each.xsl.

Make four attribute set declarations as follows:

```
<xsl:attribute-set name="col">
    <xsl:attribute name="scope">col</xsl:attribute>
```

```
    </xsl:attribute-set>

    <xsl:attribute-set name="row">
        <xsl:attribute name="scope">row</xsl:attribute>
    </xsl:attribute-set>

    <xsl:attribute-set name="th_first" use-attribute-sets="col">
        <xsl:attribute name="class" >firsthdr</xsl:attribute>
    </xsl:attribute-set>

    <xsl:attribute-set name="td_first" use-attribute-sets="row">
        <xsl:attribute name="class">firstcell</xsl:attribute>
    </xsl:attribute-set>
```

In the first two declarations, the name attribute specifies `col″ and `row″ as values, two of those allowed for scope settings for columns in table cells acting as column and row headers.

The second and third declarations use the first two, and specify class attribute values.

Now add templates to process the property values from the source XML:

```
    <xsl:template match="properties">
        <xsl:call-template name="attribute"/>
    </xsl:template>

    <xsl:template name="attribute">
        <h2>Attribute<xsl:if test="count(//property) gt 1">s</xsl:if>
        </h2>
        <table cellspacing="0">
            <tr>
                <th xsl:use-attribute-sets="th_first">Name</th>
                <th xsl:use-attribute-sets="col">Description</th>
                <th xsl:use-attribute-sets="col">Type</th>
                <th xsl:use-attribute-sets="col">Default</th>
                <th xsl:use-attribute-sets="col">Options</th>
                <th xsl:use-attribute-sets="col">Use</th>
            </tr>
            <xsl:for-each select="//property">
                <xsl:sort select="name"/>
                <tr>
                    <th xsl:use-attribute-sets="td_first">
                        <xsl:value-of select="name"/>
                    </th>
                    <td xsl:use-attribute-sets="row">
                        <xsl:apply-templates select="description"/>
                    </td>
                    <td xsl:use-attribute-sets="row">
                        <xsl:apply-templates select="type"/>
                    </td>
                    <td xsl:use-attribute-sets="row">
```

```
                    <xsl:value-of select="default"/> </td>
                <td xsl:use-attribute-sets="row">
                    <xsl:value-of select="values"/> </td>
                <td xsl:use-attribute-sets="row">
                    <xsl:value-of select="required/@state"/> </td>
            </tr>
        </xsl:for-each>
    </table>
</xsl:template>
```

The first template matches the `<properties>` element and calls the named template `attribute` with `<xsl:call-template>`.

In the called template, select all the property nodes, and sort them on the `<name>` element content. Then set out literal result elements for the `<h2>` and `<table>` elements. An `<xsl:if>` test pluralizes the heading if appropriate. In each `<tr>` element after the fixed `<th>` column headings, we iterate over each `<property>` element in turn.

Note two details. First, although there are no default attribute values in the schema declaration for `<xsl:for-each-group>`, some other elements do contain defaults, so we need to provide for them with a match for the `<default>` element. Second, the entity value ` ` is included to generate spaces in any table cells that may be empty; some browsers behave badly unless this is present.

As you write out the table cells, add attributes to them to provide style classes, and the column and row scope values for nonvisual user agents. This output is generated with the attribute `xsl:use-attribute-sets` on the `<th>` and `<td>` elements.

The next snippet shows the XHTML output for the attribute table:

```
<h2>Attributes</h2>
<table cellspacing="0">
    <tr>
        <th scope="col" class="firsthdr">Name</th>

        <th scope="col">Description</th>
        <th scope="col">Type</th>
        <th scope="col">Default</th>
        <th scope="col">Options</th>
        <th scope="col">Use</th>
    </tr>
    <tr>
        <th scope="row" class="firstcell">collation</th>
        <td scope="row">The URI of a collation to use for string comparison</td>
        <td scope="row">xs:anyURI</td>
        <td scope="row"> </td>
        <td scope="row"> </td>
        <td scope="row">optional </td>

    </tr>
    <tr>
        <th scope="row" class="firstcell">group-adjacent</th>
```

```
        <td scope="row">The common value to use if items are adjacent</td>
        <td scope="row">xsl:expression</td>
        <td scope="row"> </td>
        <td scope="row"> </td>

        <td scope="row">optional </td>
    </tr>
    <tr>
        <th scope="row" class="firstcell">group-by</th>
        <td scope="row">The common value or values to use</td>
        <td scope="row">xsl:expression</td>
        <td scope="row"> </td>

        <td scope="row"> </td>
        <td scope="row">optional </td>
    </tr>
    <tr>
        <th scope="row" class="firstcell">group-ending-with</th>
        <td scope="row">The pattern that ends a group of preceding items</td>
        <td scope="row">xsl:pattern</td>

        <td scope="row"> </td>
        <td scope="row"> </td>
        <td scope="row">optional </td>
    </tr>
    <tr>
        <th scope="row" class="firstcell">group-starting-with</th>
        <td scope="row">The pattern that starts a group of following items</td>

        <td scope="row">xsl:pattern</td>
        <td scope="row"> </td>
        <td scope="row"> </td>
        <td scope="row">optional </td>
    </tr>
    <tr>
        <th scope="row" class="firstcell">select</th>

        <td scope="row">The sequence of items to group</td>
        <td scope="row">xsl:expression</td>
        <td scope="row"> </td>
        <td scope="row"> </td>
        <td scope="row">required </td>
    </tr>
</table>
```

Monitoring the Context

As the XSLT processor iterates over the nodes, the context changes with each step. For example, if there is a variable value to output, then you need to calculate the variable value *inside* the <xsl:or-each> selection expression, or use the current() function to capture some content.

You can see this in operation by using the `position()` function to track progress through a sequence. You can do this with temporary changes to the cells containing the attribute names:

```
...
<th xsl:use-attribute-sets="td_first">

    <xsl:value-of select="concat('[',position(),'] ',name)"/>
</th>
```

The related `last()` function provides the number of items to process. You can use the following test for position to improve the output of multiple links in the XHTML. It inserts the " | " character as punctuation following the content if you haven't finished processing:

```
<xsl:for-each select="link">
    <xsl:apply-templates select="."/>

        <xsl:if test="position() ne last()">
            <xsl:text>|</xsl:text>
        </xsl:if>
</xsl:for-each>
```

Figure 4-1 shows both the improved punctuation and the output table with the first column cells numbered.

Contains

xsl:sort | sequence-constructor

Attributes

Name	Description	Type	Default	Options	Use
[1] collation	The URI of a collation to use for string comparison	xs:anyURI			optional
[2] group-adjacent	The common value to use if items are adjacent	xsl:expression			optional
[3] group-by	The common value or values to use	xsl:expression			optional
[4] group-ending-with	The pattern that ends a group of preceding items	xsl:pattern			optional
[5] group-starting-with	The pattern that starts a group of following items	xsl:pattern			optional
[6] select	The sequence of items to group	xsl:expression			required

Figure 4-1

Processing XML Code

Most documents in the XSLT Quick Reference contain examples like the following snippet. The `<examples>` element contains a `<codeblock>` element, which in turn contains a CDATA section with a code example:

```
<examples>
    <codeblock><![CDATA[
```

```
<xsl:for-each-group select="*"
    group-adjacent="if (self::speaker) then 0 else 1">
    <td class="noborder" width="50%">
        <xsl:for-each select="current-group()">
            <xsl:apply-templates select="."/>
            <xsl:if test="current-group()='0'">
                <span class="speaker"><xsl:value-of select="."/></span>
            </xsl:if>
            <xsl:if test="position() ne last()">
                <br/>
            </xsl:if>
        </xsl:for-each>
    </td>
    </xsl:for-each-group>]]></codeblock>
</examples>
```

The next Try It Out illustrates how to process this section of a reference document. You'll add two more templates to the `for-each.xsl` stylesheet to handle the output.

Try It Out   Processing CDATA

Add the following templates to handle the output of the code:

```
<xsl:template match="examples">
    <h2>Example<xsl:if test="count(codeblock) gt 1">s</xsl:if>
    </h2>
    <xsl:apply-templates/>
</xsl:template>

<xsl:template match="codeblock">
    <pre class="code">
        <xsl:value-of select="."/>
    </pre>
</xsl:template>
```

The `count()` test in the first template adds an "s" to the output if it contains more than one `<codeblock>` element.

In the second template, the `<pre>` element wraps the example. The XSLT processor will automatically escape the output, replacing the "<" and ">" characters with "<" and ">".

Here is the XHTML output:

```
<h2>Example</h2>
    <pre class="code">&lt;xsl:for-each-group select="*"
    group-adjacent="if (self::speaker) then 0 else 1"&gt;
    &lt;td class="noborder" width="50%"&gt;
        &lt;xsl:for-each select="current-group()"&gt;

        &lt;xsl:apply-templates select="."/&gt;
        &lt;xsl:if test="current-group()='0'"&gt;
```

```
    &lt;span class="speaker"&gt;&lt;xsl:value-of select="."/&gt;&lt;/span&gt;
    &lt;/xsl:if&gt;
    &lt;xsl:if test="position() ne last()"&gt;

      &lt;br/&gt;
    &lt;/xsl:if&gt;
  &lt;/xsl:for-each&gt;
&lt;/td&gt;
&lt;/xsl:for-each-group&gt;</pre>
```

Summary

This chapter explained how to make use of XSLT control structures. You learned the use of `<xsl:if>` for simple cases, and how to apply `<xsl:choose>`, `<xsl:when>`, and `<xsl:otherwise>` for more complex conditions. As an alternative, you learned that it is often possible to use if-then-else conditional expressions in XPath 2.0.

The chapter also illustrated ways of combining `<xsl:for-each>` for iterative content, together with `<xsl:apply-templates>`. You learned how to use `<xsl:attribute-set>` to apply styling and scope attribute values in tabular output, and how to process code in CDATA sections to XHTML.

Key Points

❑   When required, you can use the `<xsl:if>` and `<xsl:choose>` instructions to direct the action of the XSLT processor.

❑   When you are dealing with uniform data structures, the `<xsl-for-each>` instruction is often the best choice for driving the transformation process.

❑   Attribute sets can be specified and combined to provide a concise way of specifying attribute output.

Exercises

You'll find solutions to these exercises in Appendix A.

1.   List the types of source material and output types that lend themselves to using `<xsl:for-each>` in stylesheets.

2.   Prepare some attribute sets suitable for applying different text and background color combinations to a `<note>` element in HTML output, and show an example of how to use them in a template. The `type` attribute on the note element can be used to determine the style. Possible attribute values are "note", "caution", and "warning".

The precise colors are not critical, but I suggest black/white, blue/gray, and red/yellow combinations for text and background. Figure 4-2 shows the sort of result I have in mind, though not the colors, obviously.

Figure 4-2

The CSS stylesheet reference.css will handle the basic note style correctly.

Sorting and Grouping

Sorting content in various orders and grouping it into categories is standard fare in all manner of lists and reports. XSLT provides several useful tools that will help you get the results you want.

The sort instruction can be used in many stylesheet contexts with several sort options, and the `<xsl:for-each-group>` instruction makes it possible to group elements in a number of ways using very compact syntax.

In this chapter you'll do the following:

- ❑ Examine the options available to you for sorting and grouping content using `<xsl:sort>`, `<xsl:perform-sort>`, and `<xsl:for-each-group>`.
- ❑ Learn about the significance of datatypes and languages in sorting.
- ❑ See how to use variables in attribute value templates to create runtime values.
- ❑ Process part of a Shakespearian play marked up in XML.

Sorting Content

In earlier chapters you have used `<xsl:sort>` a couple of times with the default behavior, which is to sort as text, and to order it A–Z. Because that works well on many occasions, I did not discuss order options, multiple instructions, and so on. This section will fill in some details.

The `<xsl:sort>` instruction provides a single *sort key component* in a possible set of keys known as a *sort key specification*. For example, in the following code snippet, each of the individual sort instructions is a key component, and the pair of components together make up the key specification:

```
<xsl:for-each select="//product">
    <xsl:sort select="@store"/>
    <xsl:sort select="@sku"/>
    ...
</xsl:for-each>>
```

The instruction can apply to any sequence, not just nodes.

Here is the XSLT schema definition:

```
<xs:element name="sort">
  <xs:complexType>
    <xs:complexContent mixed="true">
      <xs:extension base="xsl:sequence-constructor">
        <xs:attribute name="select" type="xsl:expression"/>
        <xs:attribute name="lang" type="xsl:avt"/>
        <xs:attribute name="data-type" type="xsl:avt" default="text"/>
        <xs:attribute name="order" type="xsl:avt" default="ascending"/>
        <xs:attribute name="case-order" type="xsl:avt"/>
        <xs:attribute name="collation" type="xsl:avt"/>
        <xs:attribute name="stable" type="xsl:yes-or-no"/>
      </xs:extension>
    </xs:complexContent>
  </xs:complexType>
</xs:element>
```

Any keys must appear immediately after the <xsl:apply-templates>, <xsl:for-each>, <xsl:for-each-group>, or <xsl:perform-sort> instructions.

The XSLT processor does all the sorting before processing any of the other instructions in a sequence constructor. The order of sort keys is significant; they will be processed from the first/major key to the last/minor key.

Just as you'd expect, the select attribute contains an XPath expression. You can, alternatively, use an enclosed sequence constructor such as <xsl:value-of select=`@sku">. The default is select=`. " if neither is provided.

The order attribute defaults to the value "ascending"; the alternative is "descending".

Try It Out   **Sorting**

To experiment with sorting, open the products.xml file in the code folder:

```
<?xml version="1.0" encoding="UTF-8"?>
<products>
    <product sku="gdk943-46298r" color="red" units="50" store="Center"/>
    <product sku="gdk943-46298w" color="white" units="851" store="West"/>
    <product sku="gdk943-46298g" color="green" units="143" store="North"/>
    <product sku="gdk943-46298b" color="blue" units="19" store="North"/>
    <product sku="gdk943-46298p" color="purple" units="23" store="South"/>
    <product sku="gdk943-46298r" color="red" units="70" store="Center"/>
    <product sku="gdk943-46298g" color="green" units="29" store="East"/>
    <product sku="gdk943-46298w" color="white" units="203" store="South"/>
</products>
```

The requirement is to sort the content first by the stock keeping unit (SKU), and then by units available. The output is an XHTML table.

The core of the stylesheet looks very much like the table layout you used in Chapter 4 to list element attributes. This time the column headings are for "SKU," "Units," "Color," and "Store."

You might want to open `for-each.xsl` from that chapter's code and copy across some reusable components. The attribute set definitions are portable and can serve in the table, and the "head" template code will come in handy too.

Add the following code in the main template:

```
...
<xsl:template match="/">
    <html>
        <xsl:call-template name="head">
            <xsl:with-param name="title" select="title"/>
            <xsl:with-param name="style" select="$style"/>
        </xsl:call-template>
        <body>
            <h1>
                <xsl:value-of select="$title"/>
            </h1>
            <table cellspacing="0" width="50%">
                <tr>
                    <th xsl:use-attribute-sets="th_first">SKU</th>
                    <th xsl:use-attribute-sets="col">Color</th>
                    <th xsl:use-attribute-sets="col">Units</th>
                    <th xsl:use-attribute-sets="col">Store</th>
                </tr>
                <xsl:for-each select="//product">
                    <xsl:sort select="@sku"/>
                    <xsl:sort select="@color"/>
                    <tr>
                        <th xsl:use-attribute-sets="td_first">
                            <xsl:value-of select="@sku"/>
                        </th>
                        <td xsl:use-attribute-sets="row">
                            <xsl:value-of select="@units"/>
                        </td>
                        <td xsl:use-attribute-sets="row">
                            <xsl:value-of select="@color"/>
                        </td>
                        <td xsl:use-attribute-sets="row">
                            <xsl:value-of select="@store"/>
                        </td>
                    </tr>
                </xsl:for-each>
            </table>
        </body>
    </html>
</xsl:template>...
```

You'll see there are dependencies on the "head" template, on the `$title` and `$style` parameters, and on the attribute set definitions that are used to set the table's cell properties. Be sure to add this code to your template. The complete code is in `products_sort.xsl`.

The sorted table rows should look like Listing 5-1.

Listing 5-1

```html
<h1>Stock report</h1>
    <table cellspacing="0" width="50%">
        <tbody><tr>
            <th scope="col" class="firsthdr">SKU</th>
            <th scope="col">Units</th>
            <th scope="col">Color</th>
            <th scope="col">Store</th>
        </tr>
        <tr>
            <th scope="row" class="firstcell">gdk943-46298b</th>
            <td scope="row">19</td>
            <td scope="row">blue</td>
            <td scope="row">North</td>
        </tr>
        <tr>
            <th scope="row" class="firstcell">gdk943-46298g</th>
            <td scope="row">143</td>
            <td scope="row">green</td>
            <td scope="row">North</td>
        </tr>
        <tr>
            <th scope="row" class="firstcell">gdk943-46298g</th>
            <td scope="row">29</td>
            <td scope="row">green</td>
            <td scope="row">East</td>
        </tr>
        <tr>
            <th scope="row" class="firstcell">gdk943-46298p</th>
            <td scope="row">23</td>
            <td scope="row">purple</td>
            <td scope="row">South</td>
        </tr>
        <tr>
            <th scope="row" class="firstcell">gdk943-46298r</th>
            <td scope="row">50</td>
            <td scope="row">red</td>
            <td scope="row">Center</td>
        </tr>
        <tr>
            <th scope="row" class="firstcell">gdk943-46298r</th>
            <td scope="row">70</td>
            <td scope="row">red</td>
            <td scope="row">Center</td>
        </tr>
        <tr>
            <th scope="row" class="firstcell">gdk943-46298w</th>
            <td scope="row">851</td>
            <td scope="row">white</td>
            <td scope="row">West</td>
        </tr>
    </tr>
```

```
        <tr>
           <th scope="row" class="firstcell">gdk943-46298w</th>
           <td scope="row">203</td>
           <td scope="row">white</td>
           <td scope="row">South</td>
        </tr>
     </tbody>
  </table>
```

Datatypes

The `data-type` attribute is strictly required only for version 1.0 stylesheets. With an XSLT 2.0 stylesheet, the preferred approach is to cast the value in the `select` attribute to the type you require using the appropriate XML Schema value — for example, `select="xs:integer(.)"`.

However, you can use the `data-type` attribute if you wish. One of three values can be used: `"text"`, `"number"`, or a user-defined type expressed as a `QName`.

The default value is `"text"`, so if you had numeric values in some product data, such as what is shown in the following example, and you sorted on the `units` attribute value without setting a type, the resulting order would be 143, 19, 50, 851. This is because when treated as text, the key values are converted to strings before sorting.

```
<products>
    <product sku="gdk943-46298r" color="red" units="50"/>
    <product sku="gdk943-46298w" color="white" units="851"/>
    <product sku="gdk943-46298g" color="green" units="143"/>
    <product sku="gdk943-46298b" color="blue" units="19"/>
</products>
```

With `data-type="number"` or `select= "xs:integer(@units)"` you will get the items sorted by numeric value. The value `"number"` causes values to be cast as `xs:double` before sorting.

If numbers and text are mixed in the source data and you specify `data-type= "number"`, then the numbers will appear after the unsorted text values, and the opposite if the order is descending.

The result with a given user-defined `data-type` value is implementation-defined, so you need to check the processor documentation for details about any supported values.

Try It Out   Numeric Sort

In this Try It Out you'll experiment with three different combinations of type and sort orders, using the `units` attribute value in `products.xml` as sort keys.

First cast the `units` attribute value as an integer using the `xs:integer()` function and then sort the products in descending order. To use this casting method you need to have declared the XML Schema namespace in the `<xsl:stylesheet>` element.

```
<?xml version="1.0" encoding="UTF-8"?>
<xsl:stylesheet version="2.0"
    xmlns:xsl="http://www.w3.org/1999/XSL/Transform"
```

```
        xmlns:xs="http://www.w3.org/2001/XMLSchema"
    ...
<xsl:for-each select="//products">
    <xsl:sort select="xs:integer(@units)" descending/>
    ...
</xsl:for-each>
```

The products sort as 852, 203,143, and so on in the Units column.

Next, change the order by removing the `order` attribute entirely; recall that "ascending" is the default value. The order should now be 19, 23, 29, and so on.

Finally, remove the `xs:integer()` function, leaving `select= "@units"`. The values are treated as strings, resulting in 143, 19, 203, and so on.

Language Settings

Collating sequences are used in XSLT to determine the order in which to sequence string values for different languages. Not only do languages vary considerably in their sort requirements, with accented characters and such coming into play; there are often special rules to apply for publications such as dictionaries and telephone directories.

It is probable that only the English collating sequence will be supplied with the processor; certainly this is the case with the Saxon processor. However, if alternative sequences are available, you can set the `collation` attribute to a URI that specifies how strings are to be compared. The value is an attribute value template, which is an XPath expression contained in curly brackets ({}), and can contain a variable or parameter. Therefore, you can use a value like the following to represent the URI:

```
<xsl:sort collation="{$fr_uri}" select="surname"/>
```

An attribute value template is an XPath expression, where the expression is enclosed in curly brackets ({}). It is intended to contain values that can be determined only at runtime. The XSLT schema defines the type xsl:avt, which you will see used for all attributes that allow an attribute value template.

The syntax of attribute value templates, and specific rules for each attribute, are described in the XSLT 2.0 Recommendation.

Instead of the `collation` attribute, you can use the `lang` attribute to specify the language of the key, and thus provide a hint to the processor about which collating rules to use. Valid language codes are those allowed for the `xml:lang` attribute: the ISO 639-1 language codes, optionally paired with the ISO 3166-1 country values, such as `"en-GB"`, `"fr-CA"` and `"pt-BR"`.

The `case-order` attribute may also be relevant. Generally it is applied only if two compared words are equal when case is ignored, but in German, for instance, an initial capital can change the meaning of a word. Depending on requirements, the order can be specified.

By default, uppercase letters sort before lowercase; but you can use `"lower-first"` as the value of the `case-order` attribute to change the default. It determines whether uppercase letters (`"upper-first"`) are sorted before equivalent lowercase letters, or vice versa, and logically applies only to the text datatype. The effect of these values is reversed if the order is descending.

Perform a Sort

`<xsl:perform-sort>` may be used to sort items independently of other parts of a process to order information for subsequent use. Most often you will use it to create the content of a variable or parameter.

The element always contains one or more `<xsl:sort>` instructions. You may use either the `select` attribute or the element content to define the sequence to be processed.

Here is the schema definition:

```
<xs:element name="perform-sort" substitutionGroup="xsl:instruction">
  <xs:complexType>
    <xs:complexContent mixed="true">
      <xs:extension base="xsl:versioned-element-type">
        <xs:sequence>
          <xs:element ref="xsl:sort" minOccurs="1" maxOccurs=" unbounded"/>
          <xs:group ref="xsl:sequence-constructor-group" minOccurs="0"
maxOccurs="unbounded"/>
        </xs:sequence>
        <xs:attribute name="select" type="xsl:expression"/>
      </xs:extension>
    </xs:complexContent>
  </xs:complexType>
</xs:element>
```

The next code snippet shows the cast in the play *Love's Labour's Lost* by William Shakespeare. I've enclosed a copy of the play as `3L.xml`, as you'll be using part of it in the next section on grouping.

I've made some changes to the original download, applying the current version of the markup (known as P5) recommended by the Text Encoding Initiative (TEI). This project provides comprehensive schemas covering different forms of literary text. You can see the recommendations for dramatic texts at www.tei-c.org/release/doc/tei-p5-doc/html/DR.html#DRFAB.

> If you want, you can download individual plays from *The Plays of Shakespeare*, marked up by Jon Bosak in XML format, from www.ibiblio.org/bosak/.

Note that the `<div>` element name is a valid TEI element name with a similar purpose to the one in HTML:

```
<div type="cast">
  <castList>
    <head>Dramatis Personae</head>

    <castItem>Ferdinand, King of Navarre.</castItem>

    <castGroup>
```

```
            <castItem>Biron</castItem>
            <castItem>Longaville</castItem>
            <castItem>Dumain</castItem>
            <roleDesc>Lords attending on the King.</roleDesc>
        </castGroup>

        <castGroup>
            <castItem>Boyet</castItem>
            <castItem>Mercade</castItem>
            <roleDesc>Lords attending on the Princess of France.</roleDesc>
        </castGroup>

        <castItem>Don Adriano, a fantastical Spaniard.</castItem>
        <castItem>Sir Nathaniel, a curate.</castItem>
        <castItem>Holofernes, a schoolmaster.</castItem>

        <castItem>Dull, a constable.</castItem>
        <castItem>Costard, a clown.</castItem>
        <castItem>Moth, page to Armado.</castItem>
        <castItem>A Forester.</castItem>
        <castItem>The Princess of France.</castItem>

        <castGroup>
            <castItem>Rosaline</castItem>
            <castItem>Maria</castItem>
            <castItem>Katherine</castItem>
            <roleDesc>Ladies attending on the Princess.</roleDesc>
        </castGroup>

        <castItem>Jaquenetta, a country wench.</castItem>
        <castItem>Lords, attendants, &amp;c.</castItem>
    </castList>
</div>
```

If you wanted to do some further processing on the cast list immediately, you could sort from within `<xsl:apply-templates>` or `<xsl:for-each>`. However, if that were not the case, you could create a variable `$cast` to contain a pre-sorted temporary tree created with `<xsl:perform-sort>`. The following code is included in `cast.xsl`:

```
<xsl:variable name="cast">
    <xsl:perform-sort select="//castItem">
        <xsl:sort select="."/>
    </xsl:perform-sort>
</xsl:variable>
```

Later on you could list the cast or do some other processing:

```
...
<h2><xsl:value-of select="//castList/head"/></h2>
<ul class="unmarked">
    <xsl:for-each select="$cast/castItem">
        <li><xsl:value-of select="."/></li>
```

```
        </xsl:for-each>
    </ul>
    ...
```

The output should look like what is shown in Figure 5-1.

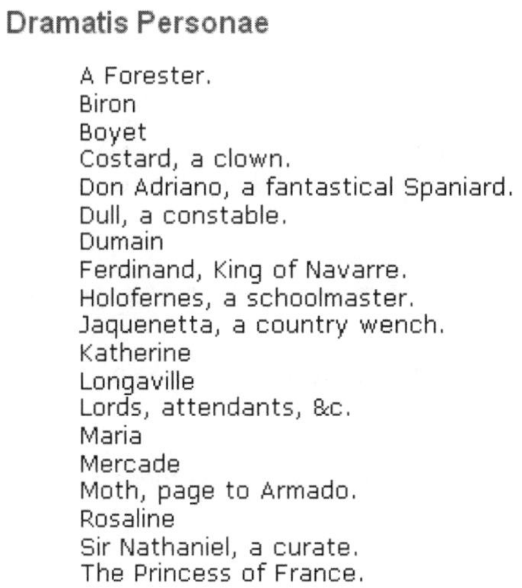

Dramatis Personae

A Forester.
Biron
Boyet
Costard, a clown.
Don Adriano, a fantastical Spaniard.
Dull, a constable.
Dumain
Ferdinand, King of Navarre.
Holofernes, a schoolmaster.
Jaquenetta, a country wench.
Katherine
Longaville
Lords, attendants, &c.
Maria
Mercade
Moth, page to Armado.
Rosaline
Sir Nathaniel, a curate.
The Princess of France.

Figure 5-1

Grouping

With the <xsl:for-each group> instruction, you can select a sequence, group the items, and treat the processing of each group separately. By comparison, <xsl:for-each> processes each selection in an identical manner.

The select attribute is required, and the result of the selection expression is known as the *population*.

The optional grouping attributes can then be used to allocate items to groups. The collation attribute works in an identical manner to that on the <xsl:sort> instruction. The schema definition follows:

```
<xs:element name="for-each-group" substitutionGroup="xsl:instruction">
  <xs:complexType>
    <xs:complexContent mixed="true">
      <xs:extension base="xsl:versioned-element-type">
        <xs:sequence>
          <xs:element ref="xsl:sort" minOccurs="0" maxOccurs="unbounded"/>
          <xs:group ref="xsl:sequence-constructor-group" minOccurs="0"
maxOccurs="unbounded"/>
        </xs:sequence>
        <xs:attribute name="select" type="xsl:expression" use="required"/>
        <xs:attribute name="group-by" type="xsl:expression"/>
        <xs:attribute name="group-adjacent" type="xsl:expression"/>
        <xs:attribute name="group-starting-with" type="xsl:pattern"/>
```

```
            <xs:attribute name="group-ending-with" type="xsl:pattern"/>
            <xs:attribute name="collation" type="xs:anyURI"/>
        </xs:extension>
      </xs:complexContent>
    </xs:complexType>
</xs:element>
```

Common Values

A typical pattern with XML data reporting is to use the `<xsl-for-each-group>` instruction with the `group-by` attribute, and to run an inner loop with `<xsl:for-each>` to output the grouped values in a table.

Grouping 1

In this exercise, the goal is to group the product information in the `products.xml` file by store, and output each store's stock in a tabular layout with a total of the units.

Use the same general stylesheet structure as you did in the last Try It Out.

Add the following code after the `<h1>` element:

```
...
<xsl:for-each-group select="//product" group-by="@store">
   <h2><xsl:value-of select="current-grouping-key()"/></h2>
   <table cellspacing="0">
   <tr>
      <th xsl:use-attribute-sets="th_first">SKU</th>
      <th xsl:use-attribute-sets="col">Color</th>
      <th xsl:use-attribute-sets="col">Units</th>
   </tr>
   <xsl:for-each select="current-group()">
      <tr>
         <th xsl:use-attribute-sets="td_first">
            <xsl:value-of select="@sku"/>
         </th>
         <td xsl:use-attribute-sets="row">
            <xsl:value-of select="@color"/>
         </td>
         <td xsl:use-attribute-sets="row">
            <xsl:value-of select="@units"/>
         </td>
      </tr>
   </xsl:for-each>
   <tr>
      <th xsl:use-attribute-sets="td_first"><strong>Total</strong></th>
      <td xsl:use-attribute-sets="row"> </td>
      <td xsl:use-attribute-sets="row">
         <xsl:value-of select="sum(current-group()/@units)"/>
      </td>
   </tr>
   </table>
```

```
</xsl:for-each-group>
 . . .
```

In the example, the products are grouped by the `store` attribute. In the `<h2>` element, the XSLT function `current-grouping-key()` returns the value shared by the members of the group — in this case, the store name.

The inner `<xsl:for-each>` loop uses the XSLT `current-group()` function to refer to each grouping. In addition to tabulating the values, the expression `sum(current-group()/@units)` will create a total value for each group. Figure 5-2 shows the output.

Stock report

Center

SKU	Color	Units
gdk943-46298r	red	50
gdk943-46298r	red	70
Total		120

West

SKU	Color	Units
gdk943-46298w	white	851
Total		851

North

SKU	Color	Units
gdk943-46298g	green	143
gdk943-46298b	blue	19
Total		162

South

SKU	Color	Units
gdk943-46298p	purple	23
gdk943-46298w	white	203
Total		226

East

SKU	Color	Units
gdk943-46298g	green	29
Total		29

Figure 5-2

The complete code is in `products_group.xsl`.

Adjacent Items

The `group-adjacent` attribute is suited to situations in which the order of items and "togetherness" is significant, as it is in many documents. It doesn't sort the selected elements, but leaves them in their original order and groups any adjacent items together.

This can be useful if you have a series of values that you know are adjacent, so you can avoid the additional processing required by `group-by`.

This is the case in the next Try It Out, where you'll make use of one of the better scenes in *Love's Labour's Lost*, a work that is renowned for its plays on words. The next snippet shows part of it. The file is act5scene1.xml.

```
...
<stage>Enter Don Adriano, Moth, and Costard</stage>

<sp>
    <speaker>Don Adriano</speaker>
    <l>Chirrah!</l>
</sp>

<stage>To Moth</stage>

<sp>
    <speaker>Holofernes</speaker>
    <l>Quare chirrah, not sirrah?</l>
</sp>

<sp>
    <speaker>Don Adriano</speaker>
    <l>Men of peace, well encountered.</l>
</sp>

<sp>
    <speaker>Holofernes</speaker>
    <l>Most military sir, salutation.</l>
</sp>

<sp>
    <speaker>Moth</speaker>
    <l><stage>Aside to Costard</stage> They have been at a great feast</l>
    <l>of languages, and stolen the scraps.</l>
</sp>

<sp>
    <speaker>Costard</speaker>
    <l>O, they have lived long on the alms-basket of words.</l>
    <l>I marvel thy master hath not eaten thee for a word;</l>
    <l>for thou art not so long by the head as</l>
    <l>honorificabilitudinitatibus: thou art easier</l>
    <l>swallowed than a flap-dragon.</l>
</sp>
...
```

Each <sp> (speech) element contains a <speaker> element followed by one or more <l> (line) elements. <stage> directions may occur at the same level as speeches, and within lines. They can also occur at the same level as lines, though that is not evident in this particular scene.

Try It Out   Grouping 2

The example that follows is partly based on one in Michael Kay's *XSLT 2.0 and XPath 2.0 Programmer's Reference* (Wrox, 2008). The goal is to create a tabular listing of speakers in column 1, and sequences of lines in column 2.

You can use the `group-adjacent` attribute to separate speakers and lines. This attribute generates an atomic value for each group, so it can be true or false, a number, a string — whatever you choose:

```
<xsl:template match="sp">
...
<xsl:for-each-group select="*" group-adjacent="if (self::speaker) then 0 else 1">
...
</xsl:template>
```

In the preceding grouping within the template for speeches, all the child elements are first selected using `select="*"`. Then in the `group-adjacent` attribute value, an if-the-else expression assigns `<speaker>` elements a grouping key of `"0"` if it is on the `self::` axis; everything else (lines and stage directions) under `<sp>` is assigned a value of `"1"`.

If you were to tabulate the grouping key values from this scene using the `current-grouping-key()` function alone, you would get output with zeros in the first column for each speaker, and ones in the second column for each of that speaker's lines:

```
...
0   1
0   1111111
0   111111
0   1
0   11111111111
0   1
0   11
...
```

However, what you want to do is tabulate the `<speaker>` and `<l>` element content and any relevant `<stage>` elements, so in each row you use the `<xsl:for-each>` and the `current-group()` function to loop through the items, creating a table cell for the speaker name and another for line/stage directions. In the second cell, use a `position()` function test to add a `<br/>` element for each new line:

```
<xsl:template match="sp">
    <table width="100%" class="noborder">
        <tr>
            <xsl:for-each-group select="*"
                group-adjacent="if (self::speaker) then 0 else 1">
                <td class="noborder" width="50%">
                    <xsl:for-each select="current-group()">
                        <xsl:apply-templates select="."/>
                        <xsl:if test="current-group()='0'">
```

```
                <span class="speaker"><xsl:value-of select="."/></span>
            </xsl:if>
            <xsl:if test="position() ne last()">

                <br/>
            </xsl:if>
        </xsl:for-each>
      </td>

      </xsl:for-each-group>
    </tr>
  </table>
</xsl:template>
```

In the output, the stage directions in this section will appear, either in their own table cells or at the start of a line. To distinguish them from the remaining text, you handle them in separate templates, marking them with square brackets "[]": one for inline and in-speech instances, and another for in-scene cases:

```
<xsl:template match="div[@type='scene']/stage">
    <table width="100%" class="noborder">
      <tr>
        <td class="noborder" colspan="2" width="50%">[<xsl:value-of
              select="."/>] </td>
      </tr>
    </table>
</xsl:template>
  <xsl:template match="stage">[<xsl:value-of select="."/>] </xsl:template> >
```

Figure 5-3 shows part of the resulting XHTML table.

[Enter Don Adriano, Moth, and Costard]	
DON ADRIANO	Chirrah!
[To Moth]	
HOLOFERNES	Quare chirrah, not sirrah?
DON ADRIANO	Men of peace, well encountered.
HOLOFERNES	Most military sir, salutation.
MOTH	[Aside to Costard] They have been at a great feast of languages, and stolen the scraps.
COSTARD	O, they have lived long on the alms-basket of words. I marvel thy master hath not eaten thee for a word; for thou art not so long by the head as honorificabilitudinitatibus: thou art easier swallowed than a flap-dragon.

Figure 5-3

The stylesheet adjacent.xsl in Listing 5-2 will process just one scene or the entire text of the play.

Listing 5-2

```
<xsl:stylesheet version="2.0"
xmlns:xsl="http://www.w3.org/1999/XSL/Transform">

    <xsl:output method="html"/>

    <xsl:param name="style">reference.css</xsl:param>
    <xsl:param name="interval" select="5"/>

    <xsl:template match="/">
        <html>
            <xsl:call-template name="head">
                <xsl:with-param name="title" select="TEI/text/front/docTitle"/>
                <xsl:with-param name="style" select="$style"/>
            </xsl:call-template>

            <body>
                <h1>
                    <xsl:value-of select="TEI/text/front/docTitle"/>
                </h1>
                <h2>
                    <xsl:value-of select="TEI/text//castList/head"
                    />
                </h2>
                <ul class="unmarked">
                    <xsl:for-each select="//castList/castItem">
                        <li>
                            <xsl:value-of select="."/>
                        </li>
                    </xsl:for-each>
                </ul>
                <xsl:apply-templates/>
            </body>
        </html>
    </xsl:template>

    <xsl:template name="head">
        <xsl:param name="title"/>
        <xsl:param name="style"/>
        <head>
            <meta http-equiv="Content-Type" content="text/xml;charset=UTF-8"/>
            <title>
                <xsl:value-of select="$title"/>
            </title>
            <link rel="stylesheet" type="text/css">
                <xsl:attribute name="href">
                    <xsl:value-of select="$style"/>
                </xsl:attribute>
            </link>
        </head>
    </xsl:template>

    <xsl:template match="div[@type='act']">
        <h2>
            <xsl:value-of select="format-number(@n,'Act 0')"/>
```

Continued

Listing 5-2: *(continued)*

```
        </h2>
        <xsl:apply-templates select="* except head"/>
    </xsl:template>

    <xsl:template match="div[@type='scene']">
        <h3>
            <xsl:value-of select="format-number(@n,'Scene 0: ')"/>
            <xsl:value-of select="head"/>
        </h3>
        <xsl:apply-templates select="* except head"/>
    </xsl:template>

    <xsl:template match="sp">
        <table width="100%" class="noborder">
            <tr>
                <xsl:for-each-group select="*"
                    group-adjacent="if (self::speaker) then 0 else 1">
                    <td class="noborder" width="50%">
                        <xsl:for-each select="current-group()">
                            <xsl:apply-templates select="."/>
                            <xsl:if test="current-group()='0'">
                                <span class="speaker"><xsl:value-of select="."/></span>
                            </xsl:if>
                            <xsl:if test="position() ne last()">
                                <br/>
                            </xsl:if>
                        </xsl:for-each>
                    </td>

                </xsl:for-each-group>
            </tr>
        </table>
    </xsl:template>

    <xsl:template match="speaker">
        <span class="speaker"><xsl:value-of select="."/></span>
    </xsl:template>

    <xsl:template match="TEI/teiHeader"/>

    <xsl:template match="TEI/text/front"/>

    <xsl:template match="div[@type='scene']/stage">
        <table width="100%" class="noborder">
            <tr>
                <td class="noborder" colspan="2" width="50%">[<xsl:value-of
                    select="."/>] </td>
            </tr>
        </table>
    </xsl:template>

    <xsl:template match="stage">[<xsl:value-of select="."/>]
</xsl:template>
</xsl:stylesheet>
```

Starting and Ending Conditions

The two remaining grouping attributes use patterns, rather than expressions, for selection; and they can be used to define conditions that begin or end a group.

Starting

To group items that include and follow a specific node, you use the `group-starting-with` attribute. You might want to do this if you have to convert from a flat structure to a nested output.

An example, which you will work with in the next exercise, is an XHTML page whose headings are at the same level as paragraphs.

Try It Out   **Starting**

Open one of the quick reference web pages you generated in Chapter 1.

The goal is to return it as closely as possible to the original quick reference structure. To do so, you need to define the `<h2>` element as the starting node, and group all the following paragraphs before the next `<h2>`.

To reconstruct the headings, capture the `<h2>` content in the `$label` variable, and use an attribute value template in the `<xsl:element>` instruction:

```
<xsl:template match="body">
   <xsl:for-each-group select="*" group-starting-with="h2">
      <xsl:variable name="label" select="."/>
      <xsl:element name="{$label}">
         <xsl:apply-templates select="current-group()"/>
      </xsl:element>
   </xsl:for-each-group>
</xsl:template>
```

If you haven't saved the output from `local.xsl`, run it again using `xsl_stylesheet.xml` as source and save the result document. Then use the stylesheet `xhtml2ref.xsl`, shown in Listing 5-3, to process that XHTML output.

Listing 5-3

```
<?xml version="1.0" encoding="UTF-8"?>
<xsl:stylesheet xmlns:xsl="http://www.w3.org/1999/XSL/Transform" version="2.0"
   xpath-default-namespace="http://www.w3.org/1999/xhtml">

   <xsl:output method="xml" encoding="UTF-8"/>

   <xsl:template match="/">
      <reference>
         <title>
            <xsl:value-of select="html/body/h1"/>
         </title>
         <body>
            <xsl:apply-templates select="html/body"/>
         </body>
```

Continued

Listing 5-3: *(continued)*

```
        </reference>
    </xsl:template>

    <xsl:template match="h1 | h2"/>

    <xsl:template match="body">
        <xsl:for-each-group select="*" group-starting-with="h2">
            <xsl:variable name="label" select="."/>
            <xsl:element name="{$label}">
                <xsl:apply-templates select="current-group()"/>
            </xsl:element>
        </xsl:for-each-group>
    </xsl:template>

    <xsl:template match="p">
        <p>
            <xsl:apply-templates/>
        </p>
    </xsl:template>

    <xsl:template match="code">
        <code>
            <xsl:value-of select="."/>
        </code>
    </xsl:template>

</xsl:stylesheet>
```

Note a few points about this stylesheet.

The value of the `xpath-default-namespace` attribute is set to `"http://www.w3.org/1999/xhtml"`. You'll recall that this is required when a default namespace is declared on an input document, but there isn't one in our XHTML source. In fact, it is hidden away in the XHTML DTD (Thanks, W3C!). Just try to remember this gotcha when you are transforming an XHTML source, and nothing is processed as a result.

Note the "do nothing" templates for `<h1>` and `<h2>`, which will stop unwanted text output.

You can't properly reconstruct the original `<element>` or `<attr>` elements from the XHTML source because the original transform `local.xsl` "lost" information that could have been captured. You could make the XHTML more "information-rich" by applying `class` attributes in `local.xsl`.

To do so, you can delete the template that currently matches the `<code>` element and add "code" to the template `match` attribute with the pattern `"attr | element"`. You can capture the element names to assign to the class attributes by using the XPath `name()` function:

```
<xsl:template match="attr | element | code">
    <code>
        <xsl:attribute name="class"><xsl:value-of select="name()"/></xsl:attribute>
        <xsl:value-of select="."/>
```

```
        </code>
    </xsl:template>
```

Then, in `xhtml2ref.xsl`, you could use these class values to name these elements, in the same manner as the headings.

Ending

The `group-ending-with` attribute matches `group-starting-with`, but seems to have fewer use cases. The order of most XML documents is "top down," with headings coming first rather than last in sequences, so there aren't too many common applications.

Summary

By now you should have a grasp of what is required to sort and group content for analysis. In the section on `<xsl:sort>`, you learned how to apply ascending and descending orders, and how to handle numbering.

You have seen that you can use `<xsl:perform-sort>` independently of other parts of a process to order information for subsequent use.

Grouping content is a common requirement in processing XML data, especially where there are clear categories to make use of. In the section on `<xsl:for-each-group>`, you learned how to use the `group-by` attribute to manipulate data grouping. Working with the `group-adjacent` attribute illustrated how to maintain order within a grouping operation. You also saw how to use `group-starting-with` to add structure to a "flat" XHTML file.

Key Points

❑   A sort specification can contain multiple `<xsl:sort>` keys, which are processed in order before other instructions in a sequence constructor.

❑   Unless you are sorting text, you need to cast sort key selections in `<xsl:sort>` to the XML Schema type that matches the data to be sorted. With user-defined datatypes, the required syntax is implementation-defined.

❑   When you are dealing with uniform data structures, the `<xsl-for-each>` instruction is often the best choice for driving the transformation process.

❑   Attribute sets can be specified and combined to provide a concise way of specifying attribute output.

Exercises

You'll find solutions to these exercises in Appendix A.

1.   In what circumstances would you use `<xsl:sort>` instructions inside `<xsl:apply-templates>`, as opposed to using it inside `<xsl:perform-sort>`?

2. Given that the default `data-type` attribute value used in an `<xsl:sort>` instruction is `"text"`, what is the correct syntax for an instruction to sort on `xs:dateTime` values in elements named `<update>`? Apart from this value, are other related settings needed to make the instruction work correctly?

3. In the last Try It Out in this chapter, I suggested some changes that could be made to the stylesheet `local.xsl`, because it "lost" information that could have been captured by applying `class` attributes. Try making these changes and verify that the `class` attributes are set correctly by looking at the XHTML source code. Then modify `xhtml2ref.xsl` to pick up those class values and output correct element names, rather than `<code>` elements.

Strings, Numbers, Dates, and Times

This chapter looks more closely at some of the more useful XSLT elements and XPath functions that you can employ to manipulate string, numeric, and datetime values.

In this chapter you'll do the following:

❑ Learn about codepoint conversion and more about collations.

❑ Use functions that support pattern-matching techniques — such as regular expressions — to find and replace text, to normalize text values, and to escape URIs.

❑ Generate simple and hierarchical numbering using <xsl:number> and format the generated values.

❑ Use another pair of tools — the <xsl:decimal-format> declaration and the XSLT format-number() function — to convert and format numeric values in source data.

❑ Work with dates and times generated from your system, which you can then process and format.

❑ Learn how to apply durations and timezone values.

String Processing

Back in Chapter 2 you were given a quick look at some of the functions that are available to you when you want to handle text strings. This section expands on that subject with a set of working examples for typical use cases.

Pay close attention here, because as I mentioned then, you will likely use string functions more often than any other category in your stylesheets, because XML is fundamentally about handling text.

About Collations

Some operations on strings need to take into account the collation sequence in use by the processor. Examples include sorting, establishing equality, and using functions such as distinct-values(), which removes duplicate items in a sequence. The use of a collation is primarily determined by language, but sometimes also by special requirements. (Recall the discussion of language in the section on sorting in Chapter 5.)

The minimum collation that XSLT processors are required to implement is the simple Unicode codepoint collation, in which strings are compared character by character using the numeric codes. This is the default collation for XPath operators and functions, but not necessarily for sorting.

If you specify a particular collation it may affect the way strings are compared. More demanding XSLT applications will have quite specific rules. The rules for comparison within a collation based on an algorithm published by the Unicode consortium, the Unicode Collation Algorithm, are more sophisticated. They involve assigning a set of weights, which first distinguish between two different characters, then between accents, and finally between uppercase and lowercase. The weighting method for non-Latin scripts is different, but the same principles apply.

General Functions

The `string()` function converts a single argument to a string. If no argument is provided, then it is the same as providing the current context item `"."`. If a sequence of more than one item is provided, then an error occurs. The following table shows some examples.

Expression	Result
`string(12.9)`	"12.9"
`string(7=7)`	"true"
`string(.)`	Returns the value of the context item
`string(*)`	Returns an error

To obtain the length of a string, you can use `string-length()`. It returns an integer value with the number of characters.

Codepoints

In the terminology used for character encoding, a *codepoint* is a numeric value in a range that makes up the set of codes, and it is intended to be distinct from a particular encoding or the representation of a character as a glyph. For example, ASCII includes 128 codepoints, and extended ASCII includes 256.

Two XPath functions handle the conversion of Unicode codepoints to and from strings. For example, you might need to generate values by algorithm, such as hexadecimal values from integers.

The `codepoints-to-string()` function takes a sequence of integers as input values and returns the equivalent string; the `string-to-codepoints` function reverses the process:

```
codepoints-to-string((88, 83, 76, 84))
```

The preceding example will return "XSLT." (Note that there are two pairs of parentheses in the example: one for the function, and another to contain the sequence of codepoints.)

Comparison

The `compare()` function enables you to perform a simple comparison between two arguments of any type. The optional collation URI may be used to identify a collation other than the default in use.

The function first converts the arguments to strings and returns an integer value, in order to be capable of expressing either argument as being greater, lesser, or equal. Possible values are -1 if the first argument is less than the second, +1 if the first value is greater than the second, and 0 if the strings are equal.

The following example returns `"-1"` in the variable `$result`:

```
<xsl:variable name = "result" select= "compare(less, greater)"/>
```

The `codepoints-equal()` function makes it possible to compare the individual characters in two strings using the Unicode codepoint collation, independent of the default collation in the context. It is therefore useful for language-independent values such as part identifiers and billing references.

The result returned is a Boolean value that is true if the strings are identical in terms of Unicode code-points.

Concatenation

The `concat()` function takes two or more comma-separated values, converts them into strings, and joins them with no punctuation or spacing.

Assuming that there are elements `<street>`, `<city>`, `<state>`, and `<zip<` in a source document, the following snippet will list them separated by commas. Typically, you'll use a `select` attribute as in the following example, which must include any inline punctuation in single quotes:

```
<xsl:variable name="address"
    select="concat(street,', ',city,', ',state,', ',zip)"/>
```

Alternatively, you can use the `<xsl:value-of>` instruction with the `separator` attribute value to provide any punctuation. The next snippet will have the same result:

```
<xsl:value-of select="street, city, state, zip" separator=", "/>
```

The `string-join()` function also allows you to provide a separator between values as a final argument. In this case, the strings are provided in a sequence as a single argument, followed by an optional separator. It has the disadvantage that you need to explicitly convert non-string values to strings beforehand, whereas `concat()` does that work for you.

The next snippet uses `string-join` with the "/" separator to output a file path:

```
<p><xsl:value-of select="string-join(('..','xslt_reference','xsl_sort.xml'),
'/')"/></p>
```

The output will look like this:

```
<p>../xslt_reference/xsl_sort.xml</p>
```

Simple Substrings

You can use several useful string functions to handle partial strings. To test whether or not one string is contained within another, you can use the `contains()` function. It takes two arguments, the first of which is the containing string. The result is a Boolean value, so it is typically used as a test inside a conditional instruction like `<xsl:if>`. For example, if `$title` has the value `"A History of France"`, then the function will return `true`:

```
<xsl:if test="contains($title,'France')>
...
</xsl:if>
```

The functions `substring-before()` and `substring-after()` return the part of a string that occurs before or after the first occurrence of a substring, respectively. The next example extracts the date part of a string representation of a datetime value:

```
<xsl:variable name="tagdate"
   select="substring-before(created,'T')"/>
```

If the `<created>` element contained `"2008-01-04T16:51:35"`, then the variable `$tagdate` would be set to `"2008-01-04"`.

The `starts-with()` and `ends-with()` functions test whether or not one string starts with or ends with another, respectively. The next example will return true if `$name` is set to the text `"Brokeback Mountain is a great film!"` If `$name` begins with `"Brother David"` or `"Browning"`, the result will be the same.

```
<xsl:variable name="name">Brokeback Mountain is a great film!</xsl:variable>
<xsl:if test="starts-with($name,'Bro')">Yes, I agree!</xsl:if>
```

You can use index and length values on strings with the more general `substring()` function, which is useful when you need to work character by character and you know the structure of the input. The function takes the form `substring(input,start,length)`. The character-position index begins at 1. The `length` argument is optional; if you omit it, the entire string following the index value is returned.

For example, you might select the three-digit area-code prefix from a North American telephone number as follows. If the number 604.873.7011 in British Columbia is assigned to the `$code` variable, the following code will pick out the prefix `"604"`:

```
<xsl:value-of select="substring($code,1,3)"/>
```

The `translate()` function replaces one substring with another, and takes three arguments. The first is the string to modify, the second is the substring to replace, and the third (which may be empty) is the list of replacement characters. If the third argument is empty, then the effect is to delete the replaced substring. The following snippet uses `translate()` to convert a string from lower to upper case.

```
translate($input, 'abcdefghijklmnopqustuvwxyz', 'ABCDEFGHIJKLOMNOPQRSTUVWXYZ')
```

Many uses of the `translate()` function, like the preceding one, are often seen in XSLT 1.0 stylesheets. The same results can be achieved more readily with functions that are not available in XSLT 1.0, such as `matches()` and `replace()` or the `uppercase()` and `lowercase()` functions.

Using Regular Expressions

Regular expressions provide a powerful way to express patterns, including potentially very complex ones, within text. For more precise matching, the XPath functions `matches()`, `replace()`, and `tokenize()` make comparisons using regular expressions, which are more powerful than simple substring operations.

They have support in many programming and schema languages — for example, in ECMAScript and RELAX NG. In XPath the pattern-matching syntax is based on that defined in the XML Schema specification, but it differs in that the XPath patterns need only match a substring, rather than the entire string.

Expression Basics

You have probably come across regular expressions somewhere in your programming life. Discussing them in any detail is outside the scope of this book, given their limited use in XSLT as a whole. However, in case you haven't seen them before, here is an outline of the syntax, which may help with understanding the use of three XPath functions described later in this section.

There is not much point in using a regular expression if you are just searching for a series of characters inside some content. The simple regular expression qwe matches "qwe," and can just as readily be done with `contains('qwe','qwe')`.

Regular expressions (or *regex* for short) are intended to help you to find content that matches a pattern, rather than a literal string. The expressions are concise, and quite powerful.

Square brackets can be used to define a group of characters. The regex `[qwe]r` matches two characters where the first is "q," "w," or "e," and the second is "r." Ranges can be expressed as `[A-Z]` or `[0-9]`.

To negate an expression, you use the `"^"` metacharacter inside a group; the regex `[^qwe]r` matches everything except those characters, and `"[^a-z]"` matches anything except lowercase letters.

To quantify the number of occurrences, you use `"?"` for zero or one, `"*"` for zero or more, and `"+"` for one or more. You can also do explicit matches with `"{value}"` — for example, `(q|w|e){3}` matches any three-character union of the three characters: "qqq" or "weq" but not "eeee."

Subexpressions can be used to divide complex ones into manageable parts — for example, a telephone number like mine, which has the pattern 99999-999999 will be matched with `([0-9]{5})-[0-9]{6})`.

In XPath, regular expressions are not anchored as they are in other languages, so `ian` matches "ian," "Debian," and "piano." The anchor metacharacters `"^"` and `"$"` may be used to anchor the match to the beginning and ending characters of the string, respectively. Therefore, `^ian` will not match only "ian," and `ian$` will not match "ian" and "Debian."

You can modify how expressions are processed by setting one or more modes with four flags. The flags can be supplied in any order in an optional argument in the `matches()`, `replace()`, or `tokenize()` functions. The flag values are the characters i, m, s, and x:

❑   i: Switches to case-insensitive mode and the match is made regardless of case. For example, the regex `ian` matches "ian," "Ian," and "IAN."

- ❑ m: Switches on multiline mode. By default, the anchor characters "`^`" and "`$`" match the beginning and ending characters of the string, respectively. Multiline mode treats the strings as though they are separated into lines marked by #x0A and the newline character, and `^` and `$` now match the start and end of any line.

- ❑ s: When this flag is used, the dot character (.) matches any character, rather than the default of any character except a newline #x0A.

- ❑ x: This flag causes whitespace in the regex to be ignored unless it is inside square brackets, "`[]`".

Matching

The `matches()` function determines whether or not an input string matches a regular expression. The next example tests for a match with a string "November 22, 2006." The escape expression "`\s`" means any whitespace character:

```
<xsl:if test="date[matches(.,'^[A-Z][a-z]+\s[0-9]+,\s[0-9]+$')])">

</xsl:test>
```

The following table shows a breakdown of the parts.

Expression	Description
^	The match is to be anchored at the start of the string.
[A-z][a-z]+	A character in the range A–Z, followed by one or more characters in the range a–z followed by any whitespace character.
\s	Any whitespace character.
[0-9]+,	One or more digits in the range 0–9, followed by a comma.
\s	Any whitespace character.
[0-9]+	One or more digits in the range 0–9.
$	The match is to be anchored at the end of the string.

Tokenizing

To split a string into its substring components or tokens, you can use the `tokenize()` function. The first argument is the input string, and the second is a regex used to match the separators in the input. As the string is processed the separators are discarded:

```
<p>Year: <xsl:value-of select="tokenize('2009-04-18', '-')[1]"/></p>
```

In the preceding example, `tokenize()` will separate the string variable $date in the form yyyy-mm-dd into its parts. The second argument, "`-`", is the separator to use, and the function returns a sequence of three tokens as "`2009`", "`04`", "`18`". The predicate "`[1]`" selects the first item in the sequence to return:

```
<p>Year: 2009</p>
```

Replacing

The XPath `replace()` function can either replace a pattern entirely with other text, or it can be used to remove a matching pattern with an empty string. The function takes three arguments: the input string, the regex, and the replacement string.

The following example will replace the day of the month in the string `"2009-01-22"` with "22." The escape expression `"\d"` means any digit, and the regex here is any two digits anchored at the end of the string:

```
replace($date,'\d\d$','22')
```

The `<xsl:analyze-string>` instruction can also be used to process an input string using a regular expression in the `regex` attribute value. It is used when text is not marked up as XML but nonetheless has a regular structure. You'll have a look at this instruction and related elements when you begin processing text without markup in Chapter 10.

If you're interested in playing around with plenty of pattern examples, take a look at the excellent website at `http://regexlib.com`.

Normalizing Values

Normalization can apply to specific processes on string values, like tidying up extra whitespace, and to resolving conflicting encodings.

The term *normalization*, unfortunately, has no fixed definition, and means different things in different contexts. Generally speaking it means performing some processing operations in a particular way, but exactly what happens depends on the specific process.

Whitespace

When content entered by users has not been validated, it is good practice to remove leading and trailing whitespace before you start working with string values. The `normalize-space()` function does just that; in addition, it replaces multiple internal spaces with single-space characters.

Given some source content like "A History of France" in a list of book titles, you could ready it for matching against another title, or for accurate sorting, by setting a value like this:

```
<xsl:value-of select="normalize-space($title)"/>
```

Unicode Values

A characteristic of some Unicode characters is that there is more than one way of encoding them. This situation is a result of reconciling the differing needs of two interest groups: one favoring fixed-length encoding, the other preferring variable-length encoding. It is quite possible to search for a character and not find it because it has a representation that differs from the one you first thought of.

The solution to this awkward problem is to apply normalization. There are, in fact, no fewer than five official algorithms available for this purpose. Details of four algorithms — C, D, KC, and KD — can be found at `www.unicode.org/reports/tr15/`. The fifth is known as "fully normalized," which is defined by the W3C at `www.w3.org/TR/charmod-norm/`.

If you have text with strings to match that might have alternative Unicode encodings for the same character, you can normalize the encoding with the `normalize-unicode()` function. It takes the input string, and an optional normalization form value, and returns a normalized version. The default value for the optional `normalization-form` parameter is NFC (normalization form C), which replaces multiple codepoint values with single ones.

For example, the character Å can be encoded either as a single codepoint x00C5 or by two codepoints, x0041 followed by x030A. NFC normalization will use x00C5. NFD will use x0041x030A.

> *Normalization form values can also be applied to output as a whole in the* `<xsl:output>` *and* `<xsl:result-document>` *elements using the* `normalization-form` *attribute.*

Escaping URIs

Often, some values in content that is intended as part of a URI will need escaping, often called *percent encoding*, before use. For example, the filename for part of a feed URI like `bxslt &amp; xpath.atom` needs fixing. The spaces and the & character are not valid. Non-ASCII characters are another example where escaping is required.

XPath 2.0 provides a number of functions that you can use for escaping URIs in your output. To apply percent encoding to characters in a URI, you can use the `encode-for-uri()` function. It first encodes the characters in UTF-8, and then represents each byte as two hexadecimal digits:

```
<p><xsl:value-of select="encode-for-uri('bxslt &amp; xpath.atom')"/></p>
```

The percent encoded output will look like this:

```
<p>bxslt%20%26%20xpath.atom</p>
```

In an XSLT application using the HTML or XHTML output methods, the final stage of the process, serialization, occurs when the result tree is written out according to the specified output method. At this time, the processor will automatically escape characters according to the HTML rules. Non-ASCII characters are escaped, but the space character is not.

However, if you have an SVG image or MathML embedded in your XHTML, the URIs will need special handling. This is because URIs may be contained in attributes defined as such in the HTML/XHTML specifications.

All URIs need encoding if you have deliberately disabled automatic escaping of URI attributes on an `<xsl:output>` declaration. This is done by setting the `escape-uri-attributes` value to no. In this case, you can use the "manual" `escape-html-uri()` function.

Ideally, to get the correct result, escaping should be applied individually to each URI component, the file path, the fragment identifier, the parameters, and so on, before assembly with the appropriate delimiters.

International Resource Identifiers (IRI), essentially URIs with non-ASCII characters, are not too common yet, though they are specified in some standards (e.g., Atom 1.0), supported in some APIs (e.g., Microsoft's .NET Framework `System.Uri` class), and recognized by most browsers. But if you need to convert an IRI to a URI, you can use the `iri-to-uri()` function. Like `encode-for-uri()`, it generates a valid URI by encoding the characters that are allowed in an IRI but not in a URI. For example, the IRI `www.w3.org/International/articles/idn-and-iri/JP納豆/引き割り納豆.html` is not a valid URI because it includes Japanese characters. To convert the IRI, you would apply the function as follows:

```
<xsl:variable name="iri">http://www.w3.org/International/articles/
idn-and-iri/JP納豆/引き割り納豆.html</xsl:variable>
<xsl:value-of select="iri-to-uri($iri)"/>
```

The last part of the resulting URI will look like this:

```
JP%E7%B4%8D%E8%B1%86/%E5%BC%95%E3%81%8D%E5%89%B2%E3%82%8A%E7%B4%8D%E8%B1%86.html
```

Numbers

Broadly speaking, there are two different methods you can apply in working with numbers in XSLT. You can generate numbers in the stylesheet using the very powerful `<xsl:number>` instruction — for example, to number headings in the output. Existing numeric values in source documents are handled differently, by converting them to strings and applying named formatting specifications.

Generating Numbers

The `<xsl:number>` instruction can be used to generate a sequential number for the current node, typically something like a series of headings. You can also use `<xsl:number>` to format the generated numbers for output, based on settings made in built-in formatting attributes. For attribute values, there is a range of tokens you can apply for styling — for example, in Arabic or Roman numbers, or ordinal values.

Here is the schema specification:

```
<xs:element name="number" substitutionGroup="xsl:instruction">
  <xs:complexType>
    <xs:complexContent mixed="true">
      <xs:extension base="xsl:versioned-element-type">
        <xs:attribute name="value" type="xsl:expression"/>
        <xs:attribute name="select" type="xsl:expression"/>
        <xs:attribute name="level" type="xsl:level" default="single"/>
        <xs:attribute name="count" type="xsl:pattern"/>
        <xs:attribute name="from" type="xsl:pattern"/>
        <xs:attribute name="format" type="xsl:avt" default="1"/>
        <xs:attribute name="lang" type="xsl:avt"/>
        <xs:attribute name="letter-value" type="xsl:avt"/>
        <xs:attribute name="ordinal" type="xsl:avt"/>
        <xs:attribute name="grouping-separator" type="xsl:avt"/>
        <xs:attribute name="grouping-size" type="xsl:avt"/>
      </xs:extension>
    </xs:complexContent>
  </xs:complexType>
</xs:element>
```

The `select` attribute selects the node for which the sequence number will be generated.

The `level` attribute determines the way the number is generated based on the current location in the tree of nodes. The possible values are `"single"`, `"any"`, and `"multiple"`.

The default value is `"single"`, which is used to number peer nodes in a hierarchy, such as all the `<h1>` elements. This is normally the node sequence integer value, though it is possible to use the `value` attribute if you want to provide a different number to be formatted.

The value `"any"` is used for sequential numbers on nodes that can appear anywhere in a document, regardless of the main hierarchy, like those that identify tables, figures, and examples.

The `"multiple"` value will output composite numbering, such as `"4.2.3"`, depending on the position of the node in a hierarchy.

Format Attribute Tokens

The `format` attribute value specifies the output format of a number. You can set a token that specifies which format you want to apply. If you specify nothing, the default value of "1" will be used. The numeric tokens apply also to any equivalent Unicode digits, and the alphabetical token will generate numbers in the appropriate language, as shown in the following table.

Token	Format	Example
1	Integers	1, 2, 3...
001	Numbers with leading zeros	001, 002, 003...
a	Lowercase Latin letters	a, b, c...
A	Uppercase Latin letters	A, B, C...
i	Lowercase Roman numerals	i, ii, iii...
I	Uppercase Roman numerals	I, II, III...
w	Number in lowercase words	one, two, three...
W	Number in uppercase words	ONE, TWO, THREE...
Ww	Number in titlecase words	One, Two, Three...

Using the `ordinal` attribute can add variety to numbers. When set to `"yes"` it will generate `"1st, 2nd, 3rd..."`, and with the token `"Ww"` it will render `"First, Second, Third..."`

Single-Level Numbers

To learn how simple numbers work, refer to the example based on the Shakespeare text from Chapter 5, `act5scene1.xml`. The goal here will be to number the lines in the scene at defined intervals, to help readers to locate specific content. Not every line needs to be numbered, so you'll set the interval to five lines.

Open the stylesheet `adjacent.xsl` and save it as `number_lines.xsl` with the following changes.

Try It Out   **Numbering Lines**

First, add a parameter declaration `$interval` to to specify how frequently you want to show the line number; I suggest every fifth line. Then, create a simple tabular layout with the text of each line, followed by the line number, provided it is a multiple of the interval value:

```
<xsl:stylesheet version="2.0" xmlns:xsl="http://www.w3.org/1999/XSL/Transform">
   <xsl:output method="html"/>
   <xsl:param name="style">reference.css</xsl:param>
     <xsl:param name="interval" select="5"/>


   ...
<xsl:template match="sp">
   <table width="100%" class="noborder">
      <td class="noborder" width="100%">
         <xsl:value-of select="speaker"/>
      </td>
      <xsl:apply-templates/>
   </table>
</xsl:template>

<xsl:template match="l">
   <tr>
      <td class="noborder" width="70%">
         <xsl:apply-templates/>
      </td>
      <td class="noborder" width="30%">
         <xsl:variable name="ln">
            <xsl:number level="any" from="div[@type='scene']"/>
         </xsl:variable>
         <xsl:if test="$ln mod $interval=0">
            <xsl:value-of select="$ln"/>
         </xsl:if>

      </td>
   </tr>
</xsl:template>
   ...
</xsl:stylesheet>
```

Inside a table cell, set up the numbering inside the `$ln` variable using the `"any"` value for the `level` attribute , and set the `from` attribute value to start the numbering within each scene. Then you select a multiple of the interval inside an `<xsl:if>` instruction.

Figure 6-1 shows part of the resulting output.

Scene 1: The King of Navarre's Park

[Enter Holofernes, Sir Nathaniel, and Dull]

HOLOFERNES

Satis quod sufficit.

SIR NATHANIEL

I praise God for you, sir: your reasons at dinner
have been sharp and sententious; pleasant without
scurrility, witty without affection, audacious without
impudency, learned without opinion, and strange with-   5
out heresy. I did converse this quondam day with
a companion of the king's, who is intituled, nomi-
nated, or called, Don Adriano de Armado.

HOLOFERNES

Novi hominem tanquam te: his humour is lofty, his
discourse peremptory, his tongue filed, his eye   10
ambitious, his gait majestical, and his general
behavior vain, ridiculous, and thrasonical. He is
too picked, too spruce, too affected, too odd, as it
were, too peregrinate, as I may call it.

SIR NATHANIEL

A most singular and choice epithet.   15

[Draws out his table-book]

HOLOFERNES

He draweth out the thread of his verbosity finer
than the staple of his argument. I abhor such
fanatical phantasimes, such insociable and
point-devise companions; such rackers of
orthography, as to speak dout, fine, when he should   20
say doubt; det, when he should pronounce debt,--d,
e, b, t, not d, e, t: he clepeth a calf, cauf;
half, hauf; neighbour vocatur nebor; neigh
abbreviated ne. This is abhominable,--which he
would call abbominable: it insinuateth me of   25
insanie: anne intelligis, domine? to make frantic, lunatic.

Figure 6-1

Multiple-Level Numbers

Using level="multiple" works well if you have a nested structure, such as parts, chapters, and sections. You use the count attribute to specify the levels to include. For example, if the document has four parts, Part 4 has three chapters, and the third chapter has five sections, you want the value generated for the very last section to be 4.3.5:

```
<xsl:template match="section">
   <xsl:number
      format=1.1.1
      level="multiple"
      count="part | chapter | section"/>
   ...
</xsl:template>
```

To get this result, you set the format attribute value to "1.1.1", the level attribute value to "multiple", and the count attribute to contain the union of the three levels: count= "part | chapter | section".

If the listing format needs to change to account for a different category of heading at the same level as a chapter (say "appendix"), then you can use a variable to establish the format, and use it in the format attribute, with an attribute value template that allows you to set a value at runtime:

```
<xsl:template match="section">
   <xsl:variable name="format" select="
      if (ancestor:chapter)
      then '1.1.1'
      else 'A.1.1'/>
   <xsl:number
      format="{$format}"

      level="multiple"
      count="part | appendix | chapter | section"/>
   ...
</xsl:template>
```

Formatting Source Numbers

As well as generating numbers, you can convert existing numeric values in source documents or data to strings, and format them for display.

Converting a Number

You use the XSLT format-number() function to do the string conversion. It takes three arguments: the number to be converted, a picture string that defines the formatting, and an optional QName that identifies an <xsl:decimal-format> declaration.

A picture string provides a character template that defines both the visible format of the number and the characters to use from the declaration. The default values for each character are shown in the following table.

Name	Default	Description
decimal-separator	.	Character used as the decimal point
digit	#	Placeholder character for significant digits
grouping-separator	,	Character that separates groups (hundreds, thousands, and so on)

Continued

Name	Default	Description
minus-sign	–	Character used as the minus sign
pattern-separator	;	Character used to separate positive and negative number patterns
per-mille	‰	Character for the per thousand sign, #x2030
percent	%	Character for the percent sign
zero_digit	0	Placeholder character for leading and trailing zeros

The following example uses the default values for the `<xsl:decimal-format>` declaration. In the picture string `"#,##0.00"`, the digit or `"#"` characters are placeholders for digits in the result string, and the `zero-digit` or `"0"` characters show how to handle significant digits.

Declaring a Format

The `<xsl:decimal-format>` declaration specifies the display appearance of a number that you have converted to a string with the `format-number()` function.

The schema definition follows:

```
<xs:element name="decimal-format" substitutionGroup="xsl:declaration">
  <xs:complexType>
    <xs:complexContent>
      <xs:extension base="xsl:element-only-versioned-element-type">
        <xs:attribute name="name" type="xsl:QName"/>
        <xs:attribute name="decimal-separator" type="xsl:char" default="."/>
        <xs:attribute name="grouping-separator" type="xsl:char" default=","/>
        <xs:attribute name="infinity" type="xs:string" default="Infinity"/>
        <xs:attribute name="minus-sign" type="xsl:char" default="-"/>
        <xs:attribute name="NaN" type="xs:string" default="NaN"/>
        <xs:attribute name="percent" type="xsl:char" default="%"/>
        <xs:attribute name="per-mille" type="xsl:char" default="&#x2030;"/>
        <xs:attribute name="zero-digit" type="xsl:char" default="0"/>
        <xs:attribute name="digit" type="xsl:char" default="#"/>
        <xs:attribute name="pattern-separator" type="xsl:char" default=";"/>
      </xs:extension>
    </xs:complexContent>
  </xs:complexType>
</xs:element>
```

The `name` attribute identifies the declaration and is used to bind the declaration to the `format-number()` function in one of its arguments. You can declare a default (unnamed) decimal format. If you do not provide the third parameter in `format-number()`, these default settings will be used. If there is no default declaration, then a built-in decimal format is used by the processor.

You'll see from the preceding specification that most of the attributes are characters used for signs and separators that will represent the number. For example, the default `decimal-separator` attribute value is a period (.), but in some European countries a comma (,) is preferred, along with the period as the `grouping-separator` attribute value for thousands:

```
<xsl:decimal-format decimal-separator="," grouping-separator="."/>
```

Having defined your formatting template, you can go on to pass the formatted values.

Try It Out   **Formatting Numbers**

As an optional final step to the previous Try It Out, use the values in the act and scene `<div>` elements to output numbering using `format-number()`.

You can render the act and scene headings with the following code. In this case, you can rely on the built-in setting of the `zero-digit` attribute on `<xsl:decimal-format>`, which is `"0"`:

```
...
<h3>
    <xsl:value-of select="format-number(@n,'Scene 0: ')"/>

    <xsl:value-of select="head"/>
</h3>
...
```

Dates and Times

Between XPath and XSLT there are plenty of functions that you can use to manipulate date and time values. Three of them provide contextual values from your system, which you can then process and format in different ways. As well as dates and times, you can work with durations and timezone values.

Contextual Dates

The XPath functions `current-date()`, `current-dateTime()`, and `current-time()` return values from your system clock and provide a current context value to which external values can be compared.

Along with any values in the source data, they will get you to the starting point for your calculations.

Here's a fragment that timestamps an update to some feed metadata. It returns an `xs:dateTime` such as `"2008-11-04T16:01:12.451Z"`:

```
<updated>
    <xsl:value-of select="current-dateTime()"/>
</updated>
```

All the datetime functions will return the same result from multiple calls in any given transformation, so you can't get one value for the beginning of a process and another for the end, for example.

Formatting

To format the information, you can use the one of the XSLT formatting functions such as `format-date()`, `format-dateTime()`, or `format-time()`. All of these return the information as a string. In the next example, the picture string `"[M]/[D]/[Y]"` returns the month/day/year format.

```
<xsl:variable name="date"
        select="format-date(current-date(),'[M]/[D]/[Y]')"/>
```

Altogether, you can use four arguments after the value to be formatted. The first is the picture string, discussed in the following section. The other three optional arguments are the language in ISO format, a code for the calendar to be used, and the ISO country code associated with the event expressed in the value. The XSLT specification contains a list of calendar codes. The optional values must be supplied together or not at all.

Picture Strings

Picture strings contain variable markers enclosed in square brackets, "[]". Any other content outside the brackets is copied to the output. Names are language-dependent. The details are presented in the following table.

Marker	Component	Default
Y	Year	Four digits
M	Month	1–12
D	Day of the month	Name
d	Day of the year	1–366
F	Day of the week	Name
W	Week of the year	1–53
w	Week of the month	1–5
H	Hour (24-hour clock)	00–23
h	Hour (12-hour clock)	1–12
P	A.M. or P.M.	Language-dependent
m	Minutes in hour	00–59
s	Seconds in minute	00–59
f	Fractional seconds	
Z	Timezone +/- hours	
z	Timezone GMT +/- hours	
C	Calendar	Name
E	Baseline from which date is calculated	Name

Date-Formatting Tokens

In addition to the tokens available for formatting numbers generated by `<xsl:number>`, the following tokens may be used for datetime formatting.

Token	Format	Output
N	Component name in uppercase	MONDAY, TUESDAY...
n	Component name in lowercase	Monday, Tuesday...
t	Traditional numbering	Language-dependent
o	Ordinal numbering	1st, 2nd, 3rd...

The following example returns the current datetime — for instance, `"January twenty-sixth at 16:30 P.M."`:

```
<xsl:variable name="datetime" select="current-dateTime()"/>
...
<xsl:value-of
    select="format-dateTime($datetime, '[MNn] [Dwo] at [H01]:[m01] pm')"/>
```

Language, Calendar, and Country

In practice, what you can get from the optional settings is quite restricted. The details of what is output are entirely implementation-dependent.

If a particular language is supported, the language argument will affect the output, so that using a value of `"fr"`, for example, will produce Lundi, Mardi, Mercredi, and so on, and the way the ordinal numbers are generated, such as 1er, 2ème, 3ème, and so on.

Saxon, for instance, looks for a user-defined Java class file that will provide language localization, and if the calendar code value is anything other than AD (Anno Domini) or ISO (ISO 8601 calendar) the default is used. Labels are output showing that the defaults are returned. The country code is used only if a timezone is specified by name, using [ZN], in the picture string. The next example shows how to use the optional values for Spanish, the Jewish calendar code AM (Anno Mundi), and Spain:

```
<xsl:value-of
    select="format-date(current-date(),'[Y]-[M01]-[D01]','es','AN','ES')"/>
```

The Saxon output follows, indicating that it has used the AD calendar and English as defaults, rather than what was required:

```
[Calendar: AD][Language: en]2009-05-15
```

Combining and Converting Values

The XPath function `dateTime()` can be used to construct an `xs:dateTime` from two input strings, an `xs:date` and an `xs:time`. Note the use of the `xs:` namespace prefix, and recall that you need to include the XML Schema namespace declaration `xmlns:xs="http://www.w3.org/2001/XMLSchema"` in your stylesheet:

```
dateTime(xs:date('2009-01-23'), xs:time('00:11;37'))
```

There is a wide range of conversion functions, such as `year-from-date()`, `minutes-from-dateTime()`, and `hours-from-time()`. Which ones you use is just a matter of which inputs you have, and what you want returned. Here's an example that illustrates how to extract the year value "2007" from a string containing a date:

```
<xsl:value-of select="year-from-date(xs:date('2007-11-03'))"/>
```

First the string is converted to a date using the `xs:date()` function, and then the year is extracted with `year-from-date()`.

Durations

Often it is necessary to work out the elapsed time since an event, and you can use a number of duration-related functions in your calculations.

XPath uses the `xs:duration` datatype, where the characters have the following meanings.

Character	Meaning
P	Period (required)
nY	Number of years
nM	Number of months
nD	Number of days
T	Begins a time section
nH	Number of hours
nM	Number of minutes
nS	Number of seconds

For these calculating durations you can use the subtraction operator (`-`) with two date values:

```
<xsl:value-of select="(xs:date("2008-06-24") - xs:date("2008-06-22"))"/>
```

The result is an `xs:dayTimeDuration` value of `P2D` (two days). Duration functions work in the opposite direction too. For example, you can use `hours-from-duration()` to get 48:

```
<xsl:variable name="hours"
    select="hours-from-duration(xs:dayTimeDuration('P2D'))"/>
```

Time zones

Timezone values are always expressed as a `dayTimeDuration` in the range `-PT14H` to `+PT14H`, representing a period of −14 to +14 hours, or 28 hours.

These values are a difference from Coordinated Universal Time (UTC), commonly known as Greenwich Mean Time (GMT), rather than a named time like "Western Daylight Time" in Western Australia, or "British Summer Time" in the United Kingdom.

I live in the United Kingdom, so the `implicit-timezone()` function always returns a timezone value from my system, specifically `PT0H` unless it is summertime, when the value is `PT1H`. In Perth, Australia, which is eight hours ahead of me, it will return `+PT08:00`.

Three functions, `adjust-date-to-timezone`, `adjust-dateTime-to-timezone`, and `adjust-time-to-timezone`, will take an input in one of the formats, with the timezone shift expressed in the second argument. Adjustment can take the form of adding or subtracting a timezone, or, if there is an existing zone value, replacing it:

```
. . .
<xsl:variable name="datetime" select="current-dateTime()"/>
<xsl:variable name="zone" select="xs:dayTimeDuration('PT2H')"/>
<xsl:variable name="est" select="xs:dayTimeDuration('-PT5H')"/>

<xsl:template match="/">
  <xsl:value-of
      select="adjust-dateTime-to-timezone($datetime + $zone,($est))"/>
</xsl:template>
. . .
```

Another trio of similar functions extract the timezone from date, time, and datetime values. They return a dayTimeDuration as you would expect. The next example uses the timezone in Western Australia, returns `"480"`, and illustrates how you can express the difference in minutes:

```
<xsl:variable name="zone"
    select="timezone-from-dateTime(xs:dateTime('2009-01-26T12:00:00+08:00'))"/>
<xsl:value-of select="$zone div xs:dayTimeDuration('PT1M')"/>
```

Summary

In this chapter you reviewed a set of XSLT elements and functions and some XPath functions for handling strings, numbers, and datetime values.

Probably the most commonly used string-manipulation functions are `concat()` and the `substring-before()` and `substring-after()` functions. You saw how these could be applied, and you looked at codepoint conversion and how regular expressions could be used with the `match()`, `tokenize()`, and `replace()` functions.

Your work on numbering involved applying the `<xsl:number>` instruction to numbering the lines of a play, and formatting the act and scene numbers using the XSLT `format-number()` function with the default `<xsl:decimal-format>` settings.

You reviewed the contextual values you can obtain from a transform using the `current-date()`, `current-dateTime()`, and `current-time()` functions. You also learned how to format these values using picture strings and tokens with `format-date()` and related functions. Finally, you learned how to operate on duration and timezone values.

Key Points

❏   There are several character-encoding issues to be aware of when working with strings. One of these is that collations other than the processor's defaults may be required to deal with language-specific or application-specific requirements.

❏   There are basic differences between the way that you work with numbering and number formatting when numbers are generated in a stylesheet, and when numeric values in an existing source document are used.

❏   Obtaining current date and time values from the system using functions like `current-date()` is often the basis for combining and comparing values, and for calculating datetime relationships such as durations.

Exercises

You'll find solutions to these exercises in Appendix A.

1.   **a.**   What is the attribute on `<xsl:number>` that determines the way in which nodes are numbered?

   b.   Create a code fragment that shows how to select and sequentially number some footnotes if the element name in the XML source is `<fn>`, and the HTML output is something like the following example.

```
<p>[4] This is the fourth footnote.</p>
```

2.   What are some implementation-related limitations on the use of the `format-date()`, `format-dateTime()`, and `format-time()` functions?

3.   Illustrate the use of the following date-related functions, making use of the XPath 2.0 Function Reference of Appendix F if required:

```
month-from-dateTime()
years-from-duration()
timezone-from-time()
```

Multiple Documents

For a good many XSLT applications you will find yourself working with different combinations of source, stylesheet, and result documents.

Because numerous development tasks are performed repeatedly, it makes sense to divide your stylesheets into reusable modules. You will also encounter cases where content can be reused, especially when that content takes the form of structured data, or is related to creating common web-page output like menus or footers.

You will also sometimes want to override rules in an existing stylesheet. By importing code into a new stylesheet, you can selectively customize it.

Finally, sometimes you'll need to produce multiple result documents, perhaps dividing a long document into smaller ones, or archiving content in one format while publishing in another.

In this chapter you'll take a look at ways to deal with all three circumstances. You'll learn how to do the following:

- ❏ Create and include modular stylesheets.
- ❏ Override existing stylesheets by importing them into a new one that provides alternative parameters, variables, and template rules.
- ❏ Load multiple XML sources using a single XSLT and XPath function, which will load one or more additional XML sources.
- ❏ Build temporary trees using `<xsl:variable>`.
- ❏ Create multiple result documents with `<xsl:result-document>`.

Modular Stylesheets

Writing stylesheet modules to contain frequently used code is a time-saving practice. It is also the case that stylesheets can become quite long and complex, and modularity can help distinguish different parts of a process.

The importing module is often called the *principal* or *main* stylesheet module.

Including Modules

In Chapters 4 and 5 you may have noticed that some of the code could well have been applied to creating almost any XHTML web page — for instance, setting up parameters or the XHTML <head> element.

A good way to handle this sort of page "furniture" and indeed any reusable content is to create several stylesheet modules, and include them as required. As time goes on, you can build up a library of routines to handle many common tasks.

The kind of content to consider includes the following:

❑ Global parameters and variables

❑ Any content that is parameterized

❑ Styling information, including banners and logos

❑ Menus and other navigation features

The <xsl:include> declaration provides the way to do this. It enables you to include any module within another, using the required href attribute to identify the stylesheet to import. This value can be an absolute or relative URI, and the included stylesheet must be a valid XSLT document. Here is the schema definition.

```
<xs:element name="include" substitutionGroup="xsl:declaration">
    <xs:complexType>
      <xs:complexContent>
        <xs:extension base="xsl:element-only-versioned-element-type">
          <xs:attribute name="href" type="xs:anyURI" use="required"/>
        </xs:extension>
      </xs:complexContent>
    </xs:complexType>
  </xs:element>
```

The included stylesheet is loaded by the processor and its declarations are inserted into the main stylesheet at the inclusion point. Included modules retain their base URI, so you need to be careful with relative paths if the base differs from the including document. Suppose that the relative path of an included stylesheet is "../common/head.xsl". Relative paths in head.xsl will be interpreted in relation to that location, not relative to the including stylesheet.

Also note that namespaces are not inherited from the main stylesheet. So if head.xsl processes an element from the atom: namespace, the included module requires its own declaration in the <xsl:stylesheet> element.

Creating Modules

You can quickly rework a transform you've already created to illustrate the point. Let's go back to for-each.xsl, save it as main.xsl, and modularize it.

Try It Out   Including Stylesheet Modules

There are several candidates for removal from `main.xsl`:

- ❑ The named template `head`
- ❑ The attribute sets listing
- ❑ The global parameters

Place all the new stylesheets in the same directory as main.xsl. Create a new stylesheet `head.xsl`, and move across the code shown next:

```
<?xml version="1.0" encoding="UTF-8"?>
<xsl:stylesheet xmlns:xsl="http://www.w3.org/1999/XSL/Transform" version="2.0">
    <xsl:template name="head">
        <xsl:param name="title"/>
        <xsl:param name="style"/>
        <head>
            <meta http-equiv="Content-Type" content="text/xml;charset=UTF-8"/>
            <title>
                <xsl:value-of select="$title"/>
            </title>
            <link rel="stylesheet" type="text/css">
                <xsl:attribute name="href">
                    <xsl:value-of select="$style"/>
                </xsl:attribute>
            </link>
        </head>
    </xsl:template>

</xsl:stylesheet>
```

The attribute sets can also be segregated into a stylesheet that deals with tabular structures. So you can create `table.xsl`, which can start off like the following example. There may be more to add later, just because table data is so pervasive:

```
<?xml version="1.0" encoding="UTF-8"?>
<xsl:stylesheet xmlns:xsl="http://www.w3.org/1999/XSL/Transform" version="2.0">

    <xsl:attribute-set name="col">
        <xsl:attribute name="scope">col</xsl:attribute>
    </xsl:attribute-set>

    <xsl:attribute-set name="row">
        <xsl:attribute name="scope">row</xsl:attribute>
    </xsl:attribute-set>

    <xsl:attribute-set name="th_first" use-attribute-sets="col">
        <xsl:attribute name="class">firsthdr</xsl:attribute>
    </xsl:attribute-set>
```

```
<xsl:attribute-set name="td_first" use-attribute-sets="row">
   <xsl:attribute name="class">firstcell</xsl:attribute>
</xsl:attribute-set>

</xsl:stylesheet>
```

Then you can separate the parameter block out to `params.xsl` as shown here:

```
<?xml version="1.0" encoding="UTF-8"?>
<xsl:stylesheet xmlns:xsl="http://www.w3.org/1999/XSL/Transform" version="2.0">

   <xsl:param name="identifier" select="reference/@xml:id"/>
   <xsl:param name="resourcelist"
      select="document(concat('reslist_',reference/@scheme,'.xml'))"/>
   <xsl:param name="meta" select="$resourcelist//entry[@xml:id eq $identifier]"/>
   <xsl:param name="title" select="$meta/title"/>
</xsl:stylesheet>
```

All that is needed in the reduced version of `main.xsl` is three lines of code to load the inclusions. It will now work in exactly the same way as `step5.xsl`:

```
<xsl:include href="params.xsl"/>
<xsl:include href="head.xsl"/>
<xsl:include href="table.xsl"/>
```

What you have gained is three reusable modules. Two of them are specific to web output, but the parameter list is quite general. Switching to a different resource list or another CSS style will be quick.

To prove the case, you could now go back to some of the other stylesheets, such as `atom-list.xsl` and `products.xsl`, and see how they might be updated to take advantage of the new modules.

A Datetime Module

Modules can also contribute to overcoming limitations that can arise with version 1.0 stylesheets. Since XSLT 2.0 will work in a backward-compatible manner with version 1.0 stylesheets, you can use version 2.0 features to handle specific processing tasks.

Date and time functions are a good example. In a version 2.0 module you can set some variables to formatted `current-date()`, `current-dateTime()`, and `current-time()` values.

Provided that you use a version 2.0 processor to run the main version 1.0 stylesheet module, it can import the date module. It is handy for version 2.0 modules too. The file `date.xsl` in Listing 7-1 contains the code.

Listing 7-1

```
<?xml version="1.0" encoding="UTF-8"?>
<xsl:stylesheet xmlns:xsl="http://www.w3.org/1999/XSL/Transform" version="2.0">
   <xsl:variable name="date"
```

```
            select="format-date(current-date(),'[Y]-[M01]-[D01]')"/>
    <xsl:variable name="time"
            select="format-time(current-time(),'[H]:[m]:[s]z')"/>
    <xsl:variable name="date_time"
            select="format-dateTime(current-dateTime(),'[Y]-[M01]-[D01]T[H]:[m]:[s]z')"/>
</xsl:stylesheet>
```

Imported Stylesheets

What can you do if you need to selectively override the behavior of an existing stylesheet? `<xsl:include>` has a cumulative effect, so it can't be used to *replace* existing functionality. `<xsl:import>`, however, does just what you need.

The declaration `<xsl:import>` also imports one module into another, but differs from `<xsl:include>` in that the declarations in the main or importing stylesheet have a higher import precedence than the imported ones. This means that if there is a template rule in two modules that matches a source node, the rule in the *importing* module is used. Often this is known as an *overlay* or *customization* layer — for, example, changing some styling or adding specific processing.

All your import declarations must appear *before* any other top-level elements in the stylesheet. This is the schema definition. Again, you use the required `href` attribute to locate the imported document:

```
<xs:element name="import">
  <xs:complexType>
    <xs:complexContent>
      <xs:extension base="xsl:element-only-versioned-element-type">
        <xs:attribute name="href" type="xs:anyURI" use="required"/>
      </xs:extension>
    </xs:complexContent>
  </xs:complexType>
</xs:element>
```

Global Parameters

A simple change of some parameter values is often all you need to do with an existing stylesheet.

Try It Out   Importing a Style

Suppose that you wanted to use a different CSS stylesheet to `reference.css` than you have used so far, without modifying the original transform.

The importing stylesheet, say `new_style.xsl`, can begin by being quite minimal:

```
<xsl:import href="main.xsl"/>
<xsl:param name="style">new.css</xsl:param>
```

Because the parameters specifying the CSS file have the same name in both stylesheets, the importing stylesheet value `new.css` will be used.

Run the quick-reference example `xsl_for_each_group.xml` (which you met in Chapter 4) with `new_style.xsl`. The essentials of the layout will be the same, with different font specifications applied. You can see the changed styles in Figure 7-1.

Templates

The same import and override technique can be applied to templates. This time in `new_style.xsl` you'll add a replacement named template to provide a simplified attribute listing, with only `name` and `description` and `type` properties in three columns. This is the named template `attribute`.

Try It Out   Importing a Template

Here are the changes to make to the called template `attribute`, cutting it down to a three-column listing.

```
<xsl:template name="attribute">
   <h2>Attribute<xsl:if test="count(//property) gt 1">s</xsl:if>
   </h2>
   <table cellspacing="0">
      <tr>
         <th xsl:use-attribute-sets="th_first">Name</th>
         <th xsl:use-attribute-sets="col">Description</th>
         <th xsl:use-attribute-sets="col">Type</th>

      </tr>
      <xsl:for-each select="//property">
         <xsl:sort select="name"/>
         <tr>
            <th xsl:use-attribute-sets="td_first">
               <xsl:value-of select="name"/>
            </th>
            <td xsl:use-attribute-sets="row">
               <xsl:apply-templates select="description"/>
            </td>
            <td xsl:use-attribute-sets="row">
               <xsl:apply-templates select="type"/>
            </td>
         </tr>

      </xsl:for-each>
   </table>
</xsl:template>
```

Run `new_style.xsl` again. The result should look like Figure 7-1.

xsl:for-each-group

Purpose

An instruction that selects a sequence of items for uniform processing, and groups them according to common values, adjacency, or in relation to other elements.

Usage

Grouping depends on which of the four attributes is specified. The attribute value is known as the group key.

The XSLT functions `current-group()` and `current-grouping-key()` may be used to process grouped items inside an `xsl:for-each` instruction.

Contains

sequence-constructor | xsl:sort

Attributes

Name	Description	Type
collation	The URI of a collation to use for string comparison	xs:anyURI
group-adjacent	The common value to use if items are adjacent	xsl:expression
group-by	The common value or values to use	xsl:expression
group-ending-with	The pattern that ends a group of preceding items	xsl:pattern
group-starting-with	The pattern that starts a group of following items	xsl:pattern
select	The sequence of items to group	xsl:expression

Figure 7-1

Activating an Imported Rule

In some situations you might want to selectively make use of specific templates from an imported stylesheet, rather than override them, or have to duplicate them in the importing stylesheet. This is more likely to be required when your customization layer is quite complex, but where perfectly useful features already exist in the imported stylesheet.

The `<xsl:apply-imports>` instruction does the trick. Here is the schema definition:

```
<xs:element name="apply-imports" substitutionGroup="xsl:instruction">
  <xs:complexType>
    <xs:complexContent>
      <xs:extension base="xsl:element-only-versioned-element-type">
        <xs:sequence>
          <xs:element ref="xsl:with-param" minOccurs="0" maxOccurs="unbounded"/>
        </xs:sequence>
      </xs:extension>
    </xs:complexContent>
  </xs:complexType>
</xs:element>
```

`<xsl:apply-imports>` searches for a rule that matches the current node and current mode and applies it, just like `<xsl:apply-templates>`. However, it looks for matches only in the immediately imported stylesheets.

Note too that you can pass parameters just as you can with `<xsl:call-template>` and `<xsl:apply-templates>`.

Here is an example of an importing stylesheet that you could provide to a reseller who required some specific customizations of your basic stylesheets. The importing stylesheet will allow them to replace the values in the original with the ones the need to use. Suppose this reseller uses different path variables than the original, such as `jlog` for logging rather than `log4j`. These paths are identified in the XML source with the `type` attribute on the `<filepath>` element. This snippet shows how:

```
<p>Several appenders are included in the <filepath
type="log">basic_log4j.xml</filepath> file.</p>
```

In the importing stylesheet, replacement variables such as `$log` are declared (the expression ``[root]`` in the path values is a placeholder representing the application root directory, and can be modified to suit the reseller's circumstances).

In the `filepath` template, `<xsl:choose>` is used to test for each of the specified types. If they are matched in the source, then the reseller's values will be applied to the output. Other `filepath` processing in the imported stylesheet should stand as is, so `<xsl:apply-imports>` is invoked inside `<xsl:otherwise>`:

```
<xsl:variable name="prod">product_name</xsl:variable>
<xsl:variable name="log">jlog.xml</xsl:variable>
<xsl:variable name="root">[root]/$prod</xsl:variable>
<xsl:variable name="bin">[root]/$prod/bin</xsl:variable>

<xsl:template match="filepath">
   <span class="filepath">
      <xsl:choose>
         <xsl:when test="@type='log'">
            <xsl:value-of select="$log"/>
         </xsl:when>
         <xsl:when test="@type='root'">
            <xsl:value-of select="$root"/>
         </xsl:when>
         <xsl:when test="@type='bin'">
            <xsl:value-of select="$bin"/>
         </xsl:when>
         <xsl:otherwise>
            <xsl:apply-imports/>
         </xsl:otherwise>
      </xsl:choose>
   </span>
</xsl:template>
```

Using `<xsl:next-match>`

There is another way to select a template that is the next lowest in priority after the current one, and it does not just apply in the case of imported stylesheets. Whereas `<xsl:apply-imports>` requires multiple stylesheet modules to be in place, the <xsl:next-match> instruction also allows several rules within a single module, which can contribute to making the stylesheet logic clearer.

The key to using this instruction is the priority of the relevant template rules. These are priorities that are either assigned by the processor or explicitly written in a stylesheet. As I suggested in Chapter 3 where you first met them, it is a good idea to make your intentions clear by setting priority attribute values.

In the next example, the first rule provides a general way to handle code elements — that is, just output plain text. The next two rules apply different class attributes depending on the context:

```
<xsl:template match="code" priority="1">
   xsl:apply-templates select="* | text()"/>
</xsl:template>

<xsl:template match="p/code" priority="2">
   <code class="black"><xsl:next-match/></code>
</xsl:template>
<xsl:template match="summary/code" priority="2">
   <code class="blue"><xsl:next-match/></code>
</xsl:template>
```

Source Documents

Just as it can make sense to use a modular structure for your stylesheets, it is often the case that source documents are structured for reuse.

You saw an example in global.xsl in Chapter 3 when you accessed the metadata in reslist_xsl.xml:

```
...
<entry xml:id="xsl_when">
   <title>xsl:when</title>
   <content src="../xslt_reference/"/>
   <category term="element_reference" scheme="resource"/>
</entry>
...
```

You used the XSLT document() function in order to obtain information for a relative URI:

```
<xsl:variable name="resourcelist" select="document('reslist_xsl.xml')"/>
```

Another case that I encountered was a complex set of warnings and cautions, maintained by a team of technical specialists, lawyers, and translators who were independent of the authors creating the main content. The solution was to develop a helper file for the warnings and cautions, and provide the authors with a guide that they used to reference individual entries as needed.

Using the document() Function

Typically you provide a single argument to the document() function: the required URI of the document to load. It returns an XML document node. In the example shown earlier, this node was assigned to the $resourcelist variable, which was then used to locate a matching Atom <entry> element node in the sequence of metadata entries.

The first argument to the function may be a sequence containing xs:string or xs:anyURI values, so a sequence of document nodes may be retrieved at once if necessary. You could, for example, load all the files refererred to with the href attribute using document(//@href).

If a base URI is needed to resolve the first URI, then you can pass it as a second argument. Assigning the document node to a variable changes the base to that of the variable, which is usually the same base as the main stylesheet.

More likely, you will find yourself working with a series of cross-references containing relative or absolute URIs.

Try It Out   Loading Glossary Terms

In this exercise you'll process a set of (very) short documents, each containing a glossary term and related alternative terms, acronyms, definitions, and cross-references, as shown in the following snippet. The files to transform are element.xml, namespace.xml (shown in the sample), css.xml, and attr.xml:

```
<?xml version="1.0" encoding="UTF-8"?>
<term xml:id="namespace" type="class">
   <label>Namespace</label>
   <definition>A URI reference which identifies an XML markup
    vocabulary.</definition>
</term>
```

To include them in an article's glossary, process the set of term references in the source document glossref.xml, which looks like this:

```
<?xml version="1.0" encoding="UTF-8"?>
<termtable>
   <dfn term="element.xml"/>
   <dfn term="namespace.xml"/>
   <dfn term="css.xml"/>
   <dfn term="attr.xml"/>
</termtable>
```

Your code to handle this list will select each <dfn> element in turn and load the file to process. The file in Listing 7-2 is gloss.xsl, and the output is shown in Figure 7-2.

Listing 7-2

```
<?xml version="1.0" encoding="UTF-8"?>
<xsl:stylesheet xmlns:xsl="http://www.w3.org/1999/XSL/Transform" version="2.0">

   <xsl:output method="xhtml" encoding="UTF-8"/>

   <xsl:template match="termtable">
      <h2>Glossary</h2>
      <xsl:for-each select="dfn">
         <xsl:apply-templates select="document(@term)"/>
      </xsl:for-each>
   </xsl:template>
   <xsl:template match="term">
```

```
    <p>
       <strong>
          <xsl:value-of select="label"/>
       </strong>: <xsl:value-of select="definition"/>
    </p>
 </xsl:template>

</xsl:stylesheet>
```

Glossary

Element: An XML vocabulary component.

Namespace: A URI reference which identifies an XML markup vocabulary.

CSS: A mechanism for adding style properties such as fonts, colors, spacing to marked up content.

Attribute: An element property.

Figure 7-2

Rather than return an entire document, you can use a *fragment identifier* to return a single node other than the root node. A fragment identifier identifies part of a resource, and follows a # character. They are commonly used in web pages to define local link targets, such as `<a href="#examples">Example</a>`. Support for this feature is implementation-defined. Here's what the Saxon processor documentation says about it:

> If the fragment identifier is a valid NCName (no colon name), it is assumed to be the ID of a node in the document, which is then located using the id() function: if no node is found, the result is an empty sequence. If the fragment identifier is not a valid NCName, it is silently ignored and the document node is returned.

XPath Alternatives

XPath 2.0 provides two light functions that you can use to return additional XML source content. One is a simplified version of the document() function. The other permits you to load multiple documents, but the XSLT specification leaves almost all the details to individual implementations.

The doc() Function

A simplified version of the document() function is the XPath doc() function. There is only one argument in this case, there being no option to pass a base URI. There is, however, a base-uri() equivalent in XPath.

Bear in mind that the XPath interface can be used in contexts other than XSLT, so some aspects of its behavior may depend on the implementation and configuration. Calling the function when the source document is missing might throw an error, so you can first verify that the XML source is there with the `doc-available()` function, which returns a Boolean value, or even report the missing document, as Listing 7-3 illustrates.

Listing 7-3

```
<xsl:if test="doc-available(@term)">
    <xsl:apply-templates select="doc (@term)"/>
<xsl:if>

<xsl:choose>
    <xsl:when test="doc-available(@term)">
        <xsl:apply-templates select="doc(@term)"/>
    </xsl:when>
    <xsl:otherwise>The resource <xsl:value-of select="@term"/>
was not found.</xsl:otherwise>
</xsl:choose>
```

The collection() Function

The XPath `collection()` function returns a collection of documents or a sequence of nodes within documents, given a URI. The implementation details are important, so check your processor documentation. The specification is quite abstract, so depending on the implementation, the collection could, for example, be a container for documents in an XML database, a file directory, or a XML catalog file.

The Saxon processor provides for the latter two alternatives, as well as allowing you to implement your own `collectionURIResolver` class.

The function also takes a string as input. If a file is identified, Saxon treats this as an XML catalog file in the form shown in the next snippet, which lists the documents in the collection. If the `stable` attribute if set to `"true"`, then a document pool is first checked to determine whether the document is already loaded. If it is not, then the document is loaded and added to the pool.

The URIs listed in the `<doc>` elements are treated like URIs passed to the `doc()` function, and the same results will be returned in subsequent calls with the same URI. Setting the `stable` attribute to `"false"` causes the document to be dereferenced directly, and the document is not added to the document pool, which means that a subsequent retrieval of the same document will not return the same node:

```
<collection stable="true">
    <doc href="element.xml"/>
    <doc href="namespace.xml"/>
    <doc href="css.xml"/>
    <doc href="attr.xml"/>
</collection>
```

If the collection URI identifies a directory, then the contents of the directory are returned. The processing options are a little more complex than I want to cover here, so I'll refer you to the Saxonica site at `www.saxonica.com/documentation/sourcedocs/collections.html` for the details.

Loading a Collection

The collection example just shown is included in the code as `glossref2.xml`. With a very small change to `gloss.xsl` (I named it `gloss_collection.xsl`), you can process this collection as follows:

```
<xsl:template match="collection">
   <h2>Glossary</h2>
      <xsl:apply-templates select="collection('glossref2.xml')"/>
</xsl:template>
```

Setting or Changing Context

When you are processing multiple documents, you might find it useful to set a global variable that locates the document node of the main source file:

```
<xsl:variable name="main" select="/"/>
```

This ensures that you can refer to any part of the main source tree when the context is in one of the other document nodes, using `$main`. Later, you can always get back to this entry point with something like the following code:

```
<xsl:for each select="main">
...
</xsl:for-each>
```

This approach to naming the document nodes of key documents can be applied to any or all of the multiple documents you have in play — for example, a helper file or a clone of a file used to process an internal cross-reference — without losing the current context. It may not always be possible to use global values, but it is better if you can identify as many resources as possible up front.

Output Documents

Generating multiple outputs is common in publishing operations. Sometimes it is a matter of breaking large files into separate chunks. Perhaps a more typical scenario is when a large website is published and hundreds of XML pages are generated in both XHTML and PDF formats; a feed update is published for new and updated documents in Atom and RSS; and XML or text "housekeeping documents" are created in the background.

In cases like this, the `<xsl-result-document>` instruction comes into play. You use it to create a new document node with a specific URI defining the location of the output. The enclosed sequence constructor forms the content of the document, and the content is output as the final result of the transform. This is the schema definition:

```
<xs:element name="result-document" substitutionGroup="xsl:instruction">
  <xs:complexType>
    <xs:complexContent mixed="true">
      <xs:extension base="xsl:sequence-constructor">
```

```
            <xs:attribute name="format" type="xsl:avt"/>
            <xs:attribute name="href" type="xsl:avt"/>
            <xs:attribute name="type" type="xsl:QName"/>
            <xs:attribute name="validation" type="xsl:validation-type"/>
            <xs:attribute name="method" type="xsl:avt"/>
            <xs:attribute name="byte-order-mark" type="xsl:avt"/>
            <xs:attribute name="cdata-section-elements" type="xsl:avt"/>
            <xs:attribute name="doctype-public" type="xsl:avt"/>
            <xs:attribute name="doctype-system" type="xsl:avt"/>
            <xs:attribute name="encoding" type="xsl:avt"/>
            <xs:attribute name="escape-uri-attributes" type="xsl:avt"/>
            <xs:attribute name="include-content-type" type="xsl:avt"/>
            <xs:attribute name="indent" type="xsl:avt"/>
            <xs:attribute name="media-type" type="xsl:avt"/>
            <xs:attribute name="normalization-form" type="xsl:avt"/>
            <xs:attribute name="omit-xml-declaration" type="xsl:avt"/>
            <xs:attribute name="standalone" type="xsl:avt"/>
            <xs:attribute name="undeclare-prefixes" type="xsl:avt"/>
            <xs:attribute name="use-character-maps" type="xsl:QNames"/>
            <xs:attribute name="output-version" type="xsl:avt"/>
        </xs:extension>
      </xs:complexContent>
    </xs:complexType>
  </xs:element>
```

You specify the URI of the output file in the href attribute.

The format attribute may be used to specify the name of the <xsl:output> declaration, which will be used to determine the output attributes. This means that if necessary, you can use multiple named <xsl:output> elements, one for each different result document. If no value is set, then any unnamed declaration you have made will be used.

You'll note that many of the serialization attribute names are mostly identical to those in <xsl:output>. That's because these attributes may be used to override those in a top-level output specification. For example, if you had an unnamed <xsl:output> declaration with the method attribute set to "xml", you could override it as follows:

```
<xsl:result-document href="output.html" method="xhtml">
...
</xsl:result-document>
```

Further, you'll see that these values may be supplied at runtime as an attribute-value template that returns the appropriate type. For instance, the href attribute could be set from a variable $output:

```
<xsl:result-document href="$output" method="xhtml">
...
</xsl:result-document>
```

The <xsl:document> *instruction also creates a document node and adds it to the result sequence, but it is not the final output from a transform. Most often it is used to perform validation on temporary trees.*

Preparing a Feed Update

Suppose you have been using the metadata file `reslist_xsl.xml` as the basis for an Atom feed for the *XSLT Quick Reference,* and you have made some recent enhancements and fixes to a number of source documents. Naturally, you want to publish an update to the feed listing. Essentially, this is a two-part process. First, you need to take the most recent version of the file and timestamp any new and revised entries with the current datetime value, and then archive the updated version. Second, you use the first output to create the feed update. Initially, you'll focus on creating the new archive.

This is a perfect task for `<xsl:result-document>` because there will be two distinct outputs. You will also be able to make use of the support in XSLT 2.0 for temporary trees, which can be used to store nodes in variables until you are ready to process them. You will store the first output (the archive data) inside a template variable before using it in the second part of the process.

Try It Out   Making a Temporary Tree

There are two inputs to part one of the transform: a task list `task_xsl.xml` itemizing the changes, and the preceding version of the quick-reference resource listing, which has a suffix of `` `_update.xml` `` in the filename. Here's the task list structure:

```
<?xml version="1.0" encoding="UTF-8"?>

<tasklist scheme="xsl">
    <topicref href="xsl_output" status="modified"/>
    <topicref href="xsl_apply_imports" status="modified"/>
    <topicref href="xsl_result_document" status="new"/>
</tasklist>
```

In the transform `update.xsl`, include `date.xsl`, shown in Listing 7-1 earlier. Among other values, it sets the `$date-time` variable:

```
<xsl:include href="date.xsl"/>
...
<xsl:variable name="resourcelist"
    select="document(concat('reslist_',tasklist/@scheme,'_update.xml'))"/>
<xsl:variable name="outputfile"
    select="concat('reslist_',tasklist/@scheme,'_new.xml')"/>
<xsl:variable name="update" select="."/>
```

Also, set up variables identifying the resource list and the output file; the naming comes from selecting the `scheme` attribute on the `<tasklist>` element. Assign the task list to the `$update` variable.

The template variable `$archive` will contain a temporary tree to hold the updated resource listing:

```
<xsl:variable name="archive">
    <collection xml:id="{$resourcelist/collection/@xml:id}" lastupdate="{$date}">
        <xsl:copy-of select="$resourcelist/collection/title"/>
        <xsl:for-each select="$resourcelist//entry">
            <xsl:variable name="match"
```

```
                            select="current()/@xml:id=$update//topicref/@href"/>
            <xsl:choose>
                <xsl:when test="$match">
                    <xsl:variable name="match2"
                        select="$update//topicref[@href=current()/@xml:id]"/>
                    <entry xml:id="{@xml:id}">
                    <xsl:choose>
                        <xsl:when test="$match2[@status='new']">
                            <xsl:apply-templates select="title | summary | content |
    category"/>

                            <published><xsl:value-of select="$date_time"/></published>
                        </xsl:when>

                        <xsl:otherwise>
                            <xsl:apply-templates select="title | summary | content |
    category | published"/>
                            <updated><xsl:value-of select="$date_time"/></updated>
                        </xsl:otherwise>
                    </xsl:choose>
                    </entry>
                </xsl:when>
                <xsl:otherwise>
                    <xsl:copy-of select="."/>
                </xsl:otherwise>
            </xsl:choose>
        </xsl:for-each>
    </collection>

</xsl:variable>
```

When a matching entry is found in the task list, most of the entry content is unconditionally copied to the output. If the `status` attribute on the `<topicref>` element in the task list is set to "new", then the `<published>` element is added to the output using the `current-dateTime()` function; otherwise, the `<updated>` element value is set or reset.

Any entries that are not referenced in the task list are copied without change.

Next, the `$outputfile` variable is used to set the `href` attribute on the `<xsl-result-document>` instruction that copies the archive to the first result tree. The code is in `update.xsl` if you want to run it with `task_xsl.xml` as the source at this stage:

```
<xsl:result-document href="{$outputfile}">
    <xsl:copy-of select="$archive"/>
</xsl:result-document>
```

In order to generate the Atom feed, you have to make only a few changes to the data in the temporary tree. Most of the work is associated with creating identifiers and converting relative URIs to absolute ones.

Try It Out   Atom Feed Tree

Before you add the second result tree, there are some more variables to define. The `$doc_url`, `$term_url`, and `$tagdomain` variables are global (because this is an exercise, the xm.net domain is fictitious):

```
<xsl:variable name="doc_url">http://xm.net/docs/</xsl:variable>
<xsl:variable name="term_url">http://xm.net/terms/</xsl:variable>
<xsl:variable name="tagdomain">xm.net</xsl:variable>
```

Still in `update.xsl`, inside another `<xsl:result-document>` instruction, define the top-level feed elements:

```
<xsl:result-document href="xslt_update.atom">

    <feed xmlns:atom="http://www.w3.org/2005/Atom">
        <author>Ian Williams</author>
        <id>
            <xsl:value-of
                select="concat('tag:',$tagdomain,',',$date,':',collection/@xml:id)"
            />
        </id>
        <link rel="self" type="application/atom+xml">
            <xsl:attribute name="href">
                <xsl:value-of select="concat($doc_url,collection/@xml:id,'.atom')"/>
            </xsl:attribute>
        </link>

        <title>
            <xsl:value-of select="collection/title"/>
        </title>
        <updated>
            <xsl:value-of select="current-dateTime()"/>
        </updated>
        ...
    </feed>
</xsl:result-document>
```

The `<id>` elements for both feed and entry elements are constructed according to the recommendation for tag URIs, which has been published as RFC 4151 (see also www.taguri.org/). In the case of the `<entry>` elements, the `<published>` date value is used with the `tagdomain` variable and the document's `xml:id` attribute value to uniquely identify each entry in the output, as shown in the following example:

```
<id>tag:xm.net,2008-11-04:xsl_apply_imports</id>.
```

Now you can use the `$archive` entry nodes to generate the Atom entries. According to the Atom specification, the order of elements is not significant, so you can suit yourself in that respect.

Note how the relative URI expressed in the `src` attribute on the source `<content>` element is expanded to an absolute value by concatenation with the `$doc_url` variable to form the `<atom:link>` element:

```
<xsl:for-each select="$archive//entry">
    <xsl:sort select="xs:dateTime(published)" order="descending"/>
    <xsl:sort select="xs:dateTime(updated)" order="descending"/>
    <xsl:variable name="tagdate" select="substring-before(published,'T')"/>
    <entry>
        <xsl:copy-of select="title"/>
        <id>
            <xsl:value-of
                select="concat('tag:',$tagdomain,',',$tagdate,':',@xml:id)"/>
        </id>
        <link rel="alternate" type="application/xhtml+xml">
            <xsl:attribute name="href">
                <xsl:value-of
                    select="concat($doc_url,substring-after(content/@src,'../'),
current()/@href,'.html')"
                    />
            </xsl:attribute>
        </link>
        <xsl:copy-of select="updated"/>
        <xsl:copy-of select="published"/>
        <xsl:for-each select="category">
            <category term="{@term}">
                <xsl:attribute name="scheme">
                    <xsl:value-of select="concat($term_url,@scheme)"/>
                </xsl:attribute>
            </category>
        </xsl:for-each>

    </entry>
</xsl:for-each>
```

The same approach is used to expand the URI for the `scheme` attribute in the `<category>` element, this time using the `$term_url` variable.

Now you can run the complete stylesheet shown in Listing 7-4 with `task_xsl.xml` as source to get both the archive listing and the Atom feed.

Listing 7-4

```
<?xml version="1.0" encoding="UTF-8"?>
<xsl:stylesheet xmlns:xsl="http://www.w3.org/1999/XSL/Transform" version="2.0"
    xmlns:xs="http://www.w3.org/2001/XMLSchema" exclude-result-prefixes="xs">

    <xsl:include href="date.xsl"/>

    <xsl:output method="xml" encoding="UTF-8" indent="yes"/>

    <xsl:variable name="resourcelist"
        select="document(concat('reslist_',tasklist/@scheme,'_update.xml'))"/>
```

```
<xsl:variable name="outputfile"
    select="concat('reslist_',tasklist/@scheme,'_new.xml')"/>
<xsl:variable name="update" select="."/>

<xsl:variable name="doc_url">http://xm.net/docs/</xsl:variable>
<xsl:variable name="term_url">http://xm.net/terms/</xsl:variable>
<xsl:variable name="tagdomain">xm.net</xsl:variable>

<xsl:template match="/">

    <xsl:variable name="archive">

        <collection xml:id="{$resourcelist/collection/@xml:id}"
            lastupdate="{$date}">
            <xsl:copy-of select="$resourcelist/collection/title"/>

            <xsl:for-each select="$resourcelist//entry">

                <xsl:variable name="match"
                    select="current()/@xml:id=$update//topicref/@href"/>

                <xsl:choose>
                    <xsl:when test="$match">
                        <xsl:variable name="match2"
select="$update//topicref[@href=current()/@xml:id]"/>
                        <entry xml:id="{@xml:id}">

                            <xsl:choose>
                                <xsl:when test="$match2[@status='new']">
                                    <xsl:apply-templates
                                        select="title | summary | content | category"/>
                                    <published>
                                        <xsl:value-of select="$date_time"/>
                                    </published>
                                </xsl:when>
                                <xsl:otherwise>
                                    <xsl:apply-templates
                                        select="title | summary | content | category
                                            | published"/>
                                    <updated>
                                        <xsl:value-of select="$date_time"/>
                                    </updated>
                                </xsl:otherwise>
                            </xsl:choose>
                        </entry>
                    </xsl:when>
                    <xsl:otherwise>
                        <xsl:copy-of select="."/>
                    </xsl:otherwise>
                </xsl:choose>
            </xsl:for-each>
        </collection>

    </xsl:variable>
```

Continued

133

Listing 7-4: *(continued)*

```
        <xsl:result-document href="{$outputfile}">
           <xsl:copy-of select="$archive"/>
        </xsl:result-document>

        <xsl:result-document href="xslt_update.atom">

           <feed xmlns:atom="http://www.w3.org/2005/Atom">
              <author>Ian Williams</author>
              <id>
                 <xsl:value-of
select="concat('tag:',$tagdomain,',',$date,':',
$archive/collection/@xml:id)"
                 />
              </id>
              <link rel="self" type="application/atom+xml">
                 <xsl:attribute name="href">
                    <xsl:value-of
                       select="concat($doc_url,$archive/collection/@xml:id,'.atom')"
                    />
                 </xsl:attribute>
              </link>
              <title>
                 <xsl:value-of select="$archive/collection/title"/>
              </title>
              <updated>
                 <xsl:value-of select="$archive/collection/@lastupdate"/>
              </updated>

              <xsl:for-each select="$archive//entry">
                 <xsl:sort select="xs:dateTime(published)" order="descending"/>
                 <xsl:sort select="xs:dateTime(updated)" order="descending"/>

                 <xsl:variable name="tagdate"
                    select="substring-before(published,'T')"/>
                 <entry>
                    <xsl:copy-of select="title"/>
                    <id>
                       <xsl:value-of
                          select="concat('tag:',$tagdomain,',',$tagdate,':',@xml:id)"
                       />
                    </id>
                    <link rel="alternate" type="application/xhtml+xml">
                       <xsl:attribute name="href">
                          <xsl:value-of
                             select="concat($doc_url,substring-after(content
                                /@src,'../'),
current()/@href,'.html')"
                          </xsl:attribute>
                    </link>
                    <xsl:copy-of select="updated"/>
                    <xsl:copy-of select="published"/>
                    <xsl:for-each select="category">
```

```
                       <category term="{@term}">
                          <xsl:attribute name="scheme">
                             <xsl:value-of select="concat($term_url,@scheme)"/>
                          </xsl:attribute>
                       </category>
                    </xsl:for-each>

                 </entry>
              </xsl:for-each>
           </feed>
        </xsl:result-document>

     </xsl:template>

     <xsl:template
        match="title | summary | content | updated | published |category">
        <xsl:copy-of select="."/>
     </xsl:template>

  </xsl:stylesheet>
```

Listing 7-5 shows part of the Atom output, which you can publish at the feed URI in the feed link
`http://xm.net/docs/xsl.atom`.

Listing 7-5

```
<?xml version="1.0" encoding="UTF-8"?>
<feed xmlns:atom="http://www.w3.org/2005/Atom">
   <author>Ian Williams</author>
   <id>tag:xm.net,2009-02-05:xsl</id>
   <link rel="self" type="application/atom+xml"
      href="http://xm.net/docs/xsl.atom"/>

   <title>XSLT elements</title>
   <updated>2009-02-05</updated>
   <entry>
      <title>xsl:result-document</title>
      <id>tag:xm.net,2009-02-05:xsl_result_document</id>
      <link rel="alternate" type="application/xhtml+xml"
         href="http://xm.net/docs/xslt_reference/.html"/>
      <published>2009-02-05T13:11:21Z</published>
      <category term="element_reference" scheme="http://xm.net/terms/resource"/>
   </entry>
   <entry>
      <title>xsl:output</title>
      <id>tag:xm.net,2008-12-19:xsl_output</id>
      <link rel="alternate" type="application/xhtml+xml"
         href="http://xm.net/docs/xslt_reference/.html"/>
      <updated>2009-02-05T13:11:21Z</updated>
      <published>2008-12-19T20:13:28Z</published>
      <category term="element_reference" scheme="http://xm.net/terms/resource"/>
   </entry>
   <entry>
      <title>xsl:apply-imports</title>
```

Continued

135

Listing 7-5: *(continued)*

```
        <id>tag:xm.net,2008-11-04:xsl_apply_imports</id>
        <link rel="alternate" type="application/xhtml+xml"
            href="http://xm.net/docs/xslt_reference/.html"/>
        <updated>2009-02-05T13:11:21Z</updated>
        <published>2008-11-04T06:58:28Z</published>
        <category term="element_reference" scheme="http://xm.net/terms/resource"/>
    </entry>
    <entry>
        <title>xsl:stylesheet</title>
        <id>tag:xm.net,2008-11-04:xsl_stylesheet</id>
        <link rel="alternate" type="application/xhtml+xml"
            href="http://xm.net/docs/xslt_reference/.html"/>
        <published>2008-11-04T06:58:28Z</published>
        <category term="element_reference" scheme="http://xm.net/terms/resource"/>
    </entry>
    ...
</feed>
```

Splitting a Document

Multiple outputs are also appropriate when a single source needs to be divided into smaller chunks. To illustrate, we'll split our play source for *Loves Labour's Lost* into separate scenes with an output file for each one. This is a case of "right-sizing" the web outputs, rather than working with temporary trees. The main (first) document will form an index with a link to each scene.

You start with a copy of `adjacent.xsl` from Chapter 5, saved as `scenes.xsl`. Perhaps you'll recall that this stylesheet uses `<xsl:for-each-group>` to group adjacent speakers and their lines. The principal change takes place in the template rule that handles `<div>` elements for scenes.

Try It Out   "Chunking" a Source File

The goal here is to chunk the play at scene boundaries into files with appropriate names, with a different result document for each scene, and to use the division points between acts as the basis for a first page index.

First, inside the scene template, define a `$file` variable in the form `[act-number][scene-number].html`:

```
<xsl:template match="div[@type='scene']">

    <xsl:variable name="file"
        select="concat('a',parent::div/@n,'s',@n,'.html')"/>

    <xsl:result-document href="{$file}">
    </xsl:result-document>
...
</xsl:template>
```

The `parent::` axis is used to obtain the act number. Each time a scene is matched, the `$file` variable is recalculated and the variable value is used to set the `href` attribute in an attribute value template on the following `<xsl:result-document>` instruction:

```
<xsl:variable name="title">
    <xsl:value-of select="format-number(parent::div/@n,'Act 0 ')"/>
    <xsl:value-of select="format-number(@n,'Scene 0: ')"/>
</xsl:variable>
```

Next, a `$title` variable is assigned for use in the `<title>` element and the `<h1>` that replaces the previous `<h3>` element.

Finally, the `<xsl:apply-templates>` instruction is wrapped in the HTML document structure:

```
<html>
    <head>
        <meta http-equiv="Content-Type" content="text/xml;charset=UTF-8"/>
        <title>
            <xsl:value-of select="$title"/>
        </title>
        <link rel="stylesheet" type="text/css">
            <xsl:attribute name="href">
                <xsl:value-of select="$style"/>
            </xsl:attribute>
        </link>
    </head>
    <body>
        <h1>
            <xsl:value-of select="$title"/>
            <xsl:value-of select="head"/>
        </h1>
        <xsl:apply-templates select="* except head"/>
    </body>
</html>
```

The same approach is used to create the links on the top-level page. These take place inside the `<div>` elements that mark the acts. This time, the `$file` variable is applied to the `href` attribute in the link:

```
<xsl:template match="div[@type='act']">
    <h2>
        <xsl:value-of select="format-number(@n,'Act 0')"/>
    </h2>
        <xsl:for-each select="div[@type='scene']">
            <xsl:variable name="file"
                select="concat('a',parent::div/@n,'s',@n,'.html')"/>
            <a href="{$file}">
                <xsl:value-of select="format-number(@n,'Scene 0: ')"/>
                <xsl:value-of select="head"/>
            </a>
            <xsl:if test="position() ne last()">
```

```
        <br/>
      </xsl:if>
    </xsl:for-each>
  <xsl:apply-templates select="* except head"/>
</xsl:template>
```

When you run the full play 3L.xml with scenes.xsl, the first page will contain an index with links to a1s1.html, a1s2.html, and so on. Figure 7-3 shows the first page, 3L.html.

Love's Labour's Lost

Dramatis Personae

> Ferdinand, King of Navarre.
> Don Adriano, a fantastical Spaniard.
> Sir Nathaniel, a curate.
> Holofernes, a schoolmaster.
> Dull, a constable.
> Costard, a clown.
> Moth, page to Armado.
> A Forester.
> The Princess of France.
> Jaquenetta, a country wench.
> Lords, attendants, &c.

Act 1

Scene 1: The King of Navarre's park.
Scene 2: The same.

Act 2

Scene 1: The same.

Act 3

Scene 1: The same.

Act 4

Scene 1: The same.
Scene 2: The same.
Scene 3: The same.

Act 5

Scene 1: The same.
Scene 2: The same.

Figure 7-3

Summary

In this chapter you learned how to make use of <xsl:include> to create modular stylesheets, making content reusable in different contexts. You also learned how to incorporate a customization layer by creating an importing module that overrides parameter values and template rules in imported stylesheets.

You used the XSLT `document()` function to access additional source documents, and learned how this function is complemented by the XPath equivalents `doc()` and `collection()`.

Then you moved on to create multiple outputs from a single source. In the first example, a small driver file was used to initiate a feed update process. A template variable was used to contain a temporary tree, which was then used to output both a new archive file and the updated feed. The second example illustrated how you can "chunk" a long XML document into smaller web segments, with a linking index page.

Key Points

❑ There is a basic distinction between the purpose of `<xsl:include>`, which aggregates stylesheet code from several modules, and `<xsl:import>`, which has the effect of customizing or overlaying the imported module code.

❑ Stylesheet modules are especially useful for creating reusable document parts. You can even mix XSLT version 1.0 and version 2.0 modules using a version 2.0 processor, because it is backward compatible.

❑ Having imported a stylesheet, you can still make selective use of template rules in it by using the `<xsl:apply-imports>` instruction.

❑ The `<xsl:result document>` element creates a final result document. You can create multiple outputs with this instruction by referring to a named `<xsl:output>` declaration and optionally overriding some of the output attribute values.

Exercises

You'll find solutions to these exercises in Appendix A.

1. What design factors and XSLT language features lend themselves to modularization?

2. If you have already declared an `<xsl:output>` element named "archive," show how you would override the declared `method` and `indent` attributes in an `<xsl:result document>` instruction.

3. Name two XSLT elements that you can use to make use of existing template rules in an imported stylesheet.

4. Complete the following table, comparing the features of the XSLT `document()` function and XPath's `doc()` function.

Values	document()	doc()
Input		
URI resolution		
Fragment identifier		
Missing document		
Result		
Other implementation issues		

Processing Text

So far in this book you've mainly been matching nodes in XML source documents to rules in stylesheets, but there is much to learn about what can be done with the text nodes that make up much of an element's content, and about processing raw text, too.

XML parsers and XSLT processors deal with whitespace-only text nodes in particular ways, and there are XSLT declarations that you can use to control how whitespace is handled inside elements.

Although XSLT is primarily designed to generate XML markup, you will find that you can use XSLT to produce plain text without markup in any convenient output format.

You may also be surprised to learn that you can do simple raw-text processing with XSLT by loading a text file and analyzing the content to find markers that you can use to construct XML elements or attributes.

In this chapter you will do the following:

❑   Learn what to expect in default whitespace character processing.

❑   Use XSLT declarations to manage, strip, or preserve whitespace in output.

❑   Make use of the `<xsl:text>` instruction to create a CSV file that can be read by a spreadsheet.

❑   Load and parse regular expressions in CSV data to create XML markup.

❑   Compare transforming CSV content with XSLT to alternatives available in a spreadsheet.

Controlling Whitespace

Whitespace-only text nodes consist entirely of any sequence of the four characters tab, newline, carriage return, or space. In XML, whitespace in element-only (or empty) elements is not considered significant. However, in elements with #PCDATA content it is significant.

In XSLT the same rules apply; there is no certainty that different XML parsers will remove the same amounts of whitespace before the XSLT processor gets to see the source data.

XML parsers will always normalize, or reduce, multiple newlines to the single newline character `"x0a"`. They will also normalize attribute values, replacing tabs or newlines with a single space, `"x20"`.

In addition, some XML parsers (MSXML, for example) will also remove whitespace-only text nodes — for example, `<para> </para>` becomes `<para/>` by default before building the source tree, so you need to check the vendor documentation to establish the details, and configure the parser accordingly.

Schema processors will also obey any schema specifications for whitespace handling.

The XSLT processor automatically merges adjacent text whitespace nodes. You can control the way the processor handles whitespace-only nodes by specifying the list of containing elements in a source document for which you wish space to be removed or preserved, using two declarations, as described in the following sections.

Stripping Space

The top-level `<xsl:strip-space>` declaration identifies the whitespace-only text nodes that are not significant and can be removed. This will prevent unwanted nodes — for example, those in element-only content — from being copied to the output. If there is a whitespace node in an element identified in the `elements` attribute, it will be stripped from the tree. This is the schema declaration.

```
<xs:element name="strip-space" substitutionGroup="xsl:declaration">
  <xs:complexType>
    <xs:complexContent>
      <xs:extension base="xsl:element-only-versioned-element-type">
        <xs:attribute name="elements" type="xsl:nametests" use="required"/>
      </xs:extension>
    </xs:complexContent>
  </xs:complexType>
</xs:element>
```

The type of each element listed in the attribute is `xsl:nametests`, which the XPath 2.0 recommendation in turn specifies in the following BNF notation:

```
NameTest  ::=  QName | Wildcard
Wildcard  ::=  "*"
               | (NCName ":" "*")
               | ("*" ":" NCName)
```

So, for example, `:title`, `atom:*`, and `atom:content` are all valid nametests.

In general, it is advisable to remove whitespace-only nodes, especially in XML data, and elements with element-only content, using the following:

```
<xsl:strip-space elements = "*"/>
```

For example, this will prevent any unnecessary space nodes from being counted and returned from the use of the `position()` function, which you were relying on to generate results based on relevant nodes.

It is not, however, a good idea for elements with mixed content — that is, with both elements and #PCDATA, because of the risk that text will be run together in some cases. In the next example, the space between the `<city>` and `<state>` elements should be preserved; otherwise, the output will read `"BangorME"`.

```
<p>Helives in <city>Bangor</city> <state>ME</atate>.</p>
```

> `<xsl:strip-space>` *will not remove extraneous space in content containing mixed text and whitespace nodes. To clean up this type of content, use the* `normalize-space()` *function that you met in Chapter 6. Recall that it removes leading and trailing spaces, and replaces multiple internal spaces with single-space characters. The* `normalize-space()` *function is shown here:*

```
<xsl:value-of select="normalize-space($title)"/>
```

Preserving Space

The `<xsl:preserve-space>` declaration has the opposite effect, and defines the nodes that are signifi-cant. The default processor action is to preserve whitespace in input documents and those loaded with the `document()` function, so you need to use it only when you want to override a value specified with `<xsl:strip-space>`. You cannot override a removal action by a parser; once the space is gone it cannot be recovered by the XSLT processor. Here is the declaration:

```
<xs:element name="preserve-space" substitutionGroup="xsl:declaration">
  <xs:complexType>
    <xs:complexContent>
      <xs:extension base="xsl:element-only-versioned-element-type">
        <xs:attribute name="elements" type="xsl:nametests" use="required"/>
      </xs:extension>
    </xs:complexContent>
  </xs:complexType>
</xs:element>
```

Again, you use the `elements` attribute, this time listing the ones to preserve. For example, to preserve space in `<atom:content>` elements, use the following top-level declarations:

```
<xsl:strip-space elements = "*"/>
<xsl:preserve-space elements = "atom:content"/>
```

Using `<xsl:text>`

If you want to control whitespace inside a literal result element, you can use the `<xsl:text>` instruction:

```
<xs:element name="text" substitutionGroup="xsl:instruction">
  <xs:complexType>
    <xs:simpleContent>
      <xs:extension base="xsl:text-element-base-type">
        <xs:attribute name="disable-output-escaping" type="xsl:yes-or-no" default="no"/>
      </xs:extension>
    </xs:simpleContent>
  </xs:complexType>
</xs:element>
```

The following example will appear in the output with all the double spacing in place. Without the `<xsl:text>` wrapper, all the whitespace would be collapsed:

```
<p><xsl:text>   some   text   here   </xsl:text></p>
```

> *Use of the* `disable-output-escaping` *attribute is deprecated, because there is no certainty that the result tree will be serialized, rather than used directly.*

XML to Text

Converting XML to delimited data that you can use in another application, such as a spreadsheet or a word processor, is very straightforward.

The next example makes use of the `products.xml` source file again, converting the attributes in each `<product>` element to a comma-separated text row in a CSV format, like the following row of data:

```
gdk943-46298r,red,50,Center
```

Try It Out   products.csv

To convert `products.xml` to `products.csv`, start a new stylesheet called `products2csv.xsl`.

The first step is to set the `method` attribute on the `<xsl:output>` declaration to `"text"`, and strip space in all elements with `<xsl:strip-space>`:

```
<xsl:output method="text"/>
<xsl:strip-space elements="*"/>
```

You need to insert a comma between values in each row. So far, you haven't made use of the separator attribute in the `<xsl:value-of>` element instruction, which can be used to insert any string value between items in a sequence.

To do so, add a `$delimiter` parameter to define the value as `","`. Then set a variable `$headers` to contain header values for each column:

```
<xsl:param name="delimiter" select="','"/>
<xsl:variable name="headers">
    <header>SKU</header>
    <header>Color</header>
    <header>Units</header>
    <header>Store</header>
</xsl:variable>
```

This enables you to select `$headers/header` as a sequence and use the `$delimiter` value as an attribute-value template in the `separator` attribute. In the product template rule, output the attribute values, commas, and a newline for each row:

```
<xsl:template match="/">
    <xsl:value-of select="$headers/header" separator="{$delimiter}"/>
    <xsl:text>&#xa;</xsl:text>
```

```
      <xsl:apply-templates/>
</xsl:template>
<xsl:template match="product">
      <xsl:value-of select="@sku"/>
      <xsl:text>,</xsl:text>
      <xsl:value-of select="@color"/>
      <xsl:text>,</xsl:text>
      <xsl:value-of select="@units"/>
      <xsl:text>,</xsl:text>
      <xsl:value-of select="@store"/>
      <xsl:text>&#xa;</xsl:text>
</xsl:template>
```

Run `products.xml` using the new stylesheet. The file `products.csv` should look like what is shown in Listing 8-1.

Listing 8-1

```
SKU,Color,Units,Store
gdk943-46298r,red,50,Center
gdk943-46298w,white,851,West
gdk943-46298g,green,143,North
gdk943-46298b,blue,19,North
gdk943-46298p,purple,23,South
gdk943-46298r,red,70,Center
gdk943-46298g,green,29,East
gdk943-46298w,white,203,South
```

The complete stylesheet code is shown in Listing 8-2.

Listing 8-2

```
<?xml version="1.0" encoding="UTF-8"?>
<xsl:stylesheet version="2.0" xmlns:xsl="http://www.w3.org/1999/XSL/Transform"
    xmlns:xs="http://www.w3.org/2001/XMLSchema">

    <xsl:output method="text"/>
    <xsl:strip-space elements="*"/>

    <xsl:param name="delimiter" select="','"/>

    <xsl:variable name="headers">
        <header>SKU</header>
        <header>Color</header>
        <header>Units</header>
        <header>Store</header>
    </xsl:variable>

    <xsl:template match="/">
        <xsl:value-of select="$headers/header" separator="{$delimiter}"/>
```

Continued

145

Listing 8-2: *(continued)*

```
        <xsl:text>&#xa;</xsl:text>
        <xsl:apply-templates/>
    </xsl:template>

    <xsl:template match="product">
        <xsl:value-of select="@sku"/>
        <xsl:text>,</xsl:text>
        <xsl:value-of select="@color"/>
        <xsl:text>,</xsl:text>
        <xsl:value-of select="@units"/>
        <xsl:text>,</xsl:text>
        <xsl:value-of select="@store"/>
        <xsl:text>&#xa;</xsl:text>
    </xsl:template>
</xsl:stylesheet>
```

Text to XML

XSLT 2.0 has a couple of very useful features that enable the process of turning delimited text into XML markup. The first of these loads a raw unparsed text file, and the second allows you to use a regular expression to analyze the content.

Loading Unparsed Text

The XSLT function unparsed-text() returns the content of an external text file as a string, so it is equivalent to the document() function for XML content. The href parameter is a string containing the URI of the file to be loaded. An optional encoding parameter may also be supplied with the value of the character encoding of the input file:

```
<?xml version="1.0" encoding="UTF-8"?>
<xsl:stylesheet version="2.0" xmlns:xsl="http://www.w3.org/1999/XSL/Transform">
    <xsl:template match="/">
        <xsl:variable name="filename" select="'census.csv'" />

        <xsl:if test="unparsed-text-available($filename)">

        <xsl:value-of select="unparsed-text($filename)"/>

        </xsl:if>
    </xsl:template>
</xsl:stylesheet>
```

To avoid an error in subsequent processing you can use the unparsed-text-available function, which will test to see whether the call will be successful.

Analyzing the Input

To process this text input you can use the <xsl:analyze-string> instruction. The content model allows for two elements, which you use to define sequence constructors for processing substrings that either match or don't match a regular expression.

Two attributes are required: the select attribute contains the text to analyze, and the regex attribute is the regular expression to use. Optionally, you can use the flags attribute to determine how that expression is interpreted. Recall from Chapter 6 that these flags control case sensitivity, the position of anchors, and how newlines and whitespace characters will be treated:

```
<xs:element name="analyze-string" substitutionGroup="xsl:instruction">
  <xs:complexType>
    <xs:complexContent>
      <xs:extension base="xsl:element-only-versioned-element-type">
        <xs:sequence>
          <xs:element ref="xsl:matching-substring" minOccurs="0"/>
          <xs:element ref="xsl:non-matching-substring" minOccurs="0"/>
          <xs:element ref="xsl:fallback" minOccurs="0" maxOccurs="unbounded"/>
        </xs:sequence>
        <xs:attribute name="select" type="xsl:expression" use="required"/>
        <xs:attribute name="regex" type="xsl:avt" use="required"/>
        <xs:attribute name="flags" type="xsl:avt" default=""/>
      </xs:extension>
    </xs:complexContent>
  </xs:complexType>
</xs:element>
```

To illustrate, your next task will be to process something a little unusual.

The FreeCEN project aims to capture all nineteenth-century U.K. census data and put it in the public domain. The project relies on volunteers entering the information in a well-defined spreadsheet format, and submitting it as CSV files. After validation, the content is loaded into a database for web access. The spreadsheet version of the data can be used for analysis by local historians. Figure 8-1 is a typical document image from which the content is transcribed.

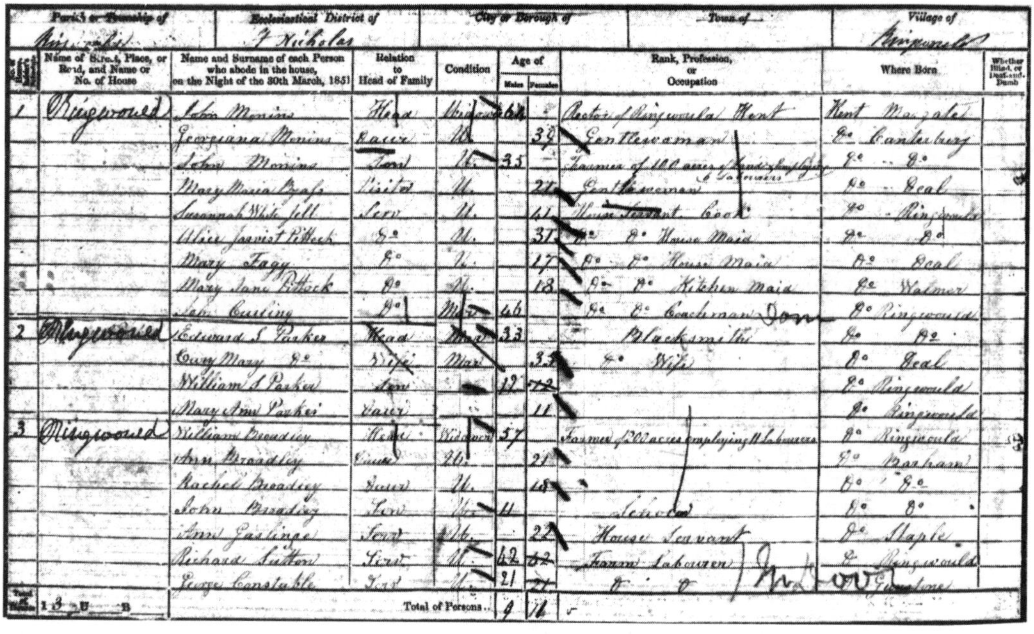

Figure 8-1

The following snippet shows a simplified example of data from an 1851 census enumerator's book. The first two values are the folio and page numbers from the source document. The third value is the house number. Following that are the occupants' names, relation to head of household, marital status (married, unmarried, widowed), sex, age, occupation, parish, and county of birth. The last value is a sequence number that can be used to restore the data to the original order after any spreadsheet processing. Note the spaces in some rows where information on occupation is not given in the original document:

```
4,1,1,Monins,John,Head,w,m,64,Rector of Ringwould Kent,Margate,KEN,1
4,1,1,Monins,Georgiana,Daughter,u,f,39,Gentlewoman,Canterbury,KEN,2
4,1,1,Monins,John,Son,u,m,35,Farmer 100 acres 6 labourers,Canterbury,KEN,3
4,1,1,Byass,Mary Maria,Visitor,u,f,21,Gentlewoman,Deal,KEN,4
4,1,1,Jell,Susannah White,Servant,u,f,41,House servant cook,Ringwould,KEN,5
4,1,1,Pittock,Alice Jarvist,Servant,u,f,31,House servant house maid,Ringwould,KEN,6
4,1,1,Fagg,Mary,Servant,u,f,17,House servant house maid,Deal,KEN,7
4,1,1,Pittock,Mary Jane,Servant,u,f,18,House servant kitchen maid,Walmer,KEN,8
4,1,1,Curling,John,Servant,m,m,46,House servant coachman,Ringwould,KEN,9
4,1,2,Parker,Edward S,Head,m,m,33,Blacksmith,Ringwould,KEN,10
4,1,2,Parker,Cary Mary,Wife,m,f,35,Blacksmith wife,Deal,KEN,11
4,1,2,Parker,William S,Son,u,m,12, ,Ringwould,KEN,12
4,1,2,Parker,Mary Ann,Daughter,u,f,11, ,Ringwould,KEN,13
4,1,3,Broadley,William,Head,w,m,57,Farmer 200 acres 11 labourers,Ringwould,KEN,14
4,1,3,Broadley,Ann,Daughter,u,f,21, ,Barham,KEN,15
4,1,3,Broadley,Rachel,Daughter,u,f,18, ,Barham,KEN,16
4,1,3,Broadley,John,Son,u,m,11,Scholar,Barham,KEN,17
4,1,3,Gaslinge,Ann,Servant,u,f,22,House servant,Staple,KEN,18
4,1,3,Sutton,Richard,Servant,u,m,43,Farm labourer,Ringwould,KEN,19
4,1,3,Constable,George,Servant,u,m,21,Farm labourer,Gunstone,KEN,20
4,1,3,Fagg,Thomas,Servant,u,m,18,Farm labourer,Barham,KEN,21
4,1,3,Benefield,John,Servant,u,m,19,Farm labourer,Barham,KEN,22
4,1,3,Lawrence,George,Servant,u,m,18,Farm labourer,Sholden,KEN,23
4,1,3,Knott,William,Servant,u,m,17,Farm labourer,St Margarets,KEN,24
```

You can read more about the FreeCEN project at http://freecen.rootsweb.com/.

Try It Out   CSV to XML

This stylesheet will need two passes through the data: one to encapsulate the content into elements representing rows and cells, and the other to create a result document containing semantic markup.

To identify the unique data source for the census information, add a parameter named $identifier. The value for this section of the 1851 census is "HO107163". Also set a value "census.csv" for the input file-name parameter $uri. Inside the main template set the $census variable using the $uri parameter value:

```
<xsl:param name="identifier"/>
<xsl:param name="uri"/>
<xsl:template match="/">
   <xsl:variable name="census" select="unparsed-text($uri)"/>
   <xsl:variable name="data">
      <list>
         <xsl:analyze-string select="$census" regex="\n">
            <xsl:non-matching-substring>
               <row>
                  <xsl:analyze-string select="." regex="," flags="x">
```

```
                <xsl:non-matching-substring>
                    <col>
                        <xsl:value-of select="normalize-space(.)"/>
                    </col>
                </xsl:non-matching-substring>
            </xsl:analyze-string>
        </row>
    </xsl:non-matching-substring>
</xsl:analyze-string>
        </list>
    </xsl:variable>
</xsl:template>
```

The $data variable will contain a temporary tree to hold the first pass at building the XML struc-
ture. The `<list>` element is the root of the tree in the variable. The first `<xsl:analyze-string>`
instruction breaks the source into lines by processing everything except line endings inside a
`<xsl:non-matching-substring>` element, with the attribute setting `regex= "\n"`. Each line will make a
`<row>` element.

The second instruction does the same with everything except commas, creating a `<col>` element for each
comma-separated value. The `flags="x"` setting tells the processor to ignore whitespace when matching.
This is also a good opportunity to normalize space in the values.

The second pass uses an `<xsl:result-document>` element to contain the final output. Given the known
structure of the CSV file from the FreeCEN specifications, it is simple to add semantic markup in the
literal result elements, and set the content using the position of the `<col>` elements:

```
<xsl:result-document href="census.xml">
    <census id="{$identifier}">
        <xsl:for-each select="$data//row">
            <person>
                <folio>
                    <xsl:value-of select="col[1]"/>
                </folio>
                <page>
                    <xsl:value-of select="col[2]"/>
                </page>
                <number>
                    <xsl:value-of select="col[3]"/>
                </number>
                <surname>
                    <xsl:value-of select="col[4]"/>
                </surname>
                <firstname>
                    <xsl:value-of select="col[5]"/>
                </firstname>
                <relation>
                    <xsl:value-of select="col[6]"/>
                </relation>
                <condition>
                    <xsl:value-of select="col[7]"/>
                </condition>
                <sex>
                    <xsl:value-of select="col[8]"/>
                </sex>
```

```
        <age>
            <xsl:value-of select="col[9]"/>
        </age>
        <occupation>
            <xsl:value-of select="col[10]"/>
        </occupation>
        <birthplace>
            <xsl:value-of select="col[11]"/>
        </birthplace>
        <county>
            <xsl:value-of select="col[12]"/>
        </county>
        <sortkey>
            <xsl:value-of select="col[13]"/>
        </sortkey>
        </person>
    </xsl:for-each>
  </census>
</xsl:result-document>
```

To process the text file in the Oxygen IDE, create a dummy XML file with just a single root element (the element name doesn't matter) and associate it with the stylesheet census.xsl. You will be able to modify the parameters that identify the census document and the URI of the CSV file in the user interface for the scenario, making it more portable over data sources.

Part of the result is contained in Listing 8-3. Listing 8-4 shows the code for census.xml.

Listing 8-3

```xml
<?xml version="1.0" encoding="UTF-8"?>
<census id="HO107163">
    <person>
        <folio>4</folio>
        <page>1</page>
        <number>1</number>
        <surname>Monins</surname>
        <firstname>John</firstname>
        <relation>Head</relation>
        <condition>w</condition>
        <sex>m</sex>
        <age>64</age>
        <occupation>Rector of Ringwould Kent</occupation>
        <birthplace>Margate</birthplace>
        <county>KEN</county>
        <sortkey>1</sortkey>
    </person>
    <person>
        <folio>4</folio>
        <page>1</page>
        <number>1</number>
        <surname>Monins</surname>
        <firstname>Georgiana</firstname>
        <relation>Daughter</relation>
```

```
            <condition>u</condition>
            <sex>f</sex>
            <age>39</age>
            <occupation>Gentlewoman</occupation>
            <birthplace>Canterbury</birthplace>
            <county>KEN</county>
            <sortkey>2</sortkey>
        </person>
        <person>
            <folio>4</folio>
            <page>1</page>
            <number>1</number>
            <surname>Monins</surname>
            <firstname>John</firstname>
            <relation>Son</relation>
            <condition>u</condition>
            <sex>m</sex>
            <age>35</age>
            <occupation>Farmer 100 acres 6 labourers</occupation>
            <birthplace>Canterbury</birthplace>
            <county>KEN</county>
            <sortkey>3</sortkey>
        </person>
        ...
        <person>
            <folio>4</folio>
            <page>1</page>
            <number>3</number>
            <surname>Knott</surname>
            <firstname>William</firstname>
            <relation>Servant</relation>
            <condition>u</condition>
            <sex>m</sex>
            <age>17</age>
            <occupation>Farm labourer</occupation>
            <birthplace>St Margarets</birthplace>
            <county>KEN</county>
            <sortkey>24</sortkey>
        </person>
</census>
```

Listing 8-4

```
<?xml version="1.0"?>
<xsl:stylesheet xmlns:xsl="http://www.w3.org/1999/XSL/Transform" version="2.0">
    <xsl:param name="identifier"/>
    <xsl:param name="uri"/>
    <xsl:template match="/">
        <xsl:variable name="census" select="unparsed-text($uri)"/>
        <xsl:variable name="data">
            <data>
                <xsl:analyze-string select="$census" regex="\n">
                    <xsl:non-matching-substring>
                        <row>
```

Continued

Listing 8-4: *(continued)*

```
                    <xsl:analyze-string select="." regex="," flags="x">
                       <xsl:non-matching-substring>
                          <col>
                             <xsl:value-of select="normalize-space(.)"/>
                          </col>
                       </xsl:non-matching-substring>
                    </xsl:analyze-string>
                 </row>
              </xsl:non-matching-substring>
           </xsl:analyze-string>
        </data>
   </xsl:variable>

   <xsl:result-document href="census.xml">
      <census xml:id="{$identifier}">
         <xsl:for-each select="$data//row">
            <person>
               <folio>
                  <xsl:value-of select="col[1]"/>
               </folio>
               <page>
                  <xsl:value-of select="col[2]"/>
               </page>
               <number>
                  <xsl:value-of select="col[3]"/>
               </number>
               <surname>
                  <xsl:value-of select="col[4]"/>
               </surname>
               <firstname>
                  <xsl:value-of select="col[5]"/>
               </firstname>
               <relation>
                  <xsl:value-of select="col[6]"/>
               </relation>
               <condition>
                  <xsl:value-of select="col[7]"/>
               </condition>
               <sex>
                  <xsl:value-of select="col[8]"/>
               </sex>
               <age>
                  <xsl:value-of select="col[9]"/>
               </age>
               <occupation>
                  <xsl:value-of select="col[10]"/>
               </occupation>
               <birthplace>
                  <xsl:value-of select="col[11]"/>
               </birthplace>
               <county>
                  <xsl:value-of select="col[12]"/>
               </county>
```

```
                <sortkey>
                    <xsl:value-of select="col[13]"/>
                </sortkey>
            </person>
        </xsl:for-each>

    </census>
  </xsl:result-document>

</xsl:template>

</xsl:stylesheet>
```

Outputting XML to CSV with `<xsl:text>` is just a starting point. JavaScript Object Notation (JSON) and other code formats are all possibilities given enough motivation and ingenuity.

Alternatives to XSLT

Because the two main examples in this chapter use the CSV format as either a target or a source format, you could argue that using XSLT and my examples are somewhat redundant. Moving data to and from spreadsheets in XML format is common enough, after all.

Of course, I have the excuse of illustrating how to output text or parse it to construct XML; but I also want to use this next short section to illustrate a number of points.

First, basic processing of spreadsheet data in XML form is not really more helpful than working with CSV and XSLT. Second, while you can develop a solution that doesn't require XSLT at all, it requires specific product knowledge and experience of XML Schema construction.

The next case uses the census example and Microsoft Excel 2003 Professional Edition. (Like many users, I'm still in an MS Office time warp.)

There are basically two options:

❑ Save the content in the generic XML format known as SpreadsheetML, which has been around even longer than Excel 2003, and then transform the result to your census target.

❑ Use your own custom schema design and map it to list objects in the spreadsheet.

Omitting the containing top-level XML instance markup, which is verbose, the following snippet reproduces the SpreadsheetML data output by the Save As function in Excel. It still requires a transform to get it to the target format, so it isn't any improvement on census.xsl:

```
<Table ss:ExpandedColumnCount="13" ss:ExpandedRowCount="24" x:FullColumns="1"
  x:FullRows="1">
  <Row>
   <Cell><Data ss:Type="Number">4</Data></Cell>
   <Cell><Data ss:Type="Number">1</Data></Cell>
   <Cell><Data ss:Type="Number">1</Data></Cell>
   <Cell><Data ss:Type="String">Monins</Data></Cell>
   <Cell><Data ss:Type="String">John</Data></Cell>
   <Cell><Data ss:Type="String">Head</Data></Cell>
   <Cell><Data ss:Type="String">w</Data></Cell>
   <Cell><Data ss:Type="String">m</Data></Cell>
```

```
  <Cell><Data ss:Type="Number">64</Data></Cell>
  <Cell><Data ss:Type="String">Rector of Ringwould Kent</Data></Cell>
  <Cell><Data ss:Type="String">Margate</Data></Cell>
  <Cell><Data ss:Type="String">KEN</Data></Cell>
  <Cell><Data ss:Type="Number">1</Data></Cell>
</Row>
<Row>
  <Cell><Data ss:Type="Number">4</Data></Cell>
  <Cell><Data ss:Type="Number">1</Data></Cell>
  <Cell><Data ss:Type="Number">1</Data></Cell>
  <Cell><Data ss:Type="String">Monins</Data></Cell>
  <Cell><Data ss:Type="String">Georgiana</Data></Cell>
  <Cell><Data ss:Type="String">Daughter</Data></Cell>
  <Cell><Data ss:Type="String">u</Data></Cell>
  <Cell><Data ss:Type="String">f</Data></Cell>
  <Cell><Data ss:Type="Number">39</Data></Cell>
  <Cell><Data ss:Type="String">Gentlewoman</Data></Cell>
  <Cell><Data ss:Type="String">Canterbury</Data></Cell>
  <Cell><Data ss:Type="String">KEN</Data></Cell>
  <Cell><Data ss:Type="Number">2</Data></Cell>
</Row>
  ...
</Table>
```

Option two requires a schema and a bit of careful work in Excel, but this approach can make good sense for many use cases, avoiding transforms partly or entirely. A lot depends on your goals and what skills you can bring to bear.

You can follow that course for the next example, and decide for yourself whether it has significant advantages or is even quicker. It is all done in the Excel user interface once the schema is prepared.

XML Maps

XML maps are objects created by Excel each time you add an XML schema to a workbook. A map describes the relationship between schema objects and spreadsheet locations. A workbook can support multiple maps, all of which have distinct names. Mapping enables a spreadsheet to exist independently of the underlying data, and separates the data in a workbook from its presentation. You can use the XML Maps dialog in Excel to define new mappings by adding, removing, and renaming schemas.

Try It Out   **Generate the Schema**

For this activity, you'll generate a census schema in the Oxygen IDE from the output created earlier. Schemas created this way are not always ideal, as they are inferred from a document instance, but the results will do for your purposes in this case.

First, generate an XML schema:

1. Open census.xml in the Oxygen IDE.
2. Choose XML ➤ Convert.

3. Choose W3C XML Schema in the dialog shown in Figure 8-2 and browse to a location to save the file as **census.xsd**.

4. Click Convert.

Figure 8-2

The schema census.xsd in Listing 8-5 is generated. Note that the schema imports xml.xsd, which should be in the same folder as census.xsd when you associate it with the Excel file.

Listing 8-5

```xml
<?xml version="1.0" encoding="UTF-8"?>
<xs:schema xmlns:xs="http://www.w3.org/2001/XMLSchema" elementFormDefault=
    "qualified">
  <xs:element name="census">
    <xs:complexType>
      <xs:sequence>
        <xs:element maxOccurs="unbounded" ref="person"/>
      </xs:sequence>
      <xs:attribute name="id" use="required"/>
    </xs:complexType>
  </xs:element>
  <xs:element name="person">
    <xs:complexType>
      <xs:sequence>
        <xs:element ref="folio"/>
        <xs:element ref="page"/>
        <xs:element ref="number"/>
        <xs:element ref="surname"/>
        <xs:element ref="firstname"/>
        <xs:element ref="relation"/>
        <xs:element ref="condition"/>
        <xs:element ref="sex"/>
        <xs:element ref="age"/>
```

Continued

155

```
          <xs:element ref="occupation"/>
          <xs:element ref="birthplace"/>
          <xs:element ref="county"/>
          <xs:element ref="sortkey"/>
       </xs:sequence>
     </xs:complexType>
   </xs:element>
   <xs:element name="folio" type="xs:integer"/>
   <xs:element name="page" type="xs:integer"/>
   <xs:element name="number" type="xs:integer"/>
   <xs:element name="surname" type="xs:NCName"/>
   <xs:element name="firstname" type="xs:string"/>
   <xs:element name="relation" type="xs:NCName"/>
   <xs:element name="condition" type="xs:NCName"/>
   <xs:element name="sex" type="xs:NCName"/>
   <xs:element name="age" type="xs:integer"/>
   <xs:element name="occupation" type="xs:string"/>
   <xs:element name="birthplace" type="xs:string"/>
   <xs:element name="county" type="xs:NCName"/>
   <xs:element name="sortkey" type="xs:integer"/>
</xs:schema>
```

XML Data in Excel

The XML features in Excel 2003 are, naturally enough, optimized for tabular data, so consistent uniform data structures are good candidates. The looser the XML structure, and the more inconsistent the data, the less likely it is a candidate for viewing or processing in a spreadsheet. You could end up with very sparse tables in extreme cases.

However, this is not a problem with the census data. To associate the schema with spreadsheet cells, you'll define an XML list with the columns containing the person-element data, add the schema you have created, and drag matching element names to the column headings.

The spreadsheet census.xls includes column headings to help you follow what to do, and an Identifier heading is added above a cell to contain the id attribute on the census element.

Try It Out   **Using the Excel GUI**

1.   Open the spreadsheet census.xls.

2.   Select the repeating elements and the headings in the spreadsheet, shown in Figure 8-3, by the bold border.

3.   Choose Data ➢ List ➢ Create List.

4.   Now choose Data ➢ XML ➢ XML Source.

5.   In the XML Maps dialog, shown in Figure 8-4, add census.xsd. Choose the <census> element as the root. The XML Source pane opens next to the spreadsheet, showing the schema structure.

6.   Select the element names under the person element one by one and drag them to the head of the matching columns.

7. Drag the `id` attribute on the census element to the cell under the Identifier heading containing `HO107163`.

8. In the XML Source pane, click Verify for export. You should get a positive response.

9. Choose Data ➢ XML ➢ Export and save the output as `census2.xml`, which should be identical to `census.xml`, the output from the previous Try It Out.

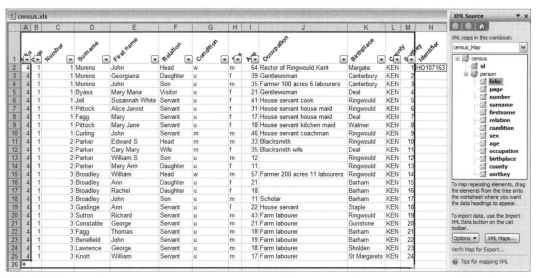

Figure 8-3

Figure 8-4

Summary

In this chapter you saw how whitespace-only text nodes are processed by default, and how to use `<xsl:strip-space>` and `<xsl:preserve-space>` to get control over processing inside element content.

Perhaps it was surprising to find that you can do simple raw-text processing with XSLT.

Loading and handling unparsed text is also possible, as you learned by processing some CSV census data. If you have a good grasp of regular expressions, it is possible to detect patterns in a range of text sources using `<xsl:analyze-string>`. A more sophisticated application of text-to-XML conversion is illustrated in Michael Kay's family-tree case study in Chapter 19 of *XSLT 2.0 and XPath 2.0 Programmers Reference* (Wrox 2008). In an activity in the next chapter, you'll use the XML census data introduced here to generate linking identifiers in a simple family tree.

To compare using spreadsheet data associated with an XML schema with XSLT conversion from CSV, you experimented with some Microsoft Excel 2003 XML features. There's more to learn here, and I encourage you to look into the detailed documentation from both the import and export perspectives.

Key Points

❏ It is important to understand how both XML parsers and XSLT processors deal with whitespace-only text nodes.

❏ You can control XSLT processor handling of whitespace using `<xsl:strip-space>` and `<xsl:preserve-space>` to specify sets of elements to exclude or include.

❏ Be careful not to use `<xsl:strip-space>` with mixed content elements.

❏ It is easy to write out delimited text files with the `<xsl:text>` instruction, but you clearly have to have a good knowledge of the target format.

❏ Regular expressions (regex) can be used to both detect patterns in raw text input and generate arbitrary XML markup.

Exercises

You'll find solutions to these exercises in Appendix A.

1. Why are the `<xsl:strip-space>` and `<xsl:preserve-space>` declarations useful?

2. Write an `<xsl:preserve-space>` declaration for appropriate elements you have seen in the XSLT Quick Reference examples.

3. Using `census.xml` as source, write a transform to convert it back to the original CSV format.

Identifiers and Keys

XSLT and XPath between them provide several ways to locate items, and to index and link them using identifiers and keys that express relationships between elements.

The id() function in XPath 2.0 enables you to find element nodes having attributes of type xs:ID, and it can be useful when the source schema or DTD is accessible. However, there are some limitations that result from the rules set by the XML specification for attribute values.

The <xsl:key> declaration and the matching XSLT key() function overcome these limitations, enabling you to locate source-tree nodes by matching either elements or attributes of any type.

When there are no obvious identifier values to use in the source data, you can use the XSLT generate-id() function to associate nodes with one another. In any single execution of a stylesheet, this function will always cause an identical unique value to be generated for a given node. This property can be used to associate related items and generate linking information.

In this chapter you will do the following:

- ❑ Review some characteristics of the ID and IDREF datatypes used in XML documents to uniquely identify items and refer to them.

- ❑ Learn how to use the XPath 2.0 id() function on ID attributes to locate source items, and appreciate its limitations.

- ❑ Use <xsl:key> and the key() function to work with more complex cross-reference structures, and locate non-unique items for processing.

- ❑ Apply the generate-id() function to index the lines of a play, and link individuals in a family tree.

- ❑ Consolidate your knowledge of both <xsl:for-each-group> and <xsl:number>.

ID Datatypes

XML Document Type Definitions (DTDs) and XML schemas both support the datatypes ID, IDREF, and IDREFS, which are most often applied as attributes. Here are some example schema declarations.

XML attributes specified as type ID have useful properties. Each element has at most one single unique identifier, and each value must be unique within the XML document:

```
<xs:attribute name="ID" type="xs:ID" use="required"/>
```

Attributes of type IDREF or IDREFS must refer to a matching ID or set of IDs. In the case of IDREFS type, the attribute contains a space-separated list of ID values:

```
<xs:attribute name="link" type="xs:IDREF" use="optional"/>
<xs:attribute name="links" type="xs:IDREFS" use="optional"/>
```

In a DTD, an ID attribute might be declared like this:

```
<!ATTLIST entry id ID #REQUIRED>
```

In an XML schema this declaration has an identical meaning:

```
<xs:element name="entry">
   ...
   <xs:attribute name="id" type="xs:ID" use="required"/>
   ...
</xs:element>
```

In XSLT you can use the XPath id() function to select elements with such IDs as long as the source nodes have the is-id property.

There are three ways for this value to be set when the source document is parsed:

❑   The source document must contain a DTD declaring an attribute as having type ID. An external DTD may not be parsed.

❑   A schema-aware processor must recognize the attribute as an xs:ID type or as one derived from xs:ID.

❑   The attribute must be named xml:id.

Attributes named xml:id are predefined as type ID, and an XSLT processor is required to set the is -id property when the source document is parsed. The W3C recommendation is xml:id Version 1.0. You can read the specification details at www.w3.org/TR/xml-id/.

Using the id() Function

The id() function enables you to select a node from the current document by specifying its unique ID value. You can also specify multiple ID values to select multiple documents. If you want to search within a different document, you can specify its root node as a second argument

The function takes two parameters, the first of which contains the required ID value or values. The first parameter may be a string containing one or more space-separated ID values, or a node with one or more values, or a sequence.

The second parameter is optional and defines the document node to be searched. If it is not supplied, then the search takes place in the same document as the context item.

Finding IDs

On each metadata `<entry>` element in the XSLT quick-reference file `reslist_xsl.xml`, the `xml:id` attribute is used as an identifier. It makes a fairly obvious candidate for using the `id()` function. As a reminder of the structure, here are entries for some elements and functions discussed in this chapter:

```
<entry xml:id="xsl_key">
    <title>xsl:key</title>
    <summary>Declares a named key to be used with the <code>key()</code>
function.</summary>
    <content src="../xslt_reference/"/>
    <category term="element_reference" scheme="resource"/>
    <category term="key" scheme="xsl"/>
</entry>
...
<entry xml:id="fn_generate_id">
    <title>generate-id</title>
    <summary>Generates an XML Name that uniquely identifies a node.</summary>
    <content src="../xslt_reference/"/>
    <category term="function_reference" scheme="resource"/>
    <category term="id" scheme="xsl"/>
</entry>
<entry xml:id="fn_key">
    <title>key</title>
    <summary>Returns the nodes with a given value for a named key, which was defined
using the <element>xsl:key</element> declaration.</summary>
    <content src="../xslt_reference/"/>
    <category term="function_reference" scheme="resource"/>
    <category term="key" scheme="xsl"/>
</entry>
```

Open the files `xsl_for_each_group.xml` and `main.xsl` again and make the following one-line change to the stylesheet, saving it as `use_id.xsl`:

```
<xsl:template match="link">
    <xsl:variable name="linkID" select="@href"/>
    <xsl:variable name="linkmeta"
        select="id($linkID,$resourcelist)"/>

    <a>
        <xsl:attribute name="href">
            <xsl:value-of select="concat($linkmeta/content/@src,$linkID,'.html')"/>
        </xsl:attribute>
        <xsl:value-of select="$linkmeta/title"/>
    </a>
</xsl:template>
```

Well, on the face of it this isn't very different from the replaced `select` attribute value:

```
$resourcelist//entry[@xml:id=$linkID] .
id($linkID,$resourcelist)"/>
```

Why bother with this change? The answer is that the first method causes the processor to perform a sequential search for this particular predicate. The second method will initiate a search in which the processor builds an index of IDs on the first search. Assuming that more than one search takes place, the index will improve performance.

The XPath function `idref()` *works in a similar fashion as* `id()`, *except that it locates all the nodes that contain* IDREF *or* IDREFS *values that refer to a given* ID *setting:*

```
idref($xref,$source)"/>
idrefs($a $b $c,$source)"/>
```

Keys

Useful as they are, there are some limitations to using XML IDs. The requirement that IDs be unique means that you have to use simple attribute values with XML names (e.g., no initial numbers or illegal characters). For example, a value like "9780470477250" (the 13-digit ISBN for this book) is an invalid ID, despite being universally used in bookselling transactions.

Keys, declared with <xsl:key>, can express node relationships with fewer limitations than IDs They can be of any datatype, and do not have to be unique in the document being searched. Keys can also return results from nodes containing multiple values, such as the names of contributors to a scientific paper.

In the declaration, you specify the name of a key and a matching pattern. The related `key()` function can then be used to return the results of any match values:

```
<xs:element name="key" substitutionGroup="xsl:declaration">
  <xs:complexType>
    <xs:complexContent mixed="true">
      <xs:extension base="xsl:sequence-constructor">
        <xs:attribute name="name" type="xsl:QName" use="required"/>
        <xs:attribute name="match" type="xsl:pattern" use="required"/>
        <xs:attribute name="use" type="xsl:expression"/>
        <xs:attribute name="collation" type="xs:anyURI"/>
      </xs:extension>
    </xs:complexContent>
  </xs:complexType>
</xs:element>
```

Two attributes are required. The `name` attribute is simply the name of a given key, and the `match` attribute defines the nodes to which the key applies. This is a pattern just like the one in the <xsl:template> `match` attribute. The `use` attribute is optional. It sets the value to be used in the key for each matching node. The following snippet names the key as `"part_id"`, and specifies nodes matching the <part> element, and the `sku` attribute as the value to use for the key:

```
<xsl:key name= "part_id" match= "part" use= "@sku"/>
```

As a mutually exclusive alternative to the use attribute, you can define a key in a contained sequence constructor.

The optional collation attribute has the same purpose as it does in <xsl:sort> and on several string-comparison functions. You saw how collations may be applied in Chapters 5 and 6. The value is the URI of the collation to use.

The key() Function

Matching is straightforward. The key() function takes up to three parameters (name, value, top). The first two are required parameters, the name and the value to find. The name parameter identifies the key to use, and will return any nodes matching the value. The third, optional top parameter may be used to specify the document node to be searched.

Try It Out   Using a Key

This time, use xsl_for_each_group.xml again and match the xml:id attribute using a key. Modify main.xsl again, saving it as use_key.xsl. First, add a key declaration that will match the <entry> elements in the XSLT quick-reference metadata using the "@xml:id" as the value in the use attribute:

```
<xsl:key name="identifier" match="entry" use="@xml:id"/>
```

Now modify the link template rule to make use of the key() function:

```
<xsl:template match="link">
    <xsl:variable name="linkID" select="@href"/>
  <xsl:variable name="linkmeta"
    select="key('identifier',$linkID,$resourcelist)"/>

  <a>
     <xsl:attribute name="href">
        <xsl:value-of select="concat($linkmeta/content/@src,$linkID,'.html')"/>
     </xsl:attribute>
     <xsl:value-of select="$linkmeta/title"/>
  </a>
</xsl:template>
```

The name parameter is 'identifier', the value to match is the $linkID variable (this will correspond to the xml:id attribute value), and the document node is $resourcelist.

In this case it is essential to use the third parameter because by default the key() function looks in the document containing the context node, and the context node is not in $resourcelist.

I haven't shown the complete code for use_id.xsl *and* use_key.xsl *here, as the changes are so small, but you'll find them in the code folder for this chapter in the downloadable code for this book on Wrox.com.*

You've no doubt see news feeds on the Web that contain tags at the end to categorize the entries. These tags have two characteristics. They aren't likely to be unique in a single feed and there are usually multiple tags per entry. The next example shows you how multiple-value, non-unique keys can work.

You will use the Atom syndication feed file you met in Chapter 1. However, this time you'll define a category key for the entries. Your goal is to filter the listing using a global parameter setting. Filtering the list focuses attention on the subset of entries that is of interest, and supplying a parameter value enables you to change the results of a search quite readily.

Using Multiple Values

Your source file is `atom.xml`. Previously, with `atom_list.xsl`, you output an unfiltered HTML table that listed authors, titles, and dates. Save a copy as `atom_key_filtered.xsl`. In the modified stylesheet, set up an `<xsl:param>` declaration `$find` to hold the parameter value `"xrx"`, which is one of the categories found in the feed. Declare a key named `category` that matches entries using the `term` attribute values on the `<category>` elements:

```
<xsl:param name="find">xrx</xsl:param>
<xsl:key name="category" match="entry" use="category/@term"/>
```

Modify the table used to list the entries as follows, adding a column to display the categories, and using the `key()` function to select the entries into the `$cat` variable:

```
<table cellspacing="0">
   <tr>
      <th xsl:use-attribute-sets="th_first">Author</th>
      <th xsl:use-attribute-sets="col">Title</th>
      <th xsl:use-attribute-sets="col">Date</th>
      <th xsl:use-attribute-sets="col">Categories</th>
   </tr>
   <xsl:variable name="cat" select="key('category',$find)"/>
   <xsl:for-each select="$cat">

      <xsl:sort select="author/name"/>
      <xsl:sort select="updated"/>
      <tr>
         <th xsl:use-attribute-sets="td_first">
            <xsl:value-of select="author/name"/>
         </th>
         <td xsl:use-attribute-sets="row">
            <xsl:apply-templates select="title"/>
         </td>
         <td xsl:use-attribute-sets="row">
            <xsl:apply-templates select="updated"/>
         </td>
         <td xsl:use-attribute-sets="row">
            <xsl:for-each select="category">
               <xsl:value-of select="@term"/>
               <xsl:if test="position() ne last()">, </xsl:if>
            </xsl:for-each>
         </td>

      </tr>
   </xsl:for-each>
</table>
```

The results should look like Figure 9-1. All the categories for an entry are listed in the table. Try changing the value of the $find parameter to get different results — for example, "iso," "odf," and "xml." A look at the category column in the output for "xml" will suggest others.

O'Reilly News: XML

Author	Title	Date	Categories
Dan McCreary	Warning: x = x + 1 May Be Hazardous to Your Brain	2008-11-18T13:18:47Z	concurrency, xml, xquery, xrx, xslt
Philip Fennell	XForms for Prototyping	2008-12-01T18:19:42Z	prototyping, xforms, xml, xrx
Philip Fennell	XForms, a pause for reflection	2008-12-17T18:05:12Z	xforms, xml, xrx

Figure 9-1

Generating Identifiers

When there are no formal identifiers in your source data and you want to relate existing nodes data to create a relationship, you can always generate identifiers.

The XSLT function generate-id() can be used to generate an XML name that uniquely identifies a node. In any given transformation the result is guaranteed to be different for every node to which it is applied. This makes generate-id() useful for creating link relationships in both XML and HTML output when the source is a single document. For example, you could generate an ID for a heading at one point in the stylesheet. Then, later (or even earlier, as the order is not significant) you can confidently refer to the heading again in an <a> element, because you know the same ID will be generated again.

There are three other aspects of using generate-id() that you should be aware of. First, the form of the identifier is implementation-specific, so you can't expect different processors to return the same values for the same source nodes. Second, while you can rely on the same processor producing unique identifiers within a given run of a stylesheet, you can't bank on it producing identical results in different runs on the same source. Third, it is possible, if unlikely, for a processor to generate an ID that was previously created in a source document (manually or otherwise). The processor is not obliged to check, and in such a case problems might arise.

Indexing Lines

The next example illustrates how to create an alphabetical index of first lines in an act of *Love's Labour's Lost* using generate-id(). There are no identifiers of any kind on the lines, so there is no way to refer to them. If an ID is added to each line, then an indexing step in the process can create the cross-references.

Try It Out   **generate-id()**

Open the XML source `a5s1.xml`. To add the index you'll modify `number_lines.xsl`. Save the changes as `index_lines.xsl`.

Each index line will be displayed as a link to the relevant line in the main body of the play, and will be processed twice to ensure that there are match identifiers.

To make the index, you need to loop through the lines selecting the first `<l>` element in each speech using the `[1]` predicate, and sort the lines in the default order. To create the links, add an `<a>` element, using the `generate-id()` function to form the value of the `href` attribute,. The value should be preceded by `"#"`.

`<xsl:apply-templates>` should have a `mode` attribute value of `"index"` so that the contents of `<sp>` elements will be processed differently from those in the main body of the play.

Next, follow each line with the name of the speaker. Because the speaker is at the same level as the lines in a speech, you need to select the speech on the `parent::` axis, and then the speaker under it:

```
<h2>Index of first lines</h2>
<xsl:for-each select="//sp/l[1]">
   <xsl:sort select="."/>
   <p><a href="#{generate-id()}">
      <xsl:apply-templates select="." mode="index"/>
   </a> [<xsl:value-of select="parent::sp/speaker"/>]</p>
</xsl:for-each>
```

The `index` mode template prevents line numbers from appearing in the index:

```
<xsl:template match="sp" mode="index">
   <table width="80%" class="noborder">
      <td class="noborder speaker" width="80%">
         <xsl:value-of select="speaker"/>
      </td>
   </table>
</xsl:template>
```

To make a link target for each index line, go to the template rule for the `<l>` element. All you need to do here is use `generate-id()` again, but this time inside an `id` attribute. The result will be an exact match with the identifier generated in the first pass through the lines. There is an overhead associated with adding an ID to every line, so apply a `position()` test for the first line. For this test to work you have to explicitly apply this template inside the `<sp>` template rule with a `select` attribute:

```
<xsl:template match="sp">
   <table width="80%" class="noborder">
      <td class="noborder speaker" width="80%">
         <xsl:value-of select="speaker"/>
      </td>
      <xsl:apply-templates select="l"/>
```

```
        </table>
    </xsl:template>
    ...
    <xsl:template match="l">
        <tr>
            <td class="noborder" width="60%">
                <xsl:if test="position() eq 1">
                    <xsl:attribute name="id" select="generate-id()"/>
                </xsl:if>
                <xsl:apply-templates/>

            </td>
            <td class="noborder" width="20%">
                <xsl:variable name="ln">
                    <xsl:number level="any" from="div[@type='scene']"/>
                </xsl:variable>
                <xsl:if test="$ln mod $interval=0">
                    <xsl:value-of select="$ln"/>
                </xsl:if>
            </td>
        </tr>
    </xsl:template>
```

In the following snippet, note in the XHTML code how the generated identifiers (in this case, `"d1e446"`) match up, first in the index where the target URL is set, and then in the play's text, where it is the target ID value:

```
<p><a href="#d1e446">Arts-man, preambulate, we will be singled from the</a>
  [Don Adriano]


<tbody>
    <tr>
        <td class="noborder speaker" width="80%">Don Adriano</td>
    </tr>
    <tr>
        <td class="noborder" id="d1e446" width="60%">Arts-man, preambulate, we
            will be singled from the</td>

        <td class="noborder" width="20%"/>
    </tr>
    ...
</tbody>
```

Figure 9-2 shows part of the web page for the Act 5 alphabetical index. Clicking on a line takes you to the location of the speech in the play where the line occurs.

Index of first lines

A most singular and choice epithet. [Sir Nathaniel]

Allons! we will employ thee. [Holofernes]

An I had but one penny in the world, thou shouldst [Costard]

An excellent device! so, if any of the audience [Moth]

Arts-man, preambulate, we will be singled from the [Don Adriano]

At your sweet pleasure, for the mountain. [Don Adriano]

Ba, most silly sheep with a horn. You hear his learning. [Moth]

Ba, pueritia, with a horn added. [Holofernes]

Bon, bon, fort bon, Priscian! a little scratch'd, [Holofernes]

Chirrah! [Don Adriano]

For the rest of the Worthies?-- [Don Adriano]

He draweth out the thread of his verbosity finer [Holofernes]

Horns. [Moth]

I do, sans question. [Holofernes]

Figure 9-2

Listing 9-1 shows the code for index_lines.xsl.

Listing 9-1

```
<xsl:stylesheet version="2.0" xmlns:xsl="http://www.w3.org/1999/XSL/Transform">

    <xsl:output method="html"/>

    <xsl:param name="style">reference.css</xsl:param>
    <xsl:param name="interval" select="5"/>

    <xsl:template match="/">
        <html>

            <xsl:call-template name="head">
                <xsl:with-param name="title" select="TEI/text/front/docTitle"/>
                <xsl:with-param name="style" select="$style"/>
            </xsl:call-template>

            <body>
                <h1>
                    <xsl:value-of select="TEI/text/front/docTitle"/>
                </h1>
                <h2>
                    <xsl:value-of select="TEI/text//castList/head"/>
                </h2>
                <ul class="unmarked">
```

```
                <xsl:for-each select="//castList/castItem">
                   <li>
                      <xsl:value-of select="."/>
                   </li>
                </xsl:for-each>
            </ul>
            <h2>Index of first lines</h2>
            <xsl:for-each select="//sp/l[1]">
               <xsl:sort select="."/>
               <p><a href="#{generate-id()}">
                      <xsl:apply-templates select="." mode="index"/>
                   </a> [<xsl:value-of select="parent::sp/speaker"/>]</p>
            </xsl:for-each>

            <xsl:apply-templates/>
         </body>
      </html>
</xsl:template>
<xsl:template name="head">
   <xsl:param name="title"/>
   <xsl:param name="style"/>
   <head>
      <meta http-equiv="Content-Type" content="text/xml;charset=UTF-8"/>
      <title>
         <xsl:value-of select="$title"/>
      </title>
      <link rel="stylesheet" type="text/css">
         <xsl:attribute name="href">
            <xsl:value-of select="$style"/>
         </xsl:attribute>
      </link>
   </head>
</xsl:template>
<xsl:template match="div[@type='act']">
   <h2>
      <xsl:value-of select="format-number(@n,'Act 0: ')"/>
   </h2>
   <xsl:apply-templates select="* except head"/>
</xsl:template>
<xsl:template match="div[@type='scene']">
   <h3>
      <xsl:value-of select="format-number(@n,'Scene 0: ')"/>
      <xsl:value-of select="head"/>
   </h3>
   <xsl:apply-templates select="* except head"/>
</xsl:template>

<xsl:template match="sp">
   <table width="80%" class="noborder">
      <td class="noborder speaker" width="80%">
         <xsl:value-of select="speaker"/>
      </td>
      <xsl:apply-templates select="l"/>
```

Continued

169

Listing 9-1: *(continued)*

```
        </table>
    </xsl:template>

    <xsl:template match="sp" mode="index">
        <table width="80%" class="noborder">
            <td class="noborder speaker" width="80%">
                <xsl:value-of select="speaker"/>
            </td>
        </table>
    </xsl:template>

    <xsl:template match="l">
        <tr>
            <td class="noborder" width="60%">
                <xsl:if test="position() eq 1">
                    <xsl:attribute name="id" select="generate-id()"/>
                </xsl:if>
                <xsl:apply-templates/>
            </td>
            <td class="noborder" width="20%">
                <xsl:variable name="ln">
                    <xsl:number level="any" from="div[@type='scene']"/>
                </xsl:variable>
                <xsl:if test="$ln mod $interval=0">
                    <xsl:value-of select="$ln"/>
                </xsl:if>
            </td>
        </tr>
    </xsl:template>

    <xsl:template match="TEI/child::teiHeader | speaker"/>

    <xsl:template match="TEI/text/front"/>

    <xsl:template match="div[@type='scene']/stage">
        <table width="100%" class="noborder">
            <tr>
                <td class="noborder" colspan="2" width="50%">[<xsl:value-of
                    select="."/>] </td>
            </tr>
        </table>
    </xsl:template>

    <xsl:template match="lg/head">[<xsl:value-of select="."
        />]<br/></xsl:template>

    <xsl:template match="stage">[<xsl:value-of select="."/>] </xsl:template>
</xsl:stylesheet>
```

Census to GEDCOM XML

In the summary of Chapter 8, I mentioned Michael Kay's family tree case study. In the later stages of the study, the content is first transformed to GEDCOM 6.0 XML, and then to XHTML.

The GEDCOM specification is maintained by the LDS Church, and is widely used in transferring genealogical data between applications. An important characteristic of the GEDCOM 6.0 structure is that it distinguishes elements for individuals from those for events in their lives, and links individuals into family elements. A census record contains all three types of information, and is quite capable of being fed into a family-tree structure.

The next Try It Out takes a set of person elements in the census output you generated in the last chapter, and builds a small family tree. There's more work with generate-id(), and a reminder of grouping and numbering too. It also illustrates the diverse results you can get with a little XSLT.

The source XML contains records for three households, but not all household members are part of the family; some are visitors and servants. Transforming data for more than one family is not typical of genealogical work, but it is useful if you want to study the history of families in one location over time — an emerging approach in local studies.

The GEDCOM 6.0 DTD is quite complex taken as a whole. I've picked only a few elements for this example. Details are available from www.familysearch.org/GEDCOM/GedXML60.pdf.

Try It Out   Building Family Trees

This task targets three of the main elements: `<FamilyRec>`, `<IndividualRec>`, and `<EventRec>`. The schema elements are shown in the next snippet. The child elements and attributes that I have highlighted are those that you will use in the transform. I won't be discussing other GEDCOM elements. Here is the code:

```
<xs:element name='FamilyRec'>
  <xs:complexType>
   <xs:sequence>
    <xs:element ref='HusbFath' minOccurs='0' maxOccurs='1'/>
    <xs:element ref='WifeMoth' minOccurs='0' maxOccurs='1'/>
    <xs:element ref='Child' minOccurs='0' maxOccurs='unbounded'/>

    <xs:element ref='BasedOn' minOccurs='0' maxOccurs='1'/>
    <xs:group ref="CommonFields"/>
   </xs:sequence>
   <xs:attribute name='Id' type='xs:ID' use='required'/>

  </xs:complexType>
 </xs:element>
 <xs:element name='IndividualRec'>
  <xs:complexType>
   <xs:sequence>
    <xs:element ref='IndivName' minOccurs='0' maxOccurs='unbounded'/>
    <xs:element ref='Gender' minOccurs='0' maxOccurs='1'/>

    <xs:element ref='DeathStatus' minOccurs='0' maxOccurs='1'/>
    <xs:element ref='PersInfo' minOccurs='0' maxOccurs='unbounded'/>
    <xs:element ref='AssocIndiv' minOccurs='0' maxOccurs='unbounded'/>
    <xs:element ref='DupIndiv' minOccurs='0' maxOccurs='unbounded'/>
    <xs:group ref="CommonFields"/>
   </xs:sequence>
   <xs:attribute name='Id' type='xs:ID' use='required'/>

  </xs:complexType>
```

171

```
      </xs:element>
      <xs:element name='EventRec'>
       <xs:complexType>
        <xs:sequence>
         <xs:element ref='Participant' maxOccurs='unbounded'/>
         <xs:element ref='Date' minOccurs='0' maxOccurs='1'/>
         <xs:element ref='Place' minOccurs='0' maxOccurs='1'/>

         <xs:element ref='Religion' minOccurs='0' maxOccurs='1'/>
         <xs:group ref="CommonFields"/>
        </xs:sequence>
        <xs:attribute name='Id' type='xs:ID' use='required'/>
        <xs:attribute name='Type' type='xs:string' use='required'/>

        <xs:attribute name='VitalType' type='VitalTypeType' use='optional'/>
       </xs:complexType>
      </xs:element>
```

Following is some sample output of the GEDCOM file showing part of the result document. Only one individual record, the related birth-event record, and the relevant family record are shown. I have highlighted lines where you use the generate-id() function to establish relationships.

You will use <xsl:number> to generate the required Id attribute values for events and families, with the numbering triggered by the sequence of persons in the source document census.xml. I've highlighted these too.

```
<GEDCOM>
   ...
   <IndividRec Id="d1e575">

      <IndivName>
         <NamePart Type="given name" Level="3">William</NamePart>
         <NamePart Type="surname" Level="1">Broadley</NamePart>
      </IndivName>
      <Gender>M</Gender>
      <PersInfo Type="occupation">
         <Information>Farmer 200 acres 11 labourers</Information>
         <Date>30 MARCH 1851</Date>
      </PersInfo>
      <PersInfo Type="residence">
         <Date>30 MARCH 1851</Date>
         <Place>
            <PlaceName>
               <PlacePart Type="country" Level="1">GBR</PlacePart>
               <PlacePart Type="county" Level="2">KEN</PlacePart>
               <PlacePart Level="4">Ringwould</PlacePart>
            </PlaceName>
         </Place>
      </PersInfo>
      <ExternalID Type="User" Id="HO107163/4/1"/>
   </IndividRec>
   <EventRec Type="birth" Id="E014">
```

```
            <Participant>
                <Link Target="IndividualRec" Ref="d1e575"/>
            </Participant>
            <Date>CAL 1794</Date>
            <Place>
                <PlaceName>
                    <PlacePart Type="country" Level="1">GBR</PlacePart>
                    <PlacePart Type="county" Level="2">KEN</PlacePart>
                    <PlacePart Level="4">Ringwould</PlacePart>
                </PlaceName>
            </Place>
        </EventRec>
        ...
    <FamilyRec Id="F014">

        <HusbFath>
            <Link Target="IndividualRec" Ref="d1e575"/>

        </HusbFath>
        <Child>
            <Link Target="IndividualRec" Ref="d1e619"/>
        </Child>
        <Child>
            <Link Target="IndividualRec" Ref="d1e662"/>
        </Child>
        <Child>
            <Link Target="IndividualRec" Ref="d1e705"/>
        </Child>
    </FamilyRec>
    ...
</GEDCOM>
```

I think it is fairly easy to see how most of the census data relates to the individual and event records, but I want to mention some less obvious points.

Places in GEDCOM are named in a hierarchy of levels for sorting purposes. They occur in both individual and event records.

In individual records, you can record residence information. You can use the ISO country code for United Kingdom (GBR), and another for Kent (KEN), an encoding of the county name used in U.K. historical data. The parish name is Ringwould. The exact day of the census is also known: 10 March 1851. The <ExternalD> element can be used to record a source identifier, and in this case I suggest you combine the census ID with the manuscript folio and page numbers from the census file.

For the event records, which will cover only the birth-event type, you need to calculate the approximate birth year of a person by subtracting the age from the census year, 1851. The individual's county and parish of birth are recorded in the census so those values go in the event details.

The mappings in the following table show how data from the census will populate the GEDCOM individual and event records. The family record carries only relationship data. Other data will have to be provided by or derived from parameter values.

Census	IndividualRec	EventRec
surname	IndividName/NamePart	Participant/Link
firstname	IndividName/NamePart	
sex	Gender	
occupation	PersInfo/Information	
age		Date (calculated)
county		PlacePart@Type
parish		PlacePart@Type

Start your transform with four date and place parameter values, which can, of course, be modified for other census contexts. The value `"KEN"` in the `$censuscounty` parameter is an encoding of the Kent county name used in U.K. historical data recording.

All the XML output is placed inside an `<xml-result-document>` instruction and a `<GEDCOM>` root element. In the `$families` variable, persons with the `"Head"`, `"Wife"`, `"Daughter"`, or `"Son"` relation value are selected. All other relationships are ignored, as they aren't supported in GEDCOM:

```
<xsl:param name="censusyear">1851</xsl:param>
<xsl:param name="censusdate">30 MARCH 1851</xsl:param>
<xsl:param name="censusplace">Ringwould</xsl:param>
<xsl:param name="censuscounty">KEN</xsl:param>

<xsl:result-document href="gedcom60.xml">
   <GEDCOM xml:id=" ">
      <xsl:variable name="families"
         select="//person[relation='Head' or relation='Wife'
         or relation='Daughter' or relation='Son']"/>
      <xsl:for-each select="$families">
      ...
      </xsl:for-each>
   </GEDCOM>
</xsl:result-document>
```

An `Id` attribute is required, and often a sequential number is used, prefixed with the initial letter of the element name. That is fine for the event and family entries, and you can use `<xsl:number>`. However, to create an `<IndividualRec>` element, you should use the `generate-id()` function you learned about earlier to set the value of the `Id` attribute. You'll use the same approach with link values in the `<EventRec>` and `<FamilyRec>` elements, making it possible to relate both to individuals.

In the `<PersInfo>` element, the `Type` attribute and an `<Information>` element will contain the details about occupation and residence. Because not every person is given an occupation in the census data, you should nest that output inside an `<xsl:if>` instruction.

The `<ExternalID>` element provides a reference to the census page containing the original data.

```
<IndividRec Id="{generate-id()}">
<IndivName>
   <NamePart Type="given name" Level="3">
      <xsl:value-of select="firstname"/>
   </NamePart>
   <NamePart Type="surname" Level="1">
      <xsl:value-of select="surname"/>
   </NamePart>
</IndivName>
<Gender>
   <xsl:value-of select="upper-case(sex)"/>
</Gender>
<xsl:if test="string-length(occupation) gt 1">
   <PersInfo Type="occupation">
      <Information>
         <xsl:value-of select="occupation"/>
      </Information>
      <Date>
         <xsl:value-of select="$censusdate"/>
      </Date>
   </PersInfo>
</xsl:if>
<PersInfo Type="residence">
   <Date>
      <xsl:value-of select="$censusdate"/>
   </Date>
   <Place>
      <PlaceName>
         <PlacePart Type="country" Level="1">GBR</PlacePart>
         <PlacePart Type="county" Level="2">
            <xsl:value-of select="$censuscounty"/>
         </PlacePart>
         <PlacePart Level="4">
            <xsl:value-of select="birthplace"/>
         </PlacePart>
      </PlaceName>
   </Place>
</PersInfo>
<ExternalID Type="User"
    Id="{concat(ancestor::census/@xml:id,'/',folio,'/',page)}"/>
</IndividRec>
```

The only event information to work out is the calculated birth year of a person. In the event records, you can work out an assumed birth year of a person by subtracting the age from the $censusyear variable value. GEDCOM recommends using the "CAL" prefix to indicate that the date is calculated:

```
<EventRec Id="" Type="birth">
   <Participant>
      <Link Target="IndividualRec" Ref="{generate-id()}"/>
   </Participant>
   <Date>
      <xsl:value-of select="concat('CAL ',$censusyear - age)"/>
   </Date>
   <Place>
```

```
            <PlaceName>
                <PlacePart Type="country" Level="1">GBR</PlacePart>
                <PlacePart Type="county" Level="2">
                    <xsl:value-of select="county"/>
                </PlacePart>
                <PlacePart Level="4">
                    <xsl:value-of select="birthplace"/>
                </PlacePart>
            </PlaceName>
        </Place>
    </EventRec>
```

The `<FamilyRec>` element consists mainly of references to individuals. On a second pass through the data, use `<xsl:for-each-group>` and the house `<number>` element to collect `<person>` nodes together. You can then use an `<xsl:choose>` filter to categorize the links as father, mother, or child:

```
<xsl:for-each-group select="$families" group-adjacent="number">
    <FamilyRec>
        <xsl:attribute name="Id">
            <xsl:value-of select=" concat('F',format-number(current-grouping-
key(),'000'))"/>
        </xsl:attribute>
        <xsl:for-each select="current-group()">
            <xsl:choose>
                <xsl:when test="relation='Head'">
                    <HusbFath>
                        <Link Target="IndividualRec" Ref="{generate-id()}"/>
                    </HusbFath>
                </xsl:when>
                <xsl:when test="relation='Wife'">
                    <WifeMoth>> <Link Target="IndividualRec" Ref="{generate-id()}"/>
                    </WifeMoth>
                </xsl:when>
                <xsl:when test="relation='Daughter' or relation='Son'">
                    <Child>
                        <Link Target="IndividualRec" Ref="{generate-id()}"/>
                    </Child>
                </xsl:when>
            </xsl:choose>
        </xsl:for-each>
    </FamilyRec>
</xsl:for-each-group>
```

GEDCOM is rather verbose, so I'm not listing the output. The complete stylesheet is `census2ged.xsl`, and is shown in Listing 9-2.

Listing 9-2

```
<?xml version="1.0"?>
<xsl:stylesheet xmlns:xsl="http://www.w3.org/1999/XSL/Transform" version="2.0">
    <xsl:param name="censusyear">1851</xsl:param>
    <xsl:param name="censusdate">30 MARCH 1851</xsl:param>
    <xsl:param name="censuscounty">KEN</xsl:param>
    <xsl:param name="censusplace">Ringwould</xsl:param>
    <xsl:template match="/">

        <xsl:result-document href="gedcom60.xml">
            <GEDCOM>
                <xsl:variable name="families"
                    select="//person[relation='Head' or relation='Wife' or relation=
                        'Daughter'or relation='Son']"/>
                <xsl:for-each select="$families">

                    <IndividRec Id="{generate-id()}">
                        <IndivName>
                            <NamePart Type="given name" Level="3">
                                <xsl:value-of select="firstname"/>
                            </NamePart>
                            <NamePart Type="surname" Level="1">
                                <xsl:value-of select="surname"/>
                            </NamePart>
                        </IndivName>
                        <Gender>
                            <xsl:value-of select="upper-case(sex)"/>
                        </Gender>
                        <xsl:if test="string-length(occupation) gt 0">
                            <PersInfo Type="occupation">
                                <Information>
                                    <xsl:value-of select="occupation"/>
                                </Information>
                                <Date>
                                    <xsl:value-of select="$censusdate"/>
                                </Date>
                            </PersInfo>
                        </xsl:if>
                        <PersInfo Type="residence">
                            <Date>
                                <xsl:value-of select="$censusdate"/>
                            </Date>
                            <Place>
                                <PlaceName>
                                    <PlacePart Type="country" Level="1">GBR</PlacePart>
                                    <PlacePart Type="county" Level="2">
                                        <xsl:value-of select="$censuscounty"/>
```

Continued

Listing 9-2: *(continued)*

```
                  </PlacePart>
                  <PlacePart Level="4">
                      <xsl:value-of select="$censusplace"/>
                  </PlacePart>
               </PlaceName>
            </Place>
         </PersInfo>
         <ExternalID Type="User"
            Id="{concat(ancestor::census/@xml:id,'/',folio,'/',page)}"
            />
      </IndividRec>

      <EventRec Type="birth">
         <xsl:attribute name="Id">
            <xsl:text>E</xsl:text>
            <xsl:number level="any" format="001"/>
         </xsl:attribute>
         <Participant>
            <Link Target="IndividualRec" Ref="{generate-id()}"/>
         </Participant>
         <Date>
            <xsl:value-of select="concat('CAL ',$censusyear - age)"/>
         </Date>
         <Place>
            <PlaceName>
               <PlacePart Type="country" Level="1">GBR</PlacePart>
               <PlacePart Type="county" Level="2">
                  <xsl:value-of select="county"/>
               </PlacePart>
               <PlacePart Level="4">
                  <xsl:value-of select="birthplace"/>
               </PlacePart>
            </PlaceName>
         </Place>
      </EventRec>
   </xsl:for-each>

   <xsl:for-each-group select="$families" group-adjacent="number">
      <FamilyRec>
         <xsl:attribute name="Id">
            <xsl:text>F</xsl:text>
            <xsl:number level="any" format="001"/>
         </xsl:attribute>
         <xsl:for-each select="current-group()">
            <xsl:choose>
               <xsl:when test="relation='Head'">
                  <HusbFath>
                     <Link Target="IndividualRec" Ref="{generate-id()}"
                     />
                  </HusbFath>
               </xsl:when>
               <xsl:when test="relation='Wife'">
```

```
                        <WifeMoth>> <Link Target="IndividualRec"
                                Ref="{generate-id()}"/>
                        </WifeMoth>
                    </xsl:when>
                    <xsl:when test="relation='Daughter' or relation='Son'">
                        <Child>
                            <Link Target="IndividualRec" Ref="{generate-id()}"
                            />
                        </Child>
                    </xsl:when>
                </xsl:choose>
            </xsl:for-each>
        </FamilyRec>
    </xsl:for-each-group>

    </GEDCOM>
    </xsl:result-document>

    </xsl:template>

</xsl:stylesheet>
```

Summary

This chapter introduced some useful concepts about the use of XML IDs and other identifying values in source data.

You learned about two options open to you when locating source-data nodes: the XPath 2.0 `id()` function, to find uniquely identified items; and `<xsl:key>` and the `key()` function, to work with more complex cross-reference structures and locate non-unique items for processing.

You saw that when there are no identifiers in source data, you can make use of the `generate-id()` function to associate related nodes and generate links between them.

Key Points

❏   XML IDs, while useful, have some limitations when it comes to naming and processing.

❏   Using the `id()` function is more efficient than a linear search using a predicate like `entry[@xml:id=$linkID]` because the processor will usually create an index.

❏   The `key()` function is also efficient for the same reason, and it enables locating element and attribute nodes of all types, including multiple non-unique values.

❏   The `generate-id()` function is guaranteed to produce the same identifier for a given node every time, but only within the same invocation of a stylesheet.

Exercises

You'll find solutions to these exercises in Appendix A.

1. Under what conditions will an XSLT processor recognize an xs:ID type and set the is-id property on a source node when parsing an input document?

2. What is the purpose of the collation attribute on the <xsl:key> declaration?

3. How consistent would you expect the results to be for a given node from the generate-id() function on the following?

   ❑ A different processing run

   ❑ A different processor

Debugging, Validation, and Documentation

Quite often the stylesheets that you write are for simple (and sometimes one-off) projects. You can just run the transform and inspect the results until it works correctly. If you hit a problem, you can inspect the code and fix it. Sometimes, however, the solution to a problem is not obvious.

Any good XSLT development environment will provide useful debugging features to help you locate problems in your code. Typically, you can step through code, set breakpoints, inspect variables, and trace execution. Then, XSLT itself provides inline messaging and error-tracing features.

Until quite recently it was not possible to validate either source or result documents within an XSLT processor. Validation, apart from passing or failing the document concerned, can help you identify stylesheet errors that you might otherwise find difficult to find, or even miss entirely.

Systematic documentation is often delivered only with the largest and most established projects. However, it is very easy to add documentation to a stylesheet and process it using XSLT.

In this chapter you'll do the following:

- ❑ Experiment with the XSLT Debugger in the Oxygen IDE.
- ❑ Write trace text with `<xsl:message>` and `<xsl:comment>`.
- ❑ Survey the features of two XPath error-handling functions.
- ❑ Learn to validate both output and input in your stylesheets using the schema-aware version of the Saxon processor.
- ❑ Use XSLTdoc, an open-source package that makes inline documentation a snap.

Debugging XSLT

A good XSLT development environment should provide debugging features that help locate problems in your code quickly. In the Oxygen IDE this involves moving from an XML editing view (or perspective) of the code to a debugging view. In the Eclipse Edition, the menu command sequence is Window ➢ Open Perspective ➢ Oxygen XSLT Debugger.

The default configuration shows the XML source, the XSLT code, and the output in three separate views. Figure 10-1 illustrates the layout.

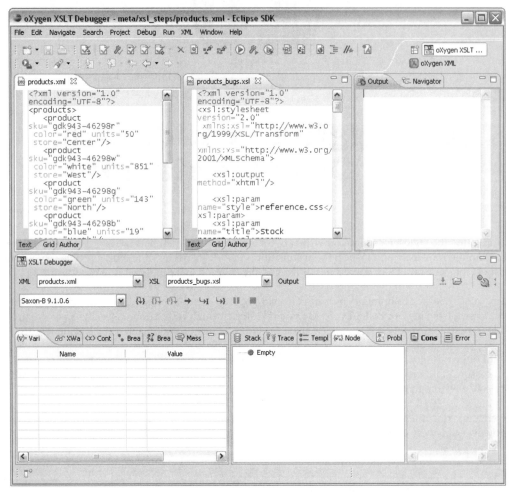

Figure 10-1

If you have just found a bug, some of the relevant files will already be open when you change to this view. If not, you can select the primary input and code files, and choose the XSLT processor. There is a full range of step-through controls that you can use. You can also set multiple breakpoints. Once the correct files are selected, you can step through the code, inspecting values in a series of inspection tabs at the bottom of the view. They include variable values, messages, process trace history, template hits, and so on.

The best way to understand the potential of a debugger is to work through a simple example, which will be the subject of your next exercise. You will work with the source file `products.xml`, introduced in Chapter 5. The stylesheet is `products_bugs.xsl`. You will step through the code, sample the variable inspection process, and view a performance profile.

This example is based on the Eclipse Edition of the IDE, which differs somewhat from the desktop editions. For example, in the desktop edition the tabs are at the bottom of the views, and the step icons are in the toolbar below the menus.

Try It Out   Debugging products.xsl

You'll perhaps recall that the original (bug-free) stylesheet tabulates product information using `<xsl:for-each-group>`. This version contains a minor, typically irritating, bug. See if you can spot it before you start.

1. Assuming you are in the Oxygen IDE XML editor, choose Window ➤ Open Perspective ➤ Oxygen XSLT Debugger.

2. In the center section of the XSLT Debugger view, open **products.xml** and **products_bugs.xsl** and select **Saxon-B 9.1.0.5** as a processor, using the drop-down lists. Refer to Figure 10-1 again to see how it should appear.

3. Choose Debug ➤ Step In. In the stylesheet, the `$style` parameter declaration is highlighted.

4. Repeat step 3 twice, and click the Trace view tab at the bottom right to see a listing of the process sequence.

5. From the Variables view tab on the far left, click the `$style` parameter. Check the Nodes/Values Set view at the bottom right, in which you should see the value of `"reference.css"`. Do the same with the `$title` parameter, which should show `"Stock report"`. The screen should look like Figure 10-2.

6. Continue stepping into the code until the `head` template is called and the `$title` parameter has been evaluated there. Check the Nodes/Values Set view again. The variable is empty, as is the `<title>` element in the output window. The problem is in the calling template; the `<xsl:with-parameter>` instruction `select` attribute value is incorrectly `"title"` when it should be `"$title"`, as shown in the next snippet:

```
<xsl:with-param name="title" select="$title"/>
```

7. Continue stepping into the code until the value of `$title` is set inside the `<h1>` element. The value is correct because the original global variable remains in scope.

8. Choose Debug ➤ Run to End to complete the transform.

183

Figure 10-2

Profiling

Some IDEs provide profiling features that analyze the amount of time the processor spends in various parts of your code. For small documents this may not be a critical matter, as you are usually working in millisecond values; but if you have a lot of information processing to do, profiling can be useful in tuning the performance of your stylesheet.

In the Oxygen IDE, two views show the results of profiling after a transform is run. The Hotspots view shows a list of all instruction calls that lie above the threshold defined in the profiler settings. Each shows the time in milliseconds or microseconds spent in the hotspot together, and how many times they have been invoked.

The Invocation view shows a top-down call tree representing how XSLT instructions are processed.

The following Try It Out illustrates the Oxygen IDE's profiling features.

Try It Out   Profiling use_key.xsl

This time you'll use the stylesheet use-key.xsl and run it with xsl_for-each-group.xml. Here are the steps:

1.   Start the debugger and load these files as you did in the previous example.

2.   In the center-right section of the interface, toggle the clock icon to turn on profiling. The Invocation view is shown at the bottom left, and the Hotspots view is displayed at the bottom right. Figure 10-3 shows the icon toggled to on.

Figure 10-3

3.   Choose Debug ➢ Run.

4.   Expand the headings in both the Invocation and the Hotspots listing. Figure 10-4 shows the analysis, highlighting the time spent evaluating the resource metadata values.

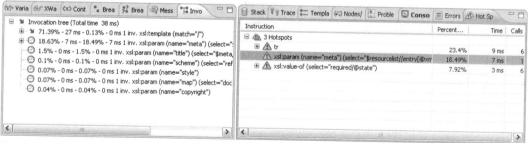

Figure 10-4

You may well get different results from mine when you profile this stylesheet. Running a profile several times with a given source seems to produce slightly different results.

Verifying XHTML Output

Back in Chapter 1 you used a processing instruction to invoke a stylesheet from a browser:

```
<?xml-stylesheet href="step1.xsl" type="text/xsl"?>
```

When you want to generate XHTML, this is often a convenient way to do a visual check of your output. For example, one of the default processing scenarios in the Oxygen IDE makes use of it. Having said that, there aren't too many other occasions when you'll need to use a processing instruction.

If you want to add a similar instruction to a result document, you can use the `<xsl:processing -instruction>` element to write a processing-instruction node to the output. Here's the schema definition:

```
<xs:element name="processing-instruction" substitutionGroup="xsl:instruction">
  <xs:complexType>
    <xs:complexContent mixed="true">
      <xs:extension base="xsl:sequence-constructor">
        <xs:attribute name="name" type="xsl:avt" use="required"/>
        <xs:attribute name="select" type="xsl:expression"/>
      </xs:extension>
    </xs:complexContent>
  </xs:complexType>
</xs:element>
```

You start with the `name` attribute, which can be expressed as an attribute-value template. Because there could be more than one processing instruction in a source document, this name identifies the processing instruction. In this case the identifier is `"xml-stylesheet"`. As you can see from the schema definition, you have the option of a `select` attribute or a contained sequence constructor to build the instruction.

You then need to create the pseudo-attributes. As you may recall from Chapter 1, these are not strictly attributes, so you cannot make use of the `<xsl:attribute>` instruction. However, you can insert the text using `<xsl:text>`.

```
<xsl:processing-instruction name="xsl-stylesheet">
   <xsl:text>href="step1.xsl" type="text/xsl"</xsl:text>
</xsl:processing-instruction>
```

Using Messages

With the `<xsl:message>` instruction you can output a diagnostic message that can assist in debugging. You can also stop the execution of a transform using the `terminate` attribute value of `"yes"`, which can take the form of an attribute value template:

```
<xs:element name="message" substitutionGroup="xsl:instruction">
  <xs:complexType>
    <xs:complexContent mixed="true">
      <xs:extension base="xsl:sequence-constructor">
        <xs:attribute name="select" type="xsl:expression"/>
        <xs:attribute name="terminate" type="xsl:avt" default="no"/>
      </xs:extension>
    </xs:complexContent>
  </xs:complexType>
</xs:element>
```

Unlike several other elements, using both the `select` attribute and the sequence-constructor methods is allowed. If you use both, the results will be joined together in a single message.

The order of execution, the format, and the destination of the output are implementation-defined. The specification merely suggests the following:

An implementation might implement xsl:message *by popping up an alert box or by writing to a log file.*

Try It Out   **Messages**

If you are using the chapter code, remove the following comment around the `<xsl:message>` instruction in `head.xsl`. Otherwise, add the code to your working copy. Then process any one of the XSLT reference files against `use_key.xsl` to see the message output.

```
<head>
    <meta http-equiv="Content-Type" content="text/xml;charset=UTF-8"/>
    <title>
        <xsl:value-of select="$title"/>
    </title>
    <link rel="stylesheet" type="text/css">
        <xsl:attribute name="href">
            <xsl:value-of select="$style"/>
        </xsl:attribute>
            <!--<xsl:message>Head section link processed</xsl:message-->

    </link>
</head>
```

Figure 10-5 shows the output, `"Head section link processed"`, which in the case of the Eclipse Oxygen IDE is in the debugger's Messages view. The same information appears in the XSLT editor's Text view.

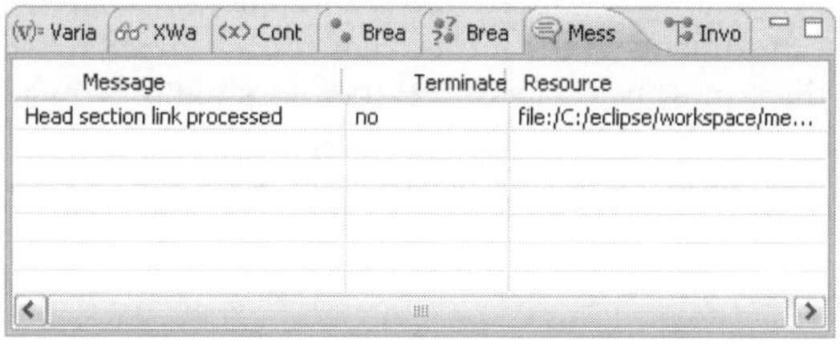

Figure 10-5

Commenting Output

To insert a comment in the output you use the `<xsl:comment>` instruction to enclose the comment text. Comments can appear anywhere inside an `<xsl:template>` instruction.

Because the order of execution of `<xsl:message>` instructions is uncertain, it may sometimes be more useful to place comment instructions in the result tree to provide diagnostics. For example, variables are often not evaluated until they are first used, so the results are hard to predict. However, you can get some idea of the sequence by stepping through the code in debug mode.

Comments have a wider utility, too. You can use them to date output, and to comment out JavaScript code in XHTML pages and even XML markup, as the following snippet shows.

```
<xsl:comment>Date created: <xsl:value-of select="format-date(current-date(),
'[Y]-[M01]-[D01]')"/>
</xsl:comment>
```

The preceding instruction produces the following output:

```
<!-- Date created: 2009-02-18 -->
```

Using the error() Function

If you are developing a large XSLT application for end users and you need to localize messages for users in different natural languages, it is worth considering making use of the XPath `error()` function.

This function enables you to specify user-defined error codes similar to those defined for XSLT and XPath. These codes, which are defined as QNames, take the form shown in the first part of the following example:

```
XTDE1110 The collation attribute of xsl:for-each-group must be a collation
recognized by the processor
```

The general idea is that user-defined error messages should follow the same pattern, using codes like this to look up localized messages for different languages.

You can use this function to handle conditions such as invalid parameters passed to a function. The function takes up to three arguments in the form `error(code, description, object)`, all of which are optional. The code, which must be cast as an `xs:QName`, should be in a user-defined namespace. The description is a string, and the object is some identifying value related to the error. The next example shows an error code in the namespace associated with the `xm:` prefix:

```
error(xs:QName('xm:821'),'Invalid parameter value')
```

Type and Schema Validation

There's a certain amount of validation you can do using XSLT's built-in datatypes. If you apply them using the `as` attribute on `<xsl:param>` elements, for example, an XSLT processor will verify that the values passed are of the correct type. If not, it will report errors, thus helping to detect coding mistakes.

Better still, you can use a schema-aware processor, such as the Saxon and AltovaXML 2008 processors. A schema-aware processor is one that can take advantage of the schemas you have defined for both input and output documents, thereby extending the range of type checking, including user-defined schema types.

Types in XSLT

Until now I haven't paid much attention to how you can declare the type of values in XSLT stylesheets: This applies to templates, variables, parameters, and functions. Here's an example, which uses the `as` attribute to define two parameters as type `xs:string` in a function:

```
<xsl:function name="xm:getentries-by-category">
   <xsl:param name="category" as="xs:string"/>
   <xsl:param name="scheme" as="xs:string"/>
   ...
</xsl:function>
```

There is no need to declare a type, but if you do, the processor has more information to work with, and will be able to check and report on any errors.

For built-in XSLT types you don't need a schema-aware processor, nor do you require validated source documents. Therefore, types like xs:integer, xs:string, and xs:date can all be declared, indicating that exactly one occurrence of the type is allowed. Otherwise, you can also show the number of occurrences allowed with the suffix characters shown in the following table.

Character	Occurrences
*	Zero or more
+	One or more
?	Zero or one

Examples include element() for an element node, attribute()+ for a sequence of one or more attribute nodes, and xs:string? for a string or an empty sequence.

Using a Schema-Aware Processor

With a schema-aware processor, the basic XSLT type system is extended to include all of the atomic types in the XML Schema — for example, derived types such as xs:nonNegativeInteger and xs:token, and any user-defined types specified in the particular schema in use.

You can use such a processor to validate both the input and the output of your stylesheet. Both aspects of validation require a declaration in your stylesheet defining the schema to be used, but they may be done independently of one another.

When an XML document is validated, apart from basic pass or fail results, element and attribute nodes in the resulting tree of nodes are associated with the type information present in the schema. This results in correct calculations — for example, when typed numeric values are compared or sorted. It also results in errors being reported at compile or run time, when incorrectly typed values are passed to a template or a function.

Importing Type Definitions

To make the schema and user-defined types available, you use the <xsl:import-schema> declaration to identify the schema. You can import multiple schema documents if required. Here's the XSLT schema definition:

```
<xs:element name="import-schema" substitutionGroup="xsl:declaration">
  <xs:complexType>
    <xs:complexContent>
      <xs:extension base="xsl:element-only-versioned-element-type">
```

```
        <xs:sequence>
          <xs:element ref="xs:schema" minOccurs="0" maxOccurs="1"/>
        </xs:sequence>
        <xs:attribute name="namespace" type="xs:anyURI"/>
        <xs:attribute name="schema-location" type="xs:anyURI"/>
      </xs:extension>
    </xs:complexContent>
  </xs:complexType>
</xs:element>
```

There are two ways to import a schema. One is to use the combination of the `namespace` and `schema-location` attributes. The `namespace` attribute is essential if there are any user-defined types in your schema. The `schema-location` attribute tells the processor where to find the schema:

```
<xsl:import-schema namespace="http://www.w3.org/1999/xhtml"
   schema-location="xhtml1-strict.xsd"/>
```

All the schemas that are relevant must be imported to one of the stylesheet modules in use. You cannot rely on one schema importing another: you must import them explicitly.

The other way is to embed the schema in `<xs:import-schema>` as a nested element, in which case you must omit the `schema-location` attribute, You may also omit the `namespace` attribute setting, as it is provided by the embedded schema declaration. If you do include the `namespace` attribute, then it must match the target namespace of the inline schema.

Validating XSLT Output

Output validation by itself is most often required in situations where your organization is publishing the information you are processing. In this context, validating the input usually takes place at the authoring stage in the production cycle. After all, that is the basic reason for having a schema in the first place.

If you validate output, any resulting errors will help you identify problems in the stylesheet, in some cases at compile time, before it is executed. This is certainly a better option than validating the result after the document is serialized, when errors thrown by a subsequent validation test will be identified in relation to their position in the result document. Fixing problems will take longer because you'll have to locate them in the output file, and try to find the matching cause in the stylesheet.

Try It Out   Validating XHTML

In the next example, you'll validate the output from `products.xml`, which you met in Chapter 5. First, make a change to the `<products>` element, referring to the schema `products.xsd`:

```
<products xmlns:xsi="http://www.w3.org/2001/XMLSchema-instance"
   xsi:noNamespaceSchemaLocation="products.xsd">
```

Here's the schema itself:

```
<?xml version="1.0" encoding="UTF-8"?>
<xs:schema xmlns:xs="http://www.w3.org/2001/XMLSchema" elementFormDefault
="qualified">
  <xs:element name="products">
    <xs:complexType>
```

```
    <xs:sequence>
      <xs:element maxOccurs="unbounded" ref="product"/>
    </xs:sequence>
  </xs:complexType>
</xs:element>
<xs:element name="product">
  <xs:complexType>
    <xs:attribute name="color" use="required" type="xs:string"/>
    <xs:attribute name="sku" use="required" type="xs:string"/>
    <xs:attribute name="store" use="required" type="xs:string"/>
    <xs:attribute name="units" use="required" type="xs:integer"/>
  </xs:complexType>
</xs:element>
</xs:schema>
```

The original stylesheet, `products.xsl`, needs only a little modification to prepare it for validation. An XHTML namespace declaration is required on the `<xsl:stylesheet>` and `<xsl:import-schema>` elements. This time you'll use the `"strict"` version of the W3C schema, and set the output method to `"XHTML"`.

The value `"strict"` means that there must be an element declaration for the output root element, in this case `<html>`, in the schema; and the content must conform to the structure of its child elements. I suggest you use a local copy of the schema, rather than access it over the Internet, to improve performance.

You will also need to import the schema `xml.xsd`, which defines an `xml:lang` attribute used in XHTML:

```
<?xml version="1.0" encoding="iso-8859-1"?>
<xsl:stylesheet version="2.0" xmlns:xsl="http://www.w3.org/1999/XSL/Transform"
    xmlns="http://www.w3.org/1999/xhtml">
  <xsl:import-schema namespace="http://www.w3.org/1999/xhtml"
      schema-location="xhtml-strict.xsd"/>
  <xs:import namespace="http://www.w3.org/XML/1998/namespace"
      schemaLocation="http://www.w3.org/2001/xml.xsd"/>
  <xsl:output method="xhtml"/>
</xsl:stylesheet>
```

Everything will be output inside an `<xsl:result-document>` element. The value `"strict"` must also be set for the `validation` attribute:

```
<xsl:result-document validation="strict">
  <html
  ...
  </html>
</xsl:result-document>
```

To run this stylesheet you need to change the default XSLT 2.0 transformer to the schema-aware version in the Oxygen IDE. Figure 10-6 shows the interface.

1. Choose Window ➤ Preferences.
2. Expand the tree to Oxygen ➤ XML ➤ XSLT-FO-XQuery ➤ XSLT.

3. Set the XSLT 2.0 Validate with drop-down to Saxon-SA (version). The version I used was 9.1.0.5.

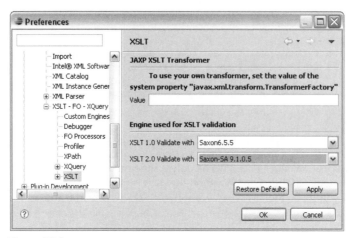

Figure 10-6

In the source code for this stylesheet, `products_valid_out.xsl`, I deliberately inserted an invalid attribute on the `<h2>` element. If you use this code, you should see the following error, which the Saxon processor reports at compile time:

```
[Saxon-SA 9.1.0.5] Attribute align is not permitted in the
content model of the complex type of element h2
@see: http://www.w3.org/TR/xslt20/#err-XTTE1510
```

The validation attribute allows three values other than `strict`. *All four values also apply to the* validation *attribute on* `<xsl:document>`, `<xsl:copy>`, *and* `<xsl:copy-of>`. *You can also specify a default value in the* default-validation *attribute on the* `<xsl:stylesheet>` *element.*

`lax` *causes the processor to validate the output against the schema only if the schema definition for the element is found.*

`preserve` *means that no validation is done at the top level. Any type annotations are passed on to the tree being constructed. This may be useful in cases where further processing is done on the tree, but clearly not in the case of serialized output.*

`strip` *removes any type annotations. Elements in the constructed tree will be annotated as* `xs:untyped`, *and attributes as* `xs:untypedAtomic`.

Specifying User-Defined Types

In a stylesheet, user-defined types are prefixed using a namespace prefix. For example, the `products.xsd` schema contains the following simple type definition derived from `xs:string`:

```
<xs:simpleType name="storetype">
  <xs:restriction base="xs:string">
```

```
        <xs:enumeration value="North"/>
        <xs:enumeration value="South"/>
        <xs:enumeration value="East"/>
        <xs:enumeration value="West"/>
        <xs:enumeration value="Center"/>
    </xs:restriction>
</xs:simpleType>
```

The `store` attribute is specified to have this type:

```
<xs:element name="product">
    <xs:complexType>
        <xs:attribute name="sku" use="required" type="xs:string"/>
        <xs:attribute name="color" use="required" type="xs:string"/>
        <xs:attribute name="units" use="required" type="xs:integer"/>
            <xs:attribute name="store" use="required" type="storetype"/>

    </xs:complexType>
</xs:element>
```

To use this type in a stylesheet, a `select` expression must be constructed using a function that returns the value as that type. This is the same approach as casting the `data-type` attribute on `<xsl:sort>` using the relevant built-in schema type, which you learned about in Chapter 5. The difference is that you would use the user-defined type in the function, as shown in the next snippet, where the product namespace prefix is p:

```
<xsl:stylesheet version="2.0" xmlns:xsl="http://www.w3.org/1999/XSL/Transform"
    xmlns:p="http://sportsproducts.eu/2009/XMLSchema">

<xsl:variable name="store" as="p:storetype" select="p:storetype('North')"/>
...
</xsl:stylesheet>
```

Complex types cannot be used directly in an `as` attribute value, but can be used in a sequence type descriptor that qualifies a node in the form of the type test `element(element_name, element_type)`.

Often, complex types are not named in schemas, which is the case in the `<product>` element in the schema `products.xsd`. For such an anonymous type you can use another construct, which casts the parameter value as an element, as follows:

```
<xsl:param name="instance" as="xs:schema-element(product)"/>
```

Source-Document Validation

The `xsi:schemaLocation` attribute on a source-document root element can be used by an XSLT processor to find the relevant schema. However, not all processors need it. The Saxon processor gets the schema location from the imported schema, and therefore does not require the attribute. The Altova processor apparently does, using it as an implicit request for validation. Consider using it if you want the stylesheet to be portable between processors.

Try It Out   **Validating XML Input**

This time you'll validate the source file `products.xml`. Save another copy of `products.xsl` as `products_valid_in.xsl`. To validate a source document you import its schema into the stylesheet:

```
<xsl:import-schema
      schema-location="products.xsd"/>
```

Then, outside the `<html>` element, you refer to the top-level element as follows, rather than the usual "/" matching the document node:

```
<xsl:template match="document-node(schema-element(products))">
...
</xsl:template>
```

The schema `products.xsd` implicitly specifies U.S.-style spelling with the name of "Center" for a store location. A U.K. author might make an error in this attribute value, as shown here:

```
<product sku="gdk943-46298r" color="red" units="70" store="Centre"/>
```

Try this or some other typing error on a `store` attribute value, and run the stylesheet. The processor should throw the following runtime error:

```
[Saxon-SA 9.1.0.5] Value "centre" contravenes the
enumeration facet "Center, West, East, South, Nor..." of
the type storetype
```

Validating Elements and Attributes

You don't have to validate at the document level. Rather, you can invoke validation of element and attribute nodes independently. This can be useful if you have valid schema definitions for some output elements but not the whole schema, or because you want to validate elements in a temporary tree. Both the `<xsl:element>` and the `<xsl:attribute>` instructions have `validation` and `type` attributes that work on those nodes individually, rather than on an entire document. The same attributes are available on literal results elements.

Suppose you want to validate a metadata entry in a literal result element that you intend to write out to the quick reference. The `validation` and `type` attributes are available but in this case they have the `xsl:` namespace prefix, `xsl:validation` and `xsl:type`.

The following example would validate the element and all of its children against the schema. If it had a named type you could alternatively use `<entry xml:id="xsl_stylesheet" xsl:type="metatype">`:

```
<entry xml:id="xsl_stylesheet" xsl:validation="strict">
   <title>xsl:stylesheet</title>
   <summary>The root element of a stylesheet.</summary>
   <content src="../xslt_reference/"/>
   <category term="element_reference" scheme="resource"/>
</entry>
```

In the case of attributes, the `validation` attribute, although allowed, is not very useful in comparison to its value in testing elements, because global attribute declarations are uncommon in schemas. On the other hand, attributes are frequently typed and can be validated against a schema type definition.

Conditional Validation

The `use-when` attribute can be used to determine whether an element and its children should be included in the stylesheet. For example, you might want to validate depending on a system property or the availability of an element. To test for a schema-aware processor, you might use the following condition to make a stylesheet more portable by placing it on all relevant declarations and instructions:

```
<xsl:import-schema  schema-location="products.xsd"
use-when="system-property('xsl:is-schema-aware')='yes'"/>
```

The functions `element-available()` and `function available()` enable you to perform selective validation as well as testing, and include or exclude code. The `element-available()` function is typically used to test for vendor or third-party extensions, such as `<saxon:output>` in the next example:

```
<xsl:when test= "element-available('saxon:ouput)">
 ...
</xsl:when>
```

In the same way, `doc-available()` and `unparsed-text-available()` provide a way to trap errors related to missing source material (you saw both in Chapters 7 and 8):

```
<xsl:if test="doc-available(@term)">
   <xsl:apply-templates select="doc (@term)"/>
<xsl:if>
```

The `type-available()` function returns `true` if a type is available for use in the static context. In practice, its use is limited to testing XML Schema types and vendor extension types, as user-defined types imported with `<xsl:import-schema>` are not available in the static context with `xsl:use-when`.

Documenting Your Stylesheets

Every programming book you read tells you to document your code, right? So I'll say it too, even if I don't always do it myself. (Similarly, when I joined the Canadian navy a long time ago, a petty officer told me, "Do as I say, not do as I do!")

I think the minimum needed is something in the form of conventional XML comments in your stylesheets, to help you recall what was intended when you wrote it. This kind of comment is, of course, distinct from `<xsl:comment>`, which puts comments in the XSLT result tree.

Comments come into their own on smaller projects, and are fine for simple notes designed for personal use, like this one:

```
<!-- head.xsl
<     xhtml head section -->
```

However, it is worth looking at alternatives that provide a systematic way of documenting code for a wider user group. The benefits of doing so are perhaps obvious for large sets of stylesheet modules, where specific tools can help you to keep track of relationships and code locations (which might otherwise be hard to do).

One such tool is XSLTdoc, an open-source tool developed with European Space Agency funding by P&P Software, and written in XSLT 2.0.

XSLTdoc is a stylesheet itself that processes stylesheets as XML source. In your stylesheet, you document the code using just a few elements in the XSLTdoc namespace, as shown in the following examples, where xd: is the namespace prefix:

```
<xd:doc>
   <xd:short>Defines the CSS stylesheet for reference pages.</xd:short>
</xd:doc>
<xsl:param name="style">reference.css</xsl:param>
...
<xd:doc>
   <xd:short>Generates a heading and selects the content of the paragraphs
   <code>purpose</code> element.</xd:short>
</xd:doc>
<xsl:template match="purpose">
   <h2>Purpose</h2>
   <xsl:apply-templates select="p"/>
</xsl:template>
```

Usually the <xd:doc> elements immediately precede the item you want to document, such as the parameter and template shown here.

When your documentation is complete, you then run your source stylesheet using XSLTdoc to produce a series of linked XHTML pages, containing the documentation that you embedded. XSLTdoc takes care of all the formatting and linking.

For the next Try It Out, you'll use it to document one of the stylesheets you have already created.

Try It Out Using XSLTdoc

Start by downloading the package from http://sourceforge.net/project/showfiles.php?group _id=124907&package_id=136566. The latest version at the time of writing was version 1.2.1.

Unzip the download and copy it to the same location as your XML project in the Oxygen IDE. Next, copy the stylesheet use_key.xsl to the XSLTdoc/xsl folder, along with the included modules head.xsl, params.xsl, and table.xsl. The included stylesheets will be processed automatically.

Rename use_key.xsl to use_key_doc.xsl.

In use_key.xsl and the other three modules, it is necessary to define a new namespace to distinguish between documentation and your XSLT source code. The URI for this namespace is http://www.pnp-software.com/XSLTdoc.

196

```
<xsl:stylesheet xmlns:xsl="http://www.w3.org/1999/XSL/Transform"
    xmlns:xd="http://www.pnp-software.com/XSLTdoc" version="2.0">
...
<xsl:stylesheet>
```

Generally, you should enclose your documentation inside an <xd:doc> element, immediately before the item concerned, though there are a couple of exceptions that I'll describe shortly. For simple text, the first sentence is treated as a short description, with any remaining sentences providing details. If you need to include XHTML in the documentation, then you must use the <xd:short> and <xd:detail> elements to contain these two sections. Inside these elements, you may also use the <xd:xml> element to contain any sample code.

The next snippet shows suggested documentation for the attribute named template:

```
<xd:doc>
    <xd:short>Generates a heading and lists the element attributes in a
        table.</xd:short>
    <xd:detail>A plural of the label is generated if the count of
        <code>property</code> elements is greater than 1. The table elements make use of
        attribute sets specified in <code>table.xsl</code>. A non-breaking
        space in each table cell ensures that table style is
        maintained.</xd:detail>
</xd:doc>
<xsl:template name="attribute">
    <h2>Attribute<xsl:if test="count(//property) gt 1">s</xsl:if></h2>
    ...
</xsl:template>
```

To describe global parameters, you can use the same approach with the optional addition of the type attribute. However, template and function parameters must have an identifying name attribute too. This is because they cannot immediately precede the function they describe; recall the XSLT rule that parameters must immediately follow a template or function declaration. I grouped the following descriptions together before the head named template in head.xsl:

```
<?xml version="1.0" encoding="UTF-8"?>
<xsl:stylesheet xmlns:xsl="http://www.w3.org/1999/XSL/Transform"
    xmlns:xd="http://www.pnp-software.com/XSLTdoc" version="2.0">
<xd:doc type="stylesheet">
    <xd:short>Specifies the processing of parameters passed to the named
        template <code>head</code>.</xd:short>
</xd:doc>
<xd:doc>
    <xd:param name="title">The value of the <code>title</code>
        element.</xd:param>
    <xd:param name="style">The value of the <code>href</code> attribute on the
 <code>link</code> element.</xd:param>
</xd:doc>
<xsl:template name="head">
    <xsl:param name="title"/>
    <xsl:param name="style"/>
    ...
```

197

```
    </xsl:template>
</xsl:stylesheet>
```

You can also document a stylesheet as a whole, as I did in the preceding code, *after* the `<xsl:stylesheet>` element (because only processing instructions should precede the root element), using the `type` attribute to identify it. The following snippet shows two additional elements you can use, which I did for the main module:

```
<xd:doc type="stylesheet">
    <xd:author>ianw</xd:author>
    <xd:copyright>Ian Williams 2002-2009</xd:copyright>
</xd:doc>
```

Save a copy of the sample XSLT configuration file `XSLTdocConfig.xml` in the same folder. I called my copy `test_config.xml`.

Edit the copied configuration file following the next example. Apart from a title and introduction, the important values to set are the relative or absolute paths of the target and source directories, and the name of the root stylesheet.

I set the `<TargetDirectory>` path attribute, used for the XSLTdoc pages, to `"../doc2"` (keeping it separate from the `doc` directory, which contains the XSLTdoc documentation):

```
<?xml version="1.0" encoding="UTF-8"?>
<XSLTdocConfig>
    <Title>Documenting XSLT</Title>
    <Introduction>
        This is a test page for XLSTDoc from Chapter 10 of Beginning XSLT and XPath.
        The source is use_key.xsl. Included modules are processed automatically.
    </Introduction>
        <TargetDirectory path="../doc2"/>
        <SourceDirectory path="./"/>
        <RootStylesheets>
            <File href="use_key_doc.xsl"/>
        </RootStylesheets>

    <AdditionalCSS>
        <File href="print.css" media="print"/>
    </AdditionalCSS>
</XSLTdocConfig>
```

Set up the transformation scenario with `test_config.xml` as the source document, and `xsltdoc.xsl` as the stylesheet. Make sure you use the basic version of the Saxon processor.

After running the transform, copy the stylesheets `xsltdoc.css` and `xmlverbatim.css` from `XSLTdoc/css` to the `doc2` directory, and open `index.html` in your browser. The result should look something like Figure 10-7.

Figure 10-7

From here you can follow the Stylesheet List link to find a module, or browse for functions and templates. Figure 10-8 shows part of the documentation from use_key_doc.xsl. Clicking on a source link takes you to a web page with the code highlighted.

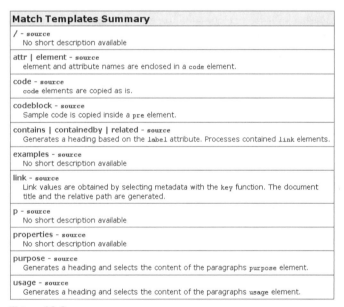

Figure 10-8

Summary

In this chapter you learned how to debug XSLT output and analyze processor performance in an IDE. You worked with the schema-aware version of the Saxon processor to validate both source and output documents, and learned how to apply validation to entire documents or individual elements and attributes. To document your code you used an inline documentation tool that uses XSLT on an XSLT source.

Key Points

❏   A debugger IDE can be a valuable tool, helping you trace the XSLT process, track variable and parameter values, and monitor code performance using profiling.

❏   You can do limited stylesheet validation using the built-in types from XML Schema.

❏   Using a schema-aware processor on both inputs and outputs will increase the robustness of your code.

❏   Validation can be applied to entire documents, individual elements, or attributes.

❏   The use-when attribute allows you to apply conditional validation in some circumstances.

❏   Providing stylesheet documentation is an important part of delivering your code to end users.

Exercises

You'll find solutions to these exercises in Appendix A.

1.   Demonstrate how to incorporate an `xsl-stylesheet` processing instruction in an XML result document.

2.   Why can using `<xsl:comment>` rather than `<xsl:message>` sometimes make it easy to trace problems in your stylesheet code?

A Case Study

This case study builds on the work you have already done with the templates for processing the XSLT 2.0 quick-reference documents found in Appendix D. The goal is to transform and combine a complete set of XSLT element and function reference documents in a single website that provides simple, clear navigation, and that makes use of the reference-document stylesheet code you have worked with so far.

However, this time the processing of links between reference pages is handed over to a small library of stylesheet modules that operate on both resource and subject metadata.

As a preliminary to explaining how the library modules can be used, I discuss the reference and metadata schemas. The reference stylesheets contain some minor changes to accommodate the use of the link modules. The link stylesheet module itself and a related function module together provide link processing. Terms are processed in a similar way to create a glossary or inline definitions.

Two examples complete the book. The first creates a quick-reference site for both XSLT elements and XSLT functions. The second outputs a sitemap conforming to the Sitemaps protocol for consumption by web crawlers.

Schema Overview

I'll be discussing several XML Schema structures in this chapter. The structure is modular with several interdependencies. The following table lists the modules A–Z, with their purpose and dependencies.

Schema	Purpose	Requires
common.xsd	Elements that are common to most of the other schemas	
iso_lang.xsd	Defines two subsets of ISO 639 language codes	

Continued

Schema	Purpose	Requires
links.xsd	Defines the link components used in other schemas	
meta.xsd	Resource and subject metadata elements	common.xsd, iso_lang.xsd, links.xsd
reference.xsd	Describes the structure and relationship of elements in any XML Schema — in this case, the quick-reference documents (Appendix D)	common.xsd, links.xsd
reslist.xsd	Container for resource metadata	meta.xsd
xml.xsd	Definitions of some XML attributes, including xml:id	

Common Elements and Attributes

The schema module common.xsd contains declarations used in both the reference and metadata modules. This schema module imports xml.xsd, where the xml:id attribute is defined.

Common Attributes

The core attribute group specifies attributes that are common to all elements: an identifier using xml:id, and class and title attributes that can be used to apply styling and labeling.

The metadata attribute group contains a single scheme attribute to be applied to root elements in several document types:

```
<xs:attributeGroup name="core">
   <xs:attribute ref="xml:id" use="optional"/>
   <xs:attribute name="class" type="xs:string" use="optional"/>
   <xs:attribute name="title" type="xs:string" use="optional"/>
</xs:attributeGroup>

<xs:attributeGroup name="metadata">
   <xs:attribute name="scheme" type="xs:string" use="optional"/>
</xs:attributeGroup>
```

Block Elements

The schema common.xsd defines a few block elements for paragraphs and notes. Both elements may be used in reference documents and term definitions:

```
<xs:element name="p">
   <xs:complexType mixed="true">
      <xs:sequence minOccurs="0" maxOccurs="unbounded">
```

```
                <xs:group ref="phrase" minOccurs="0" maxOccurs="unbounded"/>
            </xs:sequence>
        </xs:complexType>
</xs:element>

<xs:element name="note">
    <xs:complexType mixed="true">
        <xs:sequence minOccurs="0" maxOccurs="unbounded">
            <xs:group ref="phrase"/>
        </xs:sequence>
        <xs:attribute name="type" use="required">
            <xs:simpleType>
                <xs:restriction base="xs:string">
                    <xs:enumeration value="note"/>
                    <xs:enumeration value="tip"/>
                    <xs:enumeration value="caution"/>
                    <xs:enumeration value="warning"/>
                </xs:restriction>
            </xs:simpleType>
        </xs:attribute>
    </xs:complexType>
</xs:element>
```

Inline Elements

Several elements can be used in inline markup in paragraphs and notes. They may also appear in resource metadata summaries and term definitions. You have already seen the `<attr>`, `<code>`, and `<element>` elements in reference-document examples. The `<acronym>` element may be used to contain abbreviations and acronyms such as `ISO` and `CSS`. `<em>` and `<strong>`, both used for emphasis, may be familiar from XHTML:

```
<xs:group name="phrase">
    <xs:choice>
        <xs:element ref="acronym"/>
        <xs:element ref="attr"/>
        <xs:element ref="code"/>
        <xs:element ref="element"/>
        <xs:element ref="em"/>
        <xs:element ref="strong"/>
    </xs:choice>
</xs:group>

<xs:simpleType name="inline">
    <xs:restriction base="xs:string"/>
</xs:simpleType>

<xs:element name="acronym" type="inline"/>
<xs:element name="attr" type="inline"/>
<xs:element name="code" type="inline"/>
<xs:element name="element" type="inline"/>
<xs:element name="em" type="inline"/>
<xs:element name="strong" type="inline"/>
```

The Quick-Reference Schema

Until now, you have used some examples from the quick-reference documentation to develop stylesheets, and I've said very little about the formal structure of the reference documents themselves.

They contain a subset of a more complex reference vocabulary that has been in regular production use since 2004, not only for the creation of XML Schema documentation, but also for user interface, API, and web-service help. You can see some recent examples of reference documents at the Volantis Systems support gateway, for instance: `http://gateway.volantis.com/docs/admin/mcs_config_er.html`

> *This larger vocabulary was partly based on early versions of the Darwin Information Typing Architecture (DITA), an XML-based architecture for authoring, producing, and delivering technical information. DITA had its origins in IBM, and is now an OASIS standard.*
>
> *You can read more about current DITA developments and download the current version of the open toolkit at* `http://dita.xml.org/book/dita-wiki-knowledgebase`.

The quick-reference schema, `reference.xsd`, includes both `common.xsd` and `links.xsd`.

You are already familiar with the basic structure of the XSLT quick-reference documents that you worked with earlier in this book, most recently in Chapter 9, so I won't look too closely at some of the simpler elements. Figure 11-1 shows an overview.

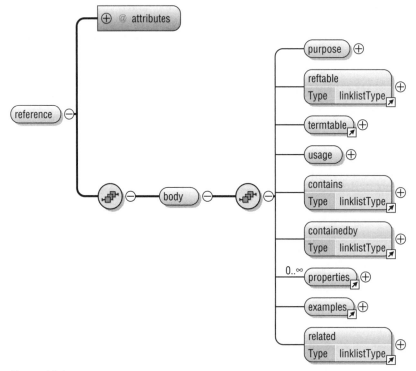

Figure 11-1

In this section I want to focus on what I call *link containers* and how they are specified, how attributes are defined in `<property>` elements, and how you can verify that link targets actually exist when you refer to them.

Link Container Elements

In the reference schema the elements in the following snippet are specified as type `linklistType`, which is defined in the included schema `links.xsd`:

```
<xs:element name="contains" type="linklistType"/>
<xs:element name="containedby" type="linklistType"/>
<xs:element name="common" type="linklistType"/>
<xs:element name="reftable" type="linklistType"/>
<xs:element name="related" type="linklistType"/>
```

You have seen the first two elements in your work so far, and you'll meet the others later in this chapter. They all have an identical structure — for example, in the reference for `<xsl:choose>` you find this content model:

```
<contains label="contains" display="inline">
    <link href="xsl_when"/>
    <link href="xsl_otherwise"/>
</contains>.
```

The `linklistType` is a deliberately general structure, supporting several different kinds of link container. They can be defined in any document type, using any convenient element name, and all the type properties will be available:

```
<xs:complexType name="linklistType">
    <xs:sequence>
        <xs:element name="description" type="xs:string" minOccurs="0"/>
        <xs:element ref="link" maxOccurs="unbounded"/>
    </xs:sequence>
    <xs:attribute name="display" use="optional" default="block">
        <xs:simpleType>
            <xs:restriction base="xs:NMTOKEN">
                <xs:enumeration value="block"/>
                <xs:enumeration value="inline"/>
            </xs:restriction>
        </xs:simpleType>
    </xs:attribute>
    <xs:attribute name="label" type="xs:string" use="optional"/>
    <xs:attribute name="role" use="optional">
        <xs:simpleType>
            <xs:restriction base="xs:NMTOKEN">
                <xs:enumeration value="navigation"/>
            </xs:restriction>
        </xs:simpleType>
    </xs:attribute>
</xs:complexType>
```

The essential part of the `linklistType` type is the `<link>` element, which can have attributes from two groups. The `linkattr` group is intended for general navigation links. The `cmattr` group state attribute can be used in addition in content-model containers to indicate whether an element is optional or required:

```
<xs:element name="link" type="linkType"/>

<xs:complexType name="linkType" mixed="true">
   <xs:attributeGroup ref="linkattr"/>
   <xs:attributeGroup ref="cmattr"/>
</xs:complexType>

<xs:attributeGroup name="linkattr">
   <xs:attribute name="href" type="xs:anyURI" use="optional"/>
   <xs:attribute name="scheme" type="xs:string" use="optional"/>
   <xs:attribute name="contexts" use="optional"/>
   <xs:attribute name="rel" use="optional">
      <xs:simpleType>
         <xs:restriction base="xs:NMTOKEN">
            <xs:enumeration value="external"/>
            <xs:enumeration value="next"/>
            <xs:enumeration value="previous"/>
            <xs:enumeration value="start"/>
            <xs:enumeration value="up"/>
         </xs:restriction>
      </xs:simpleType>
   </xs:attribute>
</xs:attributeGroup>

<xs:attributeGroup name="cmattr">
   <xs:attribute name="state" use="optional" default="optional">
      <xs:simpleType>
         <xs:restriction base="xs:NMTOKEN">
            <xs:enumeration value="optional"/>
            <xs:enumeration value="required"/>
         </xs:restriction>
      </xs:simpleType>
   </xs:attribute>
</xs:attributeGroup>
```

Property Elements

The `<properties>` element contains one or more `<property>` elements, which require a name and a description. The remaining elements are optional. The term "property" is used rather than "attribute," because in the broader schema from which this one is derived, properties are generic values that can be called attributes in one context, parameters in another, and properties in a third.

Within the `<common>` element is a link container that enables you to list attributes common to many elements in a schema. Examples from the XSLT schema are generic element attributes and validation attributes, which may be expressed on any XSLT or literal result elements.

Figure 11-2 shows the properties structure.

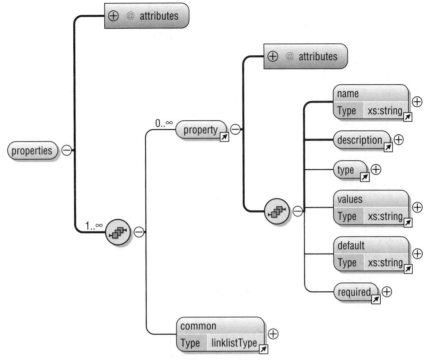

Figure 11-2

The definition of the `<property>` element follows. In the description element you can see how use is made of the `phrase` group from `common.xsd`. This makes it possible to incorporate inline markup in descriptions.

```
<xs:element name="property">
    <xs:complexType>
        <xs:sequence>
            <xs:element ref="name"/>
            <xs:element ref="description"/>
            <xs:element ref="type" minOccurs="0"/>
            <xs:element ref="values" minOccurs="0"/>
            <xs:element ref="default" minOccurs="0"/>
            <xs:element ref="required" minOccurs="0"/>
        </xs:sequence>
        <xs:attributeGroup ref="core"/>
        </xs:complexType>
</xs:element>

<xs:element name="required">
    <xs:complexType>
        <xs:attribute name="state" use="optional" default="optional">
            <xs:simpleType>
                <xs:restriction base="xs:string">
```

```
                    <xs:enumeration value="optional"/>
                    <xs:enumeration value="required"/>
                    <xs:enumeration value="deprecated"/>
                </xs:restriction>
            </xs:simpleType>
        </xs:attribute>
    </xs:complexType>
</xs:element>

<xs:element name="name" type="xs:string"/>

<xs:element name="description">
    <xs:complexType mixed="true">
        <xs:choice>
            <xs:group ref="phrase" minOccurs="0"/>
        </xs:choice>
    </xs:complexType>
</xs:element>
<xs:element name="type">
    <xs:complexType mixed="true">
        <xs:choice>
            <xs:element ref="link" minOccurs="0"/>
        </xs:choice>
    </xs:complexType>
</xs:element>

<xs:element name="default" type="xs:string"/>
<xs:element name="values" type="xs:string"/>
```

Link Verification

Because link relationships illustrating the content model are important in schema documentation, it is useful for authors to be able to verify that link-target values are correct. For the quick reference, this is done automatically during validation by checking the resource metadata file `reslist_xsl.xml`. If there is an `xml:id` attribute in a metadata entry that matches the target in the `<link>` element in the reference document, the file will validate correctly.

The cross-file validation is done by including statements in the reference schema in a language known as *Schematron*. This is a schema language based on finding patterns in the parsed document. One of its characteristics is the use of `<assert>` elements that enable you to confirm that a document conforms to a particular schema. See `www.schematron.com` for further information.

Some IDEs, such as Oxygen, allow the inclusion of Schematron assertions inside XML Schema `<xs:app-info>` elements. The next snippet shows how this is used in the quick-reference schema. In this example, the `xml:id` value on the `<reference>` element is also validated:

```
<xs:annotation>
    <xs:appinfo>
        <sch:pattern name="metadata_values">
```

```
        <sch:rule context="reference">
           <sch:assert test="@xml:id and @scheme">Both attributes must be
              present for metadata processing</sch:assert>
           <sch:assert test="document(concat('../reslist_',@scheme,'.xml'))//entry
           [@xml:id=current()/@xml:id]"
              >There is no matching identifier in the cited
              collection</sch:assert>
        </sch:rule>
     </sch:pattern>

     <sch:pattern name="link_values">
        <sch:rule context="link">
           <sch:assert test="document(concat('../reslist_',ancestor::reference
           /@scheme,'.xml'))//entry[@xml:id=current()/@href] | document
           (concat('../reslist_',@scheme,'.xml'))//entry[@xml:id=current()
           /@href]"
              >There is no matching identifier in the cited
              collection</sch:assert>
        </sch:rule>
     </sch:pattern>
  </xs:appinfo>
</xs:annotation>
```

XML Schema 1.1, now at working draft stage, has borrowed the idea of assertions from Schematron. Assertions allow Boolean conditions to be defined for any simple or complex type in XPath 2.0 syntax, as shown in the following example:

```
<xs:complexType name="arrayType">
 <xs:sequence>
  <xs:element name="entry" minOccurs="0" maxOccurs="unbounded"/>
 </xs:sequence>
 <xs:attribute name="length" type="xs:int"/>
 <xs:assert test="@length eq fn:count(./entry)"/>
</xs:complexType>
```

This assertion says that the value of the length *attribute must be the same as the number of occurrences of* <entry> *subelements. You can read about this development at* www.w3.org/TR/xmlschema11-1.

For details about a preliminary schema processor implementation for Saxon 9.1, see www.saxonica.com /documentation/schema-processing/schema11/assertions.html.

Metadata Schemas

The metadata schema meta.xsd describes the structure of two types of metadata: resource metadata and subject metadata.

By resource metadata I mean simple descriptive records for information resources of the kind you find on the Web. In this book you met these records first in Chapter 1 when you transformed an Atom feed into RSS 1.0 format. The quick reference makes use of metadata with entries for each document title in `reslist_xsl.xml`, such as the `<entry>` element that follows. You have used them for both linking and for a feed in earlier chapters.

```
<entry xml:id="xsl_namespace_alias">
   <title>xsl:namespace-alias</title>
   <summary>Declares a namespace from a stylesheet to be associated with a
      different namespace in the output.</summary>
   <content src="../xslt_reference/"/>
   <category term="element_reference" scheme="resource"/>
   <category term="namespace" scheme="xml"/>
</entry>
```

Subject metadata describes concepts and can also be used to categorize ideas into a concept hierarchy. Examples range from basic glossaries to more complex thesaurus structures. The next snippet shows the definition for the term "Attribute set", one of those used in the glossary for this book, which I'll discuss soon:

```
<term xml:id="attributeSet">
   <label>Attribute set</label>
   <definition>A named collection of attribute definitions that can be reused,
      defined by an <element>xsl:attribute-set</element> element.</definition>
</term>
```

The metadata schema and the related stylesheet library are independent of the reference schema and stylesheets. The schemas can be used alongside any XML vocabulary (not just technical-documentation vocabularies) to capture resource and subject metadata. The stylesheets can be used with other stylesheets to generate references, links, glossaries, and subject indexes.

Resource Metadata

The resource-metadata design is intended to do the following:

❑   Separate metadata from the resources described

❑   Support linking to other resource and subject metadata

❑   Generate feed documents and metadata structures in target resources conforming to vocabularies such as DITA, XHTML, and eBooks

The schema is based on Atom 1.0. Atom was originally designed as a mechanism for syndicating feeds from news sources, blogs, and other dynamic websites. In that respect it is like the many versions of RSS. But the design of Atom is more recent and includes XML features such as namespaces; as a result, it has a flexible extensibility mechanism that allows elements and relationships from other namespaces. Because of this, the use of Atom has been extended to many purposes, such as packaging descriptions of a variety of web resources.

The resource schema `meta.xsd` differs from Atom 1.0 in some respects, largely because this schema is for maintaining resource information, as opposed to publishing it in a single feed format. I've highlighted these differences in the following sections. Figure 11-3 shows the entry content model.

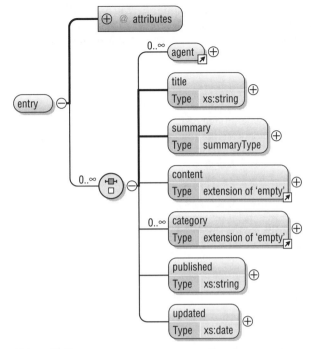

Figure 11-3

Collection

The schema `reslist.xsd` defines a container for resource metadata elements. The optional `<categories>` element can be used to list the categories supported in a collection. The `lang` attribute makes use of `iso_lang.xsd` (mentioned in the following section) to define the language used in the text of the entries. `xml:id` attributes are constrained to be unique in the `<xs:unique>` declaration:

```
<xs:element name="collection">
  <xs:complexType>
    <xs:sequence>
      <xs:element name="title" type="xs:string"/>
      <xs:element ref="entry" maxOccurs="unbounded"/>
      <xs:element ref="categories" minOccurs="0"/>
    </xs:sequence>
    <xs:attribute name="lang" type="iso_639_3" use="optional"/>
    <xs:attributeGroup ref="core"/>
    <xs:attributeGroup ref="metadata"/>
  </xs:complexType>
  <xs:unique name="entry_id">
    <xs:selector xpath="entry"/>
    <xs:field xpath="@xml:id"/>
  </xs:unique>
</xs:element>
```

The name of the `<collection>` element container for the metadata entries for a particular scheme is borrowed from the Atom Publishing Protocol (APP). APP provides (defines) a complex repository structure, and ways to POST and GET data from an Atom XML metadata store. You can find details at www.atomenabled.org/developers/protocol.

Language Values

Language-code values used in metadata are defined in iso_lang.xsd, which currently provides validation for two subsets of ISO 639 language codes covering the 23 official European Union languages. The iso_639_3 type is from the most recent alpha-3 version, and is used in lang attributes:

```
<xs:simpleType name="iso_639_3">
    <xs:restriction base="xs:string">
        <xs:enumeration value="bul"/>
        <xs:enumeration value="ces"/>
        <xs:enumeration value="dan"/>
        <xs:enumeration value="deu"/>
        <xs:enumeration value="ell"/>
        <xs:enumeration value="eng"/>
        . . .
    </xs:restriction>
</xs:simpleType>
```

Identifiers

An identifier that is unique to each entry in a collection is required, whereas an `<atom:id>` element is required to be a URI, and globally unique.

Instead of the `<atom:id>` element, an xml:id attribute is used on the `<entry>` element. This brings some XSLT-processing benefits, which I outlined in Chapter 9. Additional identifiers, if required, can be supported using the `<dc:identifier>` element from the Dublin Core namespace. Entries can be used to describe physical resources like this book. For example, if I described it for use in a citation, I could write the following:

```
<entry xml:id="b_xslt_xpath" scheme="wrox">
    <dc:indentifier scheme="isbn">978-0-470-447250</dc:identifier>
. . .
</entry>
```

Authors and Contributors

Instead of using the Atom person construct for `<atom:author>` and `<atom:contributor>`, the `<agent>` element containing an optional `<role>` specification is used. Here's how a partial example from reslist_xsl.xml might look using these elements:

```
<entry>
    <title>xsl: choose<title>
    <agent term=" williams_i" scheme="persons">
        <role term="contributor" scheme="roles"/>
    </agent>
    . . .
</entry>
```

The optional `term` attribute, defined in the `termReference` attribute group in `links.xsd`, can contain a URI that refers to individual or organization descriptions in an external file. This can be useful in domains where the same names recur frequently. Alternatively, you can provide a literal value in the element content. The schema definitions look like this. Role definitions can be user-defined and completely open-ended:

```
<xs:attributeGroup name="termReference">
   <xs:attribute name="term" type="xs:NCName" use="required"/>
   <xs:attribute name="scheme" type="xs:anyURI" use="optional"/>
</xs:attributeGroup>

<xs:element name="agent">
   <xs:complexType>
      <xs:sequence>
         <xs:element ref="role" minOccurs="1" maxOccurs="unbounded"/>
      </xs:sequence>
      <xs:attributeGroup ref="termReference"/>
   </xs:complexType>
</xs:element>

<xs:element name="role">
   <xs:complexType>
      <xs:attributeGroup ref="termReference"/>
   </xs:complexType>
</xs:element>
```

Dates

Publication-date values provided on information resources, even web resources, can vary considerably in structure and format. For example, those for the references that I included in Appendix G vary in completeness from giving just the year to a full `xs:dateTime` value, and they provide the information in several formats, too.

If you are publishing a feed, you can timestamp a description to fit the `<atom:published>` and `<atom:update>` element type, which is `xs:dateTime`. The `<datetime>` element fulfills that purpose. But metadata authors describing external resources may need to use the `<date>` element with the W3C datetime format of `yyyy-mm-dd`, and the user-defined type `vardate` with a simple pattern that allows for partial values:

```
<xs:simpleType name="vardateType">
   <xs:restriction base="xs:string">
      <xs:pattern value="[0-9]{4}(-[0-9]{2})?(-[0-9]{2})?"/>
   </xs:restriction>
</xs:simpleType>

<xs:element name="date" type="vardateType" minOccurs="0">
   <xs:annotation>
      <xs:documentation>The date of first
         publication</xs:documentation>
   </xs:annotation>
</xs:element>

<xs:element name="datetime" minOccurs="0">
```

```
       <xs:complexType>
           <xs:attribute name="type" use="optional">
               <xs:simpleType>
                   <xs:restriction base="xs:string">
                       <xs:enumeration value="published"/>
                       <xs:enumeration value="updated"/>
                   </xs:restriction>
               </xs:simpleType>
           </xs:attribute>
       </xs:complexType>
   </xs:element>
```

Content

The <content> element defines the resource URI and the type of resource. Both attributes are declared in the resourceReference attribute group in links.xsd:

```
<xs:attributeGroup name="resourceReference">
    <xs:attribute name="src" type="xs:anyURI" use="required"/>
    <xs:attribute name="type" use="optional" default="text/xml">
        <xs:simpleType>
            <xs:restriction base="xs:string">
                <xs:enumeration value="text/plain"/>
                <xs:enumeration value="text/xml"/>
                <xs:enumeration value="text/html"/>
                <xs:enumeration value="image/png"/>
                <xs:enumeration value="image/gif"/>
                <xs:enumeration value="image/jpg"/>
            </xs:restriction>
        </xs:simpleType>
    </xs:attribute>
</xs:attributeGroup>

<xs:element name="content">
    <xs:annotation>
        <xs:documentation>Locates the content of a resource</xs:documentation>
    </xs:annotation>
    <xs:complexType>
        <xs:attributeGroup ref="resourceReference"/>
    </xs:complexType>
</xs:element>
```

Subject Metadata

The subject metadata schema design is intended to do the following:

❑ Capture information about concepts such as *attribute value template* and *collation*, and organize them in a hierarchy of categories.

❑ Support linking to other resource and subject metadata, such as subject indexes.

❑ Generate inline definitions, glossaries, and subject indexes, topic maps, and Simple Knowledge Organization System (SKOS) vocabularies.

Figure 11-4 shows the content model for individual terms.

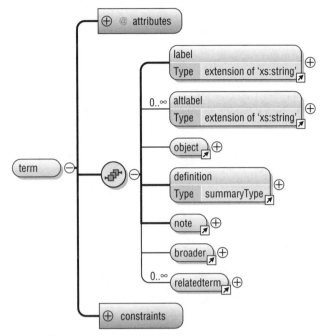

Figure 11-4

The next snippet shows the container `<terms>` element declaration. Each scheme contains a list of terms that must be unique within the scheme. Uniqueness is enforced in the same way that it is in `reslist.xsd`. Cross-references to broader terms are also validated.

```
<xs:element name="terms">
   <xs:annotation>
      <xs:documentation>Introduction followed by one or more
         terms</xs:documentation>
   </xs:annotation>
   <xs:complexType>
      <xs:sequence>
         <xs:element ref="p" minOccurs="0"/>
         <xs:sequence>
            <xs:element ref="term" minOccurs="0" maxOccurs="unbounded"/>
         </xs:sequence>
         <xs:element ref="related" minOccurs="0"/>
      </xs:sequence>
      <xs:attributeGroup ref="core"/>
      <xs:attribute name="scheme" type="xs:anyURI"/>
      <xs:attribute name="lang" type="iso_639_3" use="optional"/>
   </xs:complexType>
   <xs:unique name="term_id">
      <xs:selector xpath="term"/>
```

```
                <xs:field xpath="@xml:id"/>
        </xs:unique>
        <xs:keyref name="term_ref" refer="term_id">
            <xs:selector xpath="term/broader"/>
            <xs:field xpath="@term"/>
        </xs:keyref>
    </xs:element>
```

In each `<term>` element, the `<label>` contains the preferred term, while alternative terms such as synonyms, acronyms, and equivalents in other languages are contained in the `<altlabel>` element.

If the `lang` attribute is set to distinguish a label in another language, then that attribute value is constrained to be unique within a given term. This does not, however, prevent you from using same language alternatives, such as synonyms, in the main language of the scheme:

```
    <xs:element name="term">
        <xs:complexType>
            <xs:sequence>
                <xs:element ref="label"/>
                <xs:element ref="altlabel" minOccurs="0" maxOccurs="unbounded"/>
                <xs:element ref="object" minOccurs="0"/>
                <xs:element ref="definition"/>
                <xs:element ref="note" minOccurs="0"/>
                <xs:element ref="broader" minOccurs="0"/>
                <xs:element ref="relatedterm" minOccurs="0" maxOccurs="unbounded"/>
            </xs:sequence>
            <xs:attribute ref="xml:id" use="required"/>
            <xs:attribute name="type" type="xs:string" use="optional"/>
        </xs:complexType>
        <xs:unique name="alt_lang">
            <xs:selector xpath="altlabel"/>
            <xs:field xpath="@lang"/>
        </xs:unique>
    </xs:element>
```

References to other terms are expressed in `<broader>` and `<relatedterm>` elements, usually but not necessarily in the same scheme. Narrower relationships can be inferred and generated during processing.

```
    <xs:element name="broader">
        <xs:complexType>
            <xs:attributeGroup ref="termReference"/>
        </xs:complexType>
    </xs:element>
```

Reference Stylesheets

As you have already seen in the quick-reference stylesheets, a collection of metadata entries in a single scheme is used to maintain and process resource information, such as title and file location, and to construct links to other pages.

This case study makes use of the metadata library stylesheets, rather than directly accessing the resource collection using the `key()` function.

To begin, you will work with a stylesheet to transform a single reference file using the library.

Try It Out   **Updating the Reference Stylesheets**

To use the library, some modifications are required to the stylesheets that you last used to process quick-reference files: `use_key.xsl`, and `params.xsl`.

Two more parameters must be added to `params.xsl`. Their order does not matter:

```
<xsl:param name="scheme" select="reference/@scheme"/>
<xsl:param name="labels" select="document('labels.xml')"/>
```

The `$scheme` parameter identifies the resource scheme to use; the `$labels` parameter loads a document containing values to use for labeling headings.

Save the main stylesheet `use_key.xsl` as `reference_single.xsl`. Most of the link processing takes place in `links.xsl`, which in turn relies on some functions in a separate stylesheet, so the following declarations need to be made to `reference_single.xsl`:

```
<xsl:include href="../xsl/function.xsl"/>
<xsl:include href="../xsl/link.xsl"/>
```

Two more link containers are processed. `<common>` is added to the matches with `<contains>` and `<containedby>` to handle links to common attributes, and `<related>` will process related topics listed at the end of reference documents.

Here is the way to invoke the linking process; the parameters for the document identifier and scheme, and the label, are passed when calling a named template `getlinks` in `links.xsl`. The `label` and `display` attribute values on the container are also passed. How these values are processed is discussed in the next section:

```
<xsl:template match="contains | containedby | common">
  <xsl:call-template name="getlinks">
    <xsl:with-param name="source_id" select="$identifier" tunnel="yes"/>
    <xsl:with-param name="default_scheme" select="$scheme" tunnel="yes"/>
```

```
                <xsl:with-param name="label" select="@label"/>
                <xsl:with-param name="display" select="@display"/>
        </xsl:call-template>
    </xsl:template>

    <xsl:template match="related">
        <xsl:call-template name="getlinks">
            <xsl:with-param name="source_id" select="$identifier" tunnel="yes"/>
            <xsl:with-param name="default_scheme" select="$scheme" tunnel="yes"/>
            <xsl:with-param name="label" select="@label"/>
            <xsl:with-param name="display" select="@display"/>
        </xsl:call-template>
    </xsl:template>
```

This version of the stylesheet should also incorporate the small enhancement to the generated inline markup that I suggested at the end of Chapter 5. This involves deleting the template that currently matches the <code> element and adding the <code> element name to the template match attribute with the pattern `attr | element | code`. This will capture the element names to assign to the output class attributes by using the XPath name() function:

```
<xsl:template match="attr | element | code">
    <code>
        <xsl:attribute name="class"><xsl:value-of select="name()"/></xsl:attribute>
        <xsl:value-of select="."/>
    </code>
</xsl:template>
```

Now you can process a reference document using all the stylesheet features. Open xsl_for_each_group.xml in the code folder for this chapter. It contains more data than the earlier version you worked with. Note the following content changes. There are link references to common attribute groups, to a top-level document introducing the schema, and to a couple of related XSLT functions:

```
<properties>
    <common label="attrgroup" display="inline">
        <link href="ge_attr"/>
        <link href="version_attr"/>
    </common>
</properties>
...
<related role="navigation" label="related"  display="block">
    <link href="xsl_er"/>
    <link href="fn_current_group"/>
    <link href="fn_current_grouping_key"/>
</related>
```

Run the reference file with reference_single.xsl. The result should look like what is shown in Figure 11-5.

xsl:for-each-group

Purpose

An instruction that selects a sequence of items for uniform processing, and groups them according to common values, adjacency, or in relation to other elements.

Usage

Grouping depends on which of the four attributes is specified. The attribute value is known as the group key.

The XSLT functions current-group() and current-grouping-key() may be used to process grouped items inside an xsl:for-each instruction.

Contains elements

sequence-constructor | xsl:sort

Attributes

Name	Description	Type	Default	Options	Use
collation	The URI of a collation to use for string comparison	xs:anyURI			optional
group-adjacent	The common value to use if items are adjacent	xsl:expression			optional
group-by	The common value or values to use	xsl:expression			optional
group-ending-with	The pattern that ends a group of preceding items	xsl:pattern			optional
group-starting-with	The pattern that starts a group of following items	xsl:pattern			optional
select	The sequence of items to group	xsl:expression			required

Attribute groups

Generic element attributes | Version attributes

Example

```
<xsl:for-each-group select="*"
    group-adjacent="if (self::speaker) then 0 else 1">
    <td class="noborder" width="50%">
        <xsl:for-each select="current-group()">
            <xsl:apply-templates select="."/>
            <xsl:if test="current-group()='0'">
                <span class="speaker"><xsl:value-of select="."/></span>
            </xsl:if>
            <xsl:if test="position() ne last()">
                <br/>
            </xsl:if>
        </xsl:for-each>
    </td>
</xsl:for-each-group>
```

Related topics

XSLT elements
current-group
current-grouping-key

Figure 11-5

Link Module

The stylesheet module `link.xsl` contains the transforms for processing links between XHTML reference instances. Parameter values passed from the link containers `<contains>`, `<containedby>`, `<common>`, and `<related>` are processed, with `<h2>` heading labels generated from a helper file. Use is made of a short stylesheet, `function.xsl`, containing user-defined functions.

Link Parameters

The `getlinks` template requires four parameter values when it is called from `reference_single.xsl`:

```
<xsl:template name="getlinks">
   <xsl:param name="source_id" required="yes"/>
   <xsl:param name="default_scheme" required="yes"/>
   <xsl:param name="label" required="yes"/>
   <xsl:param name="display" required="yes"/>

   <h2>
      <xsl:value-of select="$labels//label[@name=$label]"/>
      <xsl:if test="count(current()//link)&gt;1">s</xsl:if>
   </h2>
   ...
</xsl:template>
```

They are the source document identifier, the scheme in use, and the value of the `label` and `display` attributes on the container element:

```
<xsl:template match="contains | containedby | common">
   <xsl:call-template name="getlinks">
      <xsl:with-param name="source_id" select="$identifier" tunnel="yes"/>
      <xsl:with-param name="default_scheme" select="$scheme" tunnel="yes"/>
      <xsl:with-param name="label" select="@label"/>
      <xsl:with-param name="display" select="@display"/>
   </xsl:call-template>
</xsl:template>
```

Labeling Headings

Fixed-output headings for link-container elements can sometimes be problematic — for example, having to use "Contained by" when it really should read "In substitution group." It would be useful if authors could define their own labels in some way, which also makes it easy to localize the headings for other languages.

The `label` attribute on link containers is designed to get around this problem. When the heading is output it will be more meaningful:

```
<containedby label="substitution">
   <link href="xsl_declaration"/>
</containedby>
```

The $labels parameter in params.xsl is used to load the helper document labels.xml. Here is an example:

```
<labels>
    <label name="example">Example</label>
    <label name="related">Related topic</label>
    <label name="contains">Contains element</label>
    <label name="containedby">Contained by element</label>
    <label name="attrgroup">Attribute group</label>
    <label name="external">External link</label>
    <label name="substitution">In substitution group</label>
    <label name="replacedby">Substitute</label>
    ...
</labels>
```

By editing this file, authors can produce as many labels as required. All they need to do is use the value of the name attribute in their source documents.

Scheme Selection

The value of the scheme attribute on the <reference> element of the document being processed is used to define the default metadata scheme, but the link may be to another scheme. The next snippet shows the identifier for the XSLT 2.0 specification, and identifies the scheme as "external":

```
<link href="w3c_xslt_2" scheme="external"/>
```

In these cases the default value is overridden with that of the scheme attribute on the <link> element. This takes place inside an <xsl:choose> instruction:

```
<xsl:variable name="newlist">
    <xsl:for-each select="link">
        <xsl:choose>
            <!--not the default scheme-->
            <xsl:when test="@scheme">
                <xsl:copy-of select="xm:getentry-by-id(@href,@scheme)"/>
            </xsl:when>
            <xsl:otherwise>
                <xsl:copy-of select="xm:getentry-by-id(@href,$default_scheme)"/>
            </xsl:otherwise>
        </xsl:choose>
    </xsl:for-each>
</xsl:variable>
```

A temporary tree variable $newlist is defined to contain any matching metadata entries, and the scheme and the resource identifier are used as arguments to call the stylesheet function xm:getentry-by-id in function.xsl.

Each entry in the $newlist tree is then processed with a call to the named template makelink, which handles styling of the output.

Some XML Schemas have recursive structures, so the first `<xsl:when>` test in the following code avoids creating a "self" link:

```
<p>
    <xsl:for-each select="$newlist/entry">

        <xsl:choose>
            <!-- list but don't link recursive schema references -->
            <xsl:when test="$source_id=@xml:id">
                <xsl:value-of select="title"/>
            </xsl:when>


            <xsl:otherwise>
                <xsl:call-template name="makelink">
                    <xsl:with-param name="class" select="$display"/>
                    <xsl:with-param name="url"
                        select="concat(content/@src,@xml:id,'.',$extension)"/>
                    <xsl:with-param name="linktitle">
                        <xsl:value-of select="title"/>
                    </xsl:with-param>
                </xsl:call-template>
            </xsl:otherwise>
        </xsl:choose>

        <xsl:choose>
            <xsl:when test="$display='inline'">
                <xsl:call-template name="separate">
                    <xsl:with-param name="separator"
                        >&#x00a0;|&#x00a0;</xsl:with-param>
                </xsl:call-template>
            </xsl:when>
            <xsl:otherwise>
                <xsl:if test="position() ne last()">
                    <br/>
                </xsl:if>
            </xsl:otherwise>
        </xsl:choose>

    </xsl:for-each>
</p>
```

The `$display` parameter is handled after the link is rendered. If the author intended the link style to be "inline," then the separator " | " is output (the default value is a comma). Otherwise, where the display style is "block," a `<br/>` element is output:

```
<xsl:template name="separate">
    <!--default is comma+space-->
    <xsl:param name="separator">,&#x00a0;</xsl:param>
    <xsl:if test="position() ne last()">
        <xsl:value-of select="$separator"/>
    </xsl:if>
</xsl:template>
```

Function Module

The stylesheet module `function.xsl` declares the `xm:` namespace:

```
<xsl:stylesheet xmlns:xsl="http://www.w3.org/1999/XSL/Transform"
    xmlns:xs="http://www.w3.org/2001/XMLSchema"
    xmlns:xm="http://xm.net/2007/xsl/function" version="2.0">
...
</xsl:stylesheet>
```

The prefix `xm:` is required on the `name` attribute on any `<xsl:function>` elements, and on any calls made to this module. The stylesheet function `xm:getentry-by-id` takes the `id` and `scheme` parameter values passed to it, and returns a sequence containing the required metadata entry:

```
<xsl:function name="xm:getentry-by-id">
    <xsl:param name="id" as="xs:string"/>
    <xsl:param name="scheme" as="xs:string"/>

    <xsl:variable name="linklist"
        select="document(concat('../reslist_',$scheme,'.xml'))"/>
    <xsl:variable name="linkmeta" select="$linklist//entry[@xml:id=$id]"/>
    <xsl:sequence select="$linkmeta"/>
</xsl:function>
```

I'll return to this module in the following sections.

Term Module

The stylesheet module `terms.xsl` contains the transforms for terms, and is similar in some respects to `links.xsl`. It also requires `function.xsl`.

Term containers in a main stylesheet can range from inline definitions and short glossaries to complete, controlled vocabularies used for categories.

The `<termtable>` element enables you to generate a simple glossary as a standalone page or embedded in another page, selecting content from one or more schemes.

The following example shows some of the terms from the glossary at the back of this book. These terms are listed in `xsl_terms.xml` using `<dfn>` elements:

```
<reference xml:id="xsl_terms" scheme="xsl">
    <body>
        <p>A short glossary of terms selected from those published for XSLT and
            XPath from the W3C glossary.</p>
        <termtable label="glossary">
            <dfn term="attributeSet"/>
            <dfn term="attributeValueTemplate"/>
            <dfn term="axisStep" scheme="xpath2"/>
            <dfn term="characterMap"/>
            <dfn term="collation"/>
            <dfn term="constructorFunction" scheme="xpath2"/>
            <dfn term="contextItem" scheme="xpath2"/>
```

```
                <dfn term="contextPosition" scheme="xpath2"/>
                <dfn term="currentDateTime" scheme="xpath2"/>
                <dfn term="currentGroup"/>
                <dfn term="currentGroupingKey"/>
                <dfn term="declaration"/>
                <dfn term="emptySequence" scheme="xpath2"/>
                <dfn term="extensionFunction"/>
                <dfn term="filterExpression" scheme="xpath2"/>
                <dfn term="functionParameter"/>
                <dfn term="globalVariable"/>
                <dfn term="groupingKeys"/>
                <dfn term="implicitTimezone" scheme="xpath2"/>
                <dfn term="importPrecedence"/>
                <dfn term="instruction"/>
                <dfn term="lexicalQName"/>
                ...
            </termtable>
        </body>
    </reference>
```

Notice that some <dfn> elements have a scheme attribute value of "xpath2". These settings override the default value "xsl" expressed in the scheme attribute on the <reference> element. This feature makes it possible to select terms from more than one scheme.

Figure 11-6 shows part of the resulting page.

XSLT glossary

This is short glossary of terms selected from those published for XSLT and XPath from the W3C glossary.

Glossary

Attribute set

A named collection of attribute definitions that can be reused, defined by an xsl:attribute-set element.

Attribute value template

A type of attribute value that may contain an expression surrounded with curly brackets { }, usually used to set a value with information that is only available at runtime.

Axis step

An axis step has an axis which specifies a direction of travel in the node tree such as parent:: or child:: , and a node test, which defines the nodes to select using the node name or type.

Character map

A character map allows a given character in the final result tree to be substituted by a string of characters during serialization.

Collation

A set of rules, for comparing strings, and determining how they should be ordered. Collations, which are language or application specific, are specified by a URI.

Constructor function

The constructor function for a given type is used to convert instances of other atomic types into the given type.

Context item

The item, an atomic value or node, currently being processed. When the context item is a node, it is also called the context node.

Figure 11-6

Term Parameters

In the stylesheet `terms.xsl` the named template `getterms` requires a `$default_scheme` parameter when it is called. As with links, this is normally the value of the `scheme` attribute on the root element of the document being processed. Labeling works the same way.

In the next exercise you will create a glossary using terms from the glossary in this book.

Try It Out   Creating a Glossary

To incorporate a glossary in a reference document, you need only add one template matching the `<termtable>` element to `reference_single.xsl`. Save it as `reference_gloss.xsl` and add the following code.

First include `term.xsl` in the main stylesheet:

```
<xsl:include href="term.xsl"/>
```

Then add the template:

```
<xsl:template match="termtable">
    <xsl:call-template name="getterms">
        <xsl:with-param name="default_scheme" select="$scheme"/>
        <xsl:with-param name="label" select="@label"/>
    </xsl:call-template>
</xsl:template>
```

This value together with the term identifier is used to call the `xm:getterm-by-id` function in the `function.xsl` stylesheet, which returns a term entry containing the term label and description:

```
<xsl:copy-of select="xm:getterm-by-id(@href,$default_scheme)"/>
```

It is possible to override this value with an alternative `scheme` attribute value on a term element:

```
<xsl:template name="getterms">
    <xsl:param name="default_scheme" required="yes"/>
    <xsl:param name="label" required="yes"/>

    <h2>
        <xsl:value-of select="$labels//label[@name=$label]"/>
        <xsl:if test="count(current()//link)&gt;1">s</xsl:if>
    </h2>

    <xsl:variable name="newlist">
        <xsl:for-each select="dfn">
            <xsl:choose>
                <xsl:when test="@scheme">
                    <xsl:copy-of
                        select="xm:getterm-by-id(current()/@term,current()/@scheme)"/>
                </xsl:when>
                <xsl:otherwise>
                    <xsl:copy-of
                        select="xm:getterm-by-id(current()/@term,$default_scheme)"/>
                </xsl:otherwise>
```

```
            </xsl:choose>
        </xsl:for-each>
    </xsl:variable>

    <table class="gloss">
        <tbody>
            <xsl:for-each select="$newlist/term">
                <xsl:sort select="label"/>
                <tr>
                    <th class="gloss">
                        <xsl:value-of select="label"/>
                        <xsl:if test="altlabel">
                            <xsl:text> [</xsl:text>
                            <xsl:for-each select="altlabel">
                                <xsl:value-of select="."/>
                                <xsl:if test="position()!=last()">, </xsl:if>]
                            </xsl:for-each>
                        </xsl:if> 
                        <xsl:apply-templates select="object"/>
                    </th>
                </tr>
                <tr>
                    <td class="gloss">
                        <xsl:apply-templates select="definition"/>
                    </td>
                </tr>
            </xsl:for-each>
        </tbody>
    </table>
</xsl:template>
```

When you run xsl_terms.xml with reference_gloss.xsl, the returned terms are sorted by the `<label>` element in the source terms document. Any alternative label is output in brackets, "[]".

Displaying Inline Terms

Authors can optionally incorporate terms and their definitions in the output by referring to a term and its scheme, and specifying a style in a `class` attribute. If the `class` attribute is set to `"popup"`, then a mouse-over action by an online user displays a pop-up containing the definition. In other circumstances the definition is shown inline.

Try It Out   A Definition Pop-up

To test this feature, add a definition to a copy of the reference file `xsl_character_maps.xml`. The change to the source file is simple. In the `<purpose>` element paragraph, replace the text "character map" as follows:

```
<dfn class="popup" term="characterMap" scheme="xsl"/>
```

This refers to the `characterMap` identifier in the default term scheme. When the page is rendered using reference_single.xsl, the term will be highlighted as a link, and a pop-up will display the definition. As things stand now, there is no existing link target, but I think you can see how a link to a page containing the term is formed:

```
<xsl:template match="dfn">
    <xsl:variable name="def">
        <xsl:copy-of select="xm:getterm-by-id(@term,@scheme)"/>
    </xsl:variable>
    <xsl:choose>
        <xsl:when test="@class='popup'">
            <xsl:variable name="pop" select="normalize-
                space($def/term/definition)"></xsl:variable>

            <a title="{$pop}">
                <xsl:attribute name="href"
                    select="concat('../terms_',@scheme,'/',@term,'.','.html')"/>
                <xsl:value-of select="$def/term/label"/>
            </a>

            <xsl:if test="$def/term/altlabel"> [<xsl:value-of
                select="$def/term/altlabel"/>] </xsl:if>
        </xsl:when>
        <xsl:otherwise>
            <xsl:value-of
                select="concat($def/term/label,': ',$def/term/definition)"/>
        </xsl:otherwise>
    </xsl:choose>
</xsl:template>
```

Building the Site

As I outlined in the introduction to this chapter, the overall goal is to combine all the XSLT reference pages in a single website.

Figure 11-7 shows the web-page layout, with tabs providing top-level navigation, and a table of contents with links to individual topics on the left.

The top-level navigation tabs each correspond to a `<map>` element, with the tab text coming from the element's tab attribute value. The `folder` attribute determines where the output will be written. Each `<section>` element forms a division within the table of contents.

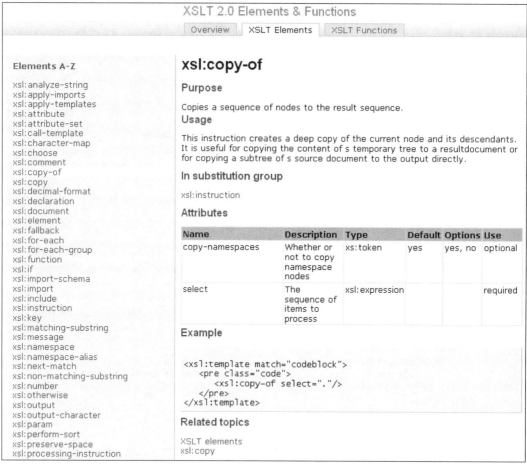

Figure 11-7

Generating the Reference Pages

To generate the site, a driver file that lists the identifiers to be processed, site_xsl.xml, is used. The href attribute values on <topicref> elements are used to locate metadata, to write the table of contents, and to open and process the individual documents. The next example shows a partial listing of the XML source:

```
<?xml version="1.0" encoding="UTF-8"?>

<site id="xsl" scheme="xsl" sitetitle="XSLT 2.0 Elements &amp; Functions">
    <map id="map_xsl_ref" folder="xslt_reference" scheme="xsl" tab="XSLT Reference">
        <section label="Introduction">
            <topicref href="xsl_er"/>
            <topicref href="xsl_functions"/>
            <topicref href="xsl_terms"/>
```

```
        </section>
     </map>
     <map id="map_elements" folder="xslt_reference" scheme="xsl" tab="XSLT Elements">
        <section label="Elements A-Z">
           <topicref href="xsl_analyze_string"/>
           <topicref href="xsl_apply_imports"/>
           <topicref href="xsl_apply_templates"/>
           <topicref href="xsl_attribute"/>
           <topicref href="xsl_attribute_set"/>
           <topicref href="xsl_call_template"/>
           ...
        </section>
        <section label="Attribute groups">
           <topicref href="ge_attr"/>
           <topicref href="version_attr"/>
           <topicref href="valid_attr"/>
        </section>
     </map>
     <map id="map_xsl_functions" folder="xslt_reference" scheme="xsl"
  tab="XSLT Functions">
        <section label="Functions A-Z">
           <topicref href="fn_current"/>
           <topicref href="fn_current_group"/>
           <topicref href="fn_current_grouping_key"/>
           <topicref href="fn_document"/>
           ...
        </section>
     </map>
  </site>
```

The main stylesheet, `site.xsl`, provides the basic structure in a series of XHTML `<div>` elements, the table of contents, and the reference content. The layout is entirely defined by the CSS stylesheet `style.css`:

```
<xsl:include href="ref2xhtml.xsl"/>

<xsl:param name="container">test_xsl</xsl:param>
<xsl:param name="logo">logo_xsl</xsl:param>

<xsl:variable name="sitetitle" select="site/@sitetitle"/>
<xsl:variable name="resourcelist"
   select="document(concat('../reslist_',site/@scheme,'.xml'))"/>
<xsl:variable name="scheme" select="site/@scheme"/>
<xsl:param name="id" select="/*/topicref[1]/@href"/>
<xsl:param name="dir">file:///c:/eclipse/</xsl:param>
<xsl:template match="/">
```

It includes `ref2xhtml.xsl`, which writes out each of the individual reference pages and sets up a number of parameter and variables:

```
<xsl:variable name="file">
  <xsl:value-of select="concat(@href,'.html')"/>
```

229

```
    </xsl:variable>

    <xsl:variable name="folder" select="ancestor::map/@folder"/>

    <xsl:result-document href="{$dir}/{$container}/{$folder}/{$file}">
```

The `href` attribute on the `<xsl:result-document>` instruction contains the target document location, constructed from `$container`, `$folder`, and `$file` parameters and variables.

Navigation Tabs

Top-level navigation is output in a table, which provides for a logo and an unnumbered list for each tab. The tab label and the first topic link in each section are obtained, and the current tab is highlighted so that it appears to be in front of the other tabs:

```
<table class="header">
    <tr>
        <td class="logo">
            <img src="{$logo}"/>
        </td>
        <td class="navcontainer">
            <ul class="navlist">
                <xsl:call-template name="tabs">
                    <xsl:with-param name="mapID"
                        select="ancestor::map/@id"/>
                </xsl:call-template>
            </ul>
        </td>
    </tr>
</table>
...
<xsl:template name="tabs">
    <xsl:param name="mapID"/>
    <xsl:for-each select="//map">
        <li>
            <xsl:variable name="linkID" select="section[1]/topicref[1]/@href"/>


            <xsl:call-template name="navtab">
                <xsl:with-param name="id" select="$linkID"/>
                <xsl:with-param name="mapID" select="$mapID"/>
                <xsl:with-param name="label" select="@tab"/>
            </xsl:call-template>

        </li>
    </xsl:for-each>

</xsl:template>

<xsl:template name="navtab">
    <xsl:param name="id"/>
    <xsl:param name="mapID"/>
    <xsl:param name="label"/>
```

```
    <xsl:variable name="linkmeta" select="$resourcelist//entry[@xml:id=$id]"/>
    <a>
        <xsl:if test="$mapID=current()/@id">
            <xsl:attribute name="class">current</xsl:attribute>
        </xsl:if>
        <xsl:attribute name="href">
            <xsl:value-of select="concat($linkmeta//content/@src,$id,'.html')"/>
        </xsl:attribute>
        <xsl:attribute name="title">
            <xsl:value-of select="$linkmeta/title"/>
        </xsl:attribute>
        <xsl:value-of select="$label"/>
    </a>
</xsl:template>
```

Table of Contents

The content of this section is the same on each page, with one exception: the link to the relevant page is highlighted if it matches the current metadata identifier:

```
<div id="pageNav">
    <xsl:for-each select="ancestor::map//section">
        <div class="relatedLinks">
            <h3>
                <xsl:value-of select="@label"/>
            </h3>
            <xsl:apply-templates select="current()//topicref"
                mode="toc">
                <xsl:with-param name="thistopic"
                    select="$identifier"/>
                <xsl:with-param name="thismeta" select="$meta"
                    tunnel="yes"/>
                <xsl:with-param name="reslist"
                    select="$resourcelist" tunnel="yes"/>
            </xsl:apply-templates>
        </div>
    </xsl:for-each>
</div>
 ...
<xsl:template match="topicref" mode="toc">
    <xsl:param name="thistopic">default</xsl:param>
    <xsl:for-each select=".">
        <xsl:variable name="topic"
            select="$resourcelist//entry[@xml:id=current()/@href]"/>
        <a>
            <xsl:attribute name="href">
                <xsl:value-of select="concat($topic/content/@src,@href,'.html')"
                />
            </xsl:attribute>
            <xsl:if test="$thistopic=current()/@href">
                <xsl:attribute name="class">currentref</xsl:attribute>
            </xsl:if>

            <xsl:value-of select="$topic/title"/>
        </a>
```

```
            <xsl:apply-templates/>
        </xsl:for-each>
    </xsl:template>
```

Content Section

The reference-page content is processed with an `<xsl:apply-templates>` instruction, with tunnel-parameter values for the document identifier and the scheme:

```
<div id="content">
    <h1>
        <xsl:value-of select="$title"/>
    </h1>

    <h2>Purpose</h2>
    <xsl:apply-templates select="$meta/summary"/>

    <xsl:apply-templates select="$resource//body/*">
        <xsl:with-param name="source_id" select="$identifier" tunnel="yes"/>
        <xsl:with-param name="default_scheme" select="$scheme" tunnel="yes"/>
    </xsl:apply-templates>
</div>
```

You may recall that tunnel parameters, if declared in a template, are passed through a chain of calls. This means that the `$source_id` and `$default_scheme` parameters will be visible to templates in ref2xhtml.xsl and links.xsl.

The section stating the purpose of an element or function is at this time obtained from the metadata `<summary>` element.

Function-Reference Pages

Function-reference pages differ somewhat from their element-reference equivalents. There is a `<syntax>` element to process. The heading is not the same, and there are fewer columns in the property table.

The type attribute on the `<properties>` element is used to call the appropriate template:

```
<xsl:template match="syntax">
    <h2>Signature</h2>
    <p>
        <span class="code">
            <xsl:value-of select="//syntax"/>
        </span>
    </p>
</xsl:template>
...
<xsl:template match="properties">
    <xsl:choose>
        <xsl:when test="@type='attribute'">
            <xsl:call-template name="attribute"/>
        </xsl:when>
        <xsl:when test="@type='parameter'">
            <xsl:call-template name="parameter"/>
        </xsl:when>
```

```
      </xsl:choose>
  </xsl:template>
  ...
  <xsl:template name="parameter">
    <h2>Parameter<xsl:if test="count(//property) gt 1">s</xsl:if>
    </h2>
    <table cellspacing="0">
      <tr>
        <th xsl:use-attribute-sets="th_first">Name</th>
        <th xsl:use-attribute-sets="col">Description</th>
        <th xsl:use-attribute-sets="col">Type</th>
        <th xsl:use-attribute-sets="col">Use</th>
      </tr>
      <xsl:for-each select="//property">
        <!-- don't sort -->
        <tr>
          <th xsl:use-attribute-sets="td_first">
            <xsl:value-of select="name"/>
          </th>
          <td xsl:use-attribute-sets="row">
            <xsl:apply-templates select="description"/>
          </td>
          <td xsl:use-attribute-sets="row">
            <xsl:apply-templates select="type"/>
          </td>
          <td xsl:use-attribute-sets="row">
            <xsl:value-of select="required/@state"/> </td>
        </tr>
      </xsl:for-each>
    </table>
  </xsl:template>
```

Landing and Glossary Pages

The Overview tab provides landing pages for each of the principal sections of the site, and a page for the glossary, and these have different content than the reference tabs. On the landing pages, the `<reftable>` element enables you to create a table of links with brief details of the entries. Listing 11-1 is the source for the XSLT-function overview.

Listing 11-1

```
<?xml version="1.0" encoding="UTF-8"?>
<?xml-stylesheet href="../xsl/dita_topic2html.xsl" type="text/xsl"?>
<reference xml:id="xsl_functions" scheme="xsl">
  <body>
    <purpose>
      <p>This section provides details of functions that may only be used with
XSLT stylesheets. These are distinct from XPath functions and user defined
functions defined with the <element>xsl:function</element> instruction.</p>
    </purpose>
    <reftable>
      <link href="fn_current"/>
      <link href="fn_current_group"/>
      <link href="fn_current_grouping_key"/>
```

Continued

Listing 11-1: *(continued)*

```
            <link href="fn_document"/>
            <link href="fn_element_available"/>
            <link href="fn_format_date"/>
            <link href="fn_format_number"/>
            <link href="fn_function_available"/>
            <link href="fn_generate_id"/>
            <link href="fn_key"/>
            <link href="fn_regex_group"/>
            <link href="fn_system_property"/>
            <link href="fn_type_available"/>
            <link href="fn_unparsed_text"/>
            <link href="fn_unparsed_entity"/>
        </reftable>
    </body>
</reference>
```

XSLT functions

This section provides details of functions that may only be used with XSLT stylesheets. These are distinct from XPath functions and user defined functions defined with the xsl:function instruction.

Name	Purpose
current	Returns the current context item
current-group	Returns the sequence of items in the current group within an xsl:for-each-group instruction
current-grouping-key	Returns the value of the group-by or group-adjacent expression for the group being processed with an xsl:for-each-group instruction. There is no key when grouping by patterns.
document	Returns the document node of the XML document located at the URI provided in the href argument
element-available	Returns true if a named XSLT instruction is available for use.
format-date, format-dateTime, format-time	Three functions that format date and time values.
format-number	Formats numbers for display using a picture string.
function-available	Returns true if a named XSLT, user-defined or extension function is available for use.
generate-id	Generates an XML Name that uniquely identifies a node.
key	Returns the nodes with a given value for a named key, which was defined using the xsl:key declaration.
regex-group	Identifies an ordered substring returned as part of a regular expression obtained from matching with xsl:analyze-string.
system-property	Returns details about the current processor in a string containing the value of a named environment property.
type-available	Tests if a given schema type is available.
unparsed-entity-public-id, unparsed-entity-uri	Two functions that access the public and system identifiers of parsed entities in the DTD of a source document.
unparsed-text, unparsed-text-available	Two functions that test for the existence of a text file, and load it for processing.

Figure 11-8

234

The link elements are processed with a call to `links.xsl`:

```
<xsl:template match="reftable">
   <xsl:param name="default_scheme" tunnel="yes"/>
   <xsl:call-template name="maketable"/>
</xsl:template>
```

Figure 11-8 shows the output for the page.

Earlier in this chapter you created the code to handle a glossary, with a template to match the `<termtable>` element. To create the glossary page in the Overview tab, you reuse this code in `ref2xhtml.xsl`.

Creating a Sitemap

Sitemaps are an easy way to provide information about pages on your website. A sitemap is an XML file that lists URLs with additional information that gives hints to web crawlers about file locations. A typical sitemap entry using the `<url>` element looks like the following snippet:

```
<?xml version="1.0" encoding="UTF-8"?>
<urlset xmlns="http://www.sitemaps.org/schemas/sitemap/0.9">
   <url>
      <loc>"http://xm.net/docs/"xslt_reference/xsl_analyze_string.html</loc>
      <lastmod>2009-05-05</lastmod>
      <changefreq>yearly</changefreq>
      <priority>0.5</priority>
   </url>

   ...
</urlset>
```

The `<urlset>` element contains a single sitemap with a `<url>` element for each page. The `<loc>` element contains the URL of the page, constrained to be no more than 2,048 characters.

An optional `<lastmod>` element gives the date of last modification in W3C datetime format, which allows you to omit the timestamp part. You can also indicate the update frequency in the optional `<changefreq>` element with values such as hourly, daily, weekly, and so on.

By setting an optional `<priority>` element value you can specify which pages you regard as most important. Valid values range from 0.0 to 1.0, with a default priority of 0.5.

To index multiple sitemaps for a series of websites, you can use a structure like the following example:

```
<?xml version="1.0" encoding="UTF-8"?>
<sitemapindex xmlns="http://www.sitemaps.org/schemas/sitemap/0.9">
   <sitemap>
      <loc>http://xm.net/xslt2_elements.xml</loc>
      <lastmod>2009-01-05</lastmod>
   </sitemap>
   <sitemap>
      <loc>http://xm.net/xpath2_functions.xml</loc>
      <lastmod>2008-11-01</lastmod>
```

```
        </sitemap>
    </sitemapindex>
```

You can find more details about the sitemap protocol at http://sitemaps.org.

The XML source for the sitemap is the same one you used to build the site: site.xml.

A standalone stylesheet, sitemap.xsl, again uses <topicref> elements in the source file to locate the <content> elements in the metadata entries and retrieve the relative URI.

Listing 11-2 shows how it works.

Listing 11-2

```xml
<?xml version="1.0" encoding="UTF-8"?>
<xsl:stylesheet xmlns:xsl="http://www.w3.org/1999/XSL/Transform" version="2.0">

    <xsl:output method="xml" encoding="UTF-8"/>
    <xsl:param name="date"
        select="format-date(current-date(),'[Y]-[M01]-[D01]')"/>
    <xsl:param name="resourcelist"
        select="document(concat('../reslist_',site/@scheme,'.xml'))"/>
    <xsl:param name="uri">"http://xm.net/docs/"</xsl:param>

    <xsl:template match="/">
        <xsl:variable name="output_file"
            select="concat('sitemap_',$date,'.xml')"/>
        <xsl:result-document href="{$output_file}">
            <xsl:variable name="resourcelist"
            select="document(concat('../reslist_',site/@scheme,'.xml'))"/>

            <urlset xmlns="http://www.sitemaps.org/schemas/sitemap/0.9">

                <xsl:for-each select="//topicref">
                    <xsl:variable name="identifier" select="@href"/>
                    <xsl:variable name="meta"
                        select="$resourcelist//entry[@xml:id=$identifier]"/>
                    <xsl:variable name="source"
                     select="substring-after(concat($meta/content/@src,@href),'../')"/>
                    <url>
                        <loc>
                            <xsl:value-of select="concat($uri,$source,'.html')"/>
                        </loc>
                        <lastmod>
                            <xsl:value-of select="$date"/>
                        </lastmod>
                        <changefreq>yearly</changefreq>
                        <priority>0.5</priority>
                    </url>
                </xsl:for-each>
            </urlset>
        </xsl:result-document>
    </xsl:template>
</xsl:stylesheet>
```

The $outputfile variable is used to set the href attribute in an `<xsl:result docment>` element. The metadata for each entry in the resource listing is processed to obtain the relative URI of the file, which is concatenated with the $uri parameter that identifies the site.

Summary

In this case study you extended your experience of XSLT by building a website for a sizeable number of reference documents. Rather than work from scratch, you made use of existing metadata schemas and an XSLT library that simplified the processing of links between documents. You also learned how to construct a simple glossary from more than one data source.

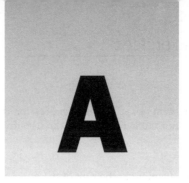

Answers to Exercises

This appendix contains suggested solutions to the exercises at the end of most of the chapters in this book.

Chapter 1

No exercises

Chapter 2

This chapter introduced XPath 2.0.

Question 1

Name some common XPath axes used to select element and attribute nodes.

Solution

Arguably the most commonly used axes are those that are used to select elements up and down the tree, probably in the following order. The `child::` axis is implicit in the majority of selections, with the `attribute::` axis coming in a close second.

- ❑ `child::`
- ❑ `attribute::`
- ❑ `parent::`
- ❑ `descendant::`
- ❑ `ancestor::`
- ❑ `self::`

Question 2

Assume that the context is in an element node. Write the expression that selects the xml:id attribute node for the element using the full and shortcut syntaxes (you can use any element name you like).

Solution

In this example I used the reference element at the root of the quick-reference documents.

```
<xsl:value-of select= `reference/@xml:id"/>
<xsl:value-of select= `reference/attribute::xml:id"/>
```

Question 3

After reviewing the string functions in XPath, create a simple XSLT stylesheet that you can use as a function test bed. Include several additional examples inside <p> elements using the following code as a guide:

```
<?xml version="1.0" encoding="iso-8859-1"?>
<xsl:stylesheet xmlns:xsl="http://www.w3.org/1999/XSL/Transform     version="2.0">
   <xsl:output method="xml" indent="yes" encoding="utf-8"/>
   <xsl:template match="/">
      <output>
         <p>
            <xsl:value-of
               select="string-join(('my', 'string', 'join', string(4.00)), '/')"/>
         </p>
      </output>
   </xsl:template>
</xsl:stylesheet>
```

Hint: You can transform the stylesheet using itself as the source document.

Solution

Here are some examples of functions I think you will use quite frequently. There is no right or wrong solution, and you may have chosen other functions.

```
<?xml version="1.0" encoding="iso-8859-1"?>
<xsl:stylesheet xmlns:xsl="http://www.w3.org/1999/XSL/Transform"
   xmlns:xs="http://www.w3.org/2001/XMLSchema" version="2.0">
   <xsl:output method="xml" indent="yes" encoding="utf-8"/>
   <xsl:template match="/">
      <output>
         <p>
            <xsl:value-of select="concat('the ','quick ','brown ','fox')"/>
         </p>
         <p>
            <xsl:value-of
               select="contains('Love&quot;s Labour&quot;s Lost','lab')"
            />
         </p>
         <p>
            <xsl:value-of select="ends-with('reslist.xml', '.xml')"/>
```

```
        </p>
        <p>
            <xsl:value-of select="normalize-space(' the  quick   brown fox ')"/>
        </p>
        <p>
            <xsl:value-of select="substring-before('reslist_xsl.xml', '.xml')"/>
        </p>
    </output>
  </xsl:template>
</xsl:stylesheet>
```

These are the results I obtained, which will be the same regardless of the source document that you use:

```
<?xml version="1.0" encoding="utf-8"?>
<output>
    <p>the quick brown fox</p>
    <p>false</p>
    <p>true</p>
    <p>the quick brown fox</p>
    <p>reslist_xsl</p>
</output>
```

Chapter 3

This chapter described the use of templates, variables, and parameters.

Question 1

List some of the benefits of using both template rules and named templates.

Solution

Template rules:

- ❏ They work like filters, comparing nodes to the rules automatically even if the source document is complex and unpredictable.
- ❏ Different modes of processing can be applied for a given match.
- ❏ Priorities can be used to cover cases when several templates match the same source.
- ❏ By default all the matching content will be output, so capturing it is fairly simple using literal-result elements.

Named templates:

- ❏ They are called by name, so they allow a degree of control not available in template rules.
- ❏ They are useful for frequently used process steps.
- ❏ The context does not move to a called template, so it can be used somewhat like a subroutine or procedure.
- ❏ Parameters can be specified and values passed, with values set at run time.

Question 2

In the `modes.xsl` stylesheet I suggested one way of formatting index values for element names. Try out two additional modes — one that produces a simple space-separated list layout, and one that indexes additional element names.

Solution

Part one of the question requires only a simple change to the `index` mode template. Instead of a list, I used <p> as the container, and followed it with an `<xsl:text>` instruction with a single space in it:

```
<xsl:template match="element" mode="index">
    <xsl:for-each select=".">
        <xsl:value-of select="."/>
        <xsl:text> </xsl:text>

    </xsl:for-each>
</xsl:template>
```

Part two first requires a change to the `<xsl:apply templates>` instruction that invokes the template. I added the source `<attr>` element to the `select` attribute value.

In the `index` mode template, I added the `<attr>` element to the `match` attribute and retained the list arrangement from the original version. (I could have added the `<code>` element too, but as it happens there isn't an instance in the source for this stylesheet.) In the listing, each index entry is prefixed with the name of the source element, using the XPath `name()` function, which comes in handy on occasions like this.

```
. . .
<body>
    <xsl:apply-templates select="reference/body"/>
    <p><strong>Element index</strong>: <xsl:apply-templates
        select="//element | //attr" mode="index"/>

    </p>
</body>
. . .
<xsl:template match="element |attr" mode="index">
    <ul>
        <xsl:for-each select=".">
            <li>
                <xsl:value-of select="name()"/>
                <xsl:text>: </xsl:text>
                <xsl:value-of select="."/>
                <xsl:text> </xsl:text>

            </li>
        </xsl:for-each>
    </ul>
</xsl:template>
```

Chapter 4

This chapter discussed using logic to drive the XSLT process.

Question 1

List the types of source material and output types that lend themselves to using `<xsl:for-each>` in stylesheets.

Solution

I tend to use iteration to process regularly structured and populated source content that you typically find in data-oriented material. Examples include name and address information, news feeds, bibliographies, and glossaries, which return output in tabular form.

Question 2

Prepare some attribute sets suitable for applying different text and background color combinations to a `<note>` element in HTML output, and show an example of how to use them in a template. The `type` attribute on the `<note>` element can be used to determine the style. Possible attribute values are `note`, `caution`, and `warning`.

The precise colors are not critical, but I suggest black/white, blue/gray, and red/yellow combinations for text and background. Figure 4-1 shows the sort of result I have in mind, though not the colors, unfortunately.

This is a note

This is a caution

This is a warning

Figure 4-1

The CSS stylesheet `reference.css` will handle the basic note style correctly.

Solution

This solution makes use of the way that you can override or supplement a CSS stylesheet with local style properties on HTML elements. Here is the definition of the `note` style in `reference.css`.

```
.note{
  padding: 5px;
  margin-bottom: 6pt;
  border: 1px solid #cccccc;
}
```

The first `<xsl:attribute-set>` definition sets the `class` attribute, and the second to fourth make use of it in the `use-attribute-sets` attribute, before declaring a `style` attribute with different values for `color` and `background-color`:

```
<xsl:attribute-set name="note">
   <xsl:attribute name="class">note</xsl:attribute>
</xsl:attribute-set>

<xsl:attribute-set name="warn" use-attribute-sets="note">
```

```
    <xsl:attribute name="style">color: red; background-color: #FFFF99;</xsl:attribute>
</xsl:attribute-set>

<xsl:attribute-set name="caution" use-attribute-sets="note">
    <xsl:attribute name="style">color: blue; background-color: #F5f7f7</xsl:attribute>
</xsl:attribute-set>

<xsl:attribute-set name="plain" use-attribute-sets="note">
    <xsl:attribute name="style">color: black;
background-color: #FFFFFF</xsl:attribute>
</xsl:attribute-set>
```

The code matching the <note> element node looks like this:

```
<xsl:template match="note">
    <xsl:choose>
        <xsl:when test="@type='warning'">
            <p xsl:use-attribute-sets="warn">
                <xsl:value-of select="."/>
            </p>
        </xsl:when>
        <xsl:when test="@type='caution'">
            <p xsl:use-attribute-sets="caution">
                <xsl:value-of select="."/>
            </p>
        </xsl:when>
        <xsl:otherwise>
            <p xsl:use-attribute-sets="plain">
                <xsl:value-of select="."/>
            </p>
        </xsl:otherwise>
    </xsl:choose>
</xsl:template>
```

Chapter 5

This chapter covered sorting and grouping of source nodes.

Question 1

In what circumstances would you use `<xsl:sort>` instructions inside `<xsl:apply-templates>`, as opposed to using it inside `<xsl:perform-sort>`?

Solution

I would use sorting in `<xsl:apply-templates>` if I intended to process the sorted output immediately using the instructions in any matching templates.

`<xsl:perform-sort>` is best applied inside a variable, when you want to "park" the sorted nodes as is without further processing.

Question 2

Given that the default `data-type` attribute value used in an `<xsl:sort>` instruction is ˋtext˝, what is the correct syntax for an instruction to sort on `xs:dateTime` values in elements named `<update>`? Apart from this value, are other related settings needed to make the instruction work correctly?

Solution

The correct syntax for `<xsl:sort>` is as follows, assuming the context item is being sorted:

```
<xsl:sort select="xs:dateTime(.)"/>
```

Because this function is in the XML Schema namespace, you must declare it in the `<xsl:stylesheet>` element:

```
xmlns:xs="http://www.w3.org/2001/XMLSchema"
```

Question 3

In the last Try It Out in this chapter, I suggested some changes that could be made to the stylesheet `local.xsl`, because it "lost" information that could have been captured by applying `class` attributes. Try making these changes and verify that the `class` attributes are set correctly by looking at the XHTML source code. Then modify `xhtml2ref.xsl` to pick up those `class` values and output correct element names, rather than `<code>` elements.

Solution

Here is the original change to generate the `class` attribute values that I suggested for `local.xsl`:

```
<xsl:template match="attr | element | code">
   <code>
      <xsl:attribute name="class">
         <xsl:value-of select="name()"/>
      </xsl:attribute>
      <xsl:value-of select="."/>
   </code>
</xsl:template>
```

Here is the replacement `code` template for `xhtml2ref.xsl`:

```
<xsl:template match="code">
   <xsl:choose>
      <xsl:when test="@class='element'">
         <element>
            <xsl:value-of select="."/>
```

```
            </element>
        </xsl:when>
        <xsl:when test="@class='attr'">
            <attr>
                <xsl:value-of select="."/>
            </attr>
        </xsl:when>
        <xsl:otherwise>
            <code>
                <xsl:value-of select="."/>
            </code>
        </xsl:otherwise>
    </xsl:choose>
</xsl:template>
```

Chapter 6

This chapter showed how to work with strings, numbers, dates, and times.

Question 1

a. What is the attribute on `<xsl:number>` that determines the way in which nodes are numbered?

b. Give a code fragment that shows how to select and sequentially number some footnotes if the element name in the XML source is `<fn>`, and the HTML output is something like the following example:

```
<p>[4] This is the fourth footnote.</p>
```

Solution

a. The `level` attribute determines the method of numbering.

b. Here I number footnotes using the value of "any" in the `level` attribute. The square brackets set off the numeric values, followed by a space inside `<xsl:text>`:

```
<xsl:template match="fn">
    <p>
        [<xsl:number level="any"/>]
        <xsl:text> </xsl:text>
        <xsl:value-of select="."/>
    </p>
</xsl:template>
```

Question 2

What are some implementation-related limitations on the use of the `format-date()`, `format-dateTime()`, and `format-time()` functions?

Solution

The settings for the optional arguments, `language`, `calendar`, and `country`, are dependent. If they are not supported, then you may get unexpected results. It is advisable to check your processor documentation and test to see if it is worth using these values.

Question 3

Illustrate the use of the following date-related functions, making use of the XPath 2.0 Function Reference of Appendix F if required:

```
month-from-dateTime()
```

```
years-from-duration()
```

```
timezone-from-time()
```

Solution

In this solution I used the following values:

```
<output>
   <p><xsl:value-of
         select="month-from-dateTime(xs:dateTime('2009-04-12T18:20:00Z'))"/></p>
   <p><xsl:value-of select="years-from-duration(xs:duration('P15M'))"/></p>
   <p><xsl:value-of select="timezone-from-time(xs:time('13:00:00+05:00'))"/></p>
</output>
```

The results looked like this:

```
<outut>
   <p>4</p>
   <p>1</p>
   <p>PT5H</p>
</output>
```

Chapter 7

This chapter demonstrated ways to handle multiple source and output documents.

Question 1

What design factors and XSLT language features lend themselves to modularization?

Solution

Typically you will use stylesheets to contain frequently used code, and avoid using long and complex stylesheets that make it hard to understand different parts of a process. Examples include global parameters, styling, and navigation features.

A second aspect of modularization is the requirement to replace or partly override parts of an existing stylesheet by writing an importing module.

Question 2

If you have already declared an `<xsl:output>` element named "archive," show how would you override the declared `method` and `indent` attributes in an `<xsl:result document>` instruction.

Solution

In this solution the `format` attribute on a `<xsl:result-document>` refers to the `<xsl:output>` declaration's `name` attribute, and overrides the two values:

```
<xsl:output name="archive" method="xml" indent="no" encoding="UTF-8"/>

<xsl:template match="/">
   <xsl:result-document format="archive" method="xhtml" indent="yes">
   ...
   </xsl:result-document>
</xsl:template>
```

Question 3

Name two XSLT elements that you can use to make use of existing template rules in an imported stylesheet.

Solution

The two instructions are `<xsl:apply-templates>` and `<xsl:next-match>`.

Question 4

Complete the following table, comparing the features of the XSLT `document()` function and XPath's `doc()` function.

Values	document()	doc()
Input		
URI resolution		
Fragment identifier		
Missing document		
Result		
Other implementation issues		

Solution

This is the table I prepared for this solution.

Values	document()	doc()
Input	Multiple document URIs	Single document URI
URI resolution	Base URI other than the context can be optionally specified	`base-uri()` function may be required in addition
Fragment identifier	Fragment identifier will return element node	Not supported
Missing document	Behavior is implementation-defined	`doc-available()` function required to verify URI exists
Result	A sequence of nodes	Document node for the URI
Other implementation issues	Fragment identifier support is implementation-specific	Behavior may depend on the implementation and configuration

Chapter 8

This chapter illustrated several aspects of processing plain text with XSLT.

Question 1

Why are the `<xsl:strip-space>` and `<xsl:preserve-space>` declarations useful?

Solution

You can use one or both of the elements to provide a list of elements where you wish to remove or return whitespace-only text.

Question 2

Write an `<xsl:preserve-space>` declaration for appropriate elements you have seen in the XSLT Quick Reference examples.

Solution

There is generally no need to preserve space unless you have specified stripping it. This solution shows two declarations: one removing it everywhere, including element-only content, the second preserving it in mixed-content elements:

```
<xsl:strip-space elements="*"/>
<xsl:preserve-space elements="p description"/>
```

Question 3

Using `census.xml` as source, write a transform to convert it back to the original CSV format.

Solution

In this solution I used the `child::` axis to select each element under `<person>`, with a comma between elements and a newline at the end:

```
<?xml version="1.0" encoding="UTF-8"?>
<xsl:stylesheet version="2.0" xmlns:xsl="http://www.w3.org/1999/XSL/Transform">

    <xsl:output method="text"/>
    <xsl:strip-space elements="*"/>

    <xsl:template match="/">
       <xsl:apply-templates/>
    </xsl:template>

    <xsl:template match="person">
       <xsl:for-each select="child::node()">
          <xsl:value-of select="."/>
          <xsl:text>,</xsl:text>
       </xsl:for-each>
       <xsl:text>&#xa;</xsl:text>
    </xsl:template>

</xsl:stylesheet>
```

Chapter 9

This chapter showed how you could use identifiers and keys to locate related nodes in source data.

Question 1

Under what conditions will an XSLT processor recognize an `xs:ID` type and set the `is-id` property on a source node when parsing an input document?

Solution

The following conditions will set this property:

❑ The source document must contain a DTD declaring an attribute as having type `ID`.

❑ If the processor is schema-aware, it must recognize the attribute as an `xs:ID` type or as one derived from it.

❑ The attribute must be named `xml:id`.

Question 2

What is the purpose of the `collation` attribute on the `<xsl:key>` declaration?

Solution

This attribute has an identical purpose to `collation` attributes on `<xsl:sort>` and on several string functions. The collation determines the rules for making sting comparisons. It can be used to provide the URI of a collation to use, other than the default collation in use by the processor. The range of supported collations is implementation-dependent.

Question 3

How consistent would you expect the results to be for a given node from the `generate-id()` function on the following?

- ❏ A different processing run
- ❏ A different processor

Solution

On a different processing run, there is no guarantee that a given processor will generate the same result for a specified node, though it might do so.

There is no requirement in the XSLT specification that processors render the result in a given format, but this is not a problem, as they are required to return the same results for a given node in the same processing run.

Chapter 10

This chapter discussed debugging, validation, and documentation.

Question 1

Demonstrate how to incorporate an `xsl-stylesheet` processing instruction in an XML result document.

Solution

If you want to create any processing instruction, you can use the `<xsl:processing-instruction>` element to write a node to the output. In this case, you define the type of instruction in the `name` attribute, and specify the remaining content inside an `<xsl:text>` instruction:

```
<xsl:processing-instruction name="xsl-stylesheet">
    <xsl:text>href="step1.xsl" type="text/xsl"</xsl:text>
</xsl:processing-instruction>
```

Question 2

Why can using `<xsl:comment>` rather than `<xsl:message>` sometimes make it easy to trace problems in your stylesheet code?

Solution

Not every XSLT processor handles message output in exactly the same sequence. For example, variables are often not evaluated until they are first used. This can mean that `<xsl:message>` content will be recorded in an unpredictable order, and may not easily be related to problem code.

In contrast, `<xsl:comment>` instructions are always evaluated in context, and can often be more helpful in resolving problems.

Chapter 11

No exercises

Extending XSLT

Having come this far and seen what is available in the standard features of XSLT, you might ask why you'd need to extend it to add functionality.

There are several possible circumstances:

- ❑ You might want to access data in a source such as a database.
- ❑ The functions you need are not available in XSLT or XPath — for example, you need to do trigonometric calculations with functions such as `tan()` or `cos()`.
- ❑ Additional instructions or attributes are needed.
- ❑ An application requires customized serialization encodings or parameters.
- ❑ A collating sequence is necessary for a language that is not provided, and you also need to localize numbers and dates in a way that is not supported.

There are a number of ways to make extensions. Some you can make yourself with stylesheet functions, and there are also open-source XSLT function libraries that you can make use of. Processor vendors may provide extensions of several kinds, including functions, instructions and declarations, additional attributes, and types. It is also possible to define your own extension, usually written in the language of the host XSLT processor.

Stylesheet Functions

A common approach to extending XSLT is to write new stylesheet functions using the `<xsl:function>` declaration, whether these are user-written or defined by a third party. These functions use XSLT and XPath, and they are called the same way as other extension functions.

The following is a schema definition. Note that as a declaration, it is a top-level element:

```
<xs:element name="function" substitutionGroup="xsl:declaration">
  <xs:complexType>
    <xs:complexContent mixed="true">
      <xs:extension base="xsl:versioned-element-type">
```

```
        <xs:sequence>
           <xs:element ref="xsl:param" minOccurs="0" maxOccurs="unbounded"/>
           <xs:group ref="xsl:sequence-constructor-group" minOccurs=
"0" maxOccurs="unbounded"/>
        </xs:sequence>
        <xs:attribute name="name" type="xsl:QName" use="required"/>
        <xs:attribute name="override" type="xsl:yes-or-no" default="yes"/>
        <xs:attribute name="as" type="xsl:sequence-type" default="item()*"/>
      </xs:extension>
    </xs:complexContent>
  </xs:complexType>
</xs:element>
```

To name a function you set the `name` attribute value to a lexical QName, which *must* have a namespace prefix that ensures it is distinct from those in the XSLT namespaces. The namespace must also be declared in the relevant `<xsl:stylesheet>` element.

You can use zero or more `<xsl:param>` elements in functions, but the `required` attribute should never be defined for a function parameter.

You call stylesheet functions from an XPath expression using the function name and a matching number of parameters, passed in as a series of comma-separated values.

Calling an Extension Function

The next example shows how to make use of a function in the FunctX stylesheet library, details of which I mention later in this appendix. You can download the XSLT 2.0–compatible version of the library from `www.xsltfunctions.com/xsl/download.html`.

I suggest that you choose the commented version for your download, which you should save in a convenient folder. It is advisable to retain the library intact, as there are some interdependencies.

The `functx:contains-word()` function works in a similar way to XPath `contains()`. It takes two string parameters: the first is the containing text string, and the second is the word to match. If a match is found, the function returns `true`. It is case-insensitive.

The word to match must be delimited by either "non-word" characters or the beginning or end of the first parameter. Most punctuation and whitespace characters are considered non-word characters, while letters and digits are word characters.

The function requires another function, `functx:escape-for-regex()`, which escapes regular expression (regex) special characters. This function is not formally declared in the calling function, as sometimes required in other languages.

Here is the code for `functx:contains-word()`.

```
<xsl:function name="functx:contains-word" as="xs:boolean"
              xmlns:functx="http://www.functx.com" >
  <xsl:param name="arg" as="xs:string?"/>
  <xsl:param name="word" as="xs:string"/>
```

```
    <xsl:sequence select="
     matches(upper-case($arg),
             concat('^(.*\W)?',
                         upper-case(functx:escape-for-regex($word)),
                         '(\W.*)?$'))
    "/>

  </xsl:function>
```

It uses the XPath functions `matches()`, `concat()`, and `upper-case()`, and calls another library function, `functx:escape-for-regex()`. The result is returned in an `<xsl:sequence>` instruction.

There is a lot of regex work going on here, and one attraction of using a library function is that you can treat it as a black box. Basically, both strings are uppercase, escaped for regex special characters, and anchored on word boundaries.

To call this function you need to ensure that the `functx:` namespace is declared in your stylesheet and that the `functx.xsl` library file is referenced in an `<xsl:include>` declaration. The following snippet illustrates how the function is called within an `<xsl:when>` test:

```
<?xml version="1.0" encoding="UTF-8"?>
<xsl:stylesheet xmlns:xsl="http://www.w3.org/1999/XSL/Transform"
    xmlns:functx="http://www.functx.com" exclude-result-prefixes="functx"

    version="2.0">

    <xsl:include href="functx.xsl"/>


    <xsl:template match="/">
        <output>
            <xsl:choose>
                <xsl:when test="functx:contains-word('now is the time for
all good men...','bad')">
                    A match was found.</xsl:when>
                <xsl:otherwise>No match in source.</xsl:otherwise>
            </xsl:choose>
        </output>
    </xsl:template>
</xsl:stylesheet>
```

Function Libraries

There are several open-source function libraries that you can make use of. This section covers two that I think you will find most useful.

EXSLT

EXSLT is a community initiative to define a standardized set of extension functions and extension elements that can be used across different XSLT processors. The functions are grouped into a number of modules. Some are written as XSLT templates or functions. Others are in JavaScript or C, depending on the platforms for which they are intended.

EXSLT developments date back to SLT 1.0 and some of its perceived weaknesses. Now, many EXSLT functions have been superseded by those in XSLT 2.0. All of them are applicable in version-1.0 stylesheets, and many are still useful in version 2.0, such as those dealing with mathematics and sets. You can download the modules from `www.exslt.org`.

FunctX

The FunctX library website lists a wide range of extension functions: strings, numbers, dates, atomic values, elements and attributes, and so on. You met one earlier in this appendix.

The library is listed A–Z and by category in both XSLT and XQuery syntax. It also includes a convenient list of XPath and XSLT functions. You can explore the library and download an XSLT 2.0–compatible version at `www.xsltfunctions.com/xsl`.

Vendor Extensions

The XSLT specification does not dictate how extension support should be provided by XSLT-processor vendors, and each vendor will have its own approaches to developing extensions. There may, for example, be different choices of languages, and a variety of language-binding mechanisms.

This section gives examples from several categories of extension provided by the Saxon processor. Full documentation can be accessed at `www.saxonica.com/documentation/extensions/intro.html`.

EXSLT Modules

Saxon provides an implementation of the EXSLT modules Common, Math, Sets, DatesAndTimes, and Random, with some restrictions. Those that overlap XSLT 2.0 functionality are still supported except where the semantics differ.

Functions

The `saxon:file-last-modified()` function takes an absolute file or HTTP URI and returns an `xs:dateTime` value, which is usually in a specific time zone. The result can then be formatted using the `format-dateTime` function, or input to arithmetic calculations or comparisons against other dates and times. It takes the following form:

```
format-dateTime(file-last-modified('input.xml'))
```

Instructions

The `<saxon:call-template>` instruction is identical to `<xsl:call-template>` except that the template name can be written as an attribute-value template, allowing the template that is called to be determined at run time:

```
<saxon:call-template name="{$template_name}"/>
```

Attributes

The `saxon:memo-function` attribute may be set on the `<xsl:function>` element. A value of `"yes"` will cache the results of calling the function; and if it is called again with the same arguments, the previous result is returned, rather than being recalculated.

Serialization Parameters

The `saxon:indent-spaces` attribute can be set on the `<xsl:output>` declaration. When the output method is XML, HTML, or XHTML with `indent="yes"`, setting an integer value will control the amount of indentation. The default value in the absence of this attribute is 3.

User-Defined Extensions

User-defined extensions (other than stylesheet functions) are generally best developed in the native language of the XSLT processor you are using — for instance, Java for Saxon, and JavaScript or C# for MSXML. The supporting facilities will depend on the processor concerned. For example, at the time of writing, Saxon supported extension functions, but not extension instructions, on the .NET platform.

MSXML uses the top-level element `<msxml:script>` to bind extension functions, which are often written inline in JavaScript, within the script element. For example, the following code provides the EXSLT `cos()` function. Note the use of the `extension-element-prefixes` attribute in the containing `<xsl:stylesheet>` declaration, which contains a space-separated list of the prefixes:

```
<xsl:stylesheet version="1.0" extension-element-prefixes="math msxsl">
...
<msxsl:script language="JavaScript" implements-prefix="math">
   function cos(arg){ return Math.cos(arg);}
</msxsl:script>
...
</xsl:stylesheet>
```

Some Java-based processors implicitly support binding of functions to Java methods. For example, Saxon recognizes the `java:` URI prefix as special and regards the value after the prefix as a Java class name. If the method is available, then it is called and the result is returned as the value from a function call. The next example shows how the external function `Math:sqrt()` would be called:

```
<xsl:template match="number">
   <result>
      <xsl:value-of select="Math:sqrt(xs:double(.))"
         xmlns:Math="java:java.lang.Math"/>
   </result>
</xsl:template>
```

Before you jump in and try developing an extension, check carefully what is already available in XSLT and XPath. Then examine the resources available in third-party XSLT function libraries. Many of these are built with XSLT and XPath, and will serve as examples of what can be achieved. Maybe they can serve as a starting point for further development work.

In addition, look at what can be done with vendor-provided extensions. As you have seen, these often go beyond additional functions alone and can cover extension attributes, instructions, and serialization properties.

XSLT Processing Model

Looked at in the abstract, the XSLT processing model can appear quite complex. I think the model is much easier to understand after you have gained some knowledge about XSLT and XPath.

This appendix expands on the brief outline of XSLT processing contained in the introduction and relates it to information that you have already encountered in several chapters of this book. While it does not contain significant new information, I hope it will draw together what you have learned in a convenient review format.

In outline, an XSLT processor parses an XML source document and a stylesheet into a source tree, applies a transform to create a result tree, and serializes the content in the specified output format.

Quite often, the process is rather more complex. Multiple source documents can be loaded, and stylesheets may be provided in modules. There may be more than one result, and multiple serializations.

In every case, each document is processed as a separate tree. Initially, a source tree is created for each input and the transformation takes place, creating one or more result trees. Finally, the result trees are serialized to one or more of the possible output formats.

The Data Model

Often the source, the stylesheet, and the result documents are in XML format. But because other input and output formats, MTML, XHTML, and text are supported, it does not make sense to use XML as an internal representation, and to possibly convert to and from XML in addition to performing the transforms. The XSLT data model therefore represents an XML document conceptually as a tree. This model is shared with XPath.

You learned about this node structure in the introduction and about the node properties in Chapter 2. Figure C-1 is a reminder of the kinds of node that are specified, in the form of a UML (Unified Modeling Language) class diagram. The rectangles represent classes and the arrows show the class relationships, in this case indicating that all the nodes are of type node.

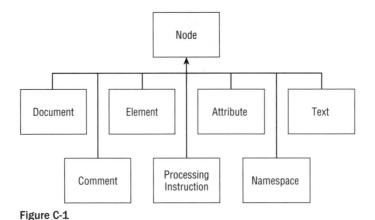

Figure C-1

The XPath data model is flat, rather than showing a hierarchy based on a particular relationship or property. Properties are defined for all nodes, even if they do not apply in every case. For example, attribute and namespace properties apply only to element nodes.

Transforming

There are several ways to invoke a stylesheet processor. In Chapter 1 you applied three methods: an xml-stylesheet processing instruction, the Oxygen IDE GUI, and the Saxon command line. The XSLT specification says nothing about how this should happen, so various types of APIs and their implementations can vary greatly.

However, the specification does say what can be passed across the interface. By now you'll have seen most of them in action: the name of the source document, the main stylesheet, and global parameters. Other values allowed include an initial named template, an initial mode, and a base URI for output.

Parsing Inputs

The XML source document is parsed and a source tree is created. The main stylesheet is parsed and, as you saw in Chapter 7, any additional stylesheets specified by <xsl:include> or <xsl:import> declarations are also loaded.

Additional XML source documents may also be loaded with the XSLT document() function, or with the XPath doc() or collection() functions. However, documents loaded this way are not part of the initialization of the source trees; this processing takes place only when one of these functions is called in a template.

At its simplest, these additional documents can be small lookup files, like the resource and subject meta-data sources you used in the case study in Chapter 11. It is also possible to handle the aggregation of a range of source documents using data values in a file that identifies the documents to process, like the one used to build the Quick Reference website.

Template Rules

You've seen what happens in template processing, discussed in detail in Chapter 4. The root node of the source tree is used as a starting point, unless an initial named template is specified.

The pattern in the `match` attribute value in an `<xsl:template>` rule is compared to those in the source document. If there is no match with the document node of the source tree, then a built-in rule is invoked.

The content of the template is a series of instructions and text nodes known as a *sequence constructor*. The sequence constructor is evaluated, and the result (which is also a sequence) is placed in the result tree in the order of the instructions in the template.

It is possible to use modes and priorities to modify the basic operation of template rules.

A mode expressed in the `mode` attribute on an `<xsl:template>` element enables a node in a source tree to be processed multiple times, each time producing a different result. Modes also allow different sets of template rules to be active when processing different trees.

Priorities, set as numeric values on a template's `priority` attribute, make it possible to resolve cases where there are several possible candidates for a match. These values will override any defaults calculated by the processor.

Variables and Parameters

Variables and parameters can be defined to have either global scope or local scope. Those with global scope can be declared as top-level elements and accessed from within all templates.

Global parameters defined with `<xsl:param>` differ from global values specified with `<xsl:variable>` in that they can be passed when the processor is invoked, and thus varied to suit the requirements of the documents being processed.

Within templates, variables can contain locally scoped values, but may not be redefined once they are set. The scope of such variables is the containing sequence constructor.

The `<xsl:variable>` instruction is also often used as a container for sequence constructors in the creation of temporary trees to be used for further processing.

Templates can contain `<xsl:param>` declarations to specify the parameters to be passed to the templates when they are processed. The instructions `<xsl:apply-templates>` and `<xsl:call template>` that invoke the templates can pass these parameter values in the `<xsl:with-param>` instruction.

Controlling Processing

Normally, source-tree nodes are processed in document order. However, as you learned in Chapter 4, it is possible to define alternative sequences in which templates are invoked.

`<xsl:apply-templates>` can take several values in the `select` attribute to determine the processing order, and can additionally specify the mode to use.

`<xsl:call-template>` calls a named template as though it were a subroutine. Whereas the context node usually moves to a template as it is matched, the context does not change with `<xsl:call-template>`.

`<xsl:if>` can be used to handle simple conditional processing. `<xsl:choose>` and the contained `<xsl:when>` and `<xsl:otherwise>` instructions provide a way to handle more complex options.

`<xsl:for-each>` may be used to process a series of nodes anywhere in the source tree, and `<xsl:for-each-group>` can be employed to group nodes in several ways.

Outputs and Serialization

In Chapter 7 you used the `<xsl:result-document>` instruction, which contains a tree of nodes, ready to serialize into one of the four supported formats supported by `<xsl:output>`. The result-document attribute values may also be set to override a named output format.

When you specify template processing using `<xsl:apply-templates>` or `<xsl:call-template>`, the constructed sequences are written to nodes as a result tree. Serialization is a distinct step and is outside the scope of the XSLT 2.0 specification.

Because serialization applies to both XSLT and XQuery, the process is the subject of a separate recommendation. See www.w3c.org/TR/xslt-xquery-serialization.

In XSLT 2.0 the attributes on the `<xsl:output>` element provide some control, in addition to template instructions, over how the result tree is turned into an output document.

D

XSLT 2.0 Quick Reference

This reference provides brief details of the XSLT 2.0 elements and functions.

The schema on which this reference is based is non-normative, which means that it is not strictly part of the XSLT 2.0 recommendation as such. The recommendation is, of course, authoritative.

A copy of the schema is in Appendix E. The online version can be found at www.w3.org/2007 /schema-for-xslt20.xsd.

There are notes on the schema in the introduction to this book, and you will find further detailed information on the use of both elements and functions in Michael Kay's *XSLT 2.0 and XPath 2.0 Programmer's Reference, Fourth Edition* (Wrox, 2008).

The content of this reference is derived from the same XML source as the material used in the case study in Chapter 11. If you chose to build the reference website described there, you can make use of the online version too.

This appendix is organized as described in the following sections.

Elements

In the schema, XSLT elements are broadly divided into two categories: *declarations* and *instructions*. These are specified as abstract elements, which never are used in stylesheets; rather, they are elements for which other elements may be substituted.

In this reference, the XSLT elements are described in alphabetical order, with notes on their purpose, their usage, and their place either in the schema content model or in the substitution spaces for declarations and instructions.

A table of attributes follows, with name, description, and type information. Any optional values and defaults are given, with a note indicating whether the attribute is required or optional.

Attribute Groups

Some attributes are common to a wide range of elements:

- ❏ Generic element attributes
- ❏ Validation attributes
- ❏ Version attributes

These are grouped together after the element entries, and referred to after the attribute listing in each entry.

Types

The XSLT schema contains a number of simple, derived datatypes. Those that are used frequently, or are complex, are described after the attribute group list, and referred to in the attribute Type column in element entries. However, those that are easily explained in the attribute table are described in place.

I also refer to one complex type representing sequence constructors.

Functions

There are several XSLT-specific functions that you can use along with those provided by XPath 2.0.

They are described following the schema type listing. XPath 2.0 functions themselves are described in another quick reference in Appendix E.

XSLT Elements

xsl:analyze-string

Purpose

An instruction that processes a string using a regular expression.

Usage

This element is useful in handling structured text that is not marked up using XML.

Note that any curly brackets in a regular expression must be escaped by doubling them, as the value of the `regex` attribute is an attribute value template.

Contains

```
xsl:matching-substring | xsl:non-matching-substring | xsl:fallback
```

In substitution group

```
xsl:instruction
```

Attributes

Name	Description	Type	Default	Options	Use
flags	Flags that determine how the expression is interpreted	xsl:avt		i, m, s, x	Optional
regex	The regular expression used to analyze the string	xsl:avt			Required
select	The string to be analyzed	xsl:expression			Required

Attribute group

Generic element attributes | Version attributes

xsl:apply-imports

Purpose

An instruction, used within a template body, to override an existing global variable or parameter, or a template rule, with one of the same name in an imported module.

Usage

<xsl:apply-imports> is useful when you want to partially override a rule, rather than replace it entirely.

<xsl:next-match> provides an alternative method of achieving the same result.

Contains

xsl:with-param

In substitution group

xsl:instruction

Attribute group

Generic element attributes | Version attributes

See also

xsl:next-match

xsl:apply-templates

Purpose

An instruction that defines a set of nodes to process.

Usage

The optional `select` attribute defines the nodes to process. If this attribute is not set, then all the children of the context node will be processed.

The `mode` attribute must match a `mode` attribute value on a matching template.

The `<xsl:sort>` element must follow immediately after the instruction.

Contains

xsl:with-param | xsl:sort

In substitution group

xsl:instruction

Attributes

Name	Description	Type	Default	Options	Use
mode	The processing mode to use	xsl:QName | xs:token		QName, #default, #current	Optional
select	The sequence of items to process	xsl:expression			Optional

Attribute group

Generic element attributes | Version attributes

xsl:attribute

Purpose

An instruction that adds attributes to literal result elements or elements created by an instruction like `<xsl:element>` or `<xsl:copy>`.

Usage

This instruction must precede other instructions used to construct an element.

The node to be added is made up of the required name and the optional namespace attributes, each of which may be expressed as attribute value templates; for example: `<xsl:attribute name="href" select="{$url}"/>`.

Either the `select` attribute or the element content should be used to define the attribute value.

Use this instruction, rather than an attribute on a literal result element, when you want the value be determined at run time.

Use the optional `type` attribute when you need to validate the value's datatype against a schema with a schema-aware processor.

Contains

`sequence-constructor`

In substitution group

`xsl:instruction`

Attributes

Name	Description	Type	Default	Options	Use
name	The name of the attribute set.	xsl:avt			Required
namespace	The namespace URI.	xsl:avt			Optional
select	The sequence of items to process.	xsl:expression			Optional
separator	Separator to be inserted between items generated in the value sequence. The default is a single space.	xsl:avt			Optional

Attribute group

`Generic element attributes` | `Version attributes` | `Validation attributes`

xsl:attribute-set

Purpose

Declares a named set of attributes and values.

Usage

To use the named set, you refer to it in the `use-attribute-sets` attribute on the `<xsl:element>` element, the `<xsl:copy>` elements, or on a literal result element.

A common use is to apply a set of fixed property values to an element, but you can also use the contained `<xsl:attribute>` elements to select values or construct sequences.

Contains

`xsl:attribute`

In substitution group

```
xsl:declaration
```

Attributes

Name	Description	Type	Default	Options	Use
name	The name of the attribute set.	xsl:QName			Required
use-attribute-sets	Used to combine other sets from the same stylesheet. The value is a space-separated list of QNames.	xsl:QNames			Optional

Attribute group

```
Generic element attributes | Version attributes
```

xsl:call-template

Purpose

An instruction that invokes a named template.

Usage

The name attribute must match the value of the name attribute on an <xsl:template> element. The context remains in the node from which the template is called, rather than moving to the called template.

The <xsl:with-param> instruction may be used to supply parameter values.

Contains

```
xsl:with-param
```

In substitution group

```
xsl:instruction
```

Attribute

Name	Description	Type	Default	Options	Use
name	The name of the template to call	xsl:QName			Required

Attribute group

```
Generic element attributes | Version attributes
```

See also

xsl:template

xsl:character-map

Purpose

Declares a named character map that determines the way characters are serialized.

Usage

In the character map, one or more specific characters are replaced by a string, each of which is defined in the contained `<xsl:output-character>` element. The character map is applied only when a `<xsl:output>` or `<xsl:result-document >` declaration refers to the map in a `use-character-maps` attribute.

Typically this element is used to create supported character entities in output.

Contains

xsl:output-character

In substitution group

xsl:declaration

Attributes

Name	Description	Type	Default	Options	Use
name	The name of the character map	xsl:QName			Required
use-character-maps	Space-separated list of the names of additional character maps to use	xsl:QNames			Optional

Attribute group

Generic element attributes | Version attributes

See also

xsl:output

xsl:result-document

xsl:choose

Purpose

An instruction that specifies a choice between alternatives, which are defined by multiple <xsl:when> instructions, and an optional terminal <xsl:otherwise> element.

Usage

Each <xsl:when> instruction has a test attribute containing an expression to evaluate.

A single <xsl:when> has the same result, as though you had used <xsl:if> for a single test.

Contains

xsl:when | xsl:otherwise

In substitution group

xsl:instruction

Attribute group

Generic element attributes | Version attributes

See also

xsl:if

xsl:comment

Purpose

An instruction that renders a comment node.

Usage

The comment may be either the value of the select attribute or contained in the constructed sequence.

In substitution group

xsl:instruction

Attribute

Name	Description	Type	Default	Options	Use
select	The comment text	xsl:expression			Optional

Attribute group

Generic element attributes | Version attributes

xsl:copy

Purpose

An instruction that copies the context item to the result sequence.

Usage

This instruction is often used in transforms when two schemas have some element structures in common.

Specified element and attribute nodes in the enclosed `<xsl:apply-templates>` instruction are added to the output as if they were created by the `<xsl:element>` or `<xsl:attribute>` instructions.

No child elements of the context node are copied, nor are its existing attributes. To do this you must use `<xsl:copy-of>`.

The selected text, processing instructions, comment, and namespace nodes are copied entirely.

In substitution group

`xsl:instruction`

Attributes

Name	Description	Type	Default	Options	Use
copy-namespaces	Whether or not to copy namespace nodes	xs:token	yes	yes, no	Optional
inherit-namespaces	Whether or not children of a copied node will inherit copied namespaces	xs:token	yes	yes, no	Optional
use-attribute-sets	The space-separated list of attribute names to use for elements	xsl:QNames			Optional

Attribute group

`Generic element attributes` | `Version attributes` | `Validation attributes`

See also

`xsl:copy-of`

xsl:copy-of

Purpose

An instruction that copies a sequence of nodes to the result sequence.

Usage

This instruction creates a deep copy of the current node and its descendants. It is useful for copying the contents of a temporary tree to a result document or for copying a subtree of a source document to the output directly.

In substitution group

xsl:instruction

Attributes

Name	Description	Type	Default	Options	Use
copy-namespaces	Whether or not to copy namespace nodes	xs:token	yes	yes, no	Optional
select	The sequence of items to process	xsl:expression			Required

Attribute group

Generic element attributes | Version attributes | Validation attributes

See also

xsl:copy

xsl:decimal-format

Purpose

A declaration that determines the display format of a source data number, which has been converted to a string by the XSLT format-number() function.

Usage

The element effectively localizes the number format for users, so you could, for example, have a group of named formats in an imported stylesheet that are used with a locale parameter to determine the formatting for a particular instance.

Contained by

xsl:declaration

Attributes

Name	Description	Type	Default	Options	Use
NaN	The string used to represent "not a number"	xs:string	NaN		Optional
decimal-separator	The character used as the decimal point	xsl:char	.		Optional
digit	The placeholder character for significant digits	xsl:char	#		Optional
grouping-separator	The character that separates groups (hundreds, thousands, and so on)	xsl:char	,		Optional
infinity	The string used to represent infinity	xs:string	infinity		Optional
minus-sign	The character used as the minus sign	xsl:char	-		Optional
name	The name of this format	xsl:QName			Optional
pattern-separator	Character used to separate positive and negative number patterns	xsl:char	;		Optional
per-mille	The character for the per thousand sign, #×2030	xsl:char	‰		Optional
percent	The character for the percent sign	xsl:char	%		Optional
zero_digit	The placeholder character for leading and trailing zeros	xsl:char	0		Optional

Attribute group

Generic element attributes | Version attributes

See also

format-number function

xsl:declaration

Purpose

An abstract element for which declaration elements may be substituted.

Usage

This element is part of the XSLT 2.0 schema, but is never used in a stylesheet.

Substitute

```
xsl:attribute-set | xsl:character-map | xsl:decimal-format | xsl:function |
xsl:import-schema | xsl:include | xsl:key | xsl:namespace-alias | xsl:output |
xsl:preserve-space | xsl:strip-space | xsl:template
```

xsl:document

Purpose

An instruction that explicitly creates a document node and adds it to the result sequence.

Usage

You should use this instruction when you need to validate a document structure in a temporary tree. In contrast, the `<xsl:result-document>` instruction creates a distinct output.

In substitution group

```
xsl:instruction
```

Attribute group

```
Generic element attributes | Version attributes | Validation attributes
```

See also

```
xsl:result-document
```

xsl:element

Purpose

Creates a named element node and writes it to the result tree.

Usage

Because the `name` attribute is an attribute value template, it is suitable for the generation of a element when the name is not known until run time.

When multiple namespaces are being used, you can use the `namespace` to provide the correct URI, without worrying about multiple prefixes getting copied to the output unnecessarily.

In substitution group

```
xsl:instruction
```

Attributes

Name	Description	Type	Default	Options	Use
inherit-namespaces	Whether or not children of a copied node will inherit copied namespaces	xs:token	yes	yes, no	Optional
name	The name of the element to create	xsl:avt			Required
namespace	The namespace URI of the element	xsl:avt			Optional
use-attribute-sets	The space-separated list of attribute set names to use for this element	xsl:QName			Optional

Attribute group

```
Generic element attributes | Version attributes | Validation attributes
```

xsl:fallback

Purpose

An instruction that defines fallback behavior when there is no implementation of a containing instruction.

Usage

Typically this element is useful when it is uncertain whether or not a particular vendor-implemented extension is available, or to define alternative processing when a version 1.0 processor encounters the version 2.0 instructions `<xsl:next-match>` or `<xsl:analyze-string>`.

In substitution group

```
xsl:instruction
```

See also

```
xsl:next-match
```

```
xsl:analyze-string
```

xsl:for-each

Purpose

An instruction that selects a sequence of items for uniform processing. The items may be either nodes or atomic values.

Usage

Each iteration through the selected sequence changes the context, so you need to remember to use appropriate expressions when constructing the sequence.

Contains

```
xsl:sort | sequence-constructor
```

In substitution group

```
xsl:instruction
```

Attribute

Name	Description	Type	Default	Options	Use
select	The sequence of items to process	xsl:expression			Required

Attribute group

```
Generic element attributes | Version attributes
```

xsl:for-each-group

Purpose

An instruction that selects a sequence of items for uniform processing, and then groups them according to common values, adjacency, or in relation to other elements.

Usage

Grouping depends on which of the four attributes is specified. The attribute value is known as the *group key*.

The XSLT functions current-group() and current-grouping-key() may be used to process grouped items inside an <xsl:for-each> instruction.

Contains

```
xsl:sort | sequence-constructor
```

In substitution group

```
xsl:instruction
```

Attributes

Name	Description	Type	Default	Options	Use
collation	The URI of a collation to use for string comparison	xs:anyURI			Optional
group-adjacent	The common value to use if items are adjacent	xsl:expression			Optional
group-by	The common value or values to use	xsl:expression			Optional
group-ending-with	The pattern that ends a group of preceding items	xsl:pattern			Optional
group-starting-with	The pattern that starts a group of following items	xsl:pattern			Optional
select	The sequence of items to group	xsl:expression			Required

Attribute group

Generic element attributes | Version attributes

See also

current-group function

current-grouping-key function

xsl:function

Purpose

Declares the name, parameters, and implementation of a custom stylesheet function.

Usage

The function may be invoked from any XPath expression.

Contains

xsl:param | sequence-constructor

In substitution group

xsl:declaration

Attributes

Name	Description	Type	Default	Options	Use
as	The datatype of the sequence produced by the function	xsl:sequence-type	item()		Optional
as	Whether or not the function overrides a vendor-specific function of the same name	xs:token	yes	yes,no	Optional
name	The name of the function	xsl:QName			Required

Attribute group

Generic element attributes | Version attributes

xsl:if

Purpose

An instruction that defines a test condition, and a sequence constructor to perform if the condition evaluates to true.

Usage

An empty sequence is returned if the test fails.

It is equivalent to if-then statements in other languages. If there are multiple conditions to test, then you should use <xsl:choose>.

Contains

sequence-constructor

In substitution group

xsl:instruction

Attribute

Name	Description	Type	Default	Options	Use
test	The XPath expression to evaluate	xsl:expression			Required

Attribute group

Generic element attributes | Version attributes

See also

xsl:choose

xsl:import

Purpose

Declaration used to import stylesheet modules, differing from `<xsl:include>` in that the declarations and rules in the importing stylesheet have a higher import precedence than those in the imported stylesheet.

Usage

`<xsl:import>` elements must precede all other declarations and user-defined data elements.

The declarations and template rules in the importing stylesheet have a higher precedence than those that are imported.

`<xsl:apply-imports>` may be used to partially override the precedence of items in the importing stylesheet.

Contained by

xsl:transform

In substitution group

xsl:declaration

Attribute

Name	Description	Type	Default	Options	Use
href	URI that identifies the stylesheet module to be imported. The way that the reference is resolved is implementation-defined.	xs:anyURI			Required

Attribute group

Generic element attributes | Version attributes

See also

```
xsl:apply-imports
```

```
xsl:include
```

xsl:import-schema

Purpose

Declaration, available only in a schema-aware processor, that identifies a schema defining the user-defined types, elements, and attributes.

Usage

Schema modules that are imported or included in the referenced schema must be explicitly declared if those definitions are required.

This element may include an inline XML schema, in which case the schema-location attribute must not be used.

In substitution group

```
xsl:declaration
```

Attributes

Name	Description	Type	Default	Options	Use
namespace	The namespace URI of the schema to be imported. This information may be enough on its own to enable an implementation to locate the required schema components.	xs:anyURI			Optional
schema-location	Indicates where the schema document is located. It is likely that a schema-aware XSLT processor will be able to process a schema document found at this location.	xs:anyURI			Optional

Attribute group

Generic element attributes | Version attributes

xsl:include

Purpose

A declaration used to include one stylesheet module within another.

Usage

The children of the included `<xsl:stylesheet>` element replace the `<xsl:include>` element in the including document; in other words, they have the same import precedence.

Multiple includes are allowed, and included stylesheets may contain further includes.

`<xsl:include>` is useful for material that is standard content in outputs over a wide range of document types.

In substitution group

`xsl:declaration`

Attribute

Name	Description	Type	Default	Options	Use
href	URI that identifies the stylesheet module to be imported. The way that the reference is resolved is implementation-defined.	xs:anyURI			Required

Attribute group

`Generic element attributes | Version attributes`

See also

`xsl:import`

xsl:instruction

Purpose

The abstract element for which instruction elements may be substituted.

Usage

This element is part of the XSLT 2.0 schema, but it is never used in a stylesheet.

Substitute

```
xsl:analyze-string | xsl:apply-imports | xsl:apply-templates | xsl:attribute |
xsl:call-template | xsl:choose | xsl:comment | xsl:copy | xsl:copy-of | xsl:document |
xsl:element | xsl:fallback | xsl:for-each | xsl:for-each-group | xsl:if | xsl:message |
xsl:namespace | xsl:next-match | xsl:number | xsl:perform-sort | xsl:processing-instruction
| xsl:result-document | xsl:sequence | xsl:text | xsl:value-of
```

xsl:key

Purpose

Declares a named key to be used with the key() function.

Usage

Using the <xsl:key> declaration simplifies code and can increase performance, as most implementations build an index the first time the key is processed.

Keys may be of any datatype, and values can be evaluated in a sequence constructor inside the <xsl:key> instead of using a use attribute setting.

Contains

```
sequence-constructor
```

In substitution group

```
xsl:declaration
```

Attributes

Name	Description	Type	Default	Options	Use
collation	The name of a collation used to compare the values of keys	xs:anyURI			Optional
match	The pattern to match	xsl:pattern			Required
name	The name of the key	xs:QName			Required
use	An expression used to determine the key value(s)	xsl:expression			Optional

Attribute group

```
Generic element attributes | Version attributes
```

See also

key function

xsl:matching-substring

Purpose

Defines the processing for a match within the `<xsl:analyze-string>` instruction.

Usage

The output is added to the result of the `<xsl:analyze-string>` instruction.

Contains

sequence-constructor

Contained by

xsl:analyze-string

Attribute group

Generic element attributes | Version attributes

See also

xsl:non-matching-substring

xsl:message

Purpose

An instruction that specifies a message to be output.

Usage

Either the `select` attribute or a sequence constructor or both may be used to create the message content. If both are used, then the results are concatenated.

Stylesheet execution may be terminated by setting the `terminate` attribute to `yes`.

The output location is implementation-dependent, but is typically either the console or a log file.

Contains

sequence-constructor

In substitution group

`xsl:instruction`

Attributes

Name	Description	Type	Default	Options	Use
select	The expression to evaluate	xsl:expression			Required
terminate	Whether or not to terminate processing after the message	xsl:avt	no	yes, no	Optional

Attribute group

`Generic element attributes | Version attributes`

See also

`xsl:comment`

xsl:namespace

Purpose

Creates a named namespace node and writes it to the result tree.

Usage

You cannot create a namespace using the `<xsl:attribute>` instruction. If you need to create a namespace declaration that is not used for any element or attribute nodes, but, for example, is used in element content, then you can use `<xsl:namespace>` for the purpose.

Contains

`sequence-constructor`

In substitution group

`xsl:instruction`

Attributes

Name	Description	Type	Default	Options	Use
name	The name of the namespace node to create	xsl:avt			Required
select	The expression to compute the namespace URI	xsl:expression			Optional

Attribute group

Generic element attributes | Validation attributes

xsl:namespace-alias

Purpose

Declares a namespace from a stylesheet to be associated with a different namespace in the output.

Usage

This is typically required in transforms that output XSLT stylesheets.

In substitution group

xsl:declaration

Attributes

Name	Description	Type	Default	Options	Use
result-prefix	The prefix to output	xs:NCName | xs:token			Required
stylesheet-prefix	A prefix used in the stylesheet	xs:NCName | xs:token			Required

Attribute group

Generic element attributes | Version attributes

xsl:next-match

Purpose

An instruction that allows more than one rule to apply to the same source node, within the same stylesheet module.

Usage

The processor looks for a rule that matches the current node and mode, and has a lower import precedence or priority than the current template.

This instruction provides considerably more flexibility than <xsl:apply-imports>.

Contains

xsl:fallback | xsl:with-param

In substitution group

xsl:instruction

Attribute groups

Generic element attributes | Version attributes

See also

XSLT elements

xsl:apply-imports

xsl:non-matching-substring

Purpose

Defines the processing for substrings that are not matched within the <xsl:analyze-string> instruction.

Usage

The output is added to the result of the <xsl:analyze-string> instruction.

Contains

sequence-constructor

Contained by

xsl:analyze-string

Attribute group

Generic element attributes | Version attributes

See also

xsl:matching-substring

xsl:number

Purpose

An instruction that numbers nodes sequentially and formats the numbers.

Usage

If a node to number is not explicitly selected in the select attribute, the context node is numbered.

The level attribute determines the numbering method. The value single is used for sibling numbering, and any is used for nodes that can appear anywhere, regardless of hierarchy. The value multiple indicates a hierarchy of numbers typical of legal documents, such as "4.2.7."

The features for formatting numbers are expressed by attribute settings, and are distinct from those in the <xsl:decimal-format> declaration and the format-number() function.

Contains

`sequence-constructor`

In substitution group

`xsl:instruction`

Attributes

Name	Description	Type	Default	Options	Use
count	Specifies which nodes are counted. The default is the same pattern as the start node.	xsl:pattern			Optional
format	The output format.	xsl:avt	1		Optional
from	Defines the point where numbering starts. The default is the root of the tree containing the start node.	xsl:pattern			Optional
grouping-separator	The character that separates groups (hundreds, thousands, and so on).	xsl:avt			Optional
grouping-size	The number of digits in each group.	xsl:avt			Optional
lang	Specifies the language to use in formatting.	xsl:avt			Optional
letter-value	Defines the numbering scheme.	xsl:avt		alphabetical, traditional	Optional
level	The method of numbering.	xs:NCName	single	single, multiple, any	Optional
ordinal	Whether or not an ordinal number is used.	xsl:avt			Optional
select	The node to number.	xsl:expression			Optional
value	A user-supplied number. If used, the level, count, and from attribute values should be omitted.	xsl:expression			Optional

Attribute group

Generic element attributes | Version attributes

See also

xsl:decimal-format

format-number function

xsl:otherwise

Purpose

An optional instruction inside an <xsl:choose> element that defines an action to take if none of the preceding <xsl:when> tests are satisfied.

Contains

sequence-constructor

Contained by

xsl:choose

Attribute group

Generic element attributes | Version attributes

xsl:output

Purpose

A declaration that determines the format of a result document that is written to the output.

Usage

If multiple outputs are required, the name attribute must be used to identify the individual format definitions, and to associate them with a format attribute value in a <xsl:result-document> instance.

Unnamed definitions and definitions with the same name are grouped together for processing.

In substitution group

xsl:declaration

Attributes

Name	Description	Type	Default	Options	Use
byte-order-mark	Defines whether or not a byte order mark is written at the start of the file.	xs:token		yes, no	Optional
cdata-section-elements	Space-separated QNames of the elements whose content is to be output inside CDATA sections.	xsl:QName			Optional
doctype-public	The public identifier to be used in any DOCTYPE declaration. Ignored unless doctype-system is also specified.	xs:string			Optional
doctype-system	The system identifier to be used in any DOCTYPE declaration.	xs:string			Optional
encoding	The character encoding of the output.	xs:string			Optional
escape-uri-attributes	Whether or not URI attributes should be escaped in HTML and XHTML output.	xs:token		yes, no	Optional
include-content-type	Whether or not a <meta> element should be should be included when the method attribute is HTML.	xs:token		yes, no	Optional

Continued

Name	Description	Type	Default	Options	Use
indent	Whether or not to indent the output.	xs:token		yes, no	Optional
media-type	The MIME type of the output file.	xs:string			Optional
method	The format to be output. If it is not one of the recognized values, it must be a prefixed lexical QName.	xsl:QName | xs:token		QName, xml, html, xhtml, text	Optional
name	The name of this format.	xsl:QName			Optional
normalization-form	Specifies how Unicode characters with multiple representations should be normalized.	xs:NMTOKEN		NFC, NFD, NFKC, NFKD, fully-normalized, none	Optional
omit-xml-declaration	Whether or not to output an XML declaration.	xs:token		yes, no	Optional
standalone	Sets the value of the standalone attribute in the XML declaration.	xs:token		yes, no, omit	Optional
undeclare-prefixes	Whether or not namespaces should be undeclared when out of scope. Applies only if the version attribute is set to '1.1'.	xs:token		yes, no	Optional
use-character-maps	Space-separated names of the <xsl:character-map> elements used in character mapping.	xs:QNames			Optional
version	The version of XML in the output document.	xs:NMTOKEN			Optional

Attribute group

`Generic element attributes`

xsl:output-character

Purpose

Defines the substitution of a single Unicode character within an `<xsl:character-map>` declaration.

Contained by

`xsl:character-map`

Attributes

Name	Description	Type	Default	Options	Use
character	The Unicode character to be replaced	xsl:char			Required
string	The replacement string to output	xs:string			Required

Attribute group

`Generic element attributes | Version attributes`

xsl:param

Purpose

A declaration used to define a global parameter to the transformation, or within `<xsl:template>` or `<xsl:function>`.

Usage

The element must appear immediately after the parent element.

A parameter supplied to a template, using `<xsl:call-template>`, `<xsl:apply-templates>`, `<xsl:apply-imports>` or `<xsl:next-match>`, is passed with `<xsl:with-param>`. A parameter, passed to a stylesheet function, is contained in an XPath expression.

Contains

`sequence-constructor`

Contained by

```
xsl:transform | xsl:template | xsl:function
```

Attributes

Name	Description	Type	Default	Options	Use
as	The type of the parameter	xsl:sequence-type			Optional
name	The parameter name	xsl:QName			Required
required	Whether or not the parameter is required	xs:token	no	yes, no	Optional
select	The default parameter value	xsl:expression			Optional
tunnel	Whether or not the parameter is a tunnel parameter	xs:token	no	yes, no	Optional

Attribute group

```
Generic element attributes | Version attributes
```

See also

```
xsl:with-param
```

xsl:perform-sort

Purpose

Used as a standalone instruction to sort items without any immediate additional processing. The element always contains one or more <xsl:sort> instructions.

Usage

You may use either the select attribute or a contained sequence constructor to define the sequence to be processed.

Contains

```
xsl:sort | sequence-constructor
```

Attribute

Name	Description	Type	Default	Options	Use
select	The sequence of items to process	xsl:expression			Optional

Attribute group

Generic element attributes | Version attributes

xsl:preserve-space

Purpose

A declaration that determines how whitespace nodes are handled.

Usage

The elements attribute lists the elements in which text-node whitespace is to be preserved.

In substitution group

xsl:declaration

Attribute

Name	Description	Type	Default	Options	Use
elements	A space-separated list of element names	xsl:nametests			Required

Attribute group

Generic element attributes | Version attributes

See also

xsl:strip-space

xsl:processing-instruction

Purpose

An instruction that outputs a processing-instruction node.

Usage

The instruction is often useful for constructing `xml-stylesheet` processing instructions for visual checking of XHTML output.

In substitution group

`xsl:instruction`

Attributes

Name	Description	Type	Default	Options	Use
name	The target of the processing instruction	xsl:avt			Required
select	The data part of the instruction	xsl:expression			Optional

Attribute group

`Generic element attributes` | `Version attributes`

xsl:result-document

Purpose

A declaration that determines the format of a result document that is written to the output.

Usage

The `href` attribute specifies the absolute or relative URI of the output file.

The `format` attribute may be used to identify a matching output-format definition in the `name` attribute value on an `<xsl:output>` declaration.

Several attributes have the same purpose as those in `<xsl:output>`, and may be used to override the respective values. These values may be supplied as attribute-value templates, returning the appropriate type.

Contains

`sequence-constructor`

In substitution group

`xsl:instruction`

Attributes

Name	Description	Type	Default	Options	Use
byte-order-mark	Defines whether or not a byte-order mark is written at the start of the file.	xsl:avt		yes, no	Optional
cdata-section-elements	Space-separated names of the elements whose content is to be output inside CDATA sections.	xsl:avt			Optional
doctype-public	The public identifier to be used in any DOCTYPE declaration. Ignored unless doctype-system is also specified.	xsl:avt			Optional
doctype-system	The system identifier to be used in any DOCTYPE declaration.	xsl:avt			Optional
encoding	The character encoding of the output.	xsl:avt			Optional
escape-uri-attributes	Whether or not URI attributes should be escaped in HTML and XHTML output.	xsl:avt		yes, no	Optional
format	The name of an <xsl:output> declaration to use.	xsl:avt			Optional
href	The location of the output file.	xsl:avt			Optional
include-content-type	Whether or not a <meta> element should be included when the method attribute is HTML.	xsl:avt		yes, no	Optional
indent	Whether or not to indent the output.	xsl:avt		yes, no	Optional
media-type	The MIME type of the output file.	xsl:avt			Optional

Continued

Name	Description	Type	Default	Options	Use
method	The format to be output. If it is not one of the recognized values, it must be a lexical QName.	xsl:avt		xml, html, xhtml, text	Optional
normalization-form	Specifies how Unicode characters with multiple representations should be normalized.	xsl:avt		NFC, NFD, NFKC, NFKD, fully-normalized, none	Optional
omit-xml-declaration	Whether or not to output an XML declaration.	xsl:avt		yes, no	Optional
output-version	The version of XML in the output document.	xsl:avt			Optional
standalone	Sets the value of the standalone attribute in the XML declaration.	xsl:avt		yes, no	Optional
type	The schema type to use in validation.	xsl:QName			Optional
undeclare-prefixes	Whether or not namespaces should be undeclared when out of scope. Applies only if the output-version attribute is set to '1.1'.	xsl:avt		yes, no, omit	Optional
use-character-maps	Space-separated QNames of the <xsl:character-map> elements used in character mapping.	xsl:QNames			Optional
validation	How any validation should be applied.	xs:token		strict, lax, preserve, skip	Optional

Attribute group

Generic element attributes | Version attributes

xsl:sequence

Purpose

An instruction that is commonly used to return the result of a stylesheet function.

Usage

The instruction also allows template rules to return atomic values.

Contains

```
xsl:fallback
```

In substitution group

```
xsl:instruction
```

Attribute

Name	Description	Type	Default	Options	Use
select	The value to be returned	xsl:expression			Required

Attribute group

```
Generic element attributes | Version attributes
```

xsl:sort

Purpose

A sort-key component, any number of which may be combined in a sort specification.

Usage

Each instruction is treated in order, with the result being processed by the containing instruction.

Contains

```
sequence-constructor
```

Contained by

```
xsl:apply-templates | xsl:for-each | xsl:for-each-group | xsl:perform-sort
```

Attributes

Name	Description	Type	Default	Options	Use
case-order	Whether uppercase or lowercase letters are collated first. The default value is language-dependent.	xsl:avt		upper-first, lower-first	Optional
collation	The URI of a collation to use for string comparison.	xsl:avt			Optional
data-type	Whether the values are collated alphabetically or numerically. The default value is 'text'. Primarily for use with XSLT 1.0 stylesheets.	xsl:avt	text	text, number	Optional
lang	Specifies the language of the sort key.	xsl:avt			Optional
order	Whether the items are arranged in ascending or descending order.	xsl:avt	ascending	ascending, descending	Optional
select	The XPath expression to evaluate.	xsl:expression			Optional
stable	Specifies whether or not the original order of equal items should be retained. Applies only to the first <xsl:sort>.	xs:token	yes	yes, no	Optional

Attribute group

Generic element attributes | Version attributes

xsl:strip-space

Purpose

A declaration that determines how whitespace nodes are handled.

Usage

The `element` attribute lists the elements in which whitespace in text nodes is not significant, and can be removed.

In substitution group

`xsl:declaration`

Attribute

Name	Description	Type	Default	Options	Use
elements	A space-separated list of element names	xsl:nametests			Required

Attribute group

`Generic element attributes` | `Version attributes`

See also

`xsl:preserve-space`

xsl:stylesheet

Purpose

The root element of a stylesheet.

Usage

The `<stylesheet>` is always the root element, even if a stylesheet is included in, or imported into, another. It must have a `version` attribute, indicating the version of XSLT that the stylesheet requires.

For a version 2.0 stylesheet, the value should be "2.0." For a stylesheet intended to execute under both XSLT 1.0 and XSLT 2.0, create a core module for each version number; then use `<xsl:include>` or `<xsl:import>` to incorporate common code, which should specify `version="2.0"` if it uses XSLT 2.0 features, or `version="1.0"` otherwise.

The `<xsl:transform>` element is allowed as a synonym. It is shown in the schema as the substitution group for `<xsl:stylesheet>`, so see that section for details of the structure.

The namespace declaration `xmlns:xsl="http//www.w3.org/1999/XSL/Transform` by convention uses the prefix `xsl`.

An element occurring as a child of the `<stylesheet>` element is called a declaration. Top-level elements are all optional, and may occur zero or more times.

In substitution group

xsl:transform

xsl:template

Purpose

Templates are the building blocks of XSLT. This element is used to declare a template for generating nodes in a result tree.

Usage

Either the `match` attribute or the `name` attribute must be present. The `match` attribute pattern is used to match nodes in the source tree, and is invoked using the `<xsl:apply-templates>` instruction. The `name` attribute explicitly names a template to call with the `<xsl:call-template>` element.

The `mode` and `priority` attributes must not be specified unless a `match` attribute is present.

Contains

xsl:param | sequence-constructor

In substitution group

xsl:declaration

Attributes

Name	Description	Type	Default	Options	Use
as	The datatype of the sequence produced by the template.	xsl:sequence	item()		Optional
match	Contains a pattern to be matched against nodes in the source tree.	xsl:pattern			Optional
mode	One or more mode names used to select a template rule among those with the same pattern. The value #all matches all modes.	xsl:QName | xs:token		QName, #default, #all	Optional
name	The name of the template.	xsl:QName			Optional
priority	A positive or negative number that sets the priority of the template in cases where multiple templates match the same node.	xs:decimal			Optional

Attribute group

Generic element attributes | Version attributes

See also

xsl:apply-templates

xsl:call-template

xsl:text

Purpose

An instruction used to add a text node to the result sequence.

Usage

The instruction may be used to control the use of whitespace. You can also disable escaping of special characters, though this usage is now deprecated because it may not work in certain cases.

In substitution group

xsl:instruction

Attribute

Name	Description	Type	Default	Options	Use
disable-output-escaping	Whether or not to escape special characters	xs:token	no	yes, no	deprecated

Attribute group

Generic element attributes | Version attributes

xsl:transform

Purpose

The name is a synonym of `<xsl:stylesheet>`.

Usage

In the XSLT schema, `<xsl:stylesheet>` element is in this substitution group, and the structure is documented under this element.

`<xsl:import>` should always be the first contained declaration if present.

Contains

```
xsl:import | xsl:declaration | xsl:param | xsl:variable
```

Attributes

Name	Description	Type	Default	Options	Use
default-validation	The validation applied to new elements and attributes when validation or type attributes are not set on an instruction	xs:token	strip	strip, preserve	Optional
id	Identifies an embedded stylesheet	xs:ID			Optional
input-type-annotations	The method of handling type annotations on input documents	xs:token	unspecified	strip, preserve, unspecified	Optional

Attribute group

```
Generic element attributes | Version attributes
```

xsl:value-of

Purpose

An instruction used to add a text node to the result sequence.

Usage

The value to output may be obtained from the select attribute or from a contained sequence constructor.

Disabling the escaping of special characters is deprecated because it may not work in certain cases.

Contains

```
sequence-constructor
```

In substitution group

```
xsl:instruction
```

Attributes

Name	Description	Type	Default	Options	Use
disable-output-escaping	Whether or not to escape special characters	xs:string	no	yes, no	deprecated
select	The value to be output	xsl:expression			Optional
separator	A string used to separate atomic values	xsl:avt			Optional

Attribute group

Generic element attributes | Version attributes

xsl:variable

Purpose

Declares a global or local variable and assigns a value to it.

Usage

The value to assign may be obtained from the select attribute or from a contained sequence constructor.

Contains

sequence-constructor

Contained by

xsl:transform

Attributes

Name	Description	Type	Default	Options	Use
as	The type of the variable	xsl:sequence-type			Optional
name	The name of the variable	xsl:QName			Required
select	The value of the variable	xsl:expression			Optional

Attribute group

Generic element attributes | Version attributes

xsl:with-param

Purpose

Sets the value of a parameter supplied to a template.

Usage

The value to assign may be obtained from the `select` attribute or from a contained sequence constructor.

Contains

sequence-constructor

Contained by

xsl:apply-imports | xsl:apply-templates | xsl:call-template | xsl:next-match

Attributes

Name	Description	Type	Default	Options	Use
as	The type of the parameter	xsl:sequence-type			Optional
name	The name of the parameter	xsl:QName			Required
select	The value of the parameter	xsl:expression			Optional
tunnel	Whether or not the parameter is a tunnel parameter	xs:token	no	yes, no	Optional

Attribute group

Generic element attributes | Version attributes

See also

xsl:param

Attribute Groups

Generic element attributes

Purpose

Generic element attributes, which may be expressed on any XSLT or literal result elements.

Attributes

Name	Description	Type	Default	Options	Use
default-collation	Used to apply styling to the element	xs:anyURI			Optional
exclude-result-prefixes	A space-separated list of namespace prefixes to exclude from the output	xs:NCName			Optional
extension-element-prefixes	A space-separated list of namespace prefixes that identify extension elements	xs:NCName			Optional
use-when	Whether or not this element and its children should be included in the stylesheet	xsl:expression			Optional
xpath_default_namespace	The namespace URI to be assumed for unprefixed names	xs:anyURI			Optional

Version attributes

Purpose

The version attribute, typically used on the <xsl:stylesheet> element. It may be used on XSLT instructions, literal result elements, and some declarations.

Attribute

Name	Description	Type	Default	Options	Use
version	The XSLT version number	xs:decimal			Optional

Validation attributes

Purpose

Validation attributes on elements.

Usage

Usually these attributes are used on the <xsl:stylesheet> element. If used on a literal result element, they should have the xsl: prefix to distinguish them from attributes in other namespaces.

Attributes

Name	Description	Type	Default	Options	Use
type	The type declaration to use for validation	xs:NCName			Optional
validation	How any validation should be applied	xs:token		strict, lax, preserve, strip	Optional

Types

The following table lists the simple types that either are used frequently in the XSLT schema or are complex. Other type definitions may be found in the schema itself in Appendix E.

Name	Description	Type	Default	Options
avt	The simple type for attributes that allow an attribute value template	xs:string		QName, #default, #current
char	A string containing exactly one character	xs:string		QName, #default, #current
expression	An XPath 2.0 expression, conforming to the pattern '.+'	xs:token		
mode	Allowed values for the mode attribute of the xsl:apply-templates instruction	xs:token		QName, #default, #current
sequence-type	The description of a datatype, conforming to the XPath 2.0 SequenceType production at http://www.w3.org/TR/xpath20/#id-sequencetype-syntax	xs:token		

XSLT Functions

The following functions are specific to XSLT 2.0, as distinct from the XPath 2.0 functions listed in Appendix F, which may also be used in XQuery.

current

Purpose

Returns the current context item.

Signature

```
current()
```

current-group

Purpose

Returns the sequence of items in the current group within an `xsl:for-each-group` instruction.

Signature

```
current-group()
```

See also

```
xsl:for-each-group
```

current-grouping-key

Purpose

Returns the value of the group-by or group-adjacent expression for the group being processed with an `xsl:for-each-group` instruction. There is no key when grouping by patterns.

Signature

```
current-grouping-key()
```

See also

```
xsl:for-each-group
```

document

Purpose

Returns the document node of the XML document located at the URI provided in the `href` argument.

Signature

```
document(href, base)
```

Parameters

Name	Description	Type	Use
href	The URI of the file to be loaded	xs:string | xs:anyURI	Required
base	The base URI to use for resolving the href parameter	node()	Optional

See also

```
unparsed-text, unparsed-text-available()
```

element-available

Purpose

Returns true if a named XSLT instruction is available for use.

Signature

```
element-available(name)
```

Parameter

Name	Description	Type	Use
name	The name of the element being tested	xsl:QName	Required

format-date, format-dateTime, format-time,

Purpose

Three functions that format date and time values.

Signature

```
format-date(value, picture, language, calendar, country)
```

Parameters

Name	Description	Type	Use
value	The date or time to format	xs:date | xs:dateTime | xs:time	Required
picture	A picture string composed of special characters showing the formatting and separators	xs:string	Required
language	The language to be used in formatting	xsl:string	Optional
calendar	The calendar to use for formatting the value	xsl:string	Optional
country	The country code associated with the value	xsl:string	Optional

format-number

Purpose

Formats numbers for display using a picture string.

Signature

```
format-number(value, picture, format)
```

Parameters

Name	Description	Type	Use
value	The number to format	xs:double | xs:float | xs:decimal	Required
picture	A picture string composed of special characters showing the grouping and separation of digits	xs:string	Required
format	Identifies an <xsl:format> declaration with further formatting information	xsl:QName	Optional

function-available

Purpose

Returns `true` if a named XSLT, user-defined, or extension function is available for use.

Signature

```
function-available(name, arity)
```

Parameters

Name	Description	Type	Use
name	The name of the element being tested	xsl:QName	Required
arity	The number of arguments of the function being tested	xs:integer	Optional

generate-id

Purpose

Generates an XML name that uniquely identifies a node.

Signature

```
generate-id (node)
```

Parameter

Name	Description	Type	Use
node	The input node. If this parameter is omitted, the context node is identified.	node()	Optional

key

Purpose

Returns the nodes with a given value for a named key, which was defined using the `xsl:key` declaration.

Signature

```
key (name, value, top)
```

Parameters

Name	Description	Type	Use
name	The name of the key defined in a declaration	xsl:QName	Required
value	The value of the key	xs:anyAtomicType	Required
top	The document node to search	node()	Optional

See also

xsl:key

regex-group

Purpose

Identifies an ordered substring returned as part of a regular expression obtained from matching with xsl:analyze-string.

Signature

regex-group (group)

Parameter

Name	Description	Type	Use
group	The substring matched by part of a regular expression, defined by the integer position of a substring contained in parentheses	xs:integer	Required

See also

xsl:analyze-string

system-property

Purpose

Returns details about the current processor in a string containing the value of a named environment property.

Signature

system-property (name)

Parameter

Name	Description	Type	Use
name	The name of the property required	xsl:QName	Required

type-available

Purpose

Tests whether a given schema type is available.

Signature

```
type-available (name)
```

Parameter

Name	Description	Type	Use
name	The name of the type to test for	xsl:QName	Required

unparsed-text, unparsed-text-available

Purpose

Two functions that test for the existence of a text file and then load it for processing.

Signature

```
unparsed-text (name)
```

Parameters

Name	Description	Type	Use
href	The URI of the file to be loaded	xs:string	Required
encoding	The character encoding of the text	xs:string	Optional

See also

document()

unparsed-entity-public-id, unparsed-entity-uri

Purpose

Two functions that access the public and system identifiers of parsed entities in the DTD of a source document.

Signature

unparsed-entity-public-id (name)

Parameter

Name	Description	Type	Use
name	The XML name of the entity	xs:string	Required

XSLT 2.0 Schema

This schema for XSLT 2.0 stylesheets is also published at www.w3.org/2007/schema-for-xslt20.xsd.

The W3C Document License follows the schema text.

```
<?xml version="1.0"?>
<xs:schema xmlns:xs="http://www.w3.org/2001/XMLSchema"
           xmlns:xsl="http://www.w3.org/1999/XSL/Transform"
           targetNamespace="http://www.w3.org/1999/XSL/Transform"
           elementFormDefault="qualified" >

<!-- ++++++++++++++++++++++++++++++++++++++++++++++++++++++++++++++++
+++++++++++++++++++++++ -->
<xs:annotation>
  <xs:documentation>

    This is a schema for XSLT 2.0 stylesheets.

    It defines all the elements that appear in the XSLT namespace; it also
provides hooks that allow the inclusion of user-defined literal result elements,
extension instructions, and top-level data elements.

    The schema is derived (with kind permission) from a schema for XSLT 1.0
stylesheets produced by Asir S Vedamuthu of WebMethods Inc.

    This schema is available for use under the conditions of the W3C Software
License published at http://www.w3.org/Consortium/Legal/2002/
copyright-documents-20021231

    The schema is organized as follows:

    PART A: definitions of complex types and model groups used as the basis for
element definitions
    PART B: definitions of individual XSLT elements
    PART C: definitions for literal result elements
    PART D: definitions of simple types used in attribute definitions
```

This schema does not attempt to define all the constraints that apply to a valid XSLT 2.0 stylesheet module. It is the intention that all valid stylesheet modules should conform to this schema; however, the schema is non-normative and in the event of any conflict, the text of the Recommendation takes precedence.

This schema does not implement the special rules that apply when a stylesheet has sections that use forwards-compatible-mode. In this mode, setting version="3.0" allows elements from the XSLT namespace to be used that are not defined in XSLT 2.0.

Simplified stylesheets (those with a literal result element as the outermost element) will validate against this schema only if validation starts in lax mode.

This version is dated 2007-03-16
Authors: Michael H Kay, Saxonica Limited
         Jeni Tennison, Jeni Tennison Consulting Ltd.

2007-03-15: added xsl:document element
            revised xsl:sequence element
            see http://www.w3.org/Bugs/Public/show_bug.cgi?id=4237

```
    </xs:documentation>
  </xs:annotation>
  <!-- ++++++++++++++++++++++++++++++++++++++++++++++++++++++++++++++++++
++++++++++++++++++++ -->

  <!--
The declaration of xml:space and xml:lang may need to be commented out because of
problems processing the schema using various tools
-->

<xs:import namespace="http://www.w3.org/XML/1998/namespace"
  schemaLocation="http://www.w3.org/2001/xml.xsd"/>

<!--
    An XSLT stylesheet may contain an in-line schema within an xsl:import-schema
element, so the Schema for schemas needs to be imported
-->

<xs:import namespace="http://www.w3.org/2001/XMLSchema"
                schemaLocation="http://www.w3.org/2001/XMLSchema.xsd"/>

<!-- ++++++++++++++++++++++++++++++++++++++++++++++++++++++++++++++++++
++++++++++++++++++++ -->
<xs:annotation>
  <xs:documentation>
    PART A: definitions of complex types and model groups used as the basis for element
definitions
  </xs:documentation>
</xs:annotation>
<!-- ++++++++++++++++++++++++++++++++++++++++++++++++++++++++++++++++++
++++++++++++++++++++ -->

<xs:complexType name="generic-element-type" mixed="true">
  <xs:attribute name="default-collation" type="xsl:uri-list"/>
```

```xml
      <xs:attribute name="exclude-result-prefixes" type="xsl:prefix-list-or-all"/>
      <xs:attribute name="extension-element-prefixes" type="xsl:prefix-list"/>
      <xs:attribute name="use-when" type="xsl:expression"/>
      <xs:attribute name="xpath-default-namespace" type="xs:anyURI"/>
      <xs:anyAttribute namespace="##other" processContents="lax"/>
</xs:complexType>

<xs:complexType name="versioned-element-type" mixed="true">
  <xs:complexContent>
    <xs:extension base="xsl:generic-element-type">
      <xs:attribute name="version" type="xs:decimal" use="optional"/>
    </xs:extension>
  </xs:complexContent>
</xs:complexType>

<xs:complexType name="element-only-versioned-element-type" mixed="false">
  <xs:complexContent>
    <xs:restriction base="xsl:versioned-element-type">
      <xs:anyAttribute namespace="##other" processContents="lax"/>
    </xs:restriction>
  </xs:complexContent>
</xs:complexType>

<xs:complexType name="sequence-constructor">
  <xs:complexContent mixed="true">
    <xs:extension base="xsl:versioned-element-type">
      <xs:group ref="xsl:sequence-constructor-group" minOccurs="0"
maxOccurs="unbounded"/>
    </xs:extension>
  </xs:complexContent>
</xs:complexType>

<xs:group name="sequence-constructor-group">
  <xs:choice>
    <xs:element ref="xsl:variable"/>
    <xs:element ref="xsl:instruction"/>
    <xs:group ref="xsl:result-elements"/>
  </xs:choice>
</xs:group>

<xs:element name="declaration" type="xsl:generic-element-type" abstract="true"/>

<xs:element name="instruction" type="xsl:versioned-element-type" abstract="true"/>

<!-- ++++++++++++++++++++++++++++++++++++++++++++++++++++++++++++++
++++++++++++++++++++ -->
<xs:annotation>
  <xs:documentation>
    PART B: definitions of individual XSLT elements
    Elements are listed in alphabetical order.
  </xs:documentation>
</xs:annotation>
<!-- ++++++++++++++++++++++++++++++++++++++++++++++++++++++++++++++
++++++++++++++++++++ -->
```

317

```
<xs:element name="analyze-string" substitutionGroup="xsl:instruction">
  <xs:complexType>
    <xs:complexContent>
      <xs:extension base="xsl:element-only-versioned-element-type">
        <xs:sequence>
          <xs:element ref="xsl:matching-substring" minOccurs="0"/>
          <xs:element ref="xsl:non-matching-substring" minOccurs="0"/>
          <xs:element ref="xsl:fallback" minOccurs="0" maxOccurs="unbounded"/>
        </xs:sequence>
        <xs:attribute name="select" type="xsl:expression" use="required"/>
        <xs:attribute name="regex" type="xsl:avt" use="required"/>
        <xs:attribute name="flags" type="xsl:avt" default=""/>
      </xs:extension>
    </xs:complexContent>
  </xs:complexType>
</xs:element>

<xs:element name="apply-imports" substitutionGroup="xsl:instruction">
  <xs:complexType>
    <xs:complexContent>
      <xs:extension base="xsl:element-only-versioned-element-type">
        <xs:sequence>
          <xs:element ref="xsl:with-param" minOccurs="0" maxOccurs="unbounded"/>
        </xs:sequence>
      </xs:extension>
    </xs:complexContent>
  </xs:complexType>
</xs:element>

<xs:element name="apply-templates" substitutionGroup="xsl:instruction">
  <xs:complexType>
    <xs:complexContent>
      <xs:extension base="xsl:element-only-versioned-element-type">
        <xs:choice minOccurs="0" maxOccurs="unbounded">
          <xs:element ref="xsl:sort"/>
          <xs:element ref="xsl:with-param"/>
        </xs:choice>
        <xs:attribute name="select" type="xsl:expression" default="child::node()"/>
        <xs:attribute name="mode" type="xsl:mode"/>
      </xs:extension>
    </xs:complexContent>
  </xs:complexType>
</xs:element>

<xs:element name="attribute" substitutionGroup="xsl:instruction">
  <xs:complexType>
    <xs:complexContent mixed="true">
      <xs:extension base="xsl:sequence-constructor">
        <xs:attribute name="name" type="xsl:avt" use="required"/>
        <xs:attribute name="namespace" type="xsl:avt"/>
        <xs:attribute name="select" type="xsl:expression"/>
        <xs:attribute name="separator" type="xsl:avt"/>
        <xs:attribute name="type" type="xsl:QName"/>
        <xs:attribute name="validation" type="xsl:validation-type"/>
      </xs:extension>
```

```
      </xs:complexContent>
    </xs:complexType>
</xs:element>

<xs:element name="attribute-set" substitutionGroup="xsl:declaration">
  <xs:complexType>
    <xs:complexContent>
      <xs:extension base="xsl:element-only-versioned-element-type">
        <xs:sequence minOccurs="0" maxOccurs="unbounded">
          <xs:element ref="xsl:attribute"/>
        </xs:sequence>
        <xs:attribute name="name" type="xsl:QName" use="required"/>
        <xs:attribute name="use-attribute-sets" type="xsl:QNames" default=""/>
      </xs:extension>
    </xs:complexContent>
  </xs:complexType>
</xs:element>

<xs:element name="call-template" substitutionGroup="xsl:instruction">
  <xs:complexType>
    <xs:complexContent>
      <xs:extension base="xsl:element-only-versioned-element-type">
        <xs:sequence>
          <xs:element ref="xsl:with-param" minOccurs="0" maxOccurs="unbounded"/>
        </xs:sequence>
        <xs:attribute name="name" type="xsl:QName" use="required"/>
      </xs:extension>
    </xs:complexContent>
  </xs:complexType>
</xs:element>

<xs:element name="character-map" substitutionGroup="xsl:declaration">
  <xs:complexType>
    <xs:complexContent>
      <xs:extension base="xsl:element-only-versioned-element-type">
        <xs:sequence>
          <xs:element ref="xsl:output-character" minOccurs="0"
maxOccurs="unbounded"/>
        </xs:sequence>
        <xs:attribute name="name" type="xsl:QName" use="required"/>
        <xs:attribute name="use-character-maps" type="xsl:QNames" default=""/>
      </xs:extension>
    </xs:complexContent>
  </xs:complexType>
</xs:element>

<xs:element name="choose" substitutionGroup="xsl:instruction">
  <xs:complexType>
    <xs:complexContent>
      <xs:extension base="xsl:element-only-versioned-element-type">
        <xs:sequence>
          <xs:element ref="xsl:when" maxOccurs="unbounded"/>
          <xs:element ref="xsl:otherwise" minOccurs="0"/>
        </xs:sequence>
      </xs:extension>
```

```
      </xs:complexContent>
    </xs:complexType>
</xs:element>

<xs:element name="comment" substitutionGroup="xsl:instruction">
  <xs:complexType>
    <xs:complexContent mixed="true">
      <xs:extension base="xsl:sequence-constructor">
        <xs:attribute name="select" type="xsl:expression"/>
      </xs:extension>
    </xs:complexContent>
  </xs:complexType>
</xs:element>

<xs:element name="copy" substitutionGroup="xsl:instruction">
  <xs:complexType>
    <xs:complexContent mixed="true">
      <xs:extension base="xsl:sequence-constructor">
        <xs:attribute name="copy-namespaces" type="xsl:yes-or-no" default="yes"/>
        <xs:attribute name="inherit-namespaces" type="xsl:yes-or-no" default="yes"/>
        <xs:attribute name="use-attribute-sets" type="xsl:QNames" default=""/>
        <xs:attribute name="type" type="xsl:QName"/>
        <xs:attribute name="validation" type="xsl:validation-type"/>
      </xs:extension>
    </xs:complexContent>
  </xs:complexType>
</xs:element>

<xs:element name="copy-of" substitutionGroup="xsl:instruction">
  <xs:complexType>
    <xs:complexContent mixed="true">
      <xs:extension base="xsl:versioned-element-type">
        <xs:attribute name="select" type="xsl:expression" use="required"/>
        <xs:attribute name="copy-namespaces" type="xsl:yes-or-no" default="yes"/>
        <xs:attribute name="type" type="xsl:QName"/>
        <xs:attribute name="validation" type="xsl:validation-type"/>
      </xs:extension>
    </xs:complexContent>
  </xs:complexType>
</xs:element>

<xs:element name="document" substitutionGroup="xsl:instruction">
  <xs:complexType>
    <xs:complexContent mixed="true">
      <xs:extension base="xsl:sequence-constructor">
        <xs:attribute name="type" type="xsl:QName"/>
        <xs:attribute name="validation" type="xsl:validation-type"/>
      </xs:extension>
    </xs:complexContent>
  </xs:complexType>
</xs:element>

<xs:element name="decimal-format" substitutionGroup="xsl:declaration">
  <xs:complexType>
    <xs:complexContent>
```

```xml
          <xs:extension base="xsl:element-only-versioned-element-type">
            <xs:attribute name="name" type="xsl:QName"/>
            <xs:attribute name="decimal-separator" type="xsl:char" default="."/>
            <xs:attribute name="grouping-separator" type="xsl:char" default=","/>
            <xs:attribute name="infinity" type="xs:string" default="Infinity"/>
            <xs:attribute name="minus-sign" type="xsl:char" default="-"/>
            <xs:attribute name="NaN" type="xs:string" default="NaN"/>
            <xs:attribute name="percent" type="xsl:char" default="%"/>
            <xs:attribute name="per-mille" type="xsl:char" default="&#x2030;"/>
            <xs:attribute name="zero-digit" type="xsl:char" default="0"/>
            <xs:attribute name="digit" type="xsl:char" default="#"/>
            <xs:attribute name="pattern-separator" type="xsl:char" default=";"/>
          </xs:extension>
        </xs:complexContent>
      </xs:complexType>
    </xs:element>

    <xs:element name="element" substitutionGroup="xsl:instruction">
      <xs:complexType mixed="true">
        <xs:complexContent>
          <xs:extension base="xsl:sequence-constructor">
            <xs:attribute name="name" type="xsl:avt" use="required"/>
            <xs:attribute name="namespace" type="xsl:avt"/>
            <xs:attribute name="inherit-namespaces" type="xsl:yes-or-no" default="yes"/>
            <xs:attribute name="use-attribute-sets" type="xsl:QNames" default=""/>
            <xs:attribute name="type" type="xsl:QName"/>
            <xs:attribute name="validation" type="xsl:validation-type"/>
          </xs:extension>
        </xs:complexContent>
      </xs:complexType>
    </xs:element>

    <xs:element name="fallback" substitutionGroup="xsl:instruction"
    type="xsl:sequence-constructor"/>

    <xs:element name="for-each" substitutionGroup="xsl:instruction">
      <xs:complexType>
        <xs:complexContent mixed="true">
          <xs:extension base="xsl:versioned-element-type">
            <xs:sequence>
              <xs:element ref="xsl:sort" minOccurs="0" maxOccurs="unbounded"/>
              <xs:group ref="xsl:sequence-constructor-group"
    minOccurs="0" maxOccurs="unbounded"/>
            </xs:sequence>
            <xs:attribute name="select" type="xsl:expression" use="required"/>
          </xs:extension>
        </xs:complexContent>
      </xs:complexType>
    </xs:element>

    <xs:element name="for-each-group" substitutionGroup="xsl:instruction">
      <xs:complexType>
        <xs:complexContent mixed="true">
          <xs:extension base="xsl:versioned-element-type">
            <xs:sequence>
```

```
                    <xs:element ref="xsl:sort" minOccurs="0" maxOccurs="unbounded"/>
                    <xs:group ref="xsl:sequence-constructor-group" minOccurs="0"
    maxOccurs="unbounded"/>
            </xs:sequence>
            <xs:attribute name="select" type="xsl:expression" use="required"/>
            <xs:attribute name="group-by" type="xsl:expression"/>
            <xs:attribute name="group-adjacent" type="xsl:expression"/>
            <xs:attribute name="group-starting-with" type="xsl:pattern"/>
            <xs:attribute name="group-ending-with" type="xsl:pattern"/>
            <xs:attribute name="collation" type="xs:anyURI"/>
          </xs:extension>
        </xs:complexContent>
      </xs:complexType>
    </xs:element>

    <xs:element name="function" substitutionGroup="xsl:declaration">
      <xs:complexType>
        <xs:complexContent mixed="true">
          <xs:extension base="xsl:versioned-element-type">
            <xs:sequence>
              <xs:element ref="xsl:param" minOccurs="0" maxOccurs="unbounded"/>
              <xs:group ref="xsl:sequence-constructor-group" minOccurs="0"
    maxOccurs="unbounded"/>
            </xs:sequence>
            <xs:attribute name="name" type="xsl:QName" use="required"/>
            <xs:attribute name="override" type="xsl:yes-or-no" default="yes"/>
            <xs:attribute name="as" type="xsl:sequence-type" default="item()*"/>
          </xs:extension>
        </xs:complexContent>
      </xs:complexType>
    </xs:element>

    <xs:element name="if" substitutionGroup="xsl:instruction">
      <xs:complexType>
        <xs:complexContent mixed="true">
          <xs:extension base="xsl:sequence-constructor">
            <xs:attribute name="test" type="xsl:expression" use="required"/>
          </xs:extension>
        </xs:complexContent>
      </xs:complexType>
    </xs:element>

    <xs:element name="import">
      <xs:complexType>
        <xs:complexContent>
          <xs:extension base="xsl:element-only-versioned-element-type">
            <xs:attribute name="href" type="xs:anyURI" use="required"/>
          </xs:extension>
        </xs:complexContent>
      </xs:complexType>
    </xs:element>

    <xs:element name="import-schema" substitutionGroup="xsl:declaration">
      <xs:complexType>
        <xs:complexContent>
```

```
        <xs:extension base="xsl:element-only-versioned-element-type">
          <xs:sequence>
            <xs:element ref="xs:schema" minOccurs="0" maxOccurs="1"/>
          </xs:sequence>
          <xs:attribute name="namespace" type="xs:anyURI"/>
          <xs:attribute name="schema-location" type="xs:anyURI"/>
        </xs:extension>
      </xs:complexContent>
    </xs:complexType>
</xs:element>

<xs:element name="include" substitutionGroup="xsl:declaration">
    <xs:complexType>
      <xs:complexContent>
        <xs:extension base="xsl:element-only-versioned-element-type">
          <xs:attribute name="href" type="xs:anyURI" use="required"/>
        </xs:extension>
      </xs:complexContent>
    </xs:complexType>
</xs:element>

<xs:element name="key" substitutionGroup="xsl:declaration">
  <xs:complexType>
    <xs:complexContent mixed="true">
      <xs:extension base="xsl:sequence-constructor">
        <xs:attribute name="name" type="xsl:QName" use="required"/>
        <xs:attribute name="match" type="xsl:pattern" use="required"/>
        <xs:attribute name="use" type="xsl:expression"/>
        <xs:attribute name="collation" type="xs:anyURI"/>
      </xs:extension>
    </xs:complexContent>
  </xs:complexType>
</xs:element>

<xs:element name="matching-substring" type="xsl:sequence-constructor"/>

<xs:element name="message" substitutionGroup="xsl:instruction">
  <xs:complexType>
    <xs:complexContent mixed="true">
      <xs:extension base="xsl:sequence-constructor">
        <xs:attribute name="select" type="xsl:expression"/>
        <xs:attribute name="terminate" type="xsl:avt" default="no"/>
      </xs:extension>
    </xs:complexContent>
  </xs:complexType>
</xs:element>

<xs:element name="namespace" substitutionGroup="xsl:instruction">
  <xs:complexType>
    <xs:complexContent mixed="true">
      <xs:extension base="xsl:sequence-constructor">
        <xs:attribute name="name" type="xsl:avt" use="required"/>
        <xs:attribute name="select" type="xsl:expression"/>
      </xs:extension>
    </xs:complexContent>
```

```
      </xs:complexType>
  </xs:element>

  <xs:element name="namespace-alias" substitutionGroup="xsl:declaration">
    <xs:complexType>
      <xs:complexContent>
        <xs:extension base="xsl:element-only-versioned-element-type">
          <xs:attribute name="stylesheet-prefix" type="xsl:prefix-or-default"
use="required"/>
          <xs:attribute name="result-prefix" type="xsl:prefix-or-default"
use="required"/>
        </xs:extension>
      </xs:complexContent>
    </xs:complexType>
  </xs:element>

  <xs:element name="next-match" substitutionGroup="xsl:instruction">
    <xs:complexType>
      <xs:complexContent>
        <xs:extension base="xsl:element-only-versioned-element-type">
          <xs:choice minOccurs="0" maxOccurs="unbounded">
            <xs:element ref="xsl:with-param"/>
            <xs:element ref="xsl:fallback"/>
          </xs:choice>
        </xs:extension>
      </xs:complexContent>
    </xs:complexType>
  </xs:element>

  <xs:element name="non-matching-substring" type="xsl:sequence-constructor"/>

  <xs:element name="number" substitutionGroup="xsl:instruction">
    <xs:complexType>
      <xs:complexContent mixed="true">
        <xs:extension base="xsl:versioned-element-type">
          <xs:attribute name="value" type="xsl:expression"/>
          <xs:attribute name="select" type="xsl:expression"/>
          <xs:attribute name="level" type="xsl:level" default="single"/>
          <xs:attribute name="count" type="xsl:pattern"/>
          <xs:attribute name="from" type="xsl:pattern"/>
          <xs:attribute name="format" type="xsl:avt" default="1"/>
          <xs:attribute name="lang" type="xsl:avt"/>
          <xs:attribute name="letter-value" type="xsl:avt"/>
          <xs:attribute name="ordinal" type="xsl:avt"/>
          <xs:attribute name="grouping-separator" type="xsl:avt"/>
          <xs:attribute name="grouping-size" type="xsl:avt"/>
        </xs:extension>
      </xs:complexContent>
    </xs:complexType>
  </xs:element>

  <xs:element name="otherwise" type="xsl:sequence-constructor"/>

  <xs:element name="output" substitutionGroup="xsl:declaration">
    <xs:complexType>
```

```
          <xs:complexContent mixed="true">
            <xs:extension base="xsl:generic-element-type">
              <xs:attribute name="name" type="xsl:QName"/>
              <xs:attribute name="method" type="xsl:method"/>
              <xs:attribute name="byte-order-mark" type="xsl:yes-or-no"/>
              <xs:attribute name="cdata-section-elements" type="xsl:QNames"/>
              <xs:attribute name="doctype-public" type="xs:string"/>
              <xs:attribute name="doctype-system" type="xs:string"/>
              <xs:attribute name="encoding" type="xs:string"/>
              <xs:attribute name="escape-uri-attributes" type="xsl:yes-or-no"/>
              <xs:attribute name="include-content-type" type="xsl:yes-or-no"/>
              <xs:attribute name="indent" type="xsl:yes-or-no"/>
              <xs:attribute name="media-type" type="xs:string"/>
              <xs:attribute name="normalization-form" type="xs:NMTOKEN"/>
              <xs:attribute name="omit-xml-declaration" type="xsl:yes-or-no"/>
              <xs:attribute name="standalone" type="xsl:yes-or-no-or-omit"/>
              <xs:attribute name="undeclare-prefixes" type="xsl:yes-or-no"/>
              <xs:attribute name="use-character-maps" type="xsl:QNames"/>
              <xs:attribute name="version" type="xs:NMTOKEN"/>
            </xs:extension>
          </xs:complexContent>
        </xs:complexType>
    </xs:element>

    <xs:element name="output-character">
      <xs:complexType>
        <xs:complexContent>
            <xs:extension base="xsl:element-only-versioned-element-type">
              <xs:attribute name="character" type="xsl:char" use="required"/>
              <xs:attribute name="string" type="xs:string" use="required"/>
            </xs:extension>
        </xs:complexContent>
      </xs:complexType>
    </xs:element>

    <xs:element name="param">
      <xs:complexType>
        <xs:complexContent mixed="true">
            <xs:extension base="xsl:sequence-constructor">
              <xs:attribute name="name" type="xsl:QName" use="required"/>
              <xs:attribute name="select" type="xsl:expression"/>
              <xs:attribute name="as" type="xsl:sequence-type"/>
              <xs:attribute name="required" type="xsl:yes-or-no"/>
              <xs:attribute name="tunnel" type="xsl:yes-or-no"/>
            </xs:extension>
        </xs:complexContent>
      </xs:complexType>
    </xs:element>

    <xs:element name="perform-sort" substitutionGroup="xsl:instruction">
      <xs:complexType>
        <xs:complexContent mixed="true">
          <xs:extension base="xsl:versioned-element-type">
            <xs:sequence>
              <xs:element ref="xsl:sort" minOccurs="1" maxOccurs="unbounded"/>
```

```
              <xs:group ref="xsl:sequence-constructor-group" minOccurs="0"
maxOccurs="unbounded"/>
            </xs:sequence>
          <xs:attribute name="select" type="xsl:expression"/>
        </xs:extension>
      </xs:complexContent>
    </xs:complexType>
  </xs:element>

  <xs:element name="preserve-space" substitutionGroup="xsl:declaration">
    <xs:complexType>
      <xs:complexContent>
        <xs:extension base="xsl:element-only-versioned-element-type">
          <xs:attribute name="elements" type="xsl:nametests" use="required"/>
        </xs:extension>
      </xs:complexContent>
    </xs:complexType>
  </xs:element>

  <xs:element name="processing-instruction" substitutionGroup="xsl:instruction">
    <xs:complexType>
      <xs:complexContent mixed="true">
        <xs:extension base="xsl:sequence-constructor">
          <xs:attribute name="name" type="xsl:avt" use="required"/>
          <xs:attribute name="select" type="xsl:expression"/>
        </xs:extension>
      </xs:complexContent>
    </xs:complexType>
  </xs:element>

  <xs:element name="result-document" substitutionGroup="xsl:instruction">
    <xs:complexType>
      <xs:complexContent mixed="true">
        <xs:extension base="xsl:sequence-constructor">
          <xs:attribute name="format" type="xsl:avt"/>
          <xs:attribute name="href" type="xsl:avt"/>
          <xs:attribute name="type" type="xsl:QName"/>
          <xs:attribute name="validation" type="xsl:validation-type"/>
          <xs:attribute name="method" type="xsl:avt"/>
          <xs:attribute name="byte-order-mark" type="xsl:avt"/>
          <xs:attribute name="cdata-section-elements" type="xsl:avt"/>
          <xs:attribute name="doctype-public" type="xsl:avt"/>
          <xs:attribute name="doctype-system" type="xsl:avt"/>
          <xs:attribute name="encoding" type="xsl:avt"/>
          <xs:attribute name="escape-uri-attributes" type="xsl:avt"/>
          <xs:attribute name="include-content-type" type="xsl:avt"/>
          <xs:attribute name="indent" type="xsl:avt"/>
          <xs:attribute name="media-type" type="xsl:avt"/>
          <xs:attribute name="normalization-form" type="xsl:avt"/>
          <xs:attribute name="omit-xml-declaration" type="xsl:avt"/>
          <xs:attribute name="standalone" type="xsl:avt"/>
          <xs:attribute name="undeclare-prefixes" type="xsl:avt"/>
          <xs:attribute name="use-character-maps" type="xsl:QNames"/>
          <xs:attribute name="output-version" type="xsl:avt"/>
        </xs:extension>
```

```
      </xs:complexContent>
    </xs:complexType>
  </xs:element>

  <xs:element name="sequence" substitutionGroup="xsl:instruction">
    <xs:complexType>
      <xs:complexContent mixed="true">
        <xs:extension base="xsl:element-only-versioned-element-type">
          <xs:sequence minOccurs="0" maxOccurs="unbounded">
            <xs:element ref="xsl:fallback"/>
          </xs:sequence>
          <xs:attribute name="select" type="xsl:expression"/>
        </xs:extension>
      </xs:complexContent>
    </xs:complexType>
  </xs:element>

  <xs:element name="sort">
    <xs:complexType>
      <xs:complexContent mixed="true">
        <xs:extension base="xsl:sequence-constructor">
          <xs:attribute name="select" type="xsl:expression"/>
          <xs:attribute name="lang" type="xsl:avt"/>
          <xs:attribute name="data-type" type="xsl:avt" default="text"/>
          <xs:attribute name="order" type="xsl:avt" default="ascending"/>
          <xs:attribute name="case-order" type="xsl:avt"/>
          <xs:attribute name="collation" type="xsl:avt"/>
          <xs:attribute name="stable" type="xsl:yes-or-no"/>
        </xs:extension>
      </xs:complexContent>
    </xs:complexType>
  </xs:element>

  <xs:element name="strip-space" substitutionGroup="xsl:declaration">
    <xs:complexType>
      <xs:complexContent>
        <xs:extension base="xsl:element-only-versioned-element-type">
          <xs:attribute name="elements" type="xsl:nametests" use="required"/>
        </xs:extension>
      </xs:complexContent>
    </xs:complexType>
  </xs:element>

  <xs:element name="stylesheet" substitutionGroup="xsl:transform"/>

  <xs:element name="template" substitutionGroup="xsl:declaration">
    <xs:complexType>
      <xs:complexContent mixed="true">
        <xs:extension base="xsl:versioned-element-type">
          <xs:sequence>
            <xs:element ref="xsl:param" minOccurs="0" maxOccurs="unbounded"/>
            <xs:group ref="xsl:sequence-constructor-group" minOccurs="0"
maxOccurs="unbounded"/>
          </xs:sequence>
          <xs:attribute name="match" type="xsl:pattern"/>
```

```
            <xs:attribute name="priority" type="xs:decimal"/>
            <xs:attribute name="mode" type="xsl:modes"/>
            <xs:attribute name="name" type="xsl:QName"/>
            <xs:attribute name="as" type="xsl:sequence-type" default="item()*"/>
          </xs:extension>
        </xs:complexContent>
      </xs:complexType>
</xs:element>

<xs:complexType name="text-element-base-type">
  <xs:simpleContent>
    <xs:restriction base="xsl:versioned-element-type">
      <xs:simpleType>
        <xs:restriction base="xs:string"/>
      </xs:simpleType>
      <xs:anyAttribute namespace="##other" processContents="lax"/>
    </xs:restriction>
  </xs:simpleContent>
</xs:complexType>

<xs:element name="text" substitutionGroup="xsl:instruction">
  <xs:complexType>
    <xs:simpleContent>
      <xs:extension base="xsl:text-element-base-type">
        <xs:attribute name="disable-output-escaping" type="xsl:yes-or-no"
default="no"/>
      </xs:extension>
    </xs:simpleContent>
  </xs:complexType>
</xs:element>

<xs:complexType name="transform-element-base-type">
  <xs:complexContent>
    <xs:restriction base="xsl:element-only-versioned-element-type">
      <xs:attribute name="version" type="xs:decimal" use="required"/>
      <xs:anyAttribute namespace="##other" processContents="lax"/>
    </xs:restriction>
  </xs:complexContent>
</xs:complexType>

<xs:element name="transform">
  <xs:complexType>
    <xs:complexContent>
      <xs:extension base="xsl:transform-element-base-type">
        <xs:sequence>
          <xs:element ref="xsl:import" minOccurs="0" maxOccurs="unbounded"/>
          <xs:choice minOccurs="0" maxOccurs="unbounded">
            <xs:element ref="xsl:declaration"/>
            <xs:element ref="xsl:variable"/>
            <xs:element ref="xsl:param"/>
            <xs:any namespace="##other" processContents="lax"/>
<!-- weaker than XSLT 1.0 -->
          </xs:choice>
        </xs:sequence>
        <xs:attribute name="id" type="xs:ID"/>
```

```
        <xs:attribute name="default-validation"
type="xsl:validation-strip-or-preserve" default="strip"/>
        <xs:attribute name="input-type-annotations"
type="xsl:input-type-annotations-type" default="unspecified"/>
      </xs:extension>
    </xs:complexContent>
  </xs:complexType>
</xs:element>

<xs:element name="value-of" substitutionGroup="xsl:instruction">
  <xs:complexType>
    <xs:complexContent mixed="true">
      <xs:extension base="xsl:sequence-constructor">
        <xs:attribute name="select" type="xsl:expression"/>
        <xs:attribute name="separator" type="xsl:avt"/>
        <xs:attribute name="disable-output-escaping"
type="xsl:yes-or-no" default="no"/>
      </xs:extension>
    </xs:complexContent>
  </xs:complexType>
</xs:element>

<xs:element name="variable">
  <xs:complexType>
    <xs:complexContent mixed="true">
      <xs:extension base="xsl:sequence-constructor">
        <xs:attribute name="name" type="xsl:QName" use="required"/>
        <xs:attribute name="select" type="xsl:expression" use="optional"/>
        <xs:attribute name="as" type="xsl:sequence-type" use="optional"/>
      </xs:extension>
    </xs:complexContent>
  </xs:complexType>
</xs:element>

<xs:element name="when">
  <xs:complexType>
    <xs:complexContent mixed="true">
      <xs:extension base="xsl:sequence-constructor">
        <xs:attribute name="test" type="xsl:expression" use="required"/>
      </xs:extension>
    </xs:complexContent>
  </xs:complexType>
</xs:element>

<xs:element name="with-param">
  <xs:complexType>
    <xs:complexContent mixed="true">
      <xs:extension base="xsl:sequence-constructor">
        <xs:attribute name="name" type="xsl:QName" use="required"/>
        <xs:attribute name="select" type="xsl:expression"/>
        <xs:attribute name="as" type="xsl:sequence-type"/>
        <xs:attribute name="tunnel" type="xsl:yes-or-no"/>
      </xs:extension>
    </xs:complexContent>
  </xs:complexType>
</xs:element>
```

```
<!-- +++++++++++++++++++++++++++++++++++++++++++++++++++++++++++++++
+++++++++++++++++++ -->
<xs:annotation>
  <xs:documentation>
    PART C: definition of literal result elements

    There are three ways to define the literal result elements
    permissible in a stylesheet.

    (a) do nothing. This allows any element to be used as a literal
        result element, provided it is not in the XSLT namespace

    (b) declare all permitted literal result elements as members
        of the xsl:literal-result-element substitution group

    (c) redefine the model group xsl:result-elements to accommodate
        all permitted literal result elements.

    Literal result elements are allowed to take certain attributes
    in the XSLT namespace. These are defined in the attribute group
    literal-result-element-attributes, which can be included in the
    definition of any literal result element.

  </xs:documentation>
</xs:annotation>
<!-- +++++++++++++++++++++++++++++++++++++++++++++++++++++++++++++++
+++++++++++++++++++ -->

<xs:element name="literal-result-element" abstract="true" type="xs:anyType"/>

<xs:attributeGroup name="literal-result-element-attributes">
  <xs:attribute name="default-collation" form="qualified" type="xsl:uri-list"/>
  <xs:attribute name="extension-element-prefixes" form="qualified"
type="xsl:prefixes"/>
  <xs:attribute name="exclude-result-prefixes" form="qualified"
type="xsl:prefixes"/>
  <xs:attribute name="xpath-default-namespace" form="qualified" type="xs:anyURI"/>
  <xs:attribute name="inherit-namespaces" form="qualified" type="xsl:yes-or-no"
default="yes"/>
  <xs:attribute name="use-attribute-sets" form="qualified" type="xsl:QNames"
default=""/>
  <xs:attribute name="use-when" form="qualified" type="xsl:expression"/>
  <xs:attribute name="version" form="qualified" type="xs:decimal"/>
  <xs:attribute name="type" form="qualified" type="xsl:QName"/>
  <xs:attribute name="validation" form="qualified" type="xsl:validation-type"/>
</xs:attributeGroup>

<xs:group name="result-elements">
  <xs:choice>
    <xs:element ref="xsl:literal-result-element"/>
    <xs:any namespace="##other" processContents="lax"/>
    <xs:any namespace="##local" processContents="lax"/>
  </xs:choice>
</xs:group>
```

```
<!-- ++++++++++++++++++++++++++++++++++++++++++++++++++++++++++++
+++++++++++++++++++ -->
<xs:annotation>
  <xs:documentation>
    PART D: definitions of simple types used in stylesheet attributes
  </xs:documentation>
</xs:annotation>
<!-- ++++++++++++++++++++++++++++++++++++++++++++++++++++++++++++
+++++++++++++++++++ -->

<xs:simpleType name="avt">
  <xs:annotation>
    <xs:documentation>
      This type is used for all attributes that allow an attribute value template.
      The general rules for the syntax of attribute value templates, and the specific
rules for each such attribute, are described in the XSLT 2.0 Recommendation.
    </xs:documentation>
  </xs:annotation>
  <xs:restriction base="xs:string"/>
</xs:simpleType>

<xs:simpleType name="char">
  <xs:annotation>
    <xs:documentation>
      A string containing exactly one character.
    </xs:documentation>
  </xs:annotation>
  <xs:restriction base="xs:string">
    <xs:length value="1"/>
  </xs:restriction>
</xs:simpleType>

<xs:simpleType name="expression">
  <xs:annotation>
    <xs:documentation>
      An XPath 2.0 expression.
    </xs:documentation>
  </xs:annotation>
  <xs:restriction base="xs:token">
    <xs:pattern value=".+"/>
  </xs:restriction>
</xs:simpleType>

<xs:simpleType name="input-type-annotations-type">
  <xs:annotation>
    <xs:documentation>
      Describes how type annotations in source documents are handled.
    </xs:documentation>
  </xs:annotation>
  <xs:restriction base="xs:token">
    <xs:enumeration value="preserve"/>
    <xs:enumeration value="strip"/>
    <xs:enumeration value="unspecified"/>
  </xs:restriction>
</xs:simpleType>
```

```
<xs:simpleType name="level">
  <xs:annotation>
    <xs:documentation>
      The level attribute of xsl:number: one of single, multiple, or any.
    </xs:documentation>
  </xs:annotation>
  <xs:restriction base="xs:NCName">
    <xs:enumeration value="single"/>
    <xs:enumeration value="multiple"/>
    <xs:enumeration value="any"/>
  </xs:restriction>
</xs:simpleType>

<xs:simpleType name="mode">
  <xs:annotation>
    <xs:documentation>
      The mode attribute of xsl:apply-templates: either a QName, or #current,
or #default.
    </xs:documentation>
  </xs:annotation>
  <xs:union memberTypes="xsl:QName">
    <xs:simpleType>
      <xs:restriction base="xs:token">
        <xs:enumeration value="#default"/>
        <xs:enumeration value="#current"/>
      </xs:restriction>
    </xs:simpleType>
  </xs:union>
</xs:simpleType>

<xs:simpleType name="modes">
  <xs:annotation>
    <xs:documentation>
      The mode attribute of xsl:template: either a list, each member being either
a QName or #default; or the value #all
    </xs:documentation>
  </xs:annotation>
  <xs:union>
    <xs:simpleType>
      <xs:list>
        <xs:simpleType>
          <xs:union memberTypes="xsl:QName">
            <xs:simpleType>
              <xs:restriction base="xs:token">
                <xs:enumeration value="#default"/>
              </xs:restriction>
            </xs:simpleType>
          </xs:union>
        </xs:simpleType>
      </xs:list>
    </xs:simpleType>
    <xs:simpleType>
      <xs:restriction base="xs:token">
        <xs:enumeration value="#all"/>
      </xs:restriction>
```

```xml
        </xs:simpleType>
      </xs:union>
    </xs:simpleType>

    <xs:simpleType name="nametests">
      <xs:annotation>
        <xs:documentation>
          A list of NameTests, as defined in the XPath 2.0 Recommendation.
          Each NameTest is either a QName, or "*", or "prefix:*", or "*:localname"
        </xs:documentation>
      </xs:annotation>
      <xs:list>
        <xs:simpleType>
          <xs:union memberTypes="xsl:QName">
            <xs:simpleType>
              <xs:restriction base="xs:token">
                <xs:enumeration value="*"/>
              </xs:restriction>
            </xs:simpleType>
            <xs:simpleType>
              <xs:restriction base="xs:token">
                <xs:pattern value="\i\c*:\*"/>
                <xs:pattern value="\*:\i\c*"/>
              </xs:restriction>
            </xs:simpleType>
          </xs:union>
        </xs:simpleType>
      </xs:list>
    </xs:simpleType>

    <xs:simpleType name="prefixes">
      <xs:list itemType="xs:NCName"/>
    </xs:simpleType>

    <xs:simpleType name="prefix-list-or-all">
      <xs:union memberTypes="xsl:prefix-list">
        <xs:simpleType>
          <xs:restriction base="xs:token">
            <xs:enumeration value="#all"/>
          </xs:restriction>
        </xs:simpleType>
      </xs:union>
    </xs:simpleType>

    <xs:simpleType name="prefix-list">
      <xs:list itemType="xsl:prefix-or-default"/>
    </xs:simpleType>

    <xs:simpleType name="method">
      <xs:annotation>
        <xs:documentation>
          The method attribute of xsl:output:
          Either one of the recognized names "xml", "xhtml", "html", "text",
          or a QName that must include a prefix.
        </xs:documentation>
```

```
      </xs:annotation>
      <xs:union>
        <xs:simpleType>
          <xs:restriction base="xs:NCName">
            <xs:enumeration value="xml"/>
            <xs:enumeration value="xhtml"/>
            <xs:enumeration value="html"/>
            <xs:enumeration value="text"/>
          </xs:restriction>
        </xs:simpleType>
        <xs:simpleType>
          <xs:restriction base="xsl:QName">
            <xs:pattern value="\c*:\c*"/>
          </xs:restriction>
        </xs:simpleType>
      </xs:union>
    </xs:simpleType>

    <xs:simpleType name="pattern">
      <xs:annotation>
        <xs:documentation>
          A match pattern as defined in the XSLT 2.0 Recommendation.
          The syntax for patterns is a restricted form of the syntax for
          XPath 2.0 expressions.
        </xs:documentation>
      </xs:annotation>
      <xs:restriction base="xsl:expression"/>
    </xs:simpleType>

    <xs:simpleType name="prefix-or-default">
      <xs:annotation>
        <xs:documentation>
          Either a namespace prefix, or #default.
          Used in the xsl:namespace-alias element.
        </xs:documentation>
      </xs:annotation>
      <xs:union memberTypes="xs:NCName">
        <xs:simpleType>
          <xs:restriction base="xs:token">
            <xs:enumeration value="#default"/>
          </xs:restriction>
        </xs:simpleType>
      </xs:union>
    </xs:simpleType>

    <xs:simpleType name="QNames">
      <xs:annotation>
        <xs:documentation>
          A list of QNames.
          Used in the [xsl:]use-attribute-sets attribute of various elements, and in the
cdata-section-elements attribute of xsl:output
        </xs:documentation>
      </xs:annotation>
      <xs:list itemType="xsl:QName"/>
    </xs:simpleType>
```

```
<xs:simpleType name="QName">
  <xs:annotation>
    <xs:documentation>
      A QName. This schema does not use the built-in type xs:QName, but rather defines
its own QName type. Although xs:QName would define the correct validation on these
attributes, a schema processor would expand unprefixed QNames incorrectly when
constructing the PSVI, because (as defined in XML Schema errata) an unprefixed
xs:QName is assumed to be in the default namespace, which is not the correct assumption
for XSLT.
      The data type is defined as a restriction of the built-in type Name, restricted
so that it can only contain one colon which must not be the first or last character.
    </xs:documentation>
  </xs:annotation>
  <xs:restriction base="xs:Name">
    <xs:pattern value="([^:]+:)?[^:]+"/>
  </xs:restriction>
</xs:simpleType>

<xs:simpleType name="sequence-type">
  <xs:annotation>
    <xs:documentation>
    The description of a data type, conforming to the SequenceType production defined
in the XPath 2.0 Recommendation
    </xs:documentation>
  </xs:annotation>
  <xs:restriction base="xs:token">
    <xs:pattern value=".+"/>
  </xs:restriction>
</xs:simpleType>

<xs:simpleType name="uri-list">
  <xs:list itemType="xs:anyURI"/>
</xs:simpleType>

<xs:simpleType name="validation-strip-or-preserve">
  <xs:annotation>
    <xs:documentation>
      Describes different ways of type-annotating an element or attribute.
    </xs:documentation>
  </xs:annotation>
  <xs:restriction base="xsl:validation-type">
    <xs:enumeration value="preserve"/>
    <xs:enumeration value="strip"/>
  </xs:restriction>
</xs:simpleType>

<xs:simpleType name="validation-type">
  <xs:annotation>
    <xs:documentation>
      Describes different ways of type-annotating an element or attribute.
    </xs:documentation>
  </xs:annotation>
  <xs:restriction base="xs:token">
    <xs:enumeration value="strict"/>
    <xs:enumeration value="lax"/>
```

```
      <xs:enumeration value="preserve"/>
      <xs:enumeration value="strip"/>
    </xs:restriction>
  </xs:simpleType>

  <xs:simpleType name="yes-or-no">
    <xs:annotation>
      <xs:documentation>
        One of the values "yes" or "no".
      </xs:documentation>
    </xs:annotation>
    <xs:restriction base="xs:token">
      <xs:enumeration value="yes"/>
      <xs:enumeration value="no"/>
    </xs:restriction>
  </xs:simpleType>

  <xs:simpleType name="yes-or-no-or-omit">
    <xs:annotation>
      <xs:documentation>
        One of the values "yes" or "no" or "omit".
      </xs:documentation>
    </xs:annotation>
    <xs:restriction base="xs:token">
      <xs:enumeration value="yes"/>
      <xs:enumeration value="no"/>
      <xs:enumeration value="omit"/>
    </xs:restriction>
  </xs:simpleType>

</xs:schema>
```

W3C® Document License

XPath 2.0 Function Reference

This reference provides brief details of the XPath 2.0 functions. These are distinct from functions that apply only to XSLT, which are detailed in Appendix D.

For the authoritative source and for details of the XPath 2.0 operators, go to the W3C recommendation *XQuery 1.0 and XPath 2.0 Functions and Operators* at www.w3.org/TR/xpath-functions.

You will find further detailed information on the use of these functions, together with additional information on XPath 2.0, in Michael Kay's *XSLT 2.0 and XPath 2.0 Programmer's Reference, Fourth Edition* (Wrox, 2008).

Functions

abs

Purpose

Returns the absolute value of a number, with the same type as the input.

Signature

abs(value)

Parameter

Name	Description	Type	Use
value	The supplied value	xs:double | xs:float | xs:decimal | xs:integer	Required

avg

Purpose

Returns the average of a sequence of numbers or durations, with the same type as the input.

Signature

```
avg (sequence)
```

Parameter

Name	Description	Type	Use
sequence	The supplied value	xs:anyAtomicType	Required

adjust-date-to-timezone, adjust-dateTime-to-timezone, adjust-time-to-timezone

Purpose

Three functions that return a supplied date, datetime, or time, with an altered time zone.

Signature

```
adjust-date-to-timezone(value, timezone)
```

Parameters

Name	Description	Type	Use
value	The date, dateTime, or time to adjust	xs:date | xs:dateTime | xs:time	Required
timezone	The time-zone value	xs:dayTimeDuration	Optional

See also

```
implicit-timezone()
```

base-uri

Purpose

Returns the base URI of a given document node.

Signature

```
base-uri(node)
```

Parameter

Name	Description	Type	Use
node	The specified node	node()	Required

boolean

Purpose

Returns the effective Boolean value of a parameter.

Signature

```
boolean(value)
```

Parameter

Name	Description	Type	Use
value	The value to evaluate	item()	Required

ceiling

Purpose

Returns the input number rounded up to the nearest whole number.

Signature

```
ceiling(value)
```

Parameter

Name	Description	Type	Use
value	The supplied value	xs:double | xs:float | xs:decimal	Required

See also

```
floor()
```

codepoint-equal

Purpose

Compares two strings character by character and returns true if the strings contain the same sequence of characters, regardless of the collation in use.

Signature

```
codepoint-equal(value1, value2)
```

Parameter

Name	Description	Type	Use
value	The values to compare	xs:string	Required

codepoints-to-string

Purpose

Takes a sequence of integer codepoint values for Unicode characters and returns the equivalent string.

Signature

```
codepoints-to-string(codepoints)
```

Parameter

Name	Description	Type	Use
codepoints	The sequence of codepoints to convert	xs:integer*	Required

collection

Purpose

Returns a sequence of documents given a URI parameter.

Signature

```
collection(uri)
```

Parameter

Name	Description	Type	Use
uri	The URI that identifies the collection	xs:string	Optional

compare

Purpose

Compares two string values. Returns +1 if the first parameter has the higher value; zero if the strings are equal; otherwise, -1.

Signature

compare(value1, value2, collation)

Parameters

Name	Description	Type	Use
value	The strings to compare	xs:string	Required
collation	A URI that identifies the collation to use	xs:string	Optional

concat

Purpose

Constructs a string from two or more parameter values, joined end to end.

Signature

concat(value, value...)

Parameter

Name	Description	Type	Use
value	A supplied value	xs:anyAtomicType	Required

count

Purpose

Returns the number of items in a sequence.

Signature

```
count(sequence)
```

Parameter

Name	Description	Type	Use
sequence	The sequence to evaluate	item()	Required

See also

```
last()
```

current-date, current-dateTime, current-time

Purpose

Three functions that return the current date, time, or both from the system clock.

Signature

```
current-date()
```

data

Purpose

Explicitly atomizes the value of a sequence.

Signature

```
data(sequence)
```

Parameter

Name	Description	Type	Use
sequence	The supplied sequence	item()	Required

dateTime

Purpose

Constructs a dateTime from supplied date and time values.

Signature

```
dateTime(date, time)
```

Parameters

Name	Description	Type	Use
date	The supplied date	xs:date	Required
time	The supplied time	xs:time	Required

day-from-date, day-from-dateTime

Purpose

Two functions that return the day of the month from a date or a dateTime.

Signature

```
day-from-date(date)
```

Parameter

Name	Description	Type	Use
date	The supplied date	xs:date | xs:dateTime	Required

days-from-duration

Purpose

Returns an integer representing the days component of a duration value.

Signature

```
days-from-duration(value)
```

Parameter

Name	Description	Type	Use
value	The supplied duration	xs:duration	Required

deep-equal

Purpose

Compares two nodes or sequences to see if they have identical content.

Signature

```
deep-equal(sequence1, sequence2, collation)
```

Parameters

Name	Description	Type	Use
sequence	A sequence to compare	item()	Required
collation	A URI that identifies the collation to use	xs:string	Optional

default-collation

Purpose

Returns the URI of the default collation.

Signature

```
default-collation()
```

distinct-values

Purpose

Removes duplicate values from a sequence.

Signature

```
distinct-values (sequence, collation)
```

Parameters

Name	Description	Type	Use
sequence	The supplied value	xs:anyAtomicType	Required
collation	A URI that identifies the collation to use	xs:string	Optional

doc, doc-available

Purpose

Two related functions: `doc()` loads an external document given a URI; `doc-available()` returns true if a call to `doc()` with the same URI will succeed.

Signature

```
doc(uri)
```

Parameter

Name	Description	Type	Use
uri	The URI of the document to be loaded	xs:string	Required

document-uri

Purpose

Returns a URI of a document node.

Signature

```
document-uri(node)
```

Parameter

Name	Description	Type	Use
node	The document node	node()	Required

empty

Purpose

Returns `true` if the argument is an empty sequence; otherwise, returns `false`.

Signature

```
empty(sequence)
```

Parameter

Name	Description	Type	Use
sequence	The supplied sequence	item()	Required

encode-for-uri

Purpose

Applies percent encoding to characters in a URI.

Signature

```
encode-for-uri(value)
```

Parameter

Name	Description	Type	Use
value	The string to encode	xs:string	Required

ends-with

Purpose

Tests whether or not a string ends with another string.

Signature

```
ends-with(value, test, collation)
```

Parameters

Name	Description	Type	Use
value	The containing string	xs:string	Required
test	The string to match	xs:string	Required
collation	A URI that identifies the collation to use	xs:string	Optional

error

Purpose

Generates an error message using the supplied values. Causes evaluation of an XPath expression, or the execution of an XSLT transform, to fail.

Signature

```
error(code, message, value)
```

Parameters

Name	Description	Type	Use
code	An error code	xs:QName	Optional
message	A message describing the error	xs:string	Optional
value	A value associated with the error condition	item()	Optional

escape-html-uri

Purpose

Applies percent encoding to non-ASCII characters in a URI.

Signature

```
escape-html-uri(value)
```

Parameter

Name	Description	Type	Use
value	The string to encode	xs:string	Required

exactly-one

Purpose

Returns the input unchanged if it is a sequence containing a single item. Otherwise, an error is reported.

Signature

```
exactly-one(sequence)
```

Parameter

Name	Description	Type	Use
sequence	The input sequence	item()	Required

exists

Purpose

Returns true only if the input sequence contains at least one item.

Signature

```
exists(sequence)
```

Parameter

Name	Description	Type	Use
sequence	The input sequence	item()	Required

false

Purpose

Returns the Boolean value false.

Signature

```
false()
```

See also

```
true()
```

floor

Purpose

Rounds down to the largest integer that is equal to or less than the input.

Signature

```
floor(value)
```

Parameter

Name	Description	Type	Use
value	The supplied value	xs:double | xs:float | xs:decimal	Required

See also

```
ceiling()
```

hours-from-dateTime, hours-from-time

Purpose

Two functions that return the hours part of a datetime or time value.

Signature

```
hours-from-dateTime(datetime)
```

Parameter

Name	Description	Type	Use
datetime	The supplied datetime	xs:dateTime	Required

See also

```
dateTime()
```

id

Purpose

Returns a sequence from a document containing all the element nodes with an xs:ID type attribute equal to the input values.

Signature

```
id(values, node)
```

Parameters

Name	Description	Type	Use
values	The supplied ID values	xs:string	Required
node	The document node to search	node()	Optional

See also

```
idref()
```

idref

Purpose

Returns a sequence from a document containing all the element nodes with an xs:IDREF or xs:IDREFS type attribute equal to the input xs:ID value.

Signature

```
idref (value, node)
```

Parameters

Name	Description	Type	Use
value	The supplied ID values	xs:string	Required
node	The document node to search	node()	Optional

See also

```
id()
```

implicit-timezone

Purpose

Returns an xs:dayTimeDuration value from the run-time context.

Signature

```
implicit-timezone()
```

See also

```
adjust-date-to-timezone(), adjust-dateTime-to-timezone(), adjust-time-to-timezone()
```

index-of

Signature

```
index-of(sequence, value, collation)
```

Purpose

Returns a sequence of integers providing the positions where a given value occurs.

Parameters

Name	Description	Type	Use
sequence	The sequence to search	xs:anyAtomicType	Required
value	The value to find	xs:anyAtomicType	Required
collation	A URI that identifies the collation to use	xs:string	Optional

implicit-timezone

Purpose

Returns a `xs:dayTimeDuration` value from the run-time context.

Signature

```
implicit-timezone()
```

See also

`adjust-date-to-timezone()`, `adjust-dateTime-to-timezone()`, `adjust-time-to-timezone()`

in-scope-prefixes

Purpose

Returns the names (namespace prefixes) of the namespace nodes for an element.

Signature

```
in-scope-prefixes(element)
```

Parameter

Name	Description	Type	Use
element	The element name for which the prefix list is required	element()	Required

insert-before

Purpose

Returns a sequence containing items inserted at the specified position in an existing sequence.

Signature

```
insert-before(sequence1, position, sequence2)
```

Parameters

Name	Description	Type	Use
sequence1	The sequence to insert into	item()	Required
position	The insertion point	xs:integer	Required
sequence2	The items to insert	item()	Required

iri-to-uri

Purpose

Converts an IRI to a URI by percent encoding special characters.

Signature

```
iri-to-uri(value)
```

Parameter

Name	Description	Type	Use
value	The string to process	xs:string	Required

lang

Purpose

Returns `true` if the language parameter matches the `xml:lang` attribute value on the specified node. If the node parameter is omitted, then the context node is tested.

Signature

```
lang(language, node)
```

Parameters

Name	Description	Type	Use
language	The language to test for	ixs:string	Required
node	The node to test	node	Optional

last

Purpose

Returns the size of the context.

Signature

```
last()
```

See also

```
count(),position()
```

local-name

Purpose

Returns a string for the part after the colon of the specified node.

Signature

```
local-name(value)
```

Parameter

Name	Description	Type	Use
node	The node for which the name is required	node()	Optional

local-name-from-QName

Purpose

Returns a xs:NCName value for the local part of the specified xs:QName.

Signature

```
local-name-from-QName(value)
```

Parameter

Name	Description	Type	Use
value	The QName from which the local name is required	xs:QName	Required

lower-case

Purpose

Converts uppercase characters to lowercase.

Signature

```
lower-case(value)
```

Parameter

Name	Description	Type	Use
value	The string to convert	xs:string	Required

See also

```
upper-case()
```

matches

Purpose

Returns true if an input string matches a regular expression.

Signature

```
matches(input,regex,flags)
```

Parameters

Name	Description	Type	Use
flags	Flags that determine how the string is interpreted	xs:string	Optional
input	The string to be analyzed	xs:string	Required
regex	The regular expression used to analyze the string	xs:string	Required

max, min

Purpose

Two functions that return a maximum or minimum value in a sequence.

Signature

```
max (sequence, collation)
```

Parameters

Name	Description	Type	Use
sequence	The supplied sequence	xs:anyAtomicType	Required
collation	A URI that identifies the collation to use	xs:string	Optional

minutes-from-dateTime, minutes-from-time

Purpose

Two functions that return the minutes part of a datetime or time value.

Signature

```
minutes-from-dateTime(datetime)
```

Parameter

Name	Description	Type	Use
datetime	The supplied datetime	xs:dateTime | xs:time	Required

See also

```
dateTime()
```

minutes-from-duration

Purpose

Returns the minutes component of a duration value.

Signature

```
minutes-from-duration(value)
```

Parameter

Name	Description	Type	Use
value	The supplied duration	xs:duration	Optional

month-from-date, month-from-dateTime

Purpose

Two functions that return a month value as an integer from an xs:date or xs:dateTime.

Signature

```
month-from-date(date)
```

Parameter

Name	Description	Type	Use
date	The supplied datetime	xs:date	Required

See also

```
current-date(), current-dateTime(), current-time()
```

months-from-duration

Purpose

Returns the months component of a duration value.

Signature

```
months-from-duration(value)
```

Parameter

Name	Description	Type	Use
value	The supplied duration	xs:duration	Required

month-from-date, month-from-dateTime

Purpose

Two functions that return a month value as an integer from an xs:date or xs:dateTime.

Signature

```
month-from-date(date)
```

Parameter

Name	Description	Type	Use
date	The supplied datetime	xs:date	Required

See also

```
current-date(), current-dateTime(), current-time()
```

name

Purpose

Returns the name of the specified node as a lexical QName.

Signature

```
name(node)
```

Parameter

Name	Description	Type	Use
node	The node for which the name is required	node	Optional

namespace-uri

Purpose

Returns a namespace URI for the specified node.

Signature

```
namespace-uri(node)
```

Parameter

Name	Description	Type	Use
node	The node for which the URI is required	node()	Optional

namespace-uri-for-prefix

Purpose

Returns the namespace URI of an in-scope namespace for a given element, identified by its prefix.

Signature

```
namespace-uri-for-prefix(node)
```

Parameters

Name	Description	Type	Use
prefix	The prefix for which the URI is required	xs:string	Required
element	The element to inspect for an in-scope declaration	element()	Required

namespace-uri-from-QName

Purpose

Returns a namespace URI for the specified `xs:QName`.

nilled

Purpose

Returns `true` if a validated element node has the `xsi:nil` attribute set to `"true"`.

Signature

```
nilled(node)
```

Parameter

Name	Description	Type	Use
node	The element node to test	node	Required

normalize-unicode

Purpose

Applies the specified Unicode normalization algorithm to a string which may contain both fixed and variable-length encodings for a given character.

Signature

```
normalize_unicode(value, normalization-form)
```

Parameters

Name	Description	Type	Use
value	The string to process	xs:string	Required
normalization-form	The algorithm to use	xs:string	Optional

not

Purpose

Returns `true` if the input is false, and `false` if the effective Boolean value is `true`.

Signature

```
not(value)
```

Parameter

Name	Description	Type	Use
value	The input value	item()	Required

number

Purpose

Converts the input to a value of type xs:double.

Signature

number(value)

Parameter

Name	Description	Type	Use
value	The input value	item()	Optional

one-or-more

Purpose

Returns a sequence unchanged if it contains one or more items. If the sequence is empty, then an error is raised.

Signature

one_or_more(value)

Parameter

Name	Description	Type	Use
value	The input value	item()	Required

position

Purpose

Returns the integer value of the context item's position in a list of items.

Signature

position()

See also

`last()`

prefix-from-QName

Purpose

Returns the `xs:NCName` prefix of a `QName`.

Signature

`prefix-from-QName(value)`

Parameter

Name	Description	Type	Use
value	The QName from which the prefix is required	xs:QName	Required

QName

Purpose

Returns an expanded `xs:QName` given a namespace URI and a lexical `form of the name`.

Signature

`QName(namespace, lexical-qname)`

Parameters

Name	Description	Type	Use
namespace	The namespace URI	xs:string	Required
lexical-qname	The lexical QName	xs:string	Required

remove

Purpose

Removes the item at the specified position from a sequence.

Signature

`remove(sequence, position)`

Parameters

Name	Description	Type	Use
sequence	The input sequence	item()	Required
position	The position of the item	xs:integer	Required

replace

Purpose

Returns a string obtained by replacing occurrences of substrings that match a regular expression with a replacement string.

Signature

```
replace(input, regex, flags)
```

Parameters

Name	Description	Type	Use
flags	Flags that determine how the string is interpreted	xs:string	Optional
input	The string to be analyzed	xs:string	Required
regex	The regular expression used to analyze the string	xs:string	Required
replacement	The string to be replaced	xs:string	Required

resolve-uri

Purpose

Converts a relative URI to an absolute URI.

Signature

```
resolve-uri(relative, base)
```

Parameters

Name	Description	Type	Use
relative	A URI reference	xs:string	Required
base	The base URI to resolve against	xs:string	Optional

resolve-QName

Purpose

Returns an expanded xs:QName containing the namespace URI corresponding to the prefix in the supplied lexical QName.

Signature

```
resolve-QName(lexical-qname, element)
```

Parameters

Name	Description	Type	Use
lexical-qname	The lexical QName	xs:string	Required
element	The name of the element node to examine	element()	Required

reverse

Purpose

Reverses the order of items in a sequence.

Signature

```
reverse(sequence)
```

Parameter

Name	Description	Type	Use
sequence	The input sequence	item()	Required

root

Purpose

Returns the root of the tree (usually the document node) to which the input node belongs.

Signature

```
root(node)
```

Parameter

Name	Description	Type	Use
node	A node in the tree	node	Optional

round

Purpose

Returns the closest integer to a numeric value of the same type as the input.

Signature

round(value)

Parameter

Name	Description	Type	Use
value	The supplied value	xs:double | xs:float | xs:decimal | xs:integer	Required

round-half-to-even

Purpose

Returns the nearest value to the input that is a multiple of 10^{-p} where p is the value of the precision argument.

Signature

round-half-to-even(value, precision)

Parameters

Name	Description	Type	Use
value	The supplied value	xs:double | xs:float | xs:decimal | xs:integer	Required
precision	The number of decimal digits after the decimal point	xs:integer	Optional

seconds-from-dateTime, seconds-from-time

Purpose

Two functions that return the seconds part of a datetime or time value.

Signature

```
seconds-from-dateTime(datetime)
```

Parameter

Name	Description	Type	Use
datetime	The supplied datetime	xs:dateTime | xs:time	Optional

See also

```
dateTime()
```

seconds-from-duration

Purpose

Returns the seconds part of a duration value.

Signature

```
seconds-from-duration(value)
```

Parameter

Name	Description	Type	Use
value	The supplied duration	xs:duration	Required

starts-with

Purpose

Tests whether or not a string begins with another string.

Signature

```
starts-with(value, test, collation)
```

Parameters

Name	Description	Type	Use
value	The containing string	xs:string	Required
test	The string to match	xs:string	Required
collation	A URI that identifies the collation to use	xs:string	Optional

static-base-uri

Purpose

Returns the base URI of the static context of an XPath expression — in XSLT terms, the element containing the expression.

Signature

```
static-base-uri()
```

string

Purpose

Converts the input value to a string.

Signature

```
string(value)
```

Parameter

Name	Description	Type	Use
value	The input value	item()	Optional

string-join

Purpose

Concatenates the strings in the input sequence, using an optional separator.

Signature

```
string-join(sequence, separator)
```

Parameters

Name	Description	Type	Use
sequence	The input sequence	xs:string	Required
separator	The separator to be used for output	xs:string	Required

See also

concat()

string-length

Purpose

Returns the number of characters in a string.

Signature

string-length(value)

Parameter

Name	Description	Type	Use
value	The input value	item()	Optional

string-to-codepoints

Purpose

Converts a string to the equivalent Unicode-character codepoints.

Signature

string-to-codepoints(value)

Parameter

Name	Description	Type	Use
value	The string to convert	xs:string	Required

subsequence

Purpose

Returns a part of a sequence identified by the `start` and `number` parameters.

Signature

`subsequence(sequence, start, number)`

Parameters

Name	Description	Type	Use
sequence	The input sequence	item()	Required
start	The first item's position	xs:double	Required
number	The number of items to be included	xs:double	Optional

substring

Purpose

Returns a part of a string identified by the `start` and `number` parameters.

Signature

`substring(value, start, number)`

Parameters

Name	Description	Type	Use
value	The contained string	xs:string	Required
start	The first character's position	xs:double	Required
number	The number of characters to be included	xs:double	Optional

substring-after

Purpose

Returns the part of a string after the specified substring.

Signature

```
substring-after(value, match, collation)
```

Parameters

Name	Description	Type	Use
value	The contained string	xs:string	Required
match	The string to match	xs:string	Required
collation	A URI that identifies the collation to use	xs:string	Optional

substring-before

Purpose

Returns the part of a string before the specified substring.

Signature

```
substring-before(value, start, collation)
```

Parameters

Name	Description	Type	Use
value	The contained string	xs:string	Required
start	The string to match	xs:string	Required
collation	A URI that identifies the collation to use	xs:string	Optional

sum

Purpose

Returns the total of a sequence of numbers or durations in the same type as the supplied sequence.

Signature

```
sum(sequence)
```

Parameters

Name	Description	Type	Use
sequence	The items to include	xs:anyAtomicType	Required
zero-value	The value and type to return if the sequence is empty	xs:anyAtomicType	Optional

timezone-from-date, timezone-from-dateTime, timezone-from-time

Purpose

Three functions that return a time-zone part from a supplied date, datetime, or time.

Signature

```
timezone-from-date(value, timezone)
```

Parameter

Name	Description	Type	Use
value	The value from which the time zone will be returned	xs:date | xs:dateTime | xs:time	Required

See also

```
implicit-timezone()
```

tokenize

Purpose

Splits a string into substrings, marked with separators, matching the regex parameter.

Signature

```
matches(input, regex, flags)
```

Parameters

Name	Description	Type	Use
flags	Flags that determine how the string is interpreted	xs:string	Optional
input	The string to be analyzed	xs:string	Required
regex	The regular expression used to analyze the string	xs:string	Required

trace

Purpose

Produces diagnostic output that is implementation-defined.

Signature

trace(value, message)

Parameters

Name	Description	Type	Use
value	A value associated with the error condition	item()	Required
message	A message describing the error	xs:string	Required

translate

Purpose

Substitutes the specified characters with replacements.

Signature

translate(value, from, to)

Parameters

Name	Description	Type	Use
value	The input string	xs:string	Required
from	The characters to replace	xs:string	Required
to	The replacement characters	xs:string	Required

true

Purpose

Returns the value `true`.

Signature

`true()`

See also

`false()`

unordered

Purpose

Specifies that a sequence need not be ordered, which is a hint to the processor that it might avoid the cost of sorting.

Signature

`unordered(sequence)`

Parameter

Name	Description	Type	Use
sequence	The input sequence	xs:anyAtomicType	Required

upper-case

Purpose

Converts lowercase characters to uppercase.

Signature

`upper-case(value)`

Parameter

Name	Description	Type	Use
value	The string to convert	xs:string	Required

See also

```
lower-case()
```

year-from-date, year-from-dateTime

Purpose

Returns the year part of a date or datetime value.

Signature

```
year-from-date(date)
```

Parameter

Name	Description	Type	Use
date	The supplied datetime	xs:date | xs:dateTime	Required

See also

```
current-date(), current-dateTime(), current-time()
```

years-from-duration

Purpose

Returns the years part of a duration value.

Signature

```
years-from-duration(value)
```

Parameter

Name	Description	Type	Use
value	The supplied duration	xs:duration	Required

zero-or-one

Purpose

Returns a sequence unchanged if it contains no more than one item. Otherwise, an error is raised.

Signature

```
zero-or-one(value)
```

Parameter

Name	Description	Type	Use
value	The input value	item()	Required

References

This short reference to online resources consolidates the references found in various chapters and adds further useful information. The descriptions are lightly edited versions of the abstracts or other information on the websites concerned.

Specifications

Associating Style Sheets with XML Documents Version 1.0. Defines how a stylesheet can be associated with an XML document by including one or more processing instructions with the target of `xml-stylesheet` in the document's prolog. `www.w3.org/TR/xml-stylesheet`

Atom Publishing Protocol. A web-application-level protocol for publishing and editing resource metadata in Atom format, using HTTP and XML. `www.atomenabled.org/developers/protocol`

Atom Syndication Format. Specifies Atom 1.0, an XML-based web content and metadata syndication format. `www.atomenabled.org/developers/syndication/atom-format-spec.php`

Cascading Style Sheets, level 2 CSS2 Specification. Defines Cascading Style Sheets, level 2 revision 1. CSS 2.1 is a stylesheet language that enables authors and users to attach styles to structured documents. `www.w3.org/TR/CSS2`

Character Model for the World Wide Web 1.0: Normalization. Provides authors of specifications, software developers, and content developers with a common reference on the use of normalization for text and string identity matching on the Web. `www.w3.org/TR/charmod-norm`

DCMI metadata terms. Specifies all the metadata terms maintained by the Dublin Core Metadata Initiative, including properties, vocabulary encoding schemes, syntax encoding schemes, and classes. `http://dublincore.org/documents/dcmi-terms`

Date and Time Formats. Defines a profile of ISO 8601, the International Standard for the representation of dates and times. ISO 8601 describes a large number of date/time formats. To reduce the scope for error and the complexity of software, it is useful to restrict the supported formats to a small number. This profile defines a few date/time formats likely to satisfy most requirements. `www.w3.org/TR/NOTE-datetime.html`

Extensible Markup Language (XML) 1.0 (Fifth Edition). The Extensible Markup Language (XML) is a subset of SGML. Its goal is to enable generic SGML to be served, received, and processed on the Web in the way that is now possible with HTML. XML has been designed for ease of implementation and for interoperability with both SGML and HTML. www.w3.org/TR/REC-xml

HyperText Markup Language (HTML). This specification defines the HyperText Markup Language (HTML), the publishing language of the World Wide Web. HTML 4 supports more multimedia options, scripting languages, stylesheets, better printing facilities, and documents that are more accessible to users with disabilities. www.w3c.org/TR/html4

ISO Schematron. A language for making assertions in XML documents. Versions are available for both version 1 and version 2 processors. www.schematron.com

P5: Guidelines for Electronic Text Encoding and Interchange. The Text Encoding Initiative (TEI) is a consortium that collectively develops and maintains a standard for the representation of texts in digital form. Its chief deliverable is a set of guidelines that specify encoding methods for machine-readable texts, chiefly in the humanities, social sciences, and linguistics. www.tei-c.org.uk/release/doc/tei-p5-doc/html

RDF Site Summary (RSS) 1.0. RDF Site Summary (RSS) is a lightweight, multipurpose extensible metadata description and syndication format. RSS is an XML application, conforms to the W3C's RDF specification, and is extensible via XML-namespace and/or RDF-based modularization. http://web.resource.org/rss/1.0/spec

RFC 4151 - The "tag" URI Scheme. Describes the "tag" Uniform Resource Identifier (URI) scheme. Tag URIs (also known as *tags*) are designed to be globally unique while being useful to humans. They are distinct from most other URIs in that they have no authoritative resolution mechanism. A tag may be used purely as an entity identifier. www.faqs.org/rfcs/rfc4151.html

RSS 2.0 Specification. RSS is a Web-content-syndication format. Its name is an acronym for Really Simple Syndication. All RSS files must conform to the XML 1.0 specification. http://cyber.law.harvard.edu/rss/rss.html

Tag URI. The tag algorithm enables people to create globally unique identifiers that no one else using the same algorithm could ever create. The identifiers conform to the URI (URL) Syntax. http://taguri.org

Unicode Normalization Forms. Specifications for four normalized forms of Unicode text. When implementations keep strings in a normalized form, they can be assured that equivalent strings have a unique binary representation. www.unicode.org/reports/tr15

Uniform Resource Identifiers (URI): Generic Syntax. Defines the generic syntax of URI, including both absolute and relative forms, and guidelines for their use; it revises and replaces the generic definitions in RFC 1738 and RFC 1808. www.ietf.org/rfc/rfc2396.txt

W3C XML Schema Definition Language (XSD) 1.1 Part 2: Datatypes. Part 2 of the specification of the XML Schema language. It defines facilities for defining datatypes to be used in XML Schemas as well as other XML specifications. The datatype language, which is itself represented in XML, provides a superset of the capabilities found in XML document type definitions (DTDs) for specifying datatypes on elements and attributes. www.w3.org/TR/xmlschema11-2

XHTML 1.0 (Second Edition). Defines the Second Edition of XHTML 1.0, a reformulation of HTML 4 as an XML 1.0 application, and three DTDs corresponding to the ones defined by HTML 4. www.w3.org/TR/xhtml1

XHTML Role Attribute Module. Role Attribute allows authors to annotate XML languages with semantic information about the purpose of an element. Use cases include accessibility, device adaptation, server-side processing, and complex data description. www.w3.org/TR/2007/WD-xhtml-role-20071004

XHTML Vocabulary Namespace. A vocabulary collection utilized by XHTML Family modules and document types using XHTML Modularization, including XHTML Role and XHTML + RDFa. www.w3.org/1999/xhtml/vocab

XQuery 1.0 and XPath 2.0 Functions and Operators. Defines constructor functions, operators, and functions on the datatypes defined in XML Schema Part 2: Datatypes, Second Edition, and the datatypes defined in XQuery 1.0 and XPath 2.0 Data Model. It also discusses functions and operators on nodes and node sequences as defined in the XQuery 1.0 and XPath 2.0 Data Model. www.w3.org/TR/xpath-functions

XSL Transformations (XSLT) Version 2.0. Defines the syntax and semantics of XSLT 2.0, a language for transforming XML documents into other XML documents. XSLT 2.0 is designed to be used in conjunction with XPath 2.0. It shares the same data model as XPath 2.0, and it uses the library of functions and operators. www.w3.org/TR/xslt20

XSLT 2.0 and XQuery 1.0 Serialization. Defines serialization of an instance of the data model as defined in XQuery 1.0 and XPath 2.0 Data Model into a sequence of octets. Serialization is designed to be a component that can be used by other specifications such as XSL Transformations (XSLT) Version 2.0 or XQuery 1.0: An XML Query Language. www.w3.org/TR/xslt-xquery-serialization

XSLT 2.0 Schema. Defines all the elements that appear in the XSLT namespace as a schema, rather than a W3C recommendation. It also provides hooks that enable the inclusion of user-defined literal result elements, extension instructions, and top-level data elements. www.w3.org/2007/schema-for-xslt20.xsd

xml:id Version 1.0. Defines the meaning of the attribute xml:id as an ID attribute in XML documents and defines processing of this attribute to identify IDs in the absence of validation, without fetching external resources, and without relying on an internal subset. www.w3.org/TR/xml-id/

Tools and Resources

EXSLT. A community initiative to provide extensions to XSLT 1.0. The extensions are broken down into a number of modules, such as date, string, and math. Many functions are superseded by equivalent XSLT 2.0 or XPath functions. www.exslt.org

FunctX XSLT Functions. Lists functions alphabetically and by category in both XSLT and XQuery syntax, and conveniently lists closely related XSLT and XPath functions too. www.xsltfunctions.com/xsl/

Jeni's XSLT Pages. The website of Jeni Tennison, which is dedicated to helping people understand and make the most of using XSLT. Includes tutorials and utilities. www.jenitennison.com/xslt/index.html

Saxonica: XSLT and XQuery Processing. Documentation that lists the standard XSLT elements, all of which are supported in Saxon stylesheets, and provides brief descriptions of

their functions. In some cases the text offers information specific to the Saxon implementation.
`www.saxonica.com/documentation/index.html`

XSL List. The open forum for the discussion of XSL — Extensible Stylesheet Language.
`www.mulberrytech.com/xsl/xsl-list`

XSLTdoc: A Code Documentation Tool for XSLT. XSLTdoc works with all versions of XSLT. It defines conventions to document XSL "code elements" directly in the source code. These are extracted to form several linked HTML pages. The XSLT source code is available with syntax highlighting. `www.pnp-software.com/XSLTdoc`

Glossary

This glossary of terms is based on a selection of those published for XSLT 2.0 and XPath 2.0 from the *W3C Glossary and Dictionary*. You can see the original entries at www.w3.org/2003/glossary. - Links to the individual glossaries are at the end of this page.

Attribute set A named collection of attribute definitions that can be reused, defined by an `xsl:attribute-set` element.

Attribute value template A type of attribute that may contain an expression surrounded with curly brackets {}, usually used to set a value with information that is available only at run time.

Axis step An axis step has an axis that specifies a direction of travel in the node tree in relation to the context node, such as `parent::` or `child::`. It also specifies a node test, which defines the nodes to select using the node name or type.

Character map A character map allows a given character in the final result tree to be substituted by a string of characters during serialization.

Collation A set of rules for determining whether two string values are equivalent, and how they should be ordered. Collations, which are language- or application-specific, are specified by a URI.

Constructor function The constructor function for a given type is used to convert instances of other atomic types into the given type.

Context item The item, an atomic value or node, currently being processed. When the context item is a node, it is also called the *context node*.

Context position The position of the context item in the sequence of items being processed. The position changes whenever the context item changes, and is used to evaluate a predicate such as `para[1]`. The `position()` function may be used to return the position's value.

Glossary

Current group The collection of related items that are processed by an `xsl:for-each-group` instruction.

Current grouping key The grouping key shared in common by all the items within the current group.

Declaration Top-level elements in the XSLT namespace and defined in the XSLT specification are known as *declarations*. Any top-level elements specified by implementers or users are called *user-defined data elements*.

Empty sequence A sequence containing zero items.

Extension function A function defined by a user, a vendor, or a third party, distinct from built-in functions specified in XSLT or XPath.

Filter expression A primary expression, such as a literal or function call, followed by zero or more predicates. The result consists of the items returned by the primary expression, filtered by applying each predicate in turn.

Function parameter A parameter defined in an `xsl:function` element. Its value can be set when the function is called in an XPath expression.

Global variable A top-level `xsl:variable` declares a global variable that is visible everywhere in a stylesheet.

Grouping keys When the `group-by` or `group-adjacent` attributes are set on the `xsl:for-each-group` element, key values are calculated for each item in the population. Those with common values are then grouped together.

Import precedence A stylesheet module loaded using `xsl:import` has a lower import precedence than a module containing the import declaration. Any matching template rules in the importing module override those in the imported stylesheet.

Instruction An XSLT element, allowed inside a sequence constructor, that causes the processor to create a result-tree fragment.

Lexical QName A qualified name with two parts: an optional namespace prefix and a colon, followed by the so-called local part of the name. For example, in `<xsl:param>`, `xsl:` is the prefix and `param` is the local name.

Literal result element An element name that is not in the XSLT namespace, written directly in a stylesheet; for example, one of the XHTML element names.

Local variable A variable defined with the `xsl:variable` element in a sequence constructor.

Mode Modes allow a node in a source tree to be processed multiple ways by the same stylesheet, each time producing a different result. They also allow different sets of template rules to be active when processing different trees.

Named template An `xsl:template` element identified with a `name` attribute.

Node One of the node types defined in XPath 2.0 — for example, document, element, or attribute.

Parameter The `xsl:param` element declares a parameter, the value of which can be set by the caller.

Path expression An XPath expression used to locate nodes within trees, which consists of one or more steps, separated by "/" or "//".

Pattern A pattern specifies a set of matching conditions on a node.

Picture string A sequence of characters used to specify digit, grouping, and separator signs when formatting numbers.

Population A sequence of items to be grouped defined in the `select` attribute on an `xsl:for-each-group` instruction.

Predicate An expression contained in square brackets, [ ] , that filters the nodes selected in a step expression.

Primary expression Expressions that are the basic primitives of the XPath language, such as a literal, variable reference, or function call.

Priority Each template rule is allocated a numeric priority value by the processor, based on the match pattern. This value is used to select which rule to evaluate when several rules match the same source node. The default priority may be overridden by explicitly setting the `priority` attribute value on the `<xsl:template>` element.

QName A node name written as a local name.

Result tree Any temporary or final result tree constructed as the result of transforming a source tree. The result tree can be either used as a source for another transformation or serialized.

Sequence An ordered collection of zero or more items.

Sequence constructor A sequence of zero or more nodes in a stylesheet that can be evaluated to return another sequence.

Serialization The process of outputting a final result tree in XML or other document formats.

Sort key component An `<xsl:sort>` element in a sort key specification.

Sort key specification A sequence of one or more `xsl:sort` elements that define the rules for sorting the items.

Source tree Any node tree provided as input to the transformation, including the document containing the initial context node, documents containing nodes supplied as parameter values, or documents returned from the results of functions.

Step Part of an XPath expression that specifies how to generate a sequence of items. The sequence may be filtered by zero or more predicates. A step may be either an axis step or a filter expression.

Glossary

Stylesheet   A transformation in the XSLT language containing one or more modules.

Stylesheet function   A function that can be called from an XPath expression within the stylesheet, defined in an `xsl:function` declaration.

Stylesheet module   A stylesheet may consist of one or more modules, each contained by an `xsl:stylsheet` or `xsl:transform` element.

Stylesheet parameter   A global `xsl:param` element, the value of which can be set when a transformation is invoked.

Template   An `xsl:template` declaration defines a template, which contains a sequence constructor for creating nodes or atomic values in a result document. It can be either a template rule containing a pattern to match, or a named template, invoked by name.

Template parameter   A local variable defined by an `xsl:parameter` element. The parameter value can be set when the template is called.

Template rule   A stylesheet contains a set of template rules. Each rule has a pattern that is matched against nodes, an optional set of template parameters, and a sequence constructor.

Temporary tree   Any node tree, usually constructed inside a variable, other than the source tree or a final result tree.

Tunnel parameter   A parameter that is recursively passed on by a called template to any further called templates.

Variable   The `xsl:variable` element declares a variable, which may be a global variable or a local variable.

Variable reference   A variable reference is a QName specified in an `<xsl:variable>` or `<xsl:param>` element, and referred to in an XPath expression. It is preceded by a $ sign to distinguish it from a reference to a source-document element name.

Whitespace text node   A text node consisting entirely of the whitespace characters #x09, #x0A, #x0D, or #x20.

Index

O

P

Q

R